Engendered Encounters

MARGARET D. JACOBS

Engendered
Encounters

Feminism and

Pueblo Cultures

1879–1934

UNIVERSITY OF NEBRASKA PRESS

LINCOLN AND LONDON

Chapter 5 appeared in a slightly
different form as "Making Savages
of Us All: White Women, Pueblo Indians,
and the Controversy over Indian Dances
in the 1920s," *Frontiers: A Journal of
Women Studies* 17:3 (1996). Chapter 6
will appear in a slightly different form
as "Shaping a New Way: White Women and
the Movement to Promote Pueblo Indian
Arts and Crafts, 1900–1935," *Journal
of the Southwest* 40 (1998).
Library of Congress Cataloging-in-
Publication Data
Jacobs, Margaret D., 1963–
Engendered encounters: feminism and
Pueblo cultures, 1879–1934 / Margaret D. Jacobs.
p. cm.—(Women in the West)
Based on the author's thesis (Ph.D.)—
University of California at Davis.
Includes bibliographical references and index.
ISBN 0-8032-2586-5 (cloth: alk. paper).—
ISBN 0-8032-7609-5 (pbk.: alk. paper)
1. Pueblo Indians—Government relations.
2. Pueblo Indians—Cultural assimilation.
3. Pueblo Indians—Public opinion.
4. Women social reformers—United States.
5. Feminists—United States.
6. Public opinion—United States.
I. Title. II. Series.
E99.P9J33 1999
305.42'0973—dc21
98-29564 CIP

In memory of Roland Marchand
and
to Cody, Riley, and Tom

Contents

Illustrations

Acknowledgments

This book started as a dissertation for the Department of History at the University of California at Davis. Thus, it is only appropriate that I start by expressing my gratitude to the dedicated scholars who guided my work there. I would first like to extend my profound appreciation to Roland Marchand, who served as my dissertation director. Not only was he unfailingly generous with his time, but his editorial skills and historical insights constantly challenged my thinking and writing. His enthusiasm for historical inquiry and his dedication to teaching also provided me with an enduring model. Vicki Ruiz introduced me to the field of Western American history and encouraged my interest in relations between white women and Native Americans. Through her breadth of knowledge and editorial acumen, she has provided me with ongoing scholarly support. In addition to her intellectual gifts, Vicki's friendship, humor, and compassion have enriched my academic and personal life. Steve Crum, as a dedicated scholar in Native American history, was invaluable in steering me to many of my most fruitful primary sources and providing me with further insight into the art of teaching. Karen Halttunen always managed to get to the essence of each of my chapter's greatest flaws. Her unflinching scholarship constantly pushed me to deepen my analysis, to bring out nuance and complexity, and to rely more on my primary sources and less on standard historical narratives.

Other scholars have also provided comments on drafts of chapters or offered lively discussion on the topic of intercultural relations among women in the American West. Thanks to Sherry Smith and Joan Jensen for their comments and insights on selected chapters. I would particularly like to recognize Peggy Pascoe for reading and commenting upon five chapters of the original manuscript. I must thank Peggy, too, for her own work, which first motivated me to study gender and race in the West.

When I first began this project, a U.C. Davis Humanities Graduate Research Award, a U.C. Davis Research Fellowship, and a Charles Redd Center for Western Studies Summer Research Grant helped me fund research trips. A Reed-Smith Fellowship from the Department of History at U.C. Davis helped me to finish writing the dissertation.

Archivists and librarians aided me greatly in my research. Michael Harrison, who has organized the Michael and Margaret B. Harrison Western Research Center at his home in Sacramento, California, allowed me to come to his home week after week to scour his collection. He also entertained me with his own stories of working in the Southwest in the 1920s and of implementing the Indian New Deal in the 1930s. Also in California, I benefited from the assistance of the staff at the Bancroft Library at the University of California, Berkeley, and the Huntington Library in San Marino. In Albuquerque, Nancy Brown aided me at the Center for Southwest Research on the University of New Mexico campus. In Santa Fe, Willow Powers of the Laboratory of Anthropology and Jane Guillentine of the School of American Research both extended great courtesy and helpfulness to me. Thanks also to the staffs at the Indian Arts Research Center and the New Mexico State Records Center and Archives. In Denver, at the Rocky Mountain Branch of the National Archives and Records Administration, Eileen Bolger provided me with great assistance. Thank you also to the staffs at the General Federation of Women's Clubs International, the American Philosophical Society, the National Anthropological Archives of the Smithsonian Institution, the Beinecke Rare Book and Manuscript Library, the Library of Congress, the Menaul Historical Library, and Special Collections at UCLA, for locating and copying material for me. I appreciate the willingness of all of these collections to permit me to quote from materials in and reproduce photographs from their collections.

Correspondence and brief encounters with the following scholars have also enriched the process of writing this book. Just as I started my project, Alfonso Ortiz supplied me with great encouragement, many sources, people to write, and even the names of cheap hotels in Santa Fe. John Kessell warmly welcomed me to Albuquerque and provided me with further leads. Stan Hordes kindly introduced me to Santa Fe and guided me to many sources. Through correspondence, Sally Hyer, Margaret Szasz, Bruce Bernstein, Richard Frost, and Molly Mullin contributed their suggestions and insights to my work. I also appreciate the careful copyediting efforts of Patricia Shelton.

Friends and colleagues made the whole process worthwhile. Laura Lovett, Matthew Lasar, Jennifer Selwyn, Lesley Burns, Lynda Payne-Bury, Cherie Barkey, Alicia Rodríquez-Estrada, Olivia Martinez-Krippner, Annette Reed-Crum, Yolanda Calderón-Wallace, and Kathy Cairns sustained me through graduate school. Since that time, I have been lucky to work with many outstanding scholars, including Carol Loats, Bea Spade, Penny Green, Cynthia Taylor, Mary Wolf, Darlis Miller, Jamie Bronstein, Ken Hammond, Margaret Malamud, Jon Hunner, John Nieto-Phillips, Ray Sadler, Bill Eamon, and Nathan Brooks.

Finally, I wish to thank my family, who, through many years, have kept the process of writing a book in perspective.

Engendered Encounters

CHAPTER ONE

White Women, Pueblo Indians, and Federal Indian Policy

Indians in olden times in trying to secure a square deal, used war-clubs. Now they use women's clubs. *Stella Atwood, chair, Indian Welfare Committee, General Federation of Women's Clubs, ca. 1924*

In 1882 a new, white, middle-class women's reform organization, the Women's National Indian Association (WNIA), petitioned the U.S. government to rectify injustices against Native Americans. The WNIA concentrated on the plight of Native American women, declaring that "the plea of Indian women for the sacred shield of law is the plea of the sisters, wives, and mothers of this nation for them, the plea of all womanhood, indeed, on their behalf to you as legislators and as men."[1] To solve the so-called Indian problem, the WNIA proposed that Native Americans should be transformed from "heathen" into "civilized" citizens of the United States. Central to their conception of this transformation was the need to overhaul gender relations among Indian tribes. White female reformers typically believed that Indian women were degraded. As Mary Dissette, a reformer who worked for decades among the Pueblo Indians of New Mexico, phrased it, Indian women, "almost hopelessly dominated by the male animal, . . . are trained from infancy to consider themselves as created solely for his use." As feminists of the female moral reform persuasion, Dissette and her peers believed Indian women deserved to be "uplifted" to a white, middle-class standard of womanhood. The WNIA and other reform organizations convinced the Bureau of Indian Affairs (BIA) to take up their agenda; for about half a century, the BIA carried out what was known as a policy of assimilation toward Native Americans. As part of this policy, it sought to transform Indian women into the middle-class ideal of the "true woman."[2] The BIA and reformers believed the Indians of the Southwest were in particular need of uplift. Still remote from Anglo America, they had for too long been exposed to Spanish and Mexican influences, particularly Catholicism.

By the 1920s, however, other white women had developed quite a different view of Native Americans. Influenced in part by the emerging anthropological profession and a growing disdain for the modernization of America, these women emphasized that many traditional Indian cultures appeared far superior to modern American society. They looked to the Southwest, precisely because of its isolation from mainstream America, as the premier spot where one could encounter an alternative, particularly among the Pueblo Indians, to the aliena-tion and fast pace of modernity. The writer Mary Austin proclaimed, "At the time Spain found them, [the Pueblos] had no rich, no poor, no paupers, no prisons, no red-light district, no criminal classes, no institutionalized orphans, no mothers of dependent children penalized by their widowhood, no one pining for a mate, who wished to be married. . . . [T]hree centuries of Christian con-tact have not quite cured them of their superior achievement."[3]

Unlike female moral reformers, this group of white women believed that among the Pueblos, women enjoyed high status and a great deal of power. Aus-tin, in fact, deemed Pueblo social structure "Mother-rule." Having rejected fe-male moral reformers' version of feminism and their vision of womanhood, Aus-tin and many other white women journeyed to the Southwest in search of a new womanhood. Here, as they attended Pueblo dances and purchased Pueblo arts and crafts, Austin and her friends concluded that they had discovered what writer Mary Roberts Coolidge called the "land of women's rights."[4] Among the Pueblos, they shaped and articulated a new type of antimodern feminism.

Many of these women took part in new reform organizations that not only championed the Pueblos' land rights and religious freedom but also challenged the assimilation policy of the BIA by seeking to preserve Native American cul-tures. In 1933 one of the most active and ardent members of the 1920s Indian reform community, John Collier, became the head of the BIA. He dramatically reshaped federal Indian policy with the passage in 1934 of the Indian Reorgani-zation Act or the Indian New Deal. This act reversed the policy of assimilation and attempted to put into practice the beliefs of 1920s white activists that In-dians should be allowed to preserve their cultures.[5]

Maria Martinez, a woman from San Ildefonso Pueblo, bore witness to these changes. Coming of age in the 1880s and 1890s as the BIA began its assimilationist policy in earnest, Martinez attended a day school set up by the BIA in her pueblo. Miss Grimes, Martinez's day-school teacher, became an important figure in her life. As an adolescent, Martinez attended a Catholic boarding school in Santa Fe. In addition to her education in non-Pueblo ways, Martinez became steeped in the heritage of her own pueblo. From her female relatives, she learned a craft that would serve her well the rest of her life—making pottery.

In 1904 Martinez, her husband, Julian, and a few other Pueblo Indians traveled to the Louisiana Purchase Exposition in St. Louis to sing and dance and to demonstrate their pottery-making skills. Intent on showing how Indians could be uplifted from their traditional "backward" state to "civilization," Congress had set aside forty thousand dollars for the construction of an "Indian building" at the exposition. One side of the building featured "traditional" Indians making their crafts; the other side displayed Indian schoolchildren attending a class and learning to take part in the modern world. Though Martinez and her husband had both attended BIA schools and learned to speak English, they found themselves on exhibit in the "traditional" side of the building.[6]

Soon after the St. Louis exposition, Martinez accompanied her husband to his new job on an archaeological dig near their pueblo. Here, she encountered archaeologists and anthropologists who were more interested in the preservation of Pueblo culture than its absorption into mainstream America. One archaeologist, Edgar Hewett, encouraged Martinez to make pottery based on shards found in the excavation. Taking Hewett's suggestion, Martinez's pottery soon became a sensation among an elite clientele of white artists and writers in New Mexico. White women in the Indian arts and crafts movement extolled her work as the most "traditional, high-quality" pottery made by a traditional Pueblo woman. Eventually, Martinez became a renowned potter, known worldwide. Together with Julian, who painted designs on most of her pottery, she entertained tourists who came to San Ildefonso in search of her famed black-on-black ware. She also traveled the continent to display her pottery at expositions and fairs. By the 1930s the exhibition of Indians at these events differed markedly from Martinez's first experience in 1904 in St. Louis. When the Martinezes attended the Century of Progress Exposition in Chicago in 1934, Julian wished to try an electric kiln of a neighboring white potter, but Maria cautioned against it because the superintendent of the Pueblos "says Indian pottery is for Indians, and it's got to be made in the Indian way."[7]

Over time Maria Martinez witnessed remarkable changes in attitude among many white Americans and in federal-government policy toward Native Americans. Once displayed in 1904 in St. Louis as a quaint "relic" of a bygone age, destined to assimilate into modern America, by the 1930s Martinez had become a symbol of an admirable culture that must be allowed to maintain itself within a modernizing America. On the surface, these changes in attitude seemed to accord Native Americans greater respect and self-determination. As the kiln episode in Chicago reveals, however, by the 1930s many white Americans had become intent on promoting their own vision of what it meant to be an Indian. The notion of assimilation may have gone out of fashion for a time, but the underlying assumption of many whites and of the BIA—that they knew what was best for the Indians—remained virtually unchanged.

This book presents a story of how and why notions about Native Americans changed in the first decades of the twentieth century, particularly among one of the groups of Americans most responsible for influencing and carrying out federal Indian policy—white women, both female moral reformers and antimodern feminists. This is also a story of what meaning and purpose Pueblo Indians gave to their experiences with white women in these same decades. By analyzing these interactions, we can gain some insight into how many Americans at the turn of the twentieth century—white and native—may have reconceptualized gender and racial differences.

The Pueblo Indians were central players in this story, yet it is no simple matter to describe the nature of Pueblo society in the late nineteenth century. Information about the Pueblos was written primarily by Spanish observers and later by Anglos, who often projected their own visions and anxieties onto the Pueblos. Most anthropological studies of the Pueblos have tended to utilize the "ethnographic present." Assuming that Pueblo life had not changed significantly for centuries, anthropologists and other observers at the turn of the century presented their observations regarding the Pueblos as the way that "traditional" Pueblos had always lived. Cultural interaction between the Pueblos and outsiders, including anthropologists, merited little attention.[8] Thus, work by white writers and anthropologists must be approached with caution.

Even the rare written archival sources by Pueblo Indians and published Pueblo autobiographies require careful analysis. Although these documents give insight into Pueblo concerns and priorities as well as glimpses of Pueblos' interactions with whites, as Gretchen Bataille and Kathleen Sands point out, in the case of Pueblo autobiographies "it must be granted that many Indian narrators are, indeed, atypical of their tribes in some measure. The very fact that they engage in a personal narrative sets them apart from those . . . who are not storytellers or whose tribal values dissuade them from putting themselves forward."[9] Autobiographies, letters, and petitions from Pueblo individuals must not be transparently assumed to reflect "the Pueblo viewpoint." It is in fact one of the unfortunate legacies of antimodern feminists that many white Americans assume that there is one monolithic Indian view. Such a notion negates the diversity of perspectives among and within Native American tribes.

Oral interviews with Pueblo Indians might have served as another source of evidence, but as this book reveals, the Pueblos have had a long history of exploitative contact with white women, from female moral reformers and BIA schoolteachers to anthropologists, writers, and tourism promoters. Frequently condemned by missionaries and reformers and often betrayed by anthropologists and other scholars, the Pueblos have placed a high value on their privacy and are often reluctant to grant outside researchers permission to conduct interviews with pueblo members. My own attempts to gain firsthand insights from the Pueblos threatened to turn into the latest manifestation of the phenomenon I describe in this book. Thus, I have relied, albeit cautiously, on written sources of and about the Pueblos.

Despite the shortcomings of available evidence, I have attempted to piece together a portrait of the Pueblos and the issues that most concerned them at the turn of the century. In 1879, on the verge of extensive contact with Anglos, nineteen different pueblos bordered the Rio Grande and dotted the landscape of western New Mexico and northeastern Arizona. The residents of these pueblos spoke (and still speak) six different languages. Anthropologists have classified the Pueblo peoples in two ways—into the Western and Eastern (or Rio Grande) Pueblos and into their respective language groups. The Western Pueblos include the Hopis of Arizona and the pueblos of Zuni, Acoma, and Laguna in western New Mexico. The Eastern Pueblos include the rest of the New Mexico Pueblos who built their villages along the Rio Grande. The Hopis and Zunis each speak a separate language. At the pueblos of Acoma, Laguna, San Felipe, Santa Ana, Zia, Santo Domingo, and Cochiti, the indigenous language is Keresan; at Jemez, it is Towa. The Tewa-speaking pueblos are Pojoaque, San Ildefonso, Santa Clara, Nambe, Tesuque, and San Juan, while at Isleta, Sandia, Picuris, and Taos the indigenous language is Tiwa. Anthropologists consider Towa, Tewa, and Tiwa to be sublanguages of the Tanoan dialect.[10]

At the time of the Spanish *entrada*, the Pueblos had lived in 134 different villages and had spoken seven different languages. Despite such linguistic variation, the Hopis and New Mexico Pueblos developed similar material cultures. All the Pueblos built multistory adobe houses and engaged in intensive agriculture; some Pueblos developed elaborate systems of irrigation. At a cultural level, the Pueblos shared what anthropologist and San Juan Pueblo member Alfonso Ortiz called "shifting clusters of experiences and meanings."[11] They exchanged many religious beliefs and practices, primarily concerned with assuring abundant harvests and with curing and healing. The kachina religion, which scholars believe originated in Mexico and was introduced into the Southwest around 1350, flourished among all of the pueblos except Taos and Picuris. Practitioners of the kachina religion believe that the kachinas, ancestors who were reborn in the underworld, serve as mediators between living beings and Pueblo gods. At one time, practitioners believe, kachinas visited their villages; when the kachinas stopped coming, they instructed the people to make masks and impersonate them during their sacred dances.[12]

The Pueblos also shared other ways of organizing and understanding their society. Prior to the arrival of the Spanish, they seem to have practiced a well-defined sexual division of labor. Men took the primary role in governing their pueblos and in performing the religious ceremonies that were believed to bring bountiful harvests. Women participated only indirectly in most religious ceremonies but could participate in women's ceremonial societies and dances. Raising children was the primary concern of women, but men played a crucial role in socializing and disciplining children. Moreover, according to Sue Ellen Jacobs, child care was "an extended family affair, if not a full community responsibility." Pueblo men were responsible for taking care of livestock and growing corn. Women were charged with preparing corn—a laborious process of grinding the grain between two stones—tending small vegetable gardens, and bringing water from wells and springs to the village. To women also fell the tasks of making pottery and plastering houses and kivas. Men traditionally wove textiles.[13]

Until recently, feminist scholars tended to assume that a strict sexual division of labor within a given society signaled a hierarchy in which men's work and activities were more highly valued than women's and in which men thus dominated women. Within the last two decades, however, many researchers have asserted that within many native societies, a clear sexual division of labor did not necessarily lead to a devaluing and subordination of women.[14] Most anthropologists have agreed that the sexual division of labor within Pueblo cultures enhanced, rather than diminished, women's status. Elsie Clews Parsons, an anthropologist who studied the Pueblos in the first few decades of the twentieth century, contended in her unpublished "Journal of a Feminist" that "how much and how little sex [differentiation] enter[s] into the Pueblos' life—it appears to count very little if at all in their personal relations, but in their occupations it is all controlling." Parsons also marveled that at some pueblos, particularly Zuni, individuals who felt ill-suited to their particular occupational role could choose to live the life of the opposite sex and become what the Zunis called a *la'mana*. More recently, both M. Jane Young and Alice Schlegel have argued that a strict division of labor along gender lines did not translate into male dominance and female subordination among the Hopis and Zunis. According to Young, both sexes were perceived as having power "in different but equal and complementary realms." Young adds that both sexes were "seen as partners operating in an interdependent manner." Similarly, Sue Ellen Jacobs, who has studied San Juan Pueblo, argues that although the pueblo had long had a "theocratically based hierarchical government," it did not order individuals in a hierarchy based on gender.[15]

The Pueblos' kinship systems and residential patterns may also have endowed Pueblo women with high status. Some scholars believe that prior to the Spanish *entrada*, all of the Pueblos organized themselves matrilineally and matrilocally.[16] Although there is no necessary correlation between matrilineality and women's power and status in any given society, in general researchers have found that matrilineal descent is correlated with benefits for women in certain areas, particularly the ownership of property. In theory all Pueblo land was owned by the village, but families acquired land-use rights and often passed the same piece of land down through generations. Among the matrilineal pueblos, women owned land-use rights as well as their houses, gardens, and household goods. Men customarily turned over the corn they cultivated to women, who were in charge of its distribution.[17]

Matrilineality also seemed to be associated with matrilocality. In matrilineal pueblos, once married, a man moved into the household of his wife's family and worked with his male in-laws. While this arrangement seems to have benefited women—who maintained close relations with their mothers and sisters and, when elderly, presided over a large extended household—it also meant, according to several anthropologists, that pressure existed for daughters to bring husbands into their households in order to ease the burden of work upon their fathers. Among the matrilocal pueblos women could become dependent upon those men who married into their families.[18] Pueblo kinship and residence patterns became a source of contention when the Spanish arrived in the Southwest.

The Pueblos had for many centuries exchanged ideas and physical goods with other Native American groups and had changed at a slow pace. In the sixteenth century their world began to change at a faster, more dramatic pace, both as the Spanish marched into their lands and as new tribes—primarily the Apaches and Navajos—migrated into their territory. They first encountered the Spanish in 1540, as Francisco Coronado led an exploratory expedition into the region. But it was not until 1598, when Don Juan de Oñate's expedition first colonized the region, that the Pueblos came into any sustained contact with the Spanish. Thereafter, Spanish *encomenderos* commandeered their labor and demanded tribute, and Franciscan friars attempted to convert them to Catholicism. The friars also worked diligently to break down the Pueblos' matrilineal kinship patterns and to replace what they characterized as the Pueblos' promiscuous sexual practices and informal marriage and divorce customs with chastity and Christian marriage.[19]

Although the Spanish could be brutal in their suppression of Pueblo religion, their interference in Pueblo social relations, and their exploitation of Pueblo labor, they did officially guarantee land rights to the Pueblos. Ruling that all settlers must respect all Indian-tilled land, they allowed each pueblo at least four square surrounding leagues.[20] To help in their effort to govern the Pueblos, the Spanish also introduced a new set of Pueblo officers—a governor (*gobernadorcillo*), lieutenant governor (*teniente*), war captain, sheriff, irrigation ditch boss (*mayordomo*), and a church warden. Before contact with the Spanish, a religious leader, known as the cacique by the Spanish, held ultimate authority in each pueblo. Under the new system of governance, the cacique continued to direct religious affairs while the new set of officers attended to the secular, day-to-day operations of the pueblo and acted as representatives to the Spanish governor.[21]

In 1680, after years of enduring forced labor and strident conversion efforts by the Spanish, the Rio Grande Pueblos organized a revolt against their conquerors, driving them out of the area until Don Diego de Vargas reconquered them in 1692. Thereafter, the Spanish and the New Mexico Pueblos seem to have reached an accommodation of sorts. The Pueblos outwardly practiced Catholicism but also continued to practice their indigenous religions, literally, underground. After 1700 the Spanish also assigned formal land grants to most of the New Mexico Pueblos. The Spanish, who had had minimal contact with the westernmost pueblos before the revolt, never reconquered the Hopis and Zunis; consequently, they did not receive land grants, and few of them practiced Catholicism.[22] For more than a century, the Pueblos' relationship with the Spanish seemed to stabilize. When Mexico gained its independence from Spain in 1821, the new Mexican government seemed less concerned with Pueblo religion. Thus the Pueblos began to perform public rituals that they had once kept secret from the Spanish. The Pueblos did not fare as well, however, in maintaining their land base as they had under the Spanish. Mexican settlers commonly trespassed on Pueblo lands, and the new government did little to protect Indian land rights.[23]

The Pueblos experienced another period of dramatic change when the United States conquered the Southwest from Mexico in 1848. Now they came into contact with a new set of government officials, missionaries, reformers, anthropologists, writers, artists, traders, developers, and tourism promoters. Under American rule the Pueblos suffered greater intrusions on their land than at any time previously. In 1848, in the Treaty of Guadalupe Hidalgo that was signed at the end of the U.S.-Mexican War, the United States agreed to legitimate Spanish land grants. In 1854 the territorial government of New Mexico confirmed Indian land grants, and in the 1890s the Supreme Court further reaffirmed them. The federal government, however, took no action when Anglo and Mexican squatters continued to encroach on Pueblo lands. Because Congress deemed the Pueblo Indians superior to so-called nomadic, "tribal" Indians, it did not consider them wards of the government. In 1876 the Supreme Court ruled that federal Indian laws did not apply to the Pueblos. This meant that Congress did not recognize Pueblo land as reservation land; therefore, their land could be preempted and purchased by non-Indians. The construction of the Atcheson, Topeka, and Santa Fe Railroad in the 1880s brought with it increasing numbers of Anglo-American settlers and tourists, who put additional pressure on the land.[24]

The Hopis and Zunis faced a different situation. Because Spain had not reconquered or assigned land grants to them, neither group could make official claims to their land when it became part of a territory of the United States. By executive order, however, the federal government established the Zuni Reservation in 1877 and the Hopi Reservation in 1882. In setting aside land for the Hopis without consulting them, the federal government created new problems. The reservation boundaries significantly reduced Hopi landholdings and did not include many of the sacred sites of the Hopis; furthermore, the government had surrounded them with the ever-expanding Navajo Indian Reservation.[25]

With their land base diminished, the traditional subsistence-based agricultural economy of the Pueblos became difficult to maintain. Mexican-Americans, who themselves were dispossessed of most of their land grants by 1912, trespassed on Pueblo land and practiced land-use policies that jeopardized the subsistence of the Pueblos.[26] The policies of the BIA exacerbated these problems. As Joseph Tafoya, a leader of one group of Indians at Santa Clara Pueblo, put it,

> the skinning off of timber from Santa Clara canon and the bad management of our watershed lands by the Indian Bureau in letting the Mexican sheep owners get away with the grass has just about ruined all of our home garden lands. These are under the Santa Clara ditch, which comes down from the Pu-Ye watershed and the skinned land. There is nothing left to hold back the water now. It runs off after every rain. In the hot months there isn't a drop of water in the ditch or else there is such a flood that the Santa Clara ditch system is all total[ly] out. We used to be celebrated for our vegetable gardens. Now we can hardly raise anything worthwhile on these lands.

Maria Martinez described a similar problem at San Ildefonso in the early 1900s; the lack of tillable land there became so pronounced in the 1920s that other pueblos, as well as Indian reform organizations, had to supply them with food.[27]

As farming became a less viable option, the Pueblos became increasingly drawn into the American economy. Seeing new markets for American goods and an opportunity to profit from growing tourist interest in Indians, white Americans, beginning in the late nineteenth century, had established a number of trading posts. Earlier, the Pueblos had traded foodstuffs or handicrafts in exchange for white American goods; now many Pueblos began purchasing food and other material goods on credit as their agricultural output decreased. To pay back their debts, or when crops failed, many Pueblo men resorted to wage-earning opportunities outside their pueblos; some joined archaeological excavations, while others went into nearby towns to find employment.[28] This may have upset the balance of men's and women's labor. Now, earning cash instead of growing corn, some Pueblo men may have become more reluctant to turn over their wages to their wives than they had been their corn.[29] On the other hand, Pueblo women also began to take part in the cash economy, primarily through selling pottery. Owing to the tourist trade, Pueblo women's traditional pottery making took on new importance. Now women too contributed cash to their households. By the 1920s, when white patrons initiated an Indian arts and crafts movement, some potters, most notably Martinez and Hopi potter Nampeyo, commanded high prices for their pottery. Among many Pueblo families in some pueblos, women's labor supplanted men's as the primary source of the family's income.[30]

Anglo-Americans not only threatened the Pueblos' land base—and therefore their ability to farm—they also interfered with the Pueblos' cultural practices. First, Anglo-American Protestant missionaries and reformers arrived in the Southwest with the belief that both Pueblo indigenous religion and Catholicism were backward and sinful. Protestant missionaries began ministering to the Pueblos of New Mexico in 1852 when a Baptist minister, Samuel Gorman, opened a mission at Laguna Pueblo. When Gorman left Laguna, having failed to gain any converts, John Menaul set up a Presbyterian mission there. In 1877 the Presbyterians established a mission and school at Zuni, and in the 1890s more Protestant churches sent missionaries to the New Mexico Pueblos. Among the Hopis, Protestant missionaries vied more competitively for Indian souls. A Mormon missionary first arrived at Hopi in 1858, followed by Moravians, Baptists, and Mennonites. By and large, however, Protestant missionaries converted few Pueblo Indians until the BIA established a network of day schools and boarding schools in the 1880s and 1890s.[31]

Only a few decades after the United States wrested the Southwest from Mexico, the BIA enacted its assimilation policy, which seemed to originate in changes in scientific notions of race and in the development of Indian reform organizations. In the late nineteenth century, white theories of racial difference underwent an important shift. Early in the nineteenth century, theorists had posited the notion of polygenesis, the idea that different races had originated from separate ancestors. This theory led its adherents to argue that Native Americans (as well as Africans and Asians) had descended from ancestors inferior to the white race's ancestor. Thus, supposed Native American inferiority originated from a biological inheritance. Beginning in the 1870s, however, some theorists asserted that all races stemmed from the same ancestor. According to these scholars, assumed Native American inferiority was not biologically determined and permanent but was conditioned by cultural evolution and environment. Lewis Henry Morgan, an early anthropologist, constructed an elaborate hierarchy of cultures, arguing that all cultures progressed through three stages: from savagery to barbarism and finally to civilization.[32]

New theories of race dovetailed with a reform movement that also emerged in the 1870s. Inspired by a Ponca chief who toured Eastern cities to relate the tragedy of Ponca removal, a group of women reformers had established the WNIA in 1879. In 1881 the publication of Helen Hunt Jackson's *A Century of Dishonor*, which documented atrocities committed against Native Americans, nourished the new reform movement. Male reformers founded the Indian Rights Association (IRA) in 1882 and in 1883 organized the Lake Mohonk conferences to develop common strategies for all reformers concerned with Indian affairs. While fighting for the enforcement of treaties and against the dissolution of Native American land bases, these new reform groups also centered their policy around the notion of cultural evolution.[33] They believed that the resolution of the "Indian problem" could be achieved only if Native Americans became fully assimilated into mainstream American society. As Mary Dissette phrased it, "[T]he greatest wrong the Ind[ian] has suffered at our hands has been his separation from our own social and national life."[34]

Taking its cue from this new, vocal, and influential group of reformers, the BIA crafted a policy designed to accelerate the progress of Indians toward civilization. This policy emphasized two elements: farming on private pieces of land and educating Indians. In 1879 General Richard Pratt opened the first Indian boarding school—Carlisle Institute in Pennsylvania—in an attempt to "kill the Indian, but save the man." Pratt's notions of assimilating Native Americans by bringing Indian children far from their homes for extended periods of time attracted many reformers and also influenced the BIA. By 1900 the government had opened twenty-five off-reservation boarding schools around the nation, mostly in the West. As one of its central strategies for assimilating Native Americans, the BIA included in its educational curriculum indoctrination in Protestant Christianity. With the additional passage of the Dawes Act in 1887, which called for the allotment of communally held Indian lands to individual Indians, reformers believed that Native Americans would soon become fully assimilated into white mainstream society. Assimilation policies also included setting up a system of Indian courts and hiring police to enforce new restrictions on Indian religious practices.[35] With the exception of the Hopis, the Dawes Act had little effect on the Pueblos, whose lands were not allotted in severalty. Yet both the BIA's assault on Indian religious practices and its Indian education program had a dramatic impact on the Pueblos.

As part of their assimilation efforts, reformers and government officials believed that gender relations among the Pueblos must be revamped. Reform organizations and the BIA touted white women as appropriate educators of Indian women in the ways of civilization. A large number of white women, many of them schooled in the tradition of female moral reform, journeyed to the Southwest as missionaries, BIA schoolteachers, field matrons, and at-large reformers. Chapter 2 analyzes two female moral reformers—Mary Dissette and Clara True—who sought to "uplift" Indian women. It also studies how three Pueblo women—Helen Sekaquaptewa, Polingaysi Qoyawayma, and Maria Martinez—may have interpreted and reshaped the white women educators' messages.

Like the Spanish, female moral reformers looked askance at matrilineality among some of the Pueblos. According to anthropologist and Santa Clara Pueblo member Edward Dozier, by the late nineteenth century kinship patterns differed substantially between the Western and Eastern Pueblos. Matrilineal Western Pueblos, who had had less exposure to the Spanish, still figured descent through mothers and assigned children to their mothers' clans. The Eastern Pueblos, however, who spoke dialects of the Tanoan language, were now bilateral, that is, lineage was determined by both parents. As for the Keresan-speaking Eastern Pueblos, Dozier argued that by the turn of the century their kinship patterns were in transition from matrilineal to bilateral relations.[36]

Most Protestant missionaries and reformers who came to the Southwest in the late nineteenth century subscribed to Lewis Henry Morgan's belief that matrilineality signaled loose sexual relations. Morgan closely tied each of his cultural stages to notions of sexuality, asserting, for example, that promiscuous intercourse "expresses the lowest conceivable stage of savagery—it represents the bottom of the scale." As a result of a supposed inability to determine the father of children, "savages" reckoned descent through the mother. In Morgan's second stage, barbarism, savage matrilineal societies had evolved toward a higher form of sexual relations—the "patriarchal family." Finally, once they reached civilization, cultures advanced to practicing a stable form of monogamous sexual relations that Morgan termed "the monogamian family." As Morgan envisioned it, "Modern society reposes upon the monogamian family. The whole previous experiences and progress of mankind culminated and crystallized in this pre-eminent institution."[37] The BIA and most reformers concerned with Indian affairs shared Morgan's view. In 1913, for example, the superintendent of the Santa Fe Indian School wrote that "among all primitive people descent is usually from the mother, owing to the fact that paternal origin is apt to be hard to trace because of the loose marital relations among such peoples."[38] And in female reformers' view of the world, loose sexual relations left Indian women vulnerable, degraded, and exploited. Up to the 1920s these reformers frequently condemned Pueblo men as sexual predators who forced sex on vulnerable Indian women. Thus, in their work to "uplift" Indian women, they sought to subvert matrilineality among those pueblos where it was still practiced. When given the opportunity, the Pueblos, as will be explored in chapter 5, hotly contested the view of their society as sexually promiscuous.

The Pueblos' allegedly casual marriage and divorce customs also elicited consternation from female moral reformers. Each pueblo had developed its own ways of organizing and formalizing marriage and divorce. As with kinship, these practices varied considerably from pueblo to pueblo by the late nineteenth century and seem to have been in flux. Among the Zunis, anthropologist Elsie Clews Parsons observed little occasion for courtship, owing to the thorough separation of boys and girls, but she also noted what she perceived to be the Zunis' casual attitudes toward both marriage and divorce. The Zunis, according to Parsons, did not conduct any wedding ceremonials; instead, "a man slips as easily as he can into the life of his wife's household." If a Zuni woman grew tired of her husband, Parsons wrote, she could simply set his belongings outside their home, signifying her desire to divorce. By contrast, Parsons contended, boys and girls at Taos found more opportunities to meet and develop intimate relationships, yet the Pueblo Council there interfered more in personal relations and rarely allowed men and women to separate once married. Further, Parsons believed there was more "marital authority" at Taos than at the other pueblos.[39] Despite the fact that each of the pueblos had developed its own standards for regulating courtship, marriage, and divorce, female moral reformers persisted in condemning all but Christian marriage. As with matrilineality, female moral reformers asserted that "casual" marriages and divorces left Indian women vulnerable.

At the turn of the century Pueblo Indians also began to encounter other white Americans who were more interested in studying and preserving Pueblo cultures than in denigrating and erasing them. Beginning in 1879 at Zuni, the Indians first met anthropologists Frank Hamilton Cushing and Matilda Coxe Stevenson. Cushing and Stevenson represented two diverging anthropological strains of thought in the late nineteenth century. Stevenson, even as she studied Zuni culture, shared the female moral reformers' views regarding the inferiority of Pueblo culture and the necessity of assimilating the Pueblos. Cushing's attempt to immerse himself in Zuni culture and his defense of the Zunis' ways prefigured the development of cultural relativism in early-twentieth-century anthropology.[40] Though many Pueblos may at first have welcomed anthropologists, who seemed to appreciate Pueblo religion, they soon became wary of these newcomers. In their quest for knowledge at all costs, many anthropologists purchased, or simply stole, sacred objects and sought information about or invaded secret ceremonies and dances, all of which violated Pueblo codes.[41]

In the early twentieth century, American anthropology developed rapidly as a profession under the guidance of Franz Boas of Columbia University. Boas had been trained in physical anthropology and had participated in many studies that sought to confirm a belief that each race differed in its mental capacities. Yet he became increasingly skeptical of such theories as he conducted fieldwork among the Eskimos, Bella Coolas, Kwakiutls, and recent immigrants to New York City. Among the Eskimos, Boas began to articulate his new orientation, "that although the character of their life is so rude as compared to civilized life, the Eskimo is a man as we are; . . . his feelings, his virtues and his shortcomings are based in human nature, like ours."[42] Between 1912 and 1930 Boas and his students led the challenge to prevailing theories of cultural evolution and white superiority and developed a new theory of cultural relativism.[43]

Cultural relativists tried to illustrate that different cultures developed divergent, but not inferior, standards. They also rejected the notion of the inheritance of certain racial traits, declaring, as Ruth Benedict did, that "what really binds men together is their culture." Boas and his students also pointed out the ways in which "whites" assumed that their culture was the norm against which all other cultures were judged and ranked. In her book *Patterns of Culture*, Benedict, a student of Boas, explained, "The white man . . . knows little of any ways of life but his own. The uniformity of custom, of outlook, that he sees spread about him seems convincing enough, and conceals from him the fact that it is after all an historical accident [that Western civilization has spread itself widely around the world]. He accepts without more ado the equivalence of human nature and his own cultural standards."[44] The Pueblos of the Southwest proved to be one of the cultural groups most studied by the cultural relativists and most cited to corroborate their new theories. Believing "primitive" cultures still intact among the Pueblos, Boas and many of his students turned to the Southwest as an appealing locale for field research.[45]

The emergence of the concept of "cultural relativism," among some whites, related to the development of its close cousin—cultural pluralism—as a model for dealing with the incredible ethnic and cultural diversity of America at the turn of the twentieth century. Rather than seeking the assimilation of all non-Anglo-Saxon, nonnative-born residents into American society, cultural pluralists, as Elsie Clews Parsons phrased it, stood "for democratic tolerance of all nationalities as against the melting-pot propaganda." Pluralists also proposed that the many different ethnicities that made up America all had something to contribute to the nation and that these disparate cultures should be seen as assets rather than as liabilities.[46]

A few writers in the Southwest had also begun to popularize these emerging relativist and pluralist views. The most famous among these was Charles Lummis. Offered a job as city editor for the *Los Angeles Times*, he decided in 1884 to "tramp across the continent" to California from his home in Ohio. On his journey he stayed briefly with the Indians of San Ildefonso Pueblo. Once in California, owing to overwork and stress, he suffered a paralytic stroke at age twenty-eight. Fed up with increasingly modernized life, in 1888 he took up residence for five years in the village of Isleta Pueblo in order to cure himself. As a result of this experience, Lummis decided to dedicate the rest of his life to defending the culture of the Pueblos. After successfully recuperating, Lummis returned to Los Angeles in 1894. Here he initiated a new magazine, *Land of Sunshine*, which later became one of the most popular western journals, *Out West*. In 1901 Lummis founded the Sequoya League, an organization devoted to Indian rights and "making better Indians." Through his articles and books, Lummis contested the view of missionaries, reformers, and the BIA that Indian cultures must be eradicated in order for Indians to progress. Lummis also promoted the Southwest as a "wonderland," full of mystery, romance, and "strange" oddities such as snake charmers, witches, and Penitentes. Popularizing the phrase "See America First" in the 1880s, he joined a rising tide of Americans who sought to break literary and intellectual ties with Europe and to articulate an American tradition.[47]

Lummis's writings also encouraged tourism to the Southwest. Before the 1880s, most Americans considered the Southwest to be a barren desert, devoid of interest, that served as a barrier between the Midwest and the coast of California. By 1881, just two years after anthropologists first arrived in the area, the Santa Fe Railway completed its line through the Southwest. Desiring a powerful symbol to attract riders, the Santa Fe Railway, according to T. C. McLuhan, "appropriated the Indian and his culture to establish for itself a meaningful emblem that would galvanize the American imagination." In 1907 the Santa Fe

Railway introduced an annual calendar that featured paintings of Pueblo Indians, represented in mystic and romantic terms.[48]

The Fred Harvey Company was also an important force in developing tourism in the Southwest. Fred Harvey first gained fame for opening a series of station restaurants, called "Harvey Houses," along the Santa Fe Railway line, at which travelers were served by Harvey Girls. Harvey eventually expanded into the hotel business, innovated gourmet dining on the trains, and got into the business of leading tours throughout New Mexico and Arizona. In 1902 the Harvey Company established an Indian Department to market Southwest Indian crafts. In 1905 Harvey opened Hopi House and El Tovar Hotel at the Grand Canyon. The Harvey corporation also motored train passengers from the Lamy station stop to a few tourist spots in New Mexico, mainly Santa Fe.[49] Tourist promoters had discovered that images of "traditional" Indians lured more tourists to the area than the BIA ideal of the assimilated Indian did. Pueblo Indians found employment and implicit support from tourist boosters for maintaining their cultural distinctiveness. Artists who had established colonies in Santa Fe and Taos also took up the cause of preserving Indian cultures. Many of these artists even rendered paintings of Pueblo Indians for the Santa Fe Railway's annual calendar.

In the 1910s and increasingly in the 1920s the Pueblos came into contact with yet another group of admiring Anglo-Americans. A significant number of white women who had been active in a wide range of social reforms and radical movements and in a new type of feminism converged on northern New Mexico, as visitors, as part-time residents, or as permanent dwellers. These women, the subject of chapter 3, included anthropologist Elsie Clews Parsons and many writers, including Mary Austin, Mabel Dodge Luhan, Alice Corbin Henderson, Elizabeth Shepley Sergeant, Ina Sizer Cassidy, and Erna Fergusson. Unlike female moral reformers, these Pueblo admirers celebrated the religious practices of the Pueblos as well as the way that the Pueblos conceived and organized gender relations. To these feminist women, matrilineality presented a remarkable curiosity. They asserted that this kinship pattern granted women greater status and power in their societies. Similarly, they looked with envy on the supposed ease with which Pueblo women could marry and divorce.

Feminist primitivists who converged on New Mexico after World War I, as will be explored in chapter 4, characterized the Pueblos as a harmonious, communal culture still steeped in the ways of its ancestors. While this may have been a Pueblo ideal, at the turn of the twentieth century, assimilation pressures, Anglo intervention in religious practices and sexual customs, rapid economic dislocation, and land conflicts all contributed to deepening divisions within the pueblos. Traditional ways of making a living and the sacred ceremonies that sought to ensure plentiful crops no longer seemed to be working. The Pueblos began to grapple with how best to meet the changed conditions. Increasingly, some Pueblo Indians began to believe that complying with new assimilation demands and adapting to new economic realities provided the best means to cope with the rapid change around them. Other Pueblo Indians believed that giving in to forced attendance at American schools, cutting their hair, and converting to Protestantism would destroy them and their culture. They preferred to resist cultural and economic change more adamantly.

Profound conflicts ensued within many pueblos.[50] This internal strife was particularly violent and painful at the Hopi village of Oraibi on Third Mesa. Here, in 1906, the "Friendlies," who supported cooperation with Anglo-Americans and BIA policy, had eventually succeeded in driving out the "Hostiles," who opposed compliance with the BIA.[51] Santa Clara Pueblo had also suffered increased divisions from the 1890s to 1935 between the Winter and Summer Moieties. The Winter Moiety, according to Dozier, claimed the right not to participate in dances, desired a separation of religious from secular activities, opposed compulsory work on the communal irrigation ditches, and favored Western dress.[52] The issue of religious versus secular governance divided many other pueblos. In the late nineteenth century in many pueblos, the caciques continued to exercise their old authority and to control the secular officers as well. Among some pueblos, members began to chafe under the cacique's power, and by the turn of the century the cacique's authority varied from pueblo to pueblo.[53] Intent on discovering and promoting their utopia, however, antimodern feminists ignored, and perhaps even aggravated, these conflicts.

Antimodern feminists also effaced other aspects of contemporary Pueblo life. Even though for decades the Pueblos had been enmeshed in the modern American economy, antimodern feminists portrayed them as a premodern, primitive people. And although Pueblo women and men were engaged in a process of redefining appropriate gender relations and sexual conduct in an evolving context, antimodern feminists portrayed Pueblo gender relations as frozen in an idyllic, preindustrial time. Pueblo women, to these white feminists, embodied their antimodern ideals and proved crucial to their emerging new conceptions of American womanhood.

In the 1920s artists, writers, anthropologists, and some tourist promoters—including many antimodern feminists—organized on behalf of the Pueblos. They established several new organizations—the New Mexico Association on Indian Affairs (NMAIA); its sister organization, the Eastern Association on Indian Affairs (EAIA); and the American Indian Defense Association (AIDA), led by an energetic Progressive reformer named John Collier. At the urging of a California reformer, Stella Atwood, and the Lakota writer Gertrude Bonnin, the General Federation of Women's Clubs (GFWC) also set up an Indian Welfare Committee in 1922 and employed John Collier as one of their researchers.[54]

These organizations first became involved in an effort to protect Pueblo land rights. In the 1913 *U.S. v. Sandoval* decision, the Supreme Court had reversed its 1876 decision, a determination that had refused to classify the Pueblos as Indians and wards of the government. Ironically, in 1913 the court declared the Pueblo Indians equally as inferior as other Indians and hence brought their lands under the protection of the federal government. The Sandoval decision meant that the government could evict squatters on Pueblo land and even return to the Pueblos land that they had sold to non-Indians. Such a possibility elicited prolonged and vehement opposition from non-Indian claimants to the land. In the 1920s, under the direction of Secretary of the Interior Albert B. Fall, New Mexico senator Holm Bursum introduced a bill to quiet title to the disputed lands. The so-called Bursum Bill would have confirmed all non-Pueblo claims of title held for more than ten years prior to 1912, the year of New Mexico statehood.[55] Rather than settling the controversy, however, the Bursum Bill motivated the Pueblos to form the All-Pueblo Council, and white writers, artists, and anthropologists to organize a successful nationwide campaign to save Pueblo lands.

In the 1920s the Pueblos found that they had become the "representative Indian" in the American imagination, temporarily displacing Plains Indians. This was no accident. As reformer Clara True remarked disapprovingly in 1924, "The Pueblo field is, on account of much advertising, the most conspicuous one in the Indian world at this time."[56] White women activists who opposed the policy of assimilation had fastened on the Pueblos during the 1920s as the quintessential "primitive." Images of the Pueblos became integral to their campaigns to promote cultural preservation as an alternative federal Indian policy.

After the Bursum Bill fight, white primitivists turned toward defending Pueblo dances against assertions by female moral reformers and the BIA that these dances were sexually immoral. This controversy, which will be explored in chapter 5, highlighted differences between female moral reformers and antimodern feminists in regard to gender and sexuality as much as to Pueblo religion. Female moral reformers alleged that the Pueblos allowed premarital sex and adultery, talked endlessly of sex subjects, and were generally a promiscuous society. Many feminist primitivists, by contrast, celebrated the Pueblos as a sexually uninhibited society, not yet encumbered with the sexual neuroses of modern Americans. Their male counterparts in the 1920s movement, equally intent on defending the Pueblos from condemnation, characterized the Pueblos as a culture that had strict sexual standards that had not yet been corrupted by modern sexual mores. For their part, Pueblo Indians also were divided over the nature and desirability of continuing their dances.

As discussed in chapter 6, a number of antimodern feminists also became active in a multifaceted movement to promote Indian arts and crafts in the 1920s and 1930s. Here they again confronted female moral reformers. Each group of white women sought to direct the arts and crafts movement to serve their own visions of womanhood. Rather than sitting by passively, Pueblo women artists also worked to shape the movement to their own purposes. Acutely aware of growing white interest in their cultures, the Pueblos used white women's attentions in order to further their own agendas. As people who stood to lose sovereignty, autonomy, land, water, and cultural control, the Pueblos recognized allies in white activists.

Eventually, white admirers of the Pueblos turned toward a larger goal of reforming the BIA and overturning assimilation policy. Owing to this new campaign, Secretary of the Interior Hubert Work appointed the Committee of 100 in 1923 to advise the government on federal Indian policy. This body, primarily made up of members of the older reform organizations such as the IRA, continued to promote assimilation. Unsatisfied, the NMAIA, EAIA, and AIDA further pressured the government for change. In 1926 the BIA responded by hiring an outside agency, the Brookings Institution, to investigate and make recommendations concerning federal Indian policy. In 1928 the Brookings Institution published its report, known popularly as the Meriam Report, which confirmed much of what the new reformers had argued. It condemned the Dawes Act, urged the government to allow Indians limited self-government, called for more monies for Indian health and education, promoted more day schools instead of boarding schools, and recommended a reorientation of Indian policy away from assimilation and toward tolerance and the appreciation of cultural differences.[57] Herbert Hoover's presidential administration made some concessions to the Meriam Report but did not fully dismantle the assimilation policy.

With the appointment in 1933 of the AIDA's John Collier as commissioner of Indian affairs under Franklin Roosevelt's administration, the federal government radically reversed its assimilation policy. In 1934 Collier submitted to Congress the Indian Reorganization Act, a sweeping bill that called for Indian self-government, the transformation of Indian education curricula to include "the study of Indian civilization," the elimination and reversal of the allotment process, and a special court on Indian affairs. Although the final bill did not include all of Collier's proposals, the so-called Indian New Deal went far in realizing the ideals of Collier and the new Indian reform organizations. Through other bills and agencies Collier also managed to increase annual appropriations to Indian peoples and to buy new lands for them, all during the Great Depression.[58]

Historians have offered five plausible causes for the transformation in attitudes and policy toward Native Americans during this period. Many scholars, particularly Kenneth Philp and Lawrence Kelly, focus almost solely on John Collier, emphasizing the force of Collier's personality, his antimodern sentiments, and his ability to lead other like-minded white individuals and Native Americans to demand reform in Indian policy.[59] Other historians, such as Elazar Barkan and George Stocking Jr., emphasize the change in anthropological theory from cultural evolution to cultural relativism.[60] Other researchers, including Robert Trennert, Marta Weigle, and T. C. McLuhan, have explained this transformation as emanating from an economic motive on the part of entrepreneurs, a desire to preserve "authentic" Indian culture as a means to lure tourists to the Southwest or to capitalize on their presence at national and international fairs.[61]

Some historians have put forth related theories that a widespread search for authenticity at the turn of the century, either as a reaction to the standardization of American industrialism or as a means to reassert masculinity, contributed to the popularity of the "old-time" Indian. In particular, intellectuals who took part in the modernist movement extolled the "primitive." And the Southwest became one place where these intellectuals, as Leah Dilworth phrases it, "focused their fantasies of renewal and authenticity."[62] Finally, a few historians have also focused on the role of Indians themselves in transforming the policy of assimilation. Devon Mihesuah, Tsianina Lomawaima, and Hazel Hertzberg all detail ways in which boarding-school indoctrination failed to produce the expected metamorphosis in Indian students, who often resisted or reinterpreted the teachings of the BIA. Hertzberg argues, in fact, that modern pan-Indian activism developed primarily as a result of the boarding-school experience. The contradictions between policy and reality gradually grew too great for the BIA, and it changed its policy.[63]

All of these explanations provide important insights into understanding the transformation in white attitudes and policy toward Native Americans. One aim of this book, however, is to provide yet another possible clue to this puzzle. By studying the large numbers of white women who took part in either upholding or overturning assimilation policy, it becomes apparent that an upheaval in white, middle-class views of proper gender roles and sexuality at the turn of the twentieth century also influenced the change in white attitudes and policy toward Native Americans. According to many women's historians, the dominant middle-class gender ideology of the late nineteenth century both confined white, middle-class women to the domestic sphere and opened up opportunities for them to play a public role. Because this ideology held that women were the moral guardians of the family, women could and did use this notion to argue for a more prominent role in enforcing public morality. As Barbara Epstein has documented, under the slogan of "Home Protection," white, middle-class women found a means to leave the home. These women often became active first in temperance crusades but moved on to other issues such as attacking prostitution, promoting health and hygiene, campaigning for women's suffrage, and engaging in Indian reform. Dominant notions about female sexuality played a key role in white, middle-class women's association with morality. Much of late-nineteenth-century prescriptive literature held that women's sexual passion lay dormant, and thus women were better able to control it than men. Many white, middle-class women appear to have accepted this view of female sexuality and to have used it to justify further forays into the public sphere, often to enforce their vision of sexuality and morality among women who were neither middle-class nor white.[64]

By the first decades of the twentieth century, more American women began to contest these notions of "woman's proper role" and "female sexual purity." As increasing numbers of working-class, and some middle-class, women entered the paid labor force, particularly in new unskilled and service-sector jobs, old conceptions of "woman's sphere" eroded. Furthermore, several generations of middle-class women obtained a higher education; some of them carved out careers for themselves in the new fields of sociology and anthropology or in the growing public sector. A drastic decline in the birth rate, increasing use of birth control, and an astounding rise in divorce, especially among middle- and upper-class women, also undermined older views of women's proper roles. Campaigns for women's suffrage and progressive reform pushed the boundaries of woman's sphere ever outward. Some white, middle-class women began to challenge the view of women as sexually pure beings who were morally superior to men. New Freudian conceptions of sexuality, working-class women's articulation of a competing vision of female sexuality, advertising, and commercialized leisure all contributed to a breakdown of Victorian ideals of female sexual purity, leading to what some researchers have deemed a "modern" view of women.[65]

In studying this upheaval in notions of womanhood at the turn of the twentieth century, women's historians have tended to concentrate on changes in either feminist ideology or notions of women's sexuality. Some scholars have focused on charting how white, middle-class women's-rights advocates defined themselves—as inherently different from, or absolutely equal to, men.[66] Other scholars have described the transition from a nineteenth-century society that denied and repressed women's sexuality to a twentieth-century culture that championed women's sexual liberation.[67] Still other historians have questioned this narrative, arguing that neither were Victorian American women so repressed nor were "new women" who underwent the "revolution in manners and morals" so liberated.[68]

While this focus on feminist ideology and sexuality has been valuable, women's historians have neglected another important dimension of this twentieth-century transformation in women's roles—what it meant in the realm of race relations. Many women's historians have studied the interplay between late-nineteenth-century gender ideology and race. Peggy Pascoe, in particular, has studied the racial assumptions behind notions of gender in this period and how they affected white, female moral reformers' interactions with Native American women and Chinese prostitutes. Mihesuah, Lomawaima, and Lisa Emmerich have each examined this ideology's effect on Native American women, while Vicki Ruiz and George Sanchez have studied its implications for Mexican-American women. Evelyn Brooks Higginbotham has looked at how black Baptist women both subscribed to and reshaped the Victorian ideology of "respectability."[69] Yet there has been no concomitant outpouring of research on the emerging gender roles of the 1910s and 1920s and the development of new views of racial difference and intercultural relations.[70] Rather than seeing these as two separate and distinct cultural developments, I perceive these as two linked phenomena. As some women began to question the nineteenth-century gender notions that had conditioned their experience and identity, they also began to undermine the assumptions about race that accompanied those notions. Shifting ideas about racial difference also encouraged these same white women to reconceptualize white womanhood. Driven by both feminist and antimodern ideals, these women found in their depictions of and interactions with Pueblo women an arena in which to reenvision womanhood.

The Southwest, like the American West as a whole, presents a particularly fertile field for exploring the intersections of race and gender.[71] To the white women who journeyed, sojourned, or settled in New Mexico after World War I, the region represented a refuge from modernity, gender restrictions, sexual conventions, and racial prejudice. As they discovered, however, the forces that they had fled were alive and well in the Southwest; rather than retreating to the Southwest, they engaged in new battles there. And ironically, antimodernist feminists helped to usher the area into the modern life they so detested. Intent on preserving the Pueblos' cultures, they contributed to the romanticization and commodification of the region.

Antimodern feminists in the Southwest also seem to have generated an enduring legacy as well. Much of what non–Native Americans accept as true in the last years of the twentieth century about all Native Americans emanated from antimodern feminists' romantic representations of the Pueblos in this era. Many white feminists still seek out utopian visions within Native American cultures, oblivious to the full range of contemporary Native American concerns and even more unaware of how their quest is part of an ongoing historical relationship of cultural appropriation and negotiation. Ultimately, this book asks how we can get beyond the scripted roles for white women and Indians that were written at the turn of the century. This task will not be achieved simply by white women writing a new script but rather through a new interaction based on mutual improvisation. Perhaps by analyzing white women's historical interactions with the Pueblos in close detail, this book may contribute in some small way to breaking free of the script.

CHAPTER TWO

Uplifting Indian Women

In the course of their education in schools provided by our Government, . . . the young of the Indian race . . . have presented for their acceptance a new moral standard which includes many things, notably personal chastity, respect for women, unselfishness on many lines. This standard is directly opposed to the practices in vogue in their own tribal customs and ceremonials, where the male is supreme and all that contributes to his comfort or pleasure is his by right of his male supremacy. The female is taught this from early childhood.   *Mary Dissette, 1924*

I have read your powerful plea against the union of Oklahoma . . . and most heartily agree with you. I wish I could help the cause but as a woman has no political status, and is classed with the Indians she is helping to raise to the dignity of citizens, I am helpless. In fact I have not been able to protect myself in the work I have given my life to from the influence of coarse politicians, how then can I help the Indians?   *Mary Dissette to Herbert Welsh, president, Indian Rights Association, 1906*

As Mary Dissette's first comment suggests, many white women who worked for Indian reform perceived the Indian woman as a victim of Indian male supremacy. In contrast, they often extolled the high status white, middle-class women supposedly enjoyed. White women such as Dissette believed that they had a special mission to uplift Indian women to their own higher station and in the process to elevate the entire Indian race. Yet as Mary Dissette's second remark reveals, in caustic terms, many white women who worked with Indian women also considered white women's supposedly higher status a cruel hypocrisy. Many female reformers chafed under the very standards they sought to instill in Indian women. Enlisted by reform organizations, mission societies, and the Bureau of Indian Affairs (BIA) to uplift Indian women to a static early-nineteenth-century view of womanhood, white women actually transmitted a more complex, fluid notion of gender to Indian women.

Early in the nineteenth century, coincidental with the rise of a market economy, middle-class Americans had developed an ideology that endowed the ideal woman with the qualities of Christian piety, sexual purity, submissiveness, and domesticity. Those who trumpeted this ideology, such as the writer Catherine Beecher, asserted that middle-class women's role as cultural and moral guardian in the home made women equal, if not superior, to men. Dubbed by historians the "cult of true womanhood," "the cult of domesticity," and the doctrine of "separate spheres," this ideology seems to have functioned both as a normative constraint on middle-class women's lives and as a concept that middle-class women used to promote a visible public role for themselves in the realm of social reform. Inadvertently, the notion of a woman's private sphere seemed to create unexpected new opportunities for homosocial bonding and intimacy between middle-class women. Additionally, as Mary Ryan, Christine Stansell, and other historians have shown, middle-class women also employed the ideology as a means of promoting their class interests and of attempting to enforce their standard of morality on working-class women.[1]

By the late nineteenth century, with the entrance of large numbers of working-class women into industrial labor and of middle-class women into colleges and universities, the reality of women's lives had grown increasingly discordant with the model of separate spheres. Once graduated from college, women often sought an arena in which they could put their educational training to use. Yet many careers were still virtually closed to women. Middle-class, college-educated women found an outlet for their career aspirations in reform and the new women's clubs. While women such as Jane Addams became engaged in settlement-house work and in labor issues, others became involved in temperance, antiprostitution, and other antivice and social-purity movements. Here, they could justify their presence in the public arena by claiming that they were acting on the ideal of true womanhood that associated women with morality and purity. In order to protect these values in the private sphere of the home, these women reasoned, it was necessary to extend them to the public sphere. Thus in the late nineteenth century, women's reform and a particular form of feminism flourished. Although they did not use the term "feminism," many female moral reformers conceived of women as an oppressed class of people who, by virtue of their supposed moral superiority to men, deserved greater authority in society.[2]

Some middle-class women became concerned with Indian policy. The founders of the Women's National Indian Association (WNIA), Mary Bonney and Amelia Stone Quinton, were veteran reformers. Bonney had also founded the

Chestnut Street Female Seminary in Philadelphia, worked as an active member of the Woman's Union Missionary Society of Americans for Heathen Lands, and served as the president of the Women's Home Mission Circle. Quinton had equally impressive reform credentials; she had worked in asylums, almshouses, infirmaries, prisons, and women's reformatories and had been a state organizer for the Woman's Christian Temperance Union. During its first three years, the WNIA concentrated on lobbying the federal government to meet its treaty obligations and to prevent further white encroachments onto Indian land. By 1882, however, when Herbert Welsh founded a comparable men's organization—the Indian Rights Association (IRA)—the WNIA had begun to articulate a new position. The WNIA now denounced the reservation system and called for efforts to assimilate Native Americans into the mainstream of American society through education, citizenship, and the allotment of communally held Indian land to individuals and families. Forfeiting the work of lobbying to the men of the IRA, the WNIA adopted missionary work among Indian tribes and highlighted the need to uplift Indian women and transform their pagan households into Christian homes.[3]

Together with the Quakers and other religious denominations, the WNIA encouraged the BIA to institutionalize this "women's work for women" into a field matron program. Responding to their pressure, the BIA created the position of field matron in the 1890s "in order that Indian women may be influenced in their home life and duties, and may have done for them in their sphere what farmers and mechanics are supposed to do for Indian men in their sphere."[4] Thus the BIA, the WNIA, and religious mission groups seemed to support the belief in separate spheres and sought to extend and enforce these spheres among Indian peoples. However, even the BIA's job description for the field matron reflected in part the ways that the notion of separate spheres had broken down. Although the BIA expected its female employees to demonstrate femininity and self-sacrifice, it also defined the work of the field matron as a "skilled and demanding job requiring hardiness, self-sufficiency, and a large degree of professional autonomy." In such words it celebrated traits more appropriate to the notion of the male sphere. In addition, rather than employing married women who could model appropriate female behavior, the BIA at first preferred to hire single women as field matrons.[5]

By the late nineteenth century, white women reformers had not only trespassed into the supposed sphere of men, but they had also undermined a key tenet of true womanhood—the notion that women should be submissive to men. As Barbara Epstein has found, the temperance and social purity movements took a decidedly antagonistic stand toward men. These reformers believed that male intemperance and sexual license, afforded through the double standard, harmed middle-class women in the home. Thus, as part of their brand of feminism, many of these women's reform movements sought to enforce the single standard of morality associated with true womanhood.[6]

The tenet of women's sexual and moral purity, while still normatively powerful, also was undergoing a transformation. The doctrine of separate spheres had encouraged women to define their social lives around other women. Even as separate spheres blurred in the late nineteenth century, many women continued to rely on homosocial bonds with other women. The myriad of women's reform movements helped to encourage these ties. Many college-educated women who chose not to marry also found intimacy and companionship with other women. Yet at the same time, marriage manuals and some popular literature had begun to stress the ideal of romantic love in marriage and the notion that women and men should find companionship with each other, not with their peers. Along with this new ideal came new notions about women's sexuality. While a consensus in both medical and popular literature in the late nineteenth century still insisted that sex should be confined to marriage, there emerged growing disagreement as to whether women actually possessed less passion and sexual desire than men.[7]

Despite the upheaval in middle-class notions of proper gender relations in the late nineteenth century, the BIA and many Indian-reform organizations continued to extol true womanhood as the key to uplifting Indian women. The BIA charged field matrons with visiting Indian women in their homes to instruct them in "civilized home life, stimulating their intelligence, rousing ambition, and cultivating refinement." Not expected to set their sights too high, Indian women's ambitions, according to the BIA, should revolve around "bettering" their home. The BIA's job description for field matrons called for them to educate Indian women in the "care of a house, keeping it clean and in order, . . . and suitably furnished," in "cleanliness and hygienic conditions," and in "preparation and serving of food." The BIA also expected field matrons to teach proper skills in "adorning the home, both inside and out, with pictures, curtains, home-made rugs, flowers, grassplots, and trees"; in sewing, laundry, caring of the sick, and raising little children; in keeping and care of domestic animals; and in proper observance of the Sabbath. In general, the field matron was to "lend her aid in ameliorating the condition of Indian women."[8]

The BIA also hired many women as schoolteachers to educate both Indian girls and boys. In addition to teaching children English and mathematics and giving them Protestant religious instruction, these teachers were entrusted with imparting appropriate middle-class standards of conduct between men and women. Ironically, just as the BIA tried to turn Indian men into self-sufficient, individualistic farmers at a time when farming was becoming increasingly untenable for most Americans, they also tried to transform Indian women into "true" women when this ideal had become increasingly anachronistic.

The BIA never achieved its grandiose plan to assimilate Native Americans through uplifting Indian women. Several historians have noted that by the 1910s the BIA's field matron program focused more on promoting public health on Indian reservations than on converting Indian women to "true womanhood." According to these historians, the BIA abandoned its emphasis on white women as civilizers of Indian women owing to the realities of reservation life; that is, the health needs of Indian peoples eventually overshadowed reformers' original goals. Field matrons' limited training in health care pointed to the need for trained professionals.[9] Other scholars have explored both the overt and more subtle ways in which Indian women resisted the civilizing mission.[10] Analyzing another dimension of the issue, in her book on the Cherokee Female Seminary, *Cultivating the Rosebuds*, Devon Mihesuah argues that many Cherokee women did strive to meet the "true woman" ideal, touting temperance and Christianity and believing that it was their duty to uplift the Cherokee Nation. Mihesuah argues, however, that most Cherokee women could not "realistically aspire to the ideal of a 'true woman'" because the ideal could only be attained by white women and those Indian women who looked white. In *They Called It Prairie Light*, Tsianina Lomawaima argues similarly that white women's efforts to instill the "cult of domesticity" really only prepared Indian women to serve as domestic servants for white women.[11]

For all of their important insights, these works have assumed, for the most part, that the white women who sought to instill true womanhood among Indian women followed its tenets themselves, that they both modeled and enforced the notions of separate spheres, domesticity, submissiveness, piety, and purity. Yet, given the upheaval in gender relations among white, middle-class Americans in the late nineteenth century, it was not a given that white women would preach or model true womanhood to Native American women.[12] Notwithstanding the instructions of the BIA, just what would white women teach Indian women and men, boys, and girls about the proper relationship between the sexes? Having themselves taken a public role, would female schoolteachers and field matrons preach to Indian women that they should follow the ideal of domesticity and remain in a private sphere? Would they instruct Indian women to be submissive to Indian men, even when they believed Indian men degraded their women? Would they continue to value homosocial relations between women, or would they promote romantic love between men and women? Would they uphold sexual purity as an ideal or accept that women should express sexual desires? And if Indian people chose to adopt some of what their teachers sought to impart to them, what exactly would they imbibe?

This chapter seeks to explore the nature of interaction between white female reformers and Pueblo women at the turn of the century. A close examination of the lives of two women reformers among the Pueblo Indians, Mary Dissette and Clara True, reveals a great chasm between the doctrines they were hired to preach and their actual behavior. By taking on male roles and challenging male authority in the BIA, both True and Dissette defied the very notions of separate spheres and female submissiveness they were supposed to teach Indian women. Some historians have asserted that female moral reformers' critique of gender relations in Native American society precluded them from challenging gender inequality in their own culture.[13] This was certainly not true in the case of True and Dissette, who vigorously challenged women's oppression in white American society. Some women who were employed by the BIA went even further and began to question the entire civilizing mission itself. Whatever their particular beliefs, True, Dissette, and other female moral reformers imparted more to their Indian women charges than the goals of true womanhood; they also transmitted their desire for independence and their rebellion against social norms.

We can only understand the nature of the "true womanhood" mission by examining the other side of the interaction as well, that is, how Pueblo women viewed and acted upon female reformers' teachings. Unfortunately, it is impossible to find extensive records of the Pueblo women who were the pupils of Dissette and True. Other Pueblo women, however, left evidence of how they interpreted white women's instruction. The autobiographies of two Hopi women, Polingaysi Qoyawayma and Helen Sekaquaptewa, as well as an extensive biography of the San Ildefonso potter Maria Martinez, provide insight into the ways in which Indian women constructed their own notions of womanhood from the messages and models of female schoolteachers and field matrons.

In 1888 the Presbyterian Board of Home Missions sent Mary Dissette to convert and civilize the Indians at Zuni Pueblo. Dissette stayed at Zuni for almost twelve years, working first as the Presbyterian mission schoolteacher, then as superintendent of the Presbyterians' Zuni Industrial School, then as a BIA schoolteacher, later as a nurse during the smallpox epidemic of 1898–99, and finally as a field matron. For the next thirty years, Dissette worked in various aspects of Indian education, serving as superintendent of Pueblo day schools in the early 1900s, teaching at Paguate Day School near Laguna Pueblo and at Santo Domingo Pueblo in the 1910s, and in the 1920s, working as a librarian at the Santa Fe Indian School. Later, she was employed at Chilocco Indian School in Oklahoma before returning to live in Santa Fe.[14]

During the course of her career in Indian work, Dissette befriended another female reformer—Clara True—who had come to New Mexico to convert and civilize the Pueblo Indians. Born in Kentucky, True attended college in Missouri. She became involved in Indian-reform work in the 1890s, when she was stationed at the Lower Brule Agency on the Sioux Reservation. There she served as principal of the boarding school for six years. From 1902 to 1907 True taught at the day school at Santa Clara Pueblo. From 1908 to 1910 she served as the superintendent of the Mission Indians at the Morongo Reservation near Banning in southern California. Around 1910 she returned to New Mexico to settle in the Española Valley, close to Santa Clara Pueblo. Here she owned and operated a series of ranches and managed an apple, hay, and livestock business. From 1910 until the 1940s, although True did not work in an official capacity with the Santa Clara Indians, she involved herself intensely in their affairs.[15]

In the 1910s True and Dissette joined forces to crusade against corruption and sexual immorality within the BIA. They focused their efforts mainly on the suppression of liquor traffic to Indians and on purging the BIA of employees they deemed sexually immoral. In the 1920s, in an abrupt reversal of their position in the 1910s, Dissette and True became ardent defenders of the BIA against the new group of white activists who challenged the policy of assimilation. Dissette and True turned the focus of their crusade against sexual immorality upon the Pueblo Indians themselves, suddenly finding in their traditional dances gross obscenity and debauchery.

Like most reformers who carried out Indian work at the turn of the century, Dissette and True evinced a combination of pity and contempt toward the Indians. Dissette believed that the Zunis lived in "gross animalism" but had "been too long neglected" and that they should be helped by the government. True asserted, "[T]he [Indian] people are to be pitied for their ignorance and for the injustice they suffer."[16] Aiming to "civilize" and convert the Indians to Christianity, True and Dissette particularly condemned Pueblo dances and belief in witchcraft as impediments to the Pueblos' progress. Dissette reported during the Shalako ceremony at Zuni that "dancing and debauchery are all they think of at this time." True condemned the dances as occasions for "drunken carousals." At Zuni, Dissette intervened to rescue an old woman who had been accused of and punished for witchcraft. She had the woman's four accusers arrested. After this incident, the BIA dispatched a troop of soldiers to guard Dissette and other white employees at Zuni for six months. Finally, because the

BIA feared a reprisal against Dissette and believed that she could no longer teach effectively in such a situation, it transferred her from Zuni to Santa Fe in 1898.[17]

Both Dissette and True also detested the traditional healing practices of Pueblo doctors. Both women faced their greatest challenges at Zuni and at Santa Clara in fighting the outbreak and spread of deadly epidemics: smallpox at Zuni in 1898 and 1899 and diphtheria at Santa Clara in 1903. Dissette's and True's attempts to dispense medicine, quarantine patients, and vaccinate children met with opposition from tribal doctors and their supporters, who preferred to treat patients in their traditional ways and resented Dissette's and True's visible contempt for them.[18] In January 1899 Mary Dissette pressured the BIA to send her back to that "village of horrors," as she referred to Zuni, "to assist as Nurse" during the smallpox epidemic. Though truly concerned with the plight of the Zunis who suffered from smallpox, Dissette had an ulterior motive in returning to Zuni. "This is a terrible scourge," Dissette remarked, "but it can be used as a great educator to those people if anyone will take the pains and it is going to show them who their real friends are."[19] Dissette saw the epidemic as an opportunity to succeed in her mission, which had been cut short by her transfer, to educate and civilize the Indians.

The Zunis, however, did not cooperate. When Dissette tried to nurse the Zunis through the epidemic, many of them proved unwilling to take medicine from her.[20] Since the Zunis believed that if a child "falls sick and is cured by a medicine man of the medicine order of a society she must be 'given' to the family of the medicine man or to his society," many Zunis may have been reluctant to accept Dissette's medicine.[21] The schoolteacher at Zuni, Elmira Greason, observed that "the Zunis have refused [Dissette's] goods for the reason, sufficient for them, that the bestowal of relief goods was accompanied by the intimation that it involved personal obligation to her. As one expressed it, 'she want to buy us.'" Several Zuni officials wrote a petition to their Indian agent, a Major Walpole, objecting to the continued presence of Dissette at Zuni. "Miss Dissette here many years and Zuñis don't want her," the Zuni petitioners wrote. "Miss Dissette was not kind to the people and we don't like her and we don't want her here. Maybe she go away and the Zuñis will be happy."[22]

In 1902 at Santa Clara, True encountered problems similar to those Dissette had faced at Zuni. According to True, the two parties in the pueblo took differing stands over whether to cooperate with True and the doctor. One party pledged to cooperate, but the other was "reluctant to openly give up their last tribal custom—that of 'making medicine.'" As the proportions of the epidemic increased, True found herself "unable to manage the epidemic. . . . In the case now suspected the father stations himself by his little one and . . . says that he will fight to the limit to prevent any interference whatever." True could not enforce an effective quarantine. Desperate for help, she believed that only federal troops could alleviate the situation in Santa Clara.[23]

True and Dissette faced enormous challenges in their bouts with the smallpox and diphtheria epidemics. It would have been difficult for any person to know how to save lives while respecting the wishes of Indians who did not trust white medicine. Still, both women displayed enormous ignorance of and contempt for the cultures of the Indians with whom they lived. "I have located the 'medicine' den," True told Superintendent Crandall, "a house without doors and windows, access being through the roof."[24] True seemed to be so unfamiliar with Pueblo culture that she did not recognize this doorless, windowless structure, the "medicine den," as the Pueblos' equivalent of a church—a kiva, a subterranean chamber used to perform sacred ceremonies. She viewed the kiva as just another house where the Indians tried to hide victims of disease from her.

Interpreting everything through the lens of their own ideology, True and Dissette utterly failed to see the significance of Indian religion—which included curing and healing ceremonies. According to True, medicine men resented white American doctors, not because they saw them as a threat to their religious and cultural system, but because the tribal doctors desired money. "The secret of the opposition here," said True, "is that the medicine men get a pretty good living out of their practice and Dr. Holterman was disturbing this happy arrangement." Because both True and Dissette utterly dismissed the strong religious beliefs of the Indians as whim, they could not understand that the Pueblo Indians took their religion very seriously and would not easily abandon it.[25]

A few white women reformers, however, did manage to display sensitivity to Indian religion while providing medical care. The Indians did not object to all white influence, and they did not reject all field matrons or other BIA employees. In fact, the Zunis who petitioned the government in 1899 wrote: "We like a nice Field Matron here to give Medicine that is all right. We like the kind women in school that's all right and we like Mr. Bennet the Indian Trader and his store but we don't like people who are not kind."[26] Thus, most Indians did not reject Western medicine per se, just as they did not object to many western material goods. Many Indians did, however, resist the ways in which some white reformers dispensed medicine and the assumptions of superiority and paternalism that guided the civilizing mission of women such as True and Dissette.

To fight what they deemed the backward practices of the Pueblos, Dissette and True posed a Christian education and inculcation in the values of hard work and thrift as the solution to "the Indian problem." To Dissette, education could transform the most "heathen" and recalcitrant of Indians. In the case of a fifteen-year-old Zuni boy caught stealing supplies from the school and breaking into a house, Dissette wrote to the military official in charge of the Pueblo Agency: "I have concluded that the boy . . . needs schooling worse than arrest and imprisonment. He is as wild as a rabbit and about as responsible but not worse than many boys who have developed well when placed under proper conditions."[27] Believing the Indians lazy, Dissette and True also sought to instill a self-help ethic among them. Although Dissette sought aid for the starving Zunis during the harsh winter of 1895, she worried that if they were given unconditional government handouts, they would never learn to help themselves. Dissette also saw a bright spot in the Zunis' plight. Many new children had shown up in her school hungry and in search of food and had traveled to the Albuquerque Indian School in order to obtain their meals. "These Inds. have been so opposed to sending any one away to school before," Dissette wrote, "that I cannot but feel that their dire necessity will prove a blessing in the end."[28]

As part of their educational efforts, True and Dissette subscribed to the views of reform organizations and the BIA: in order to bring about the civilization of Indians, it would be necessary to transform relations between Indian men and women. As Sen. Henry Dawes declared to a group of reformers at the 1897 Lake Mohonk conference, "[U]ntil in every Indian home, wherever situated, the wife shall sit by her hearthstone clothed in the habiliments of true womanhood, and the husband shall stand sentinel at the threshold panoplied in the armor of a self-supporting citizen of the United States,—then and not till then, will your work be done."[29] If Indian homes could be rebuilt in the style of white homes, complete with wife at the hearth and husband at the threshold, reformers reasoned, civilization would soon be accomplished.

White women reformers adopted a particular mission for themselves in reorienting Indian women to a new gender role. The president of the WNIA, Amelia Stone Quinton, argued that "this Indian work is but the Christian motherhood of the nation obeying its instincts toward our native heathen." White, middle-class women supposedly possessed the high moral standards, piety, and purity necessary to uplift Indian women.[30] The BIA seemed to accept Quinton's view. White women teachers could, according to Commissioner of Indian Affairs John D. C. Atkins, "rescue [Indian women] as far as possible from the life of mental and physical drudgery to which they have been hitherto held by the customs of their people."[31]

While the BIA and the WNIA may have seemed to have identical missions, there was an important difference between their agendas. The WNIA and female moral reformers who comprised its membership framed their endeavor as a feminist project, though of course few of them labeled it as such. As feminists, they believed women as a class to be universally oppressed. Considering themselves part of a great sisterhood of women that cut across racial lines, the "patriotic Christian women" of the WNIA could hear the "cry of suffering, undefended, ever-endangered Indian women" and believed that "the pleas of Indian women for the sacred shield of law [was] the plea of the sisters, wives, and mothers of this nation for them, the plea of all womanhood."[32] While they believed that all women were oppressed, female moral reformers seemed to assert that some women were less oppressed than others. White, middle-class gender norms, they believed, had given women like themselves a measure of status and control unknown to their non-Christian, non-middle-class sisters. As these women saw it, they had a duty to improve the status and raise the consciousness of other women in order that these less fortunate women would also participate in this great sisterhood of women. Female moral reformers were not just attempting to "uplift" Indian women; they were also hoping to recruit them to their movement. The BIA, of course, had no such intentions. It merely believed that transforming gender relations constituted one important part of the civilizing agenda.

When True and Dissette took up their posts in New Mexico, they projected two contradictory pictures of Indian women—the lazy Indian mother and the Indian woman as victim of Indian male dominance. In Dissette's view Indian women proved themselves lazy when they relied on their young daughters to take care of younger children and to help with housework. She complained that "when a lazy Ind. mother can take a ten year old girl out of school to mind the baby so that she can idle and gossip it is time that she was shown that such things would not be permitted."[33] Accustomed to a style of parenting that emphasized the centrality of mothers, Dissette could not imagine or condone child-raising practices that relied on a network of caregivers. Dissette, too, seemed unaware of the demanding domestic duties Pueblo women engaged in daily. In Dissette's view, lazy Indian women acted as an obstacle to the progress of the race.

More commonly, Dissette and True portrayed Indian women as victims of Indian men. Dissette believed that among the Pueblos, "the male is supreme and all that contributes to his comfort or pleasure is his by right of his male supremacy." While working at Santo Domingo Pueblo, she claimed that the Indian women there were "almost hopelessly dominated by the male animal" and were "trained from infancy to consider themselves as created solely for his use."[34] Dissette suggested that male supremacy and female subordination among the Pueblos derived from sexual immorality. In a 1924 letter, she described a dance in which she saw "little boys holding long-necked gourds in place to represent their sex organs." Soon after the dance, one of the little boys, a pupil in her school, "said to a girl who had outdistanced him in her schoolwork, 'You think you are so smart, but pretty soon you'll be having babies for us boys and then what good will all your schooling do you?'" Dissette promptly slapped the boy.[35] By juxtaposing these two incidents, Dissette created the impression that what she regarded as male sexual immorality served as the basis for male dominance of Pueblo women in other arenas of life.

Dissette's view of Pueblo gender relations echoed that of other white reformers in the nineteenth century. Helen Bannan writes that in contrast to the cult of domesticity that supposedly elevated white, middle-class American women, reformers imagined Indian women as imprisoned in a "cult of degraded drudgery." They portrayed Indian women as the victims of paganism, immorality, forced subservience, and "abusive overwork outside the home and ignorance within it."[36] Indeed, many reformers in this period characterized virtually all non-Protestant, non-middle-class, and non-white peoples in similar terms— as victims of "intellectual deprivation, domestic oppression, and sexual degradation." Women in the WNIA, the home-mission movement, and the foreign-mission movement believed that the relations between the sexes in any given race served as a prime indicator of the degree to which that race was civilized. Such a conceptualization of non-Protestant women—from Native American women to Chinese and Muslim women—created the impression that, as Joan Jacobs Brumberg phrases it, Protestant "American women enjoyed a unique and enviable position."[37]

Female moral reformers' tendency to universalize all women's experience led them to believe they could speak for all women. They believed they understood the plight of Native American women and the solution to their problems. This tendency allowed them to represent themselves as the all-knowing, active subjects and to portray Native American women as victimized objects. Seeing the problems of Native American women in terms of their gender oppression also meant that female moral reformers were often oblivious to the many other forms of racial, class, and colonialist oppression that figured in the experience of Native American women. In essence, female moral reformers did not recognize their own collusion in other forms of power that oppressed Native American women.[38]

True and Dissette also did not recognize the contradiction between their two representations of Indian women. In fact, they proposed the same solution— education—for both the victimized and the lazy Indian woman. Dissette believed that education in government schools presented Pueblo children with a "new moral standard" that included "respect for women." On another occasion Dissette remarked that "realizing that the Indian women are the real barriers to

all progress, we have emphasized the need of girls' education and with such success that our brightest, best pupils are girls and we always have more girls than
boys in school."[39]

Female moral reformers' work to transform Native American gender relations, however, also involved much more than in-class lessons. It also entailed
the "rescue" of Indian women in allegedly immoral situations. True often took
the initiative to rescue young Indian women from supposedly nefarious Indian
men. When she served as superintendent on the Morongo Reservation, True
claimed credit for rescuing Indian girls in southern California from a life of vice:
"I robbed the Los Angeles Red Light and got back the [Indian] girls, many of
them Sherman Institute educated but gone wrong from a bad start. Only one
proved incorrigible and I had to let her go to the ultimate bad. I made Southern
California pretty safe for Indians."[40]

In 1919 True took up the cause of a Santa Clara woman, Monica Silva, who
had fallen in love with a man from Santo Domingo Pueblo, married him, and
become pregnant. According to True, however, Silva had become suspicious
that her husband was being unfaithful to her and had decided to return to Santa
Clara. Before she could leave, the Santo Domingo council summoned her and
ordered her not to leave. True alleged that when Silva refused to stay, the council beat her nearly to death and branded her on the neck and other parts of the
body with a knife. "Truly the training the Pueblos have had in the past is beginning to show itself," True declared. "We MUST get somewhere soon if we save
any of the race here to decency." True also championed the cause of a fifteen-
year-old Santa Clara girl, Patricia Naranjo, whose father allegedly left her alone
in their cabin at night while he went to feasts at other pueblos and on the Jicarilla
Apache Reservation. Declaring the girl "bright and industrious" but "sadly neglected," True wished to rescue the child from her father, sure that harm would
come to her if she did not interfere.[41]

At first, believing in the utter depravity of most Indian men, True also sought
to protect white womanhood from Indian male lust. Writing in 1902, True told
her supervisor, Superintendent Crandall, that an Anglo woman in Denver, Cora
Marie Arnold, was in love with a Santa Clara Indian, Albino Naranjo, and had
asked for her help in courtship. True told Crandall that she refused to help the
couple, that her "reply is good Anglo-Saxon . . . and that I would not willingly
dishonor womanhood." In the late 1920s True no longer seemed to find it necessary to protect white womanhood. She now referred to the vocal group of white
women who had begun to champion Indian culture as a "school of Indian uplifters (feminine gender) who think a lot of the picturesqueness of the buck" and as
a "party of buck-struck society women."[42] Using the derogatory term for Indian

men, True seemed to ridicule more than condemn potential liaisons between white women and Indian men.

Even when no longer employed by the BIA, Dissette and True worked to provide what they believed to be an uplifting environment for Indian girls. While at Zuni, Dissette adopted a young Zuni girl, whom she called Daisy Schuman, who had lost both her parents. From 1888 to 1895, Daisy lived with Dissette at Zuni and went with her on her annual vacations to Santa Fe. In 1895 Dissette sent Daisy to live with a former Zuni schoolteacher's family in Washington DC, where Dissette believed she would "learn in that cultured Christian home such lessons as are most necessary, and which our limitations and situation make impossible to her in Zuni."[43] Daisy Schuman later returned to New Mexico, where she joined Dissette at Paguate Day School and Santo Domingo as a teacher's assistant and married a Pueblo man named Ed Thomas. In the 1930s she became the head schoolteacher at Paguate Day School.[44] In the 1910s Dissette built on an addition to her Santa Fe home so that during her summer vacations she could care for her "family of five orphan Ind. girls and train them in sanitary thrifty habits." Describing her endeavor, Dissette explained: "We have about five acres, only a few blocks from the Capitol, in fruit and alfalfa, and here we bring our Ind. girls every summer, our cow, chickens, ponies and pets, and they have a chance to put into actual practise [sic], under the right conditions, the training they receive in Govt. Schools. They are girls I have rescued from the worst moral and sanitary conditions and who have no other home than mine. Some of them have been supported by me for eight years, until old enough to send out to Board. School, and all but one are still dependent, and supported by me during the vacation months."[45]

True also continued her "rescue" efforts in an unofficial capacity. In 1924, even though she no longer worked for the BIA, True ran a free employment agency for Indians in Santa Fe and rented rooms to young Indians there. She also kept a sewing machine in a back room where the Indian girls employed in town could make their clothing. True designed the agency and hostel particularly for girls who had left school after the eighth grade. "Many of [the Indian girls] go into domestic service in the city," True explained, "and a mile from where they have received their education at government expense, they strike the primrose path head on and go to speedy destruction with few exceptions. Some try abortion and die horribly. Some go home to become mothers of Mexican or American babies, unhonored and unwelcome anywhere in the world." Whether or not unwed pregnancy was a common occurrence among Pueblo girls who attended boarding school, True envisioned her enterprise as a means to counter "the primrose path."[46]

True and Dissette seem to fit the pattern of many white women who chose to become missionaries, both in America and abroad, or were hired by the BIA to inculcate true womanhood in Indian women and to uplift them to a "higher civilization."[47] For the most part scholars have assumed that women like True and Dissette unquestioningly carried out their duties, instructing Indian women in the values associated with true womanhood. While True and Dissette certainly never lost the sense that Indians should be civilized, they did diverge drastically from the true-womanhood agenda. They lived in a time when such notions were breaking down, and indeed they contributed to their erosion. While they believed in the goal of uplifting Indian women, they did not necessarily share their employer's view of the meaning of "uplift." Rather than preparing Indian women for a life of domesticity and true womanhood, True's and Dissette's notions of "uplift" emphasized independence, autonomy, and education—their own feminist goals.

The BIA's job description for field matrons prescribed that white women would teach Indian women the domestic skills necessary to transform their pagan households into Christian homes. In 1896 Dissette taught several Indian girls to sew quilts and derived great satisfaction when the "ten or eleven little girls . . . proudly marched through the town two and two last Eve. each bearing a bright quilt of her own making on her arm." Yet Dissette's own attitude toward domesticity might have undermined her teachings. In a letter to a male friend, Dissette revealed, "I am rejoiced to hear that [your wife] has a good cook for I know how she dislikes cooking and though I am rather fond of baking and dabbling in the kitchen, once in a while, I'd have to love a man, more than my selfish soul is capable of in order to agree to cook him three meals a day for 365 days in the year and at the same time preserve my usual? placidity of temper."[48]

Although Dissette did teach domestic skills to the Zuni girls in her school, she valued their acquisition of these skills for reasons beyond their utility in maintaining a Christian home. Dissette wished to train the girls in spinning and weaving, she said, because "I want to provide my girls with some practical paying employment which their people will recognize as a benefit. 'What do you do for your people? You don't even stay at home and grind [corn] in order to help them,' is the taunt that is flung in the faces of the few girls who have the courage to stay by the school. . . . I feel that we owe it to these girls to put into their hands a weapon of defense which shall be an unanswerable argument in favor of education." While Dissette wished to train the Indian girls in a traditionally feminine occupation (at least in white American society), her purpose was to enable them to develop a skill that could make them independent wage earners. Although Dissette had been charged with educating Indian girls to keep "civilized" homes, her promotion of spinning and weaving for wages was designed to make Indian girls independent and capable of leaving their homes.[49]

Other white women employed by the BIA may have simply failed in their mission to instruct Indian women in domestic skills. For example, though field matron Ellen Stahl visited ninety-five Zuni families from 16 August to 20 September 1895, when filling out the BIA field matron report form, she reported "none" under the category of "names of women induced to adopt civilized practices in their household." When asked to list the "number of Indian women actually instructed" in domestic duties, Stahl recounted showing three women how to make yeast bread, pies, and biscuits and teaching one girl to wash and another to sew. Curiously, Stahl also mentioned that she taught two men "to do all kinds of American cooking," instructed two men in sewing and two in knitting, and showed one man how to keep a house clean.[50] Even given explicit instructions, Stahl did not appear to have any compunction about instructing Indian men in domestic skills or reporting that she did so to her superiors. Some Indian men also seemed to have no idea that the new skills being offered by field matrons should be exclusive to Indian women. In fact, given that weaving had traditionally been a male endeavor among Pueblo men, it is not surprising that Indian men would have been interested in learning sewing and knitting skills.

Like Ellen Stahl, Clara True found nothing upsetting about evidence of Indian men engaging in domestic duties associated with "true women"; in fact, she lauded it. In her first encounter with Pueblo Indians at Santa Clara Pueblo, True admired the domesticity of Pedro Cajete, who allowed a school building to be constructed on his land and helped to build it as well. Of Cajete, True wrote, "The school was in confusion incident to plastering and whitewashing. Pedro apologized profusely saying that the late rains made building difficult. . . . We have an extra man and a girl hired and Pedro's family are all at work except Pedro who has to mind the baby. Pedro is a jewel. We like him very much indeed. . . . He got up from the dinner table to do the work when he heard we wanted it done."[51]

Curiously, True, who rarely complimented anyone in her letters, admired Pedro, not only because he showed a willingness to work, but also because he minded the baby. The fact that Pueblo women had an essential part in the building of Pueblo dwellings—that of plastering and whitewashing—elicited no comment at all from True. Yet part of her job was to instill the notion of white, separate spheres into the Pueblos, which surely would not countenance men minding babies while women plastered houses.

Both True's and Stahl's support for Indian male domesticity reveals the enormous gap between stated BIA policies and the actual notions of proper gender relations and roles held by the white women employed by the BIA. Although the BIA still proposed that women and men should be confined to separate spheres, one private and the other public, its female employees had developed different standards. Barbara Epstein observes that the Woman's Christian Temperance Union (WCTU), of which both True and Dissette became members, promoted a "white life" crusade that included, among other things, a belief that men should become more nurturing and take a larger role in parenting.[52] Interestingly, True's brand of feminism not only sought women's invasion of the public sphere but also wished for men's inclusion in the domestic sphere.

Although the BIA model for womanhood envisioned the Indian woman becoming a dutiful and dependent wife, many of the women it hired were themselves single and did not model this behavior. As single white women, seemingly without any other source of support, both True and Dissette sought financial independence and security. Learning business skills that the "true woman" would have left to her husband, True and Dissette bought property and supported themselves on their BIA earnings and on profits from their farming and ranching ventures. When Dissette bought five acres of property in Santa Fe, she displayed a remarkable competence in financial matters. She managed her venture financially through a few donations from friends and relatives but mostly supported herself from her salary and the cultivation of winter apples and small fruits, the raising of some Jersey cows, and the renting of houses on her property. After 1910 True also became a property owner and a skilled rancher. In addition to carrying out her Indian reform activities, she managed an apple, hay, and livestock business.[53]

The true-womanhood ideal had also emphasized women's submissiveness to men. As Peggy Pascoe has pointed out, by the late nineteenth century this "virtue" was all but obsolete.[54] Certainly, Dissette and True did not model submission to men. Dissette resented the expectation that she should defer to male judgment and feign dependence upon, and inferiority to, men. When soldiers were employed to protect her at Zuni in 1897, she came into conflict with a lieutenant. Dissette became irritated at him because "he talked to me on all topics as if I were a 14 yr. old school girl or some 'pore white-trash' that had been born and raised here." During her conversation with the lieutenant, Dissette "preserved with difficulty my attitude of respectful attention." But the next morning, Dissette composed a letter to the lieutenant, using one of the "salient points in his harangue," that he was "a man perfectly capable of forming his own opinions." In her letter Dissette remarked, "I was a woman capable of doing the same thing and of expressing them [opinions] too when I had an opportunity. Then I proceeded to do so forcibly, yet politely and the result was that my gallant Sir-know-it-all made an 'Additional Report.'"[55]

Dissette developed an acute critique of the gender policies of the BIA. "The truth is these pueblos have been and are grossly neglected," she complained. "The poor teachers (women) have risked their lives daily to help the people while the Agent was in Pueblo, Colorado attending to his banking interests and the Supervising teacher sat in his office chair assisting the clerk with the Agent's office work and writing peremptory letters to these same long suffering little appreciated women." Other women employees in the BIA developed similar gendered critiques of their work. In 1895 one field matron wrote, "[I]t is evident to any person who ever spent one week among Indians that those Matron Report [forms] were gotten up by some *man* who probably never saw an Indian at his home and who had no conception of the way in which they live" (emphasis in original).[56] Perhaps Ellen Stahl's apparent difficulty in filling out her field matron report form confirms this woman's complaint. Clearly, Dissette and some other female employees of the BIA resented the hold of men in the BIA over all the most powerful positions. Meanwhile, they believed, women carried out the "real" work in the field and received little of the credit or financial compensation.

True also resented male power and privilege. She showed great ambition to rise through the ranks in the Indian Service and to attain leadership positions that previously only men had held. When she was thwarted by high officials in the BIA, who appointed men instead of her, she became bitter. While she was stationed at the Lower Brule Agency as principal of the boarding school, her superior recommended that she be made superintendent of the school. According to True, the Catholic bishop, the outgoing and incoming Indian agents, and the Indians themselves supported True's promotion. The commissioner of Indian affairs, however, appointed one of his friends to the job. True believed that the commissioner told the new appointee "that the job would be a snap as 'Miss True will do all the work.'" Embittered, True recalled, "I had my first lesson in Indian Service politics then."[57]

Like many other women in the late nineteenth century, Dissette and True believed that women, as a class of people, were morally superior to, but unjustly oppressed by, men.[58] Viewing themselves as members of a victimized class, feminists such as True and Dissette also perceived themselves to be part of a great sisterhood of women who needed to look out for one another and work together to challenge male dominance. It was with other women that both Dissette and True felt most comfortable and could be most intimate. In asking the Presbyterian Board to send observers to Zuni, Dissette explicitly asked them to send a woman because, she said, "there are many things which I can discuss only with a woman." She also suggested to a benevolent society that "a thoroughly trained medical missionary—a woman—would be the greatest earthly boon" for Zuni. Dissette believed that women had equal if not superior intelligence to men; thus she supported women in positions of power and authority. Looking back on her work in the BIA, Dissette commented that "there used to be a bunch of intelligent sympathetic teachers in the day schools, women of course."[59]

True and Dissette were also part of a large group of white, middle-class women in the late nineteenth century who found intimacy and companionship with other women rather than with men.[60] During her tenure at Morongo, True met Mary Bryan, a "woman of wealth and position," who served as treasurer of the Redlands Indian Association. When True took over the superintendency at Morongo, Bryan volunteered to help her on the reservation, working as a financial clerk. True and Bryan became very close friends. Bryan "was so closely connected with all of my work," True declared, "that we slept, ate and camped as well as worked together. At the close of my official life, she elected to keep up the intimacy." True and Bryan spent the rest of their lives together in New Mexico. Dissette also found companionship with other women. During her annual vacation to Santa Fe, she asked other white women who worked among the Indians of the Southwest to spend vacations with her.[61]

Rather than submit to the BIA status quo of male cronyism and dominance and female sacrifice and subservience, both Dissette and True sought to gain greater authority and power through this sisterhood of women and through their association with morality. After she was transferred from Zuni in 1898, Dissette persisted in behind-the-scenes maneuvering until the agent eventually reappointed her to Zuni. As the agent had feared, however, once reassigned to Zuni as nurse in 1899, Dissette attempted to gain ultimate power and authority, not just over the Zuni people, but over other BIA employees. She viewed the fight against the epidemic as a competition between herself and other BIA employees, and she set out to prove that the new schoolteacher and the field matron were incompetent and negligent in their duties.[62] True sought a much broader range of power than did Dissette. In 1913 she made a bid for a position as assistant commissioner in the Indian Service. She counted on support from the IRA and from individuals she had worked with in California, including Stanford University president David Starr Jordan and another prominent Indian reformer, Annie E. K. Bidwell. Dissette also wrote True a letter of support.[63] Again, as in the 1890s, True was passed over for the assignment.

Though True did not attain the powerful position in the BIA that she longed for, she did find other means to assert authority. Acting as a constant thorn in the side of the BIA, True continually aired her opinions about BIA personnel and policy. When she was accused of meddling, she publicized the charges as a badge of honor, bragging that "the Administrative Secretary of the Interior recently stated that 'Miss True has given us more trouble than all the rest of the [Indian Service] put together.'" Despite her reputation as a meddler, True became relatively powerful in Indian-reform circles. The IRA often asked her advice about matters pertaining to Pueblo Indians, and she worked for them briefly in 1924 and 1925.[64] She also became known internationally for her efforts. In 1920 the Mexican government offered her "a most attractive and important part in an Indian program." Additionally, True became intensely involved in New Mexico state politics. Even before women's suffrage had passed, True exerted power in the New Mexico state legislature, working on matters regarding Pueblo lands that were largely seen (until the 1920s) as the exclusive province of male attorneys.[65] In 1926 True became chairperson of the New Mexico North Central Accrediting Committee, in charge of the certification of teachers in public schools. In 1927 she also obtained a position as supervisor of public high schools in New Mexico. These positions suited her career ambitions and her longing for power and authority. She enjoyed her power to "pass upon the qualifications of all teachers in accredited schools," proclaiming, "I do not give approval to anybody who does not deserve it."[66]

In their bids for power and authority, Dissette and True often attacked men in the BIA for their alleged lack of morality. Though they implicitly rejected some of the old tenets of true womanhood—that women should play a submissive role in a separate domestic sphere—they still clung fiercely to the notion of women's exalted moral position and sexual purity. Like other moral reformers of their time, True and Dissette sought to instill a single standard of sexual behavior among both men and women, that sexual activity should be engaged in only for procreative purposes within the confines of a Christian marriage.[67] In the mid-1910s True and Dissette joined forces to clean up the BIA, focusing on two issues in particular—stopping the liquor traffic to Indians and ending sexual immorality within the BIA. True and Dissette first targeted Pueblo superintendent Crandall, charging him with encouraging the liquor traffic to Indians. In the late 1910s and 1920s True and Dissette redirected their efforts to clean up the BIA and focused on the new superintendent of the Pueblo Agency, Philip T. Lonergan. They charged Lonergan with allowing sexual immorality within the ranks of BIA employees under his supervision.[68] True and Dissette also campaigned against Superintendent Lonergan because they believed his "right-hand man," a Mexican-American named Chavez, had syphilis. According to True, Chavez "visit[ed] the pueblos upon business for the Superintendent and women day school teachers ha[d] to entertain him in their homes." True claimed, "I have never known such vileness in the Indian Service. . . . It seems that nothing can be done with these vicious employees whose low morals are giving tone to the Indians."[69]

Dissette, True, and other female moral reformers viewed venereal disease as a primary cause of women's sterility and blamed the spread of the disease on immoral men. Impure husbands who frequented houses of prostitution might contract the disease and infect their pure wives with it. In their rhetoric, social hygienists and purity crusaders alike portrayed middle-class women as innocent, weak, and helpless. Even "fallen women," prostitutes who were seen as the source of the disease, were characterized as victims who had been forced or enticed into prostitution through the "white slave trade."[70] True and Dissette also sought a "concerted campaign to clean up incipient venereal disease" among the Indians in Indian schools, believing that there could be "no sound mind in a dirty body." Tellingly, however, whereas they represented Chavez as an evil menace, they portrayed the potentially infected Indians as "victims," who "can be treated and cured without unpleasant publicity."[71] Just as doctors and moral reformers cast white men as the villains and white women as the victims in the spread of venereal disease, True and Dissette depicted Indians as a race, up until 1920, as the helpless and innocent victims of both Mexican and white men.

Even Indian men, whom Dissette and True had often depicted as degenerate sexual predators, became helpless victims of venereal disease. True blamed the BIA for inflicting "a brute of a superintendent upon so many helpless people."[72] During her early years at Santa Clara, True seemed to sympathize with the plight of Indian women, blaming their degradation on Indian men. She saw herself as an older sister who could rescue her younger Indian sisters from their condition. But by the time True began her ranching operation, rather than accusing Pueblo men of abusing Pueblo women, she turned her attention more toward exposing officials in the BIA as the true victimizers of all Indians. In this way, up to the 1920s, True and Dissette seemed to code Native Americans as a "feminine" race, as a long-suffering, victimized class of people. Dissette drew broad analogies between the conditions of women and of Native Americans, as when she bitterly quipped, "[A] woman has no political status, and is classed with the Indians she is helping to raise to the dignity of citizens."[73]

To protect both its decent employees and the Indians, True believed "there should be a frequent housecleaning in the [Indian] Service."[74] True's gendered metaphor of housecleaning is especially relevant here. She was supposed to teach the virtues of domesticity associated with housecleaning to Indian women, but True became more and more intent on broadening the meaning of women's work and the arena in which women could use their skills. She implied

44

that only upright Christian women could accomplish the thorough cleaning the BIA needed to save the Indians. Thus, using the rhetoric of women's sexual purity, True and Dissette argued for an enlarged role for women. Their growing interest in the sexual misconduct of BIA employees revealed a growing anxiety about what they perceived to be changing sexual mores; their unrest would become intensified in the 1920s.

Dissette and True shared many of the same perspectives—an aversion to domesticity, a refusal to submit to male dominance, a faith in women's moral superiority, a sense of sisterhood with other women, a commitment to crusade against male abuse of power, a desire to attain power themselves, and an unshakeable belief in the need to civilize Pueblo Indians. Yet they diverged in one area of Indian reform in the 1910s and 1920s. While Dissette continued her focus on the uplift of Indian women, True eventually became more involved in the affairs of Indian men than of Indian women. Rather than maintaining her view that all Indian men sought to degrade Indian women, True began to make distinctions between those Indian men who corrupted Indian women and those who were "good."[75] In True's mind "bad" Indian men clung to their traditional ways, while "good" men renounced their "heathenism."

From 1910 to the 1930s, True worked intensely to organize a group of so-called progressive men in Santa Clara Pueblo. In a letter to the president of the Progressive Pueblo Indian Council, True reminisced about her role with the young Indians:

If I have steered you past the rocks until your boat is in smooth water, I am glad to have been of help to my old boys of the little day school in Santa Clara where I carried some of you on my back when you were too little to walk to a school picnic. I made the first "pants" many of you ever wore. Most of you have boys of your own now. It is probably impossible for any outsider to understand the close bond of friendship you and I have for each other. It seems but yesterday since I ran the clippers over your hair by order of the Indian Bureau. I have spanked a good many of you. As you grew up, we were companions in hunting and fishing and gardening and "busting" broncos. Later on in life, most of you worked for me on my ranch. We have been almost like the same family for nearly thirty years. . . . You are always my "boys." Don't forget that, whatever happens.[76]

True's paternalistic letter to the council reveals how much more she identified with the activities of men—hunting, fishing, and "busting" broncos—than she did with those of women. She may have become more involved in the affairs of Indian men than with women because she was more interested in village politics—the province of Pueblo men—than with the home lives of Pueblo women.

Further, whereas she lamented her lack of power in relation to white men, she clearly believed she could exert dominance and authority over some Indian men, whom she believed were "always my 'boys.'" It seems that True, at least in her own mind, moved from her role as older sister to Indian women to that of father to Indian men.

Thus, True and Dissette cannot be easily categorized as purveyors of true womanhood to Indian women; they modeled, instead, a configuration of fluid and often contradictory values and qualities. Both in their behavior and in their teachings Dissette and True urged Indian women to become independent and self-sufficient wage earners rather than dependent wives. True's and Dissette's decisions not to marry and to rely on their relationships with other women for companionship may have offered alternative paths to Indian women as well. Rather than stressing the importance of women's submissiveness to men, Dissette and True also modeled that women could challenge men. In addition, they showed no compunction about participating in the public arena of business and politics. But there were limits to how much the two women would transform the mission of the BIA and challenge the norms associated with true womanhood. They continued to stress the value of women's sisterhood and sexual purity throughout their lives. In fact, they often attacked male privilege and power based on its association with sexual immorality. Most importantly, they maintained the notion that assimilation into American society was the only option for Pueblo Indians and that white women had a key role to play in accomplishing this.

True and Dissette were not alone among female schoolteachers and field matrons in broadcasting a complicated message about womanhood to Indian girls and women. As we have seen, in failing to reach Indian women and instead teaching domestic skills to Indian men, Ellen Stahl did not transmit the BIA's desired message to Native Americans. There were countless other white women who served as field matrons and as schoolteachers who undoubtedly shared many of True's and Dissette's feminist and assimilationist views. To understand the meaning of these white women's work with Indians, it is necessary to look at the other side of the encounter: the perspective of Indian women. White women had redefined their mission to Indian women and men; what would Indian women take from their encounters with these white women? To be sure, some took nothing at all, preferring to distance themselves as much as possible from white women and their civilizing mission. Dissette lamented losing her "oldest and most reliable girl," who "was married Indian fashion." Dissette speculated that either her student's new husband had forbidden her to go to Sunday School or the girl wished "to sever all relations with the Mission" and stay away. Others may have selectively chosen certain aspects of white women's teachings while ignoring others. For example, three girls who attended Dissette's classes often missed school because they had "special ceremonies to perform in the dances, and their attendance had always been a matter of contention between their parents and us."[77]

Yet other Pueblo women seemed to develop meaningful relationships with their white women teachers and field matrons. Daisy Schuman Thomas, for example, lived with Dissette for many years. Unfortunately, Thomas and other native women who knew Dissette and True left only a faint trail of written records. The accounts of two Hopi women, Helen Sekaquaptewa and Polingaysi Qoyawayma, however, yield insights into how some Pueblo women interpreted their encounter with white female moral reformers. In addition, a biography of the San Ildefonso potter Maria Martinez also sheds light on this subject. These narratives must be approached with caution, however. Both Sekaquaptewa's and Qoyawayma's books are "as told to" autobiographies. Each woman told her story to a white woman—Louise Udall and Vada Carlson, respectively—who then framed and shaped their stories. The master narrative of each book seems to be one of how each native woman struggled to overcome the "backwardness" of Hopi life in order to achieve success in the modern world. At the same time, each woman eventually reconciles with and "salvages" some aspects of her culture. It is possible, though, to use evidence in these books without accepting the overall framing of each of the women's stories. Likewise, Alice Marriott's biography of Maria Martinez provides an overall structure that reflects Marriott's vision more than that of Martinez. Nevertheless, we can glean from this source important insights into Martinez's view of her interactions with white women.[78]

Both Polingaysi Qoyawayma and Helen Sekaquaptewa were born and grew up in the Hopi village of Oraibi. Sekaquaptewa was born in 1898 and Qoyawayma in the early 1890s.[79] Both girls were born to "Hostile" families who opposed cooperation with white missionaries and BIA officials and who fought bitterly with the "Friendlies" of the village who favored adaptation to white ways. In 1906 both girls experienced the violent schism in Oraibi between the Hostiles and the Friendlies that led to the Hostiles being exiled to Hotevilla.[80] Against the wishes of their parents, both Sekaquaptewa and Qoyawayma were "caught" and taken down the mesa to attend day school at New Oraibi. Although Qoyawayma's parents had tried to hide her when white officials and the Navajo police rounded up Hopi children to bring them to day school, Qoyawayma allowed herself to be caught.[81] Once the two girls arrived at school, white teachers christened Talashongnewa's young daughter Helen and the Qoyawayma girl Elizabeth Ruth, or Bessie for short.

Despite the taunts of the Friendly children and the adjustment to school life, both girls liked school. Sekaquaptewa attended the day school only briefly before she was "caught" again, at age seven, and sent away to the on-reservation boarding school at Keams Canyon. After attaining only a sixth-grade education during ten years there, she wanted to continue her schooling. But because she was still a minor, she needed her parents' permission to attend another school. Knowing that her parents would refuse to let her attend another school so far from home, Sekaquaptewa managed to cajole BIA officials into letting her attend Phoenix Indian School for three years without her parents' permission. Similarly, Qoyawayma looked forward to educational opportunities beyond the New Oraibi day school. Learning of a wagon that was bound for Sherman Institute, an Indian boarding school in Riverside, California, Qoyawayma stowed herself away in it. When she was discovered the day the wagon was to leave, Qoyawayma refused to get out of the wagon until her parents signed a permission slip allowing her to go.[82]

After many years away, with little contact with their parents, both Qoyawayma and Sekaquaptewa returned to the Hopi mesas. As neither wanted to return to a Hopi lifestyle or participate in Hopi ceremonies, each had trouble adjusting to her return and felt ill at ease in her parents' home. After failed attempts to get her mother to use pots and pans and to make American-style dishes, Qoyawayma moved in with the Freys, a white missionary family.[83] Helen Sekaquaptewa soon met another returned student, Emory Sekaquaptewa, whom she married in both Hopi and American fashion. Although Emory came to live with Helen's family, as was customary, soon neither Helen nor Emory could tolerate the tension present in the household. They moved out on their own, taking jobs first at an Indian school in Idaho and then returning to the Hopi Reservation where they also worked off and on at other federal institutions. Eventually, they acquired a ranch away from their village on the border of the Hopi and Navajo Reservations. Sekaquaptewa bore ten children, two of whom died in infancy, and raised two Navajo boys as well. She also became an active member of the Mormon church.[84]

Qoyawayma followed a different path, serving as a missionary for many years and then becoming a schoolteacher among the Hopis and Navajos. She married a Cherokee man, but the couple soon divorced. Qoyawayma's methods of teaching Indian children eventually became a model under the Indian New Deal of the 1930s. With her earnings, she built her own house, complete with running water, heating, and electricity, and with modern conveniences such as a stove and washing machine. She also acquired a piano.[85]

Maria Martinez, born in the 1880s in San Ildefonso Pueblo, attended day school there and later was sent to a Catholic boarding school in Santa Fe. Unlike Qoyawayma's and Sekaquaptewa's parents, Martinez's parents approved of her obtaining a white education. Upon her return from boarding school, Martinez wrestled with the idea of becoming a schoolteacher but instead married Julian Martinez. The couple struggled to eke out a living from farming but supplemented their farm income with Julian's wages from work on an anthropological dig and as a janitor in Santa Fe. When anthropologists and traders expressed interest in Martinez's pottery skills, however, the couple's fortune changed. Perfecting her pottery-making techniques, Martinez became a famous potter and the richest person in her village. A number of other women joined in the pottery-making enterprise, and eventually the pueblo prospered as an art center. In the 1920s and 1930s pottery making began to surpass agriculture as the greatest source of wealth in the village.[86]

In their personal odysseys, Martinez, Qoyawayma, and Sekaquaptewa all came into contact with white women schoolteachers and field matrons. Martinez's day-school teacher, Miss Grimes, made a lasting impression on her. According to Martinez, Miss Grimes had endeared herself to the pueblo because she was "nice and friendly. She visited all the houses, and she knew everybody in the pueblo by name. If she went to a house at mealtime, she sat down and ate with the family, and afterwards she helped wash the dishes. She was never cross, and she never refused to help people who were in trouble."[87] Similarly, when she returned from thirteen years away at boarding schools, Sekaquaptewa became very close to one of the white women on the Hopi Reservation, Miss Sarah Abbott, a field matron who acted as both resident field nurse and overseer of the community laundry and sewing rooms. As Sekaquaptewa described it, Miss Abbott provided her a refuge from the difficulties she faced when she returned home from boarding schools. Sekaquaptewa admired Miss Abbott because she "endeavored to learn and understand the ways and customs of the people." Interestingly, Sekaquaptewa measured Abbott by the same standard Martinez applied to Grimes. "During her visits [to the sick], if a family should be eating," Sekaquaptewa wrote, "and if they should invite her to stay and eat with them, she would sit down and eat." To both Martinez and Sekaquaptewa, sharing a meal offered by a Pueblo family showed signs of respect and friendship. Sekaquaptewa concluded that Abbott "was a good angel in my life . . . until she retired in 1925."[88]

The white women whom these three Indian women encountered seemed on the surface to follow the mission of the BIA—to uplift Indian women; they instilled in Martinez, Qoyawayma, and Sekaquaptewa the importance of being a "lady." Martinez described one of the many conversations she had with Miss Grimes about becoming a lady:

"My mother says that you aren't like other white women," [Maria] said. "Nobody else we ever knew was as easy to be with as you are."

"Your mother is easy to be with, too," Miss Grimes answered. "She is a real lady."

"Is a lady a grownup?" Maria wanted to know.

"A lady is a person who is friendly and helpful and kind, and who treats people nicely. . . ," answered Miss Grimes. "You have to keep . . . thinking and trying, and not ever stop, if you truly want to be a lady."

. . . [Maria replied], "I'm going to keep trying and trying to be a lady like my mother and you."[89]

Clearly, Grimes valued "ladylike" behavior, but she left the concept ill defined and open to interpretation.

Their white teachers' efforts to stress the importance of ladylike behavior led many young Indian women students to strive to emulate white ladies. Martinez and her sister would imagine their dolls were "little ladies." When she wore her white confirmation dress, Martinez mused that now she would have to be a lady. When Martinez's mother dressed her and her sister in new American clothes for their stay at St. Catherine's Indian School in Santa Fe, Martinez asked if they looked like ladies in them. At boarding school with her sister, she wondered if it was unladylike of her to let her sister write letters home for her. In class, when she was about twelve, Sekaquaptewa and a playmate imagined themselves as two "eastern society women." Taking on the roles of "Mrs. Judson of New York City" and "Mrs. Holmes of Philadelphia," they passed notes to each other regarding the books they had read and their families.[90]

It was one thing to play "lady"; it was another to be a lady. When these three Indian women tried to apply the lessons of ladyhood—the female moral reformers' ideal of womanhood—to their own lives, how did they define what it meant to be a lady? Weaving together their own culture's conceptions of gender with the lessons they had learned from white women schoolteachers and field matrons, these Indian women crafted their own notion of womanhood. As one of their precepts of womanhood, all three Indian women stressed the value of attaining an education, and a "white woman's education" at that. When she sought to transfer to the Phoenix Indian School, Sekaquaptewa commented, "I still loved to study and learn." Qoyawayma shared Sekaquaptewa's zeal for learning, attending several educational institutions throughout her early life and eventually becoming a schoolteacher. After returning from boarding school at Sherman Institute, Qoyawayma noted that "her former Sherman schoolmates had returned, married, and were living the traditional life. She was still reaching out for education. What for? they would have asked."[91]

In 1899, when Martinez returned from boarding school, she had a telling conversation with her old teacher, Miss Grimes. Miss Grimes asked her what she wanted to do with her life. At a loss, Martinez replied,

"Just what most ladies do, I guess. Get married and have a house and take care of babies."

"That's a fine life if it's what you want," said Miss Grimes slowly, "but you don't have to live it if you don't want to. You are a bright girl, and you work and study hard. If you wanted to, you could go to school and college and learn to be a teacher yourself."

Overhearing the conversation, Miss Grimes's sister piped up that teaching was "a lonely life for a woman. . . . Your first choice is the best one, Maria. Live like other ladies." Martinez considered Miss Grimes's suggestion seriously. She discussed it with her mother and one of her sisters. Her mother told her that "it's the right life for a woman, to have her own house and her own children and her own man. It's right to be at home, in your own pueblo with your own people." Her sister Desideria responded more harshly, "Why do you want to be a teacher? . . . That's all right for white people. But Indian girls don't have to be teachers. They have houses and babies to take care of."[92] Martinez wrestled with her choices and eventually did opt for marriage. Formal American education seemed to hold little value to many Pueblo Indian women. But for some Pueblo women who came into prolonged contact with white women, including Qoyawayma, Sekaquaptewa, and Martinez, education became a prime value in their concept of womanhood. At a time when middle-class white women had begun to demand a college education for themselves, it was not surprising that as teachers they would emphasize this value to Indian women.

As another tenet of their standard of womanhood, Qoyawayma, Sekaquaptewa, and Martinez stressed the importance of women's independence and the ability to earn one's own wages in the new economy into which the Pueblos were rapidly becoming enmeshed. Qoyawayma was overjoyed when she learned that her benefactors at Riverside planned to pay her for her work. "She who had never before had money . . . was to have money of her own." Because she enjoyed learning and earning her own money as a housekeeper, Qoyawayma did not want to go home to her village during the summer and "almost dreaded" returning to her village after her stint at Sherman Institute. Later, as a BIA schoolteacher, she liked getting her own paycheck and the feeling of independence it gave her.[93] With the money she earned from her work, Qoyawayma built her own home. While at Phoenix Indian School, Sekaquaptewa put to use the

American domestic skills she had learned. Because she had to earn all of her own spending money, Sekaquaptewa claimed that "my hands were never still. I was always doing embroidery or crochet or tatting, making things to sell."[94] From an early age, Martinez showed an interest in earning her own wages. At age five, she told her mother she wanted to own and operate a trading post when she grew up. When anthropologists and traders became interested in her pottery, Martinez realized a means to gain financial independence and security.[95]

At least one of the lessons Qoyawayma, Martinez, and Sekaquaptewa had learned from their teachers was the acceptability of being "independent" and of earning one's own wage, concepts that would have been meaningless before the Pueblos had become integrated into the American economy. Before ever attending American schools, Qoyawayma and Martinez already evinced a rebelliousness and independence. Rather than squelching these tendencies, American education with white women actually reinforced them. All three of these Pueblo women learned from their encounters with white women teachers how to put domestic skills to a commercial purpose. Instead of teaching them that their place was solely in the home, white women teachers encouraged Indian women to earn wages in the economy outside their pueblo and strive for economic independence.

On the subject of marriage, the three women were divided. When Qoyawayma returned home, her parents wished her to marry and have children, but Qoyawayma resisted. According to her autobiography, marriage

had never entered Polingaysi's mind. She wanted to save money. She wanted to build a house of her own someday, but she was not ready for marriage. The image of herself, down on her knees in the grinding room, laboriously reducing the blue cornmeal to fine flour for the piki wedding bread, was appalling to Polingaysi. . . .

She was not yet willing to become a living seed pod for her Hopi people. She loved children but was not ready to assume the role of mother. . . .

And for no man, she told herself with spirit, would she grind corn on her knees.

Clearly, a traditional Hopi marriage did not appeal to Qoyawayma. Neither did a traditional American marriage. She wished to avoid the life of drudgery she believed had been assigned to women, both among the Hopis and in the larger American society. Observing German farm women during a trip with her missionary employer to Kansas, Qoyawayma "thought of the Hopi women, slaving at their grinding stones, and the German women slaving over their washboards, and wondered which were to be more pitied." Qoyawayma recoiled from what she regarded as the domestic slavery inherent in marriage in general.

When her brief marriage failed, Qoyawayma rationalized that "she had been independent too long, and had fought too hard for her precious independence, to take second place in her home."[96]

Qoyawayma's attitudes toward marriage and the role expected of women within it almost echo Mary Dissette's sentiments.[97] Qoyawayma probably had not acquired her yen for independence and her aversion to domesticity among the Hopis in Oraibi. Rather her white women teachers, many of whom must have shared Dissette's ambivalence about domesticity and who themselves never married, may have imbued her with a criticism of women's domestic role within late-nineteenth-century Victorian marriages.[98] Obviously, if the BIA intended to instruct Indian women in true womanhood, something had gone awry.

Martinez and Sekaquaptewa did not hold such aversions to marriage. Both women represented their marriages as working partnerships in which women potentially found fulfillment in working closely with their husbands. Helen's marriage to Emory Sekaquaptewa embodied the precepts of working together to contribute earnings to the family economy. Shortly after their marriage, the couple went to work together at an Indian school in Idaho. When they returned to Arizona, they bought a ranch that they sustained together. Sekaquaptewa sewed for money, worked as a domestic in Phoenix, and helped with farming. In her autobiography Sekaquaptewa presented her marriage as an ideal and harmonious partnership. This depiction of her marriage in such terms may have derived both from Hopi concepts of proper relations between the sexes and emerging white models of companionate marriage.

Anthropologists have stressed that though men and women have had distinctly separate roles and responsibilities in Hopi society, the men have not generally subordinated women; relationships between men and women have been complementary and equitable.[99] Both Qoyawayma's and Sekaquaptewa's autobiographies make clear, however, that traditionally, Hopi men and women socialized separately. Therefore, while Helen's depiction of her marriage to Emory may have been based on Hopi notions, it also may have been influenced by exposure to white female teachers' new emphasis on companionate marriage. Martinez also portrayed her marriage as a partnership, but a much more troubled one than that of the Sekaquaptewas. When Martinez began making pottery for commercial sale, she enlisted Julian to paint designs on the finished product. Together they ran their pottery business. Yet Julian struggled with a drinking problem throughout his life. Martinez constantly tried to coax him to take a greater part in the pottery business as a means to wean him from his habit. Her expectation that her husband should work closely with her suggests that she, too, might have imbibed notions from her teachers that valued a companionate marriage.

Though Martinez, Qoyawayma, and Sekaquaptewa undoubtedly absorbed some of the lessons white women imparted regarding women's possibilities, they did not accept all the views white women offered. Their own accounts constantly countered the notions that Indian women were lazy. Both Sekaquaptewa and Qoyawayma emphasized how hard Indian women worked, particularly at grinding corn. Martinez's book also stressed the constant round of women's domestic chores and child care. To varying degrees, all three women also challenged white women reformers' notion that their cultures degraded them. While rejecting many aspects of their cultures, Sekaquaptewa and Qoyawayma nevertheless defended many of the fundamental beliefs of the Hopis. As Sekaquaptewa put it, she was not interested in the ritual part of Hopi religion because she believed it "crude," but "the things my parents taught me about the way to live were good." These included remaining a virgin until marriage and being faithful to one's spouse.[100] Qoyawayma, Sekaquaptewa, and Martinez had not become "true women." Yet neither had they remained "traditional" Indian women. Their encounters with white women had led them to seize upon lessons that they found most useful to their own situations and to shape a unique, multicultural view of womanhood.

While gender roles were in flux at the turn of the century, notions about race and culture were also undergoing a significant transformation. In 1912 one observer challenged the whole basis for the field matron program. As Charles Saunders, a writer who favored the preservation of Pueblo cultures, put it, "Finding the Pueblo women leisurely with their work instead of rushing about it like victims of Americanitis, [the field matron] sets them down as lazy; and because their dress bears the stain of the prevailing dust of the Southwest they are, in her eyes, dirty. So perfectly convinced that Pueblo women are as 'benighted' as the authorities in Washington think they are, she proceeds to revolutionize the Pueblo household."[101] Saunders worried that the field matrons, as well as the whole host of other BIA employees and missionaries, would ultimately destroy the culture of the Pueblos that he found so worthy of preserving. But Saunders need not have worried; some field matrons had reached conclusions similar to his own.

In the late 1890s the field matron at Zuni, May Faurote, came into conflict with Mary Dissette. They quarreled over the issue of where to conduct classes in spinning and weaving and then over the handling of the smallpox epidemic. In a letter to Herbert Welsh, the president of the IRA, in which she defended herself against Dissette's charges, Faurote revealed how one field matron's views of the

civilizing mission were transformed by her experience. While Dissette continued to assume she knew what was best for the Indians, Faurote believed that

> [i]f the object in view is to help the Indian it is certainly better to know him
> before dictating the policy that shall govern him. . . . These people are
> certainly savages and do believe in witches and occasionally act upon their
> belief, but if history be true, our own ancestors did the same when they
> were supposed to be an enlightened Christian people, this belief is their
> worst fault and must be dealt with firmly until they have outgrown it; aside
> from this they are gentle, peaceable, affectionate and much kinder than
> many so-called Christians. I have been with them daily in their homes, and
> have seen their family life and nowhere have I seen more instances of self-
> sacrificing love between members of the same family than in Zuni. . . .
> Zuni is certainly dirty and its inhabitants are the victims of disease and
> filth, but they are men and women and I believe constant threatening and
> bulldozing not only unwise but positively detrimental in its effects.[102]

A few other field matrons and female schoolteachers also reexamined their attitudes toward Native Americans. In northern California, field matrons Mabel
Reed and Mary Arnold also questioned their assigned role in the assimilation
plan. After being adopted by Karok families, Reed and Arnold wrote of a
Christmas celebration: "These were our own people. They were our
friends. . . . [The Indians] could be as gay and as Indian as they chose without
any loss of dignity, because we had been adopted . . . and were not white any
longer but Indians like themselves."[103] Faurote's, Reed's, and Arnold's views
would become increasingly popular. Faurote's nascent cultural relativism—her
ability to see the "savage" in her own culture and the "civilization" in the Zuni's
society—foreshadowed the new vision of anthropologists, artists, and writers
who would discover the Southwest in the 1910s and 1920s. Reed's and Arnold's
shared belief that they could assume an Indian identity also prefigured how this
new group of primitivists would attempt at times to play Indian. As Dissette and
True labored in the Southwest to civilize the Pueblo Indians and impart to them
their own notions of transformed gender relations, a new group of white women
began to articulate a position that fully exploded the Victorian ideal of womanhood and the racial assumptions that underlay the civilizing mission. Although
True and Dissette were shocked by these women, it was really female moral reformers who, in their own lives, had taken the first steps that would eventually
lead to their successors' open repudiation of the assumptions of true womanhood.

CHAPTER THREE

Antimodern Feminists and the
Emergence of Cultural Relativism

New Mexico had been discovered by artists. In a frenetic effort to escape the complications of Western cities, they were seeking not only the peace of the desert, but the refreshment of primitive life. What a relief to turn from the War and its drives to softly mellowed pueblos where brown men raised what they ate in peace. From feminism, free love, and flaming books to a sanely humorous people who took sex as simply as weather.   *Erna Fergusson, 1936*

In 1910, as she was traveling from Santa Fe to Española by train, Clara True befriended a sociologist on her first informal field trip to the Southwest. She invited the woman, Elsie Clews Parsons, to stay at her ranch near Santa Clara Pueblo while Parsons's husband, a congressman, met with the chief forester of the United States at the Grand Canyon. True provided Parsons with a pony and an Indian guide and encouraged her to dig for Pueblo pottery remains in the ruins nearby. Parsons wrote admiringly that True traded horses with the Indians, had restored the old apple orchard on her ranch, marketed apples all over the Southwest, and was the first woman elected to the irrigation committee of her river valley. Parsons also noted that True was the first white woman in the valley to run a ranch "with Indians, without a White man on it. She liked Indian men," she once told Parsons. "With White men, she always felt ill at ease." Parsons concluded that True "liked women to whom she could play the man." She was, in Parsons's view, "a feminist of the militant type, although she did not know it. She was rather against woman suffrage than for it: of my habits of smoking and of wearing riding-breeches she much disapproved." Indeed, True wrote Parsons in 1912, "I wish you wouldn't smoke and that you'd eat a big beefsteak everyday."[1]

Although True disapproved of some of Parsons's practices, she apparently identified with Parsons. Both women had overcome many of the restraints placed on women at the turn of the century; both pursued their interests and ca-

56

reers independent of men. True had chosen not to marry and found a lifelong companion in another woman. Parsons had married and borne six children, but due to her wealth and her decision to resist tradition, she hired caretakers for her children, which allowed her to pursue her career. Both women also were intensely interested in Indians. When Parsons returned to the Southwest in 1912, she and True "rode horseback through the desert . . . to the great Apache Dance." On that trip Parsons also collected ceremonial objects from Santa Clara Pueblo for museums in the East. True agreed to procure more objects after Parsons left. In 1915, on another of Parsons's field trips to the area, the two women met again. Until 1922 True wrote Parsons frequent, gossipy, and lengthy letters, but True and Parsons would not remain friends.[2] The women clashed when Parsons acquired True's Pajarito Ranch after True defaulted on a loan Parsons had made to her.[3] Eventually, too, True became aware of how significantly Parsons disagreed with two of True's most cherished beliefs—that white women were morally pure and therefore had a duty to enforce purity among others and that Indian cultures were in need of uplift to the standards of white civilization. In her work, first as a sociologist and then as an anthropologist, Parsons openly challenged both positions.

Parsons, of course, was not alone. She followed and also led a number of other white women in the early twentieth century who rejected sexual purity and women's quest for moral authority and instead articulated a new vision of feminism based on individual self-fulfillment and "sex expression." Parsons also contributed to the growing discourse of cultural relativism and primitivism that sought to destroy the racial hierarchies of the nineteenth century. Several other like-minded women joined Parsons in New Mexico; most prominent among them were the Greenwich Village salon hostess Mabel Dodge Luhan and her friend Mary Austin, a writer. Other lesser-known white women who had been active in social reform and feminism also journeyed to or settled in Santa Fe or Taos—Alice Corbin Henderson, Elizabeth Shepley Sergeant, Ina Sizer Cassidy, and Amelia Elizabeth White. Erna Fergusson, born and raised in New Mexico, returned to live there after attending college in the East.[4]

The commitment of these women both to a new type of feminism and to cultural relativism was not coincidental. Erna Fergusson, who noted that the group of artists and writers who had descended on Santa Fe had turned "from feminism, free love, and flaming books" to the "refreshment of primitive life," drew connections between this new group's avowed interest in defining a new type of womanhood and their discovery of Indian culture. Clara True also perceived this connection; she ridiculed this new group of white women as "rich women who have graduated from Birth Control and the Soviet to find a thrill in Native

Art." As Fergusson commented, these bohemians also sought to "escape the complications of Western cities" and the "War and its drives."[5] Their newfound primitivism was animated by both their growing sentiment against industrialization and modernization *and* their redefinition of womanhood, feminism, and women's sexuality.[6] I use the term "antimodern feminism" to describe the unique vision these women conceived in the first decades of the twentieth century.[7] Through a close examination of the lives of Mary Austin, Mabel Dodge Luhan, and Elsie Clews Parsons, this chapter examines the integral link between antimodern feminists' reconceptualization of womanhood and their antimodern sensibilities.

A number of the white women who traveled to and settled in northern New Mexico after World War I oriented themselves toward the Pueblo peoples in a different manner than had most white women who had gone to New Mexico as BIA schoolteachers and field matrons or as Protestant missionaries. Whereas the earlier generation of female reformers had sought the assimilation of Indians into the mainstream of American society, many of the white women who arrived in New Mexico after World War I called for the preservation of Indian culture as both a valuable asset to white Americans and a model for them. Rather than seeing the Pueblos as backward peoples in need of uplift, many of these women questioned the notion of white superiority. Mary Austin stressed the contributions that Native Americans, and especially Pueblo Indians, had made to America. Like her mentor, Charles Lummis, Austin touted the Pueblos as the key to discovering a unique American heritage.

Austin and other white women also upheld the Pueblos as a model society for a modern white America that had gone awry. Luhan invited old friends to her home in Taos to arouse in them the same sympathy and admiration for the Pueblos that she felt. She persuaded English novelist D. H. Lawrence and his wife, Frieda, to come to Taos, believing Lawrence to be the writer who could best interpret the meaning of the Pueblos to a wide audience. In her own writing Luhan represented Pueblo society as an antidote for modern America's problems. "Oh, fellow mortals out there in the world!" she proclaimed in her memoirs. "Until you learn how to join together once more, to fuse your sorrowful and lonely hearts in some new communion, you can never make true music. The sounds you produce will continue to be but the agonized expression, called 'modern,' of separate and unshared life, the wistful, sorrowing complaint of individualism before it has reached the new communal level for which it has been creating itself."[8]

Not only did the antimodern feminists challenge the notion of white superiority, they also reversed the common notion that Indians were a vanishing race.

Luhan conceptualized the white and the Indian race on a great wheel. "I saw the huge wheel turning slowly," she imagined, "weighted down with all the accretions of our civilization: the buildings and machinery, the multitudinous objects we had invented and collected about us, and ourselves fairly buried under the heavy load, muffled, stifled, going under. On the other side of the wheel, rising, bare-limbed and free, heads up bound with green leaves, sheaves of corn and wheat across their shoulders, this dark race mounting."[9]

New attitudes toward Indians among white women also reached beyond bohemian circles. In the 1920s the highly educated Lakota (Sioux) writer, Gertrude Bonnin (or Zitkala-Ša), urged the General Federation of Women's Clubs (GFWC) to organize an Indian Welfare Committee. The new GFWC committee chose Stella Atwood, a woman active in Indian policy reform in California, as its head. At first the committee also conceived of itself as part of the federation's nationwide Americanization campaign and took as one of its slogans "Americanize the First Americans." Unlike the moral reformers, however, who would have taken such a phrase to mean cultural assimilation, Atwood and her committee interpreted the slogan as "citizenship rights for the American Indians and . . . the protection of their property."[10] Why had this new view of the Pueblos taken hold? Why, in particular, had some white women who had been so associated with the work of uplifting Indian peoples to "civilization" begun to articulate and act on this new view?

Growing sentiment against industrialization and modernization in America provides one answer. As anthropologist Peter Nabokov has observed, if Indians didn't exist, white Americans would have "somehow come around to inventing them, as a utopian antithesis to so much that alienated us."[11] Anthropologists, writers, and artists who were disgruntled by World War I and the rapid pace of American industrialization found solace in northern New Mexico, where many of the Indian and Mexican people still engaged in subsistence agriculture and devoutly practiced their religions. As writer Charles Saunders put it, "[T]his slow life [of the Pueblos] looked rather pleasant to us fresh from the world of skyscrapers, department stores, and automobiles."[12]

Many of the white women who arrived in New Mexico, including Parsons, Luhan, and Austin, had developed an acute critique of modern industrial life. All three traveled in radical anticapitalist circles in Greenwich Village that were opposed to "tendencies in American life . . . of standardization, mechanization, and materialism."[13] As Austin quoted approvingly to Luhan from a lecture she had heard, "Material progress, invention, manufactures, science, which does not bring with them increased consciousness, are not progress but impediments." When one of Luhan's psychoanalysts, Dr. A. A. Brill, told her that she should learn to adjust to city life, Luhan objected, arguing, "Why should one accept a perfectly uncivilized environment?"[14] As can be seen by these comments, antimodern feminists commonly stood notions of "progress" and "civilization" on their heads. Tales of the Pueblo Indian cultures piqued these women's interest in finding an alternative to modernizing America. Austin herself recognized that white people were perhaps lured to the Pueblos out of nostalgia, as is evidenced by her belief that Taos Pueblo's "essential primitiveness, its vital pagan quality, [gathers] to itself the nostalgia of house-bred, book-fed peoples."[15]

Anti-industrial sentiment and a nostalgia for an agrarian past account for part of the transformation in some white women's attitudes toward Native American peoples in general and Pueblo cultures in particular. But they cannot fully explain why many white women became so involved in the defense of Indian cultures. To understand this involvement, it is important to analyze how many of these same white women had also begun to undermine the very tenets upon which female moral reformers such as Clara True and Mary Dissette had built their work for the uplift of Indian cultures. Women such as True and Dissette had based their mission partly on the notion of women's perceived sexual purity. When other women, such as Parsons, Luhan, and Austin, began in varying degrees to celebrate women's sexuality, they eroded the basis for female moral reformers' mission to uplift non-middle-class, non-Christian, and non-white women from their supposedly degraded sexual condition. Moreover, these women included freer sexuality in their vision of "the primitive," thereby forming the foundation for their new admiration of Native American cultures.[16] The emergence and popularization of cultural relativism thus cannot be fully understood without examining changing gender and sexual mores at the turn of the century.

To make such a broad connection between the development of admiration for Indian cultures and the abandonment of notions of women's moral superiority and sexual purity risks glossing over important differences among the white women who began to champion Pueblo culture in the 1920s. One of the most prominent women in the 1920s Indian reform movement, Stella Atwood, appeared to lead a rather conventional, upper-middle-class clubwoman's life and seemed neither to scorn modernization nor to have any interest in feminism of any kind. Writing to Luhan, Atwood declared, "I am conservative myself and I keep putting on the brakes a little bit." Rather, Atwood's defense of Indian culture seemed to derive from her staunch commitment to extending the rights of citizenship to all Americans.[17]

Atwood, though, was not reflective of most of the white women who participated in the 1920s movement. As Clara True and Erna Fergusson aptly noted, most of these women had, indeed, "graduated from Birth Control and the Soviet," advocated free love and feminism, and read "flaming books." Many of them had been and continued to be involved in redefining feminism and in championing other radical causes. The early-twentieth-century media defined these women as "New Women." Although this label had been used since the 1890s to describe any woman who took on a public role, by the 1920s it connoted a young, independent, self-defined, intelligent, sexually expressive, white, middle-class or upper-middle-class woman who was no longer bound by the notion of separate spheres or by perceived biological or intellectual limitations. While the media and many historians have focused on young women as the "new women" of the 1920s, the lives of Parsons, Luhan, and Austin contradict this image.[18] "New women" of the first decades of the twentieth century supposedly advocated self-development, self-expression, and personal satisfaction over the older notion of women's self-sacrifice. The "new woman" of the 1920s diverged most significantly from feminists at the turn of the century in her advocacy of women's sexuality.[19]

Yet the white women who championed simultaneously cultural preservation and a new type of feminism differed subtly in their views of sexuality. Of the three women featured in this chapter, Mary Austin perceived herself as a kind of transitional figure between the moral reform feminism of her mother and the sexually expressive feminism she would encounter among many of her peers. Despite her many affairs and her sometimes open advocacy of free love and "sex expression," Mabel Dodge Luhan never fully embraced this new type of feminism, and she resisted the labels of "new woman" and "feminist." Walter Lippmann, a journalist and close friend of Luhan, called her "the unclassified . . . not belonging to any type, a sport."[20] In both her personal life and her sociological and anthropological writings, Elsie Clews Parsons confidently identified herself as a feminist and consistently crusaded for women's self-fulfillment and sexual expressiveness. She defined the "new woman" as "bent on finding out for herself, unwilling to live longer at secondhand, dissatisfied with expressing her own will to power merely through ancient media, through children, servants, younger women, and uxorious men. She wants to be not only a masterless woman, one no longer classified as daughter or wife, she wants a share in the mastery men arrogate."[21]

The eldest of the three women, Mary Austin struggled to break away from notions of women's moral authority and sexual purity but never completely accepted women's sexual expressiveness as the key to women's equality and liberation. Caught between two eras of feminism, Austin wrote, "[T]here were women like Anna Howard Shaw who kept to the old restrictions, and younger women who let them go. I found myself going with the younger women. The one whose pace I kept most faithfully was Charlotte Perkins Gilman." Austin did, indeed, break with some of the "old restrictions," but her reluctance to name these restrictions or to discuss sexuality openly reveals her discomfort with the emerging values of women's "sex expression." Instead, like her friend Charlotte Perkins Gilman, she emphasized work and economic independence as the foundation of women's emancipation.[22]

Born in Carlinville, Illinois, in 1868 to a bookish father and a temperance-crusading mother, Mary Hunter Austin was influenced by both her father's love of literature and her mother's notion of women's moral superiority. She also developed a great interest in the natural world around her. Like many other middle-class white women of her generation, she attended college, where she suffered a nervous breakdown. As was common at the turn of the century, her doctor attributed her mental breakdown to overtaxing her brain. Defying her doctor's prescriptions, Austin eventually graduated from Blackburn College, intent on teaching in the local school. After her father's death in 1888, however, her older brother devised plans to move with their mother to California. During her first months in California, Austin suffered another bout of depression and mental breakdown. In the deserts of California, however, she recovered by studying the natural and cultural phenomena of her new environment and by beginning to write.[23]

In the West, in what she deemed to be the "country of lost borders," Austin found the courage she needed to break with conventions. "Out there where the borders of conscience break down, where there is no convention, and behavior is of little account except as it gets you your desire," Austin believed "almost anything might happen." Writing about herself in the third person in her autobiography, Austin asserted that she "suffered from the contempt in which woman's talent was held. . . . But growing up as she did at the western edge of American culture, suffered less than might have been the case farther East from the repressive conventions hedging femininity on every side."[24]

While True and Dissette had implicitly undermined the doctrine of separate spheres through their own examples, Austin explicitly challenged it. She rebelled against what she called "three pet sex superstitions": "that the work a human being may do in the world is determined by sex, . . . that the social value of a woman is established by what some man thinks of her, . . . and that one man alone must 'support' the family."[25] Austin believed in combining a career with marriage. Looking back on her life from the 1920s, Austin wrote, "I wished to be married. Contrary to the popular conception about literary women, I like do-

mestic life and have a genuine flair for cooking. And I wanted children profoundly."[26] In 1890, hoping to fulfill her longings for domesticity, children, and
a supportive companion, she married Wallace Austin.

In her marriage Austin found neither the domestic bliss nor the support for
her writing that she had expected. Her new husband constantly strove to strike
it rich. He moved his new wife to Lone Pine in the Owens Valley on the eastern
side of the Sierra Nevadas, where he hoped to profit from a new water irrigation
scheme. Because her husband's money-making schemes almost always failed to
pay off, Austin went back to work as a schoolteacher. She soon became pregnant
and gave birth to a daughter. Desiring to devote more attention to writing, Austin became increasingly unhappy with her married life, domesticity, and caring
for her young daughter, who had begun to show signs of a severe mental disabil-
ity.

Austin, however, found much to stimulate her outside her home. It was in
Owens Valley that she first became interested in Native Americans. With her
daughter in a knapsack on her back, she explored the country around her and
befriended the women of the Paiute Indian band that lived in the area. She also
collected material and wrote many stories based on the customs, traditions, and
lifestyles of the local miners, shepherds, and Mexicans. Austin's interactions
with the non-middle-class residents in her vicinity earned her the disapproval of
Lone Pine's "respectable" women. In Bishop, where she moved to get away
from her husband and to support herself as a schoolteacher, she again experienced this disapproval. When townspeople learned that Austin left her three-
year-old daughter chained to a chair while she taught school, they were appalled
at her seeming lack of maternal instincts. Austin eventually found another arrangement—boarding the child with a neighboring farm family. The townspeople also condemned Austin's other defiances of convention. When, in celebration of Chinese New Year, she gave a cake to Sing Lee, a Chinese man who did
her laundry, a group of ladies visited her personally to scold her.[27]

Risking social disgrace again, Austin eventually separated from, and later divorced, her husband. Many female moral reformers perceived the increasing
frequency of divorce as exploitative of women, but Austin and many other new
feminists of the 1910s and 1920s supported the liberalization of divorce laws.[28]
After separating from her husband, Austin institutionalized her mentally dis-
abled daughter and went to live in Los Angeles, where she found a literary mentor in Charles Lummis and a friend in Charlotte Perkins Gilman. There and in
San Francisco she pursued her writing career and social reform efforts. In 1903
she moved to the new artist's colony in Carmel. That same year she published
her first book, *Land of Little Rain*, based on her experiences in Owens Valley.

Continuing to write about nature, spirituality, women, Indians, and Hispanics, she gained a modest amount of fame. She also became active in the woman's suffrage movement, serving as director of publicity and lecturer for the National American Woman's Suffrage Association (NAWSA). Having become part of the literary establishment, Austin also traveled to Europe and New York City, where she campaigned to pressure New York editors, critics, and intellectuals "to admit the Indian among American influences."[29]

After the dissolution of her marriage, Austin experimented with new sexual possibilities. In New York City she had a brief affair with the muckraking journalist Lincoln Steffens. With Steffens she attended Mabel Dodge Luhan's salons and became close friends with her. At one point she wrote Luhan of her two lovers, one of whom had gone to Jerusalem and the other who was her New York "steady." She also supported women's right to birth control. "The stability of women's hold on the work of the world," Austin contended, "depends on her control of the liability of child-bearing. Maternity must be voluntary. . . . There must be no more mystery about sex if there is to be mastery."[30] Austin, like many other middle-class American women, had begun to question and shed older notions regarding the necessity of women's sexual purity.[31] Yet for Austin the transition from her Victorian upbringing to the emerging sexual mores of the 1910s and 1920s proved difficult. She described the process as follows:

> In those late nineteenth-century decades all the disabilities of excessive child-bearing were charged up to the horrid appetites of the husband. Not only did the current phrases of birth control and contraceptives not come into use until the women of the pioneer generations [of feminists] were past being interested in them, but nobody . . . had yet suggested that women are passionately endowed even as men are. . . . That sexual desire was something to which God in his inscrutable wisdom had sacrificed all women, was so certainly believed by my mother's generation. . . . But my own generation still lacked even a vocabulary by which measures of escape could be intelligently discussed.

Austin sensed the dangers to women inherent in the emerging standards of sexuality. "I came too late into the social scheme to have cared for love without responsibility," Austin declared. "And of the men who so early accepted love without obligation, too many had rejected other things along with it, truth, integrity, intention, the shared sacrifice."[32]

As an alternative to sex without obligation or love, Austin conceived of sexuality as a spiritual act. As with many other "new women," Austin expressed an interest in finding spiritual satisfaction through love and sex, writing Mabel Dodge Luhan that "the bond formed by two people giving themselves wholly, is real, has substance, spiritual substance which involves the spiritual integrity of both parties."[33] Searching for a link between spirituality and sexuality, Austin challenged institutionalized Christianity and instead sought a new expression of religion, believing it to be the "natural motion of [the] heart to express something of [its] feeling and experience with the invisible universe." Together with Luhan, Austin pursued her interest in alternative spirituality.[34]

Austin's renunciation of the notion of female sexual purity and Christian piety contributed to her skepticism regarding the need for middle-class women to uplift their downtrodden "sisters." Brought up by a temperance-crusading mother and admiring of the Woman's Christian Temperance Union (WCTU), Austin sympathized with women's quest for moral authority. "In all my life I have not seen anything so single-minded, so gallant, so truly Crusading, as those women and their Union," Austin wrote. She believed that the temperance movement, by exposing "the possibilities that a drunken father was believed to visit on his unborn offspring," had unwittingly allowed the "question of divorce and the right of women to choose when and under what conditions" they would bear children to be "admitted to the Protestant consciousness in the United States." At the same time, Austin "was not really liking, not personally approving or agreeing with Frances Willard," the energetic head of the WCTU. By the time she wrote her autobiography in the early 1930s, Austin described herself "as a feminist not wholly given over to the conviction of the innate superiority of women." Instead, she resisted the notion that it was woman's duty to "raise the world from all that's low!"[35]

Austin's questioning of nineteenth-century notions of women's sexual purity and moral authority served to deepen her interests in protecting Native American cultures from moral reformers and assimilationists. After World War I, like so many intellectuals, Austin sought a respite from the rigors of modern life. She accepted invitations from her friends Luhan, Ina Sizer Cassidy, and Gerald Cassidy to visit them in New Mexico. Together with the Cassidys, she toured the Southwest in search of material for the book on both Indians and Hispanos she published in 1924 as *The Land of Journey's Ending*. That same year she settled permanently in Santa Fe, living out the remaining ten years of her life there. From 1924 to 1934 she wrote ten books, defended Pueblo lands and religion, and promoted Pueblo and Hispano/Mexican arts and crafts. Known for her eccentricity, egotism, and arrogance, Austin was tagged even by her friends as "God's mother-in-law."

Austin's friend Mabel Dodge Luhan broke more decidedly with dominant late-nineteenth-century sexual mores; yet she never felt completely comfortable in her symbolic role as a sexually emancipated woman. She was born in 1879 as

Mabel Ganson to an elite, upper-class family in Buffalo. In 1900 she married Karl Evans and bore a son, John. Unhappy in her marriage and as a mother, she soon became involved intimately with her gynecologist. After the death of Karl Evans in a hunting accident, Luhan's affair with the gynecologist became an open scandal. Luhan's mother shipped her off to Europe.[36] On board ship she met her second husband, Edwin Dodge. Together they set up housekeeping at Villa Curonia in Florence, where they entertained intellectuals, artists, and nobles. In Luhan's bedroom, a trapdoor from Edwin's dressing room above opened over her bed; she hoped Edwin would appear and climb down a silken ladder into her arms. Edwin, however, never used the ladder. Dismayed, Luhan attempted to seduce other men.

In 1911 she encountered Gertrude and Leo Stein, who introduced her to the new intellectual movement of modernism. Drawn to this new movement, Mabel moved back to New York City with Edwin in 1912, where she befriended a group of radicals, including Elsie Clews Parsons, who condemned bourgeois American industrial capitalism. Luhan launched a salon in her Fifth Avenue apartment and gathered together this new group of radical intellectuals, activists, and artists to discuss the important issues of the day. During this time she met John Collier, who was active in promoting the preservation of immigrant cultures and in documenting poor industrial conditions in New York City. Luhan also became involved in efforts to organize the Modernist Art Exhibit at the Armory and to publicize the modern literary style of Gertrude Stein. She believed that modern art and literature would help to "shake up and make over the fixed patterns of life."[37] Together with the young radical journalist John Reed, Luhan helped to organize the Paterson Strike Pageant at Madison Square Garden, a reenactment of the silk workers' strike in New Jersey, which attracted about fifteen thousand viewers. When World War I broke out, she opposed it and enlisted in the Women's Peace Party. Luhan became interested in Freud and psychoanalysis; she underwent treatment herself and helped to popularize Freudian views by writing a weekly column for the Hearst papers.[38]

Luhan's wealth enabled her to pursue both domesticity and a career, but she chose to avoid both. Although she wrote several books, she never characterized herself as a career woman and never came out as forcefully as Austin and Parsons did for the right of women to pursue public careers. Nevertheless, she did critique the notion of separate spheres in subtle ways. When her lover John Reed took an assignment to cover the Mexican Revolution, she decided secretly to join him. But when she met him in Chicago en route to Mexico, "he looked merely rather glad instead of overjoyed. The man in him was already on the job. The woman's place was in the home!"[39]

Both Parsons and Austin openly proclaimed themselves feminists, but Luhan never identified herself in that way. She may have disliked the connotations the term "feminism" had developed by the 1920s. According to Susan Ware, the National Woman's Party, in their bid for the Equal Rights Amendment, had appropriated the term. To some "modern" women, Dorothy Dunbar Bromley wrote in 1927, the term had come to suggest the "old school" of women "who wore flat heels and had very little feminine charm, or the current species who antagonize men with their constant clamor about maiden names, equal rights, [and] woman's place in the world."[40] Though Luhan eschewed the label, she participated in many women's radical causes. She helped provide meeting space and money to defend Margaret and William Sanger when they were indicted for promoting birth control.

Luhan also joined a unique organization, the Heterodoxy Club, that she described as a club "for unorthodox women, that is to say, women who did things and did them openly."[41] Based in Greenwich Village between 1912 and 1940, the Heterodites held luncheons on a number of topics, from pacifism to African American rights to the Russian Revolution. They avidly followed the new psychological and sexual theories of Havelock Ellis and Sigmund Freud. The club included progressive reformers involved in the Women's Trade Union League and the National Association for the Advancement of Colored People as well as socialists such as Elizabeth Gurley Flynn and Crystal Eastman. Historian Judith Schwarz asserts that belief in a certain type of feminism united all Heterodoxy members. To these women, feminism embodied the right to individual fulfillment; members of the group experimented with novel social and sexual arrangements, which they believed would enhance their personal freedom. The Heterodites abandoned an earlier view of women's moral superiority and sexual purity. Spoofing member Elsie Clews Parsons's sociological and anthropological work, one Heterodite even wrote "Marriage Customs and Taboo among the Early Heterodites," which asserted that the "tribe of Heterodites is known as a tabooless group. There is the strongest taboo on taboo. Heterodites say that taboo is injurious to free development of the mind and spirit."[42]

Because of her many open love affairs, Luhan gained the reputation as a sexually emancipated, self-directed "new woman."[43] After arriving back in New York in 1912, she separated from and divorced Edwin Dodge. After the Paterson Strike Pageant, John Reed sailed with Luhan and other friends to spend the summer at Villa Curonia, where Reed and Luhan became lovers. To Luhan's satisfaction, Reed used the silken ladder that Edwin Dodge would not. Back in New York, they moved in together without marrying and conducted an on-again, off-again affair. In 1915, however, while Reed covered the war in Europe,

Mabel found a new love interest in Maurice Sterne, a Russian immigrant painter. She lived with him at Finney Farm in Croton-on-Hudson, New York, until she succumbed to pressure from her neighbors and impulsively married him one day. Almost immediately, she regretted her decision and sent him on a "honeymoon" alone out West.

Despite her apparent unconcern for social conventions, in her memoirs, Luhan revealed a more complicated perspective. She struggled to shed what she called the "curse" of restrictive views on female sexuality and to avoid the potential perils of emerging sexual mores. Luhan credited birth control pioneer Margaret Sanger with transforming her views on sexuality. She considered Sanger "an ardent propagandist for the joys of the flesh," who voiced "a new gospel of not only sex knowledge in regard to conception, but sex knowledge about copulation and its intrinsic importance." Until she discussed sex at length with Sanger, there had usually been a "certain hidden, forbidden something" in Luhan's feelings about sex. "I really got something from [Sanger]," Luhan wrote, "something new and releasing and basic . . . about the possibilities in the body for 'sex expression'"; as she "unfolded the mysteries and mightiness of physical love, it seemed to [me that I] had never known it before as a sacred and at the same time a scientific reality." Luhan added that Sanger helped her "to get rid of some old, old prohibitions" and that she taught her "the way to a heightening of pleasure and of prolonging it."[44]

Though she embraced women's "sex expression," Luhan carefully qualified her views on sex and love. "By love I do not mean only the ultimate sexual act," Luhan wrote, "though this is perhaps the cornerstone of any life, and its chief reality. . . . Coition alone never released or satisfied anyone, lacking the needed intrinsic elements of what we call love." Luhan spoke from her own experience. Shortly after separating from Edwin Dodge and before becoming involved with John Reed, Luhan decided that she needed "sex-expression" in her life. "Finally I came to the conclusion," she recounted in her memoirs, "that I was very old-fashioned and that what I needed and had never admitted to myself was this sex-expression other people were so intent upon." Thinking a young male friend of hers could "transform [her] into a completely independent woman," Luhan and her young lover attempted to have sex first in her apartment and then in a hotel room. Once in the hotel room, "I did feel rather more like an emancipated women and I forced myself impassively to undress and get into the ugly bed. . . . [But] he had suddenly become a dose of medicine I must take, a kind of medicine that would usher me into the world of free souls."[45] Luhan, like Austin, never fully embraced women's "sex expressiveness."

By the time she moved to New Mexico in 1917, Luhan's new orientation toward women and sexuality, as well as her antimodern stance, prepared her to admire, rather than condemn, the Pueblo Indians. In her memoirs Luhan characterized her decision to move to New Mexico as a mystical confluence of forces. When her husband Maurice Sterne was in the Southwest, Luhan visited a medium who foresaw that she was "surrounded by many people . . . dark people . . . dark faces—they are Indians. . . . You are to help them—you are for them." That evening she dreamed that an Indian face replaced the face of Maurice. A few days later Maurice wrote her from Santa Fe, "Do you want an object in life? Save the Indians, their art-culture—reveal it to the world!"[46]

Once in Taos, Luhan became immediately interested in the Indians at Taos Pueblo and became infatuated with one particular Taos Indian, Tony Luhan. Eventually, Sterne and Mabel separated, and Mabel lived openly with Tony, beginning in 1920. When Mabel became involved in the campaign to defend Pueblo lands in 1922, her scandalous interracial affair became a liability to the movement. Her old friend from New York, Mary Austin, intervened, encouraging both Mabel and Tony to divorce their spouses and marry one another and Mabel to "make an allowance for Tony's wife."[47] Despite occasional marital problems, Mabel and Tony lived together the rest of their lives.[48] Like Austin, Luhan became active in defending Pueblo lands and religion and in promoting their art. Both women also used their writing to popularize the emerging theory of cultural relativism.

Of the three women featured here, Elsie Clews Parsons most directly challenged women's moral superiority and sexual purity. Through her sociological and anthropological work, she also provided the most articulate support for cultural relativism and its relation to a new gender orientation. An immensely prolific writer, she wrote eighty-five articles and two books between 1915 and 1917 alone.[49] Born in 1874 to a wealthy family in New York City, Parsons early on evinced a willingness to challenge conventions. As a young woman, she appeared on the beach near her family's summer home in Newport, Rhode Island, without any stockings. When she waded into the surf bare-legged, according to Rosemary Zumwalt, Newport society was shocked. In 1892 Parsons defied her parents when she demanded to go to college at Barnard College, a newly opened women's college affiliated with Columbia University. Here she became interested in the new discipline of sociology, which appealed to her because it combined intellectual development with an active social role. For her master's thesis, she examined relief efforts for the poor in New York City, and for her doctorate she pursued an interest in the history of education and government and wrote a dissertation entitled "The Educational Legislation and Administration of the Colonies."

When she completed her doctorate in 1899, her former sociology professor, Franklin Giddings, hired her as an assistant in his sociology course. In 1900 Elsie Clews married Herbert Parsons, a lawyer and up-and-coming progressive politician, but continued to teach at Barnard until her husband was elected to Congress in 1905. Even more outside the norms of convention for a woman of her class, Parsons continued to work after having children. She bore two children while teaching at Barnard. All in all, she gave birth to six children, only four of whom survived childhood. As Rosalind Rosenberg has pointed out, Parsons could never have accomplished such a feat if it had not been for her husband's tolerant attitude and her class position, which afforded her a large number of servants.[50]

As evidenced in her life and writing, Parsons attacked the notion that men and women should occupy separate spheres. She hoped that in the future, "it ceases to be 'funny' for a man to thread a needle or shop or hold a baby, or for a woman to cast a ballot or sit on a jury or introduce a bill," when "domesticity and politics will become optional for both." By studying gender differences cross-culturally, Parsons concluded that in every society the sexes were separated, but not in the same way. For example, she noted that in northwest Siam (Thailand), women worked iron and poled boats. Thus, she argued that sexual roles were a matter of social convention, not biological destiny.[51]

Parsons also rebelled against the notion that women had little sexual passion and that sex should be confined to marriage. In an eight-page section of *The Family*, which she published in 1906, Parsons advocated trial marriages and sexual expressiveness for women as well as men. She called for an end to the double standard and suggested that premarital sex was acceptable for both women and men. Ministers, journalists, and other public speakers seized on this section and "regarded [*The Family*] as a threat to the moral fiber of the nation."[52] Parsons saw monogamy as another restrictive social convention. In her ideal of "an unconventional society," she wrote, "the impulses of sex will not be restricted in their expression to conjugality, nor will conjugality itself be considered as necessarily a habit for a lifetime." In her own marriage she openly carried on a series of flirtations and engaged in at least one long-term extramarital affair, with the novelist Robert Herrick in New Mexico, who immortalized her in his novel *The End of Desire*. Perhaps not fully reconciled to her ideals, however, Parsons became angry when her husband engaged in his own flirtations and alleged affairs.[53]

Parsons also believed that children, especially girls, should be taught about sex at a young age. "Boys escape from the nursery and learn, or mislearn, of sex," she asserted, "but for girls who commonly do not leave their nursery until they start to make another there is little opportunity to hear anything at all about sex."[54] Supporting contraception and abortion, Parsons declared that "no woman . . . should have to bear a child against her will." Despite her radical stance on sexual issues, Parsons implicitly recognized the potential dangers of sexual liberation for women—that once it was seen as natural for women to have and act on sexual desires, women might become expected to be sexual all the time. Parsons hoped that one day, "even during that part of life which is highly charged with sex, it may be treated as the impulse it is, varying in quantity, sometimes lacking altogether."[55]

Parsons openly challenged the notion of women's moral superiority. She objected to attempts to legislate morality and disagreed with the goals of moral reformers and purity crusaders to involve the state in enforcing moral standards. She particularly condemned the racial assumptions of the female quest for moral authority.[56] Her body of sociological work focused on comparing the social conventions of middle- and upper-class Americans with those of supposedly savage or primitive cultures around the world. In *The Old-Fashioned Woman: Primitive Fancies about the Sex*, Parsons focused on similarities across cultures in the treatment of women. Rather than arguing that "heathen" men degraded women in ways foreign to and unthinkable in American society, as the moral reformers did, Parsons exposed the similarities between so-called primitive societies' treatment of women and Americans' conventional treatment of women. For example, she compared cloisters and harems with women's sphere in American homes and female infanticide with a preference for boy babies.[57]

Parsons's interest in gender and cross-cultural analysis and her disdain for women's quest for moral authority reinforced her growing advocacy of cultural pluralism and relativism. After her husband's election to Congress in 1905, Parsons moved with her family to Washington DC until 1911. Despite her distance from academic life, Parsons maintained her interest in sociology and also read widely in ethnology. She was drawn particularly to the work of Franz Boas and gradually became more absorbed with anthropology than with sociology. She especially relished fieldwork; in addition to her informal field trips to the Southwest in 1910, 1912, and 1913, Parsons also traveled to the Yucatan in 1912 under Boas's sponsorship.[58] In 1911 she returned to live in New York, where she mingled with Greenwich Village radicals, such as Max Eastman and Charlotte Perkins Gilman, and attended Mabel Dodge Luhan's salons. Parsons shared the Village radicals' identification with socialism, their desire for spiritual, artistic, and sexual liberation, their admiration for Freud, and their contempt for Victorian morality. Parsons also promoted women's suffrage and ardently supported pacifism. Severely disillusioned by World War I, Parsons retreated from sociology and public life and immersed herself at war's end in anthropological field-work, mostly among the Pueblos and among blacks in the Caribbean.[59]

Despite their different conceptualizations of women's sexuality and femi-nism, all three of these women shared an aversion to the quest for women's moral authority. Along with their sentiments against industrialization, their new view of women, gender relations, and sexuality prepared them to look at Native Americans, particularly Indian women, in different ways than white women reformers had. When these women came to New Mexico, searching for an alternative to the standards under which they had grown up and trying to make sense of new gender conventions, they envisioned Pueblo society as a kind of feminist utopia.[60] Parsons claimed that "only twice through my association with Pueblo Indians has it occurred to me to be a feminist." Along with many other women who sojourned in New Mexico after World War I, Parsons be-lieved the Pueblos to have an egalitarian society, a "land of women's rights."[61] Some male writers agreed; Charles Saunders noted that the Pueblo civilization had achieved "equality of woman."[62] This view of Pueblo culture as a feminist utopia overturned the perspectives of women such as Dissette and True, who believed that Pueblo women were degraded within their cultures and in need of uplift to white civilized womanhood.

What, in the eyes of these antimodern feminists, signaled Pueblo women's equality? Matrilineality and matrilocality among some of the Pueblos provided the basis for much of the antimodern feminists' belief that Pueblo women en-joyed a higher status than white women. Although some scholars assert that all or most of the Pueblos had traditionally figured descent through the female line and expected men who married to move to their wife's household, by the turn of the twentieth century, greater variability existed in these customs. Among the Western Pueblos of Hopi, Zuni, Acoma, and Laguna, matrilineal clans, female ownership of houses and gardens, and matrilocal residence persisted, but among the Eastern Pueblos matrilineal clans no longer existed, and men owned the houses and gardens.[63] Yet, with the exception of Parsons, antimodern femi-nist writers focused on matrilineality and matrilocality as fixed and unvarying Pueblo traditions.

Early anthropologist Lewis Henry Morgan, the BIA, and most nineteenth-century reformers had viewed matrilineality as a sign of the backwardness and savagery of those Native Americans who practiced it.[64] But the white women who came to New Mexico after World War I inverted these assumptions. They interpreted what moral reformers had called "loose marital relations" as sexual liberation and argued instead that matrilineality and matrilocality granted women power that they were denied in white American society. Owning property constituted the basis of this power. To the Pueblo wife, Austin asserted, "belongs the house, the furniture, the garnered grain, the marriage rights of her children."[65] Following from the ownership of property, some antimodern feminists believed that Pueblo women enjoyed absolute dominion. "The house . . . was the house-mother's," Austin wrote. "Seldom her daughters left her, but brought husbands home, and built on another room and another, until the clustered house heap took on that pyramidal form you may observe at Zuñi or Taos." Austin referred to this absolute dominion as "Mother-rule" and believed that it explained the seemingly harmonious communalism of the Pueblos. "Perhaps the most stabilizing fact of Pueblo Constitution is its retention of the matriarchal formula for its social pattern," contended Austin. "Peace and stability, these are the first fruits of Mother-rule."[66]

Many antimodern feminists, who had themselves experienced the difficulty of obtaining a divorce, also characterized the pueblos as feminist utopias because of the ease by which most Pueblo women could end an unsuitable marriage. As Austin described it, "Every house is a Mother Hive, to which the daughters bring home husbands, on terms of good behavior; or dismiss them with the simple ceremony of setting the man's private possessions—his gun, his saddle, his other pair of moccasins—outside the door." Austin's view contrasted greatly with the interpretations of some male writers. In 1925 Charles Lummis remarked approvingly that the Pueblos "do not believe in divorce."[67] Who was right? Actually, both writers were. At the turn of the century, divorce customs varied greatly from pueblo to pueblo.[68] Yet, as with matrilineality and matrilocality, women popularizers of the Pueblos, such as Luhan and Austin, portrayed ease of divorce as a universal, unvarying Pueblo trait.

They also depicted divorce among the Pueblos as a painless process that benefited women. Yet the actual experience of Indian women sometimes belied this portrayal of Pueblo-style divorce. One of Parsons's most important informants at Zuni was a part-Cherokee, part-white woman named Margaret Lewis, who had been a schoolteacher at Zuni and then married a Zuni man who became governor of the pueblo. Lewis wrote Parsons when her husband decided to leave her. "I am all broken up," Lewis confessed. "I am having a hard time my children to support and raise—Everything is so high I will have a hard time in trying to keep the wolf from the door."[69] Obviously, as an outsider who had married into Zuni, Lewis did not experience all the supports other Pueblo women would have enjoyed. Yet divorce among the Pueblos by the turn of the twentieth century was not as simple as antimodern feminists represented it. Antimodern feminists condemned missionaries, moral reformers, and BIA bureaucrats for their attempts to undermine Pueblo marriage and divorce patterns. They often noted

73

approvingly that children born out of wedlock suffered no stigma in Pueblo cultures, and they questioned why missionaries and reformers should try to disturb this idyllic arrangement. "By breaking down Indian custom marriage," Austin declared, "the missionaries have contrived to increase the number of unsatisfactory settlements, and added to the irregularities, formerly at a minimum for their populations."[70]

Since the white women feminists who came to New Mexico after World War I had all championed a breakdown of separate spheres in white society, they might also have been expected to see Pueblo societies as models of a society in which gender distinctions had blurred. Though there existed ample evidence of distinctly separate gender roles in Pueblo society, to some extent antimodern feminists did find in Pueblo culture the "separate sphereless" society they advocated. In her unpublished "Journal of a Feminist," Parsons detailed the sexual division of labor in Pueblo society but argued that sex differentiation counted "very little if at all in personal relations."[71] Parsons took an interest in Pueblo men and women who took on roles of the other gender, often called "berdaches" by outside observers and "*la'mana*" by the Zuni. Parsons suspected that a Zuni woman named Nancy, who dressed and acted like a man and worked in the house of the Zuni governor where she stayed, was a *la'mana*. "She was, I concluded a 'strong-minded woman,' a Zuñi 'new woman,' a large part of her male." Of men who chose to do women's work, Parsons noted that this was a "curious commentary . . . on that thorough-going belief in the intrinsic difference between the sexes which is so tightly held to in our own culture."[72]

Parsons also recounted other occasions in which men's and women's roles could be reversed. In a dispute over pastureland, Parsons's informant Margaret Lewis worked as an interpreter for her husband, the Zuni governor, and the Pueblo Council. Soon, however, she served as a mediator. As Parsons recalled, "Presently when the baby began to cry she asked the Governor to take it out to quiet it. The Governor had ingratiating ways with the baby. . . . While Lewis looked after the baby, Margaret transacted the business of the meeting to the satisfaction alike of farmer and agent." Even after Margaret Lewis divorced her husband, the Pueblo council kept coming to her for advice and finally made her an officer of the council.[73] Parsons does not make clear if such a role would have been possible for any Pueblo woman, or if Margaret Lewis's status as a non-Pueblo enabled her to attain such a position. In any event, Parsons revealed that Pueblo men were accustomed to engaging in domestic activities relegated to "women's sphere" in white American society.

Austin, too, delighted in what she believed to be men's domestic role in Pueblo culture. The traditional Pueblo man, she wrote, wove and spun, minded the young children, and sang to his women as they bent over the neatly boxed metates in the milling room.

There were always these three smoothed stone slabs, for the three grades of fineness of the meals demanded by the discriminating housewife, and the three manos or hand-stones resting on them, in a clean little room by itself, or perhaps several of them grouped together where the women of one hive could be found plump-plumping to the rhythm of the grinding-song, sung by the young men between pleasant quips and cheerful laughter. . . .

At evening when the light breaks, before it dies, into unimaginable splendor, there is a stir of cheerful domestic life, smell of cooking, laughter of women.[74]

While Austin and Parsons both portrayed Pueblo men as fluid in their role, Austin differed from Parsons in that she rarely showed Pueblo women acting outside the home. Instead, Austin idealized Pueblo women's role in the home as powerful and satisfying.

Like Austin, Luhan idealized the Pueblo home as a site where women figured prominently, found community with each other, and experienced sensual satisfaction in their work. She described how Pueblo women cleaned the wheat, "little by little, standing upon a clear sheet and holding a basket overhead, letting the grain pour slowly downwards past their faces like a sheet of yellow rain." Luhan believed that Pueblo women's work brought women together in a convivial community. "Out in the Pueblo the Indian women sit together cozily," Luhan wrote, "in great heaps of corn, shucking the ears. They strip off the harsh husks and their sensitive fingers enjoy the pleasant contact with the ivory-hard, polished ears." Further, Luhan asserted, "[T]hey feel like queens, sitting with these riches surrounding them."[75] As Luhan imagined it, the sensual and sexually suggestive task of shucking corn fulfilled Pueblo women.

Luhan and Austin expressed great admiration and even longing for the Pueblo homes they depicted. On first seeing Taos Pueblo, Luhan declared, "Now, strange to say, although the village seemed austere and certainly anything but domestic, yet one got a feeling of home from it. The very essence of it was of the home. . . . That was the feeling it gave out richly. A stab of longing and of nostalgia went through me like lightning." Luhan desired to replicate what she believed to be the Pueblo home: a place of production, community, and sensuality. She attempted to make her home productive through canning fruits and vegetables. "Something left over in me from my grandmother has made me turn back to these earlier ways of living," Luhan wrote, "made me to enjoy my storerooms full of the fruit of the earth, though it has meant so much hard work to stock these dark cellars and these storeroom shelves, and has, probably, cost more to fill them than to buy the efficient products of the shops."[76] Luhan failed to mention whether it was she or her Indian and Mexican servants who had actually done the work of canning. Luhan did attempt at one point to engage in some productive household labor without her servants. At the urging of D. H. Lawrence, who told her she should not have servants, Luhan tried to scrub her own living-room floor and bake bread. "My Indian girls stood round looking half-distressed and half amused," Luhan remembered. "I frowned and paid no attention to them, because I wanted this to be real. I didn't want to experiment, I wanted to be really washing the floor." On another occasion, Luhan asserted, "I am perfectly content to sit in the window and knit and knit and knit and ponder and remember and get into a kind of even rhythm."[77]

Yet try as she might, Luhan did not always find her own home to be the productive and sensually satisfying paradise she envisioned. Her floor-scrubbing experiment did not meet with success, and Luhan reverted to her nonproductive role in the household. In *Winter in Taos*, she alternately portrayed her home as cozy and inviting and then as lonely and unfulfilling. Luhan felt sorry for "people who float around the world in hotels and boarding houses, . . . who are without roots. . . . [I]t is inconceivable that they don't know enough to find a little house somewhere that will be their very own, . . . where the kettle sings on the hearth and the flower blooms in the window." Luhan believed her own adobe home, patterned after Pueblo architecture, was "the essence of homeliness and comfort," "nestle[d] close to the earth and seem[ing] to be rooted in it."[78] On other occasions, however, while she imagined her friend's winter home "where the fire snoozed in the chimney" and everything "smelled sweet with butter and spices," Luhan lamented that her own "house was utterly still below me, and I felt lonesome and drear." As if to talk herself into remaining at home, Luhan wrote, "It really isn't worth it, I thought to live here in this solitude, shut in by the winter, when everyone has gone somewhere else and is having an interesting time! But alas! I remembered that I was here because I chose to be, and that no other kind of time anyone was having meant a thing to me, compared with my life, the way I had built it here. This was best for me, this home in the valley. . . . Like always, no matter how miserable, I'd rather be home!"[79]

While Austin had seen the Pueblo home as a place of women's power, where men and women shared domesticity, Luhan saw it as an arena in which to reassert traditional gender roles. In *Edge of Taos Desert*, the fourth volume of her memoirs, Luhan asserted that "from the first, I never disputed [Tony's] decisions. It was as though I couldn't impose my will against his, he always seeming stronger than I, and his judgment better than mine. It was certainly a rare thing for me to recognize the authority in a man, and a great satisfaction. I'd always wanted to have that submissive feeling but I never really could." When D. H. and Frieda Lawrence came to Taos, Luhan competed with Frieda for Lawrence's attention. She dressed the way Lorenzo, as she called him, preferred, wearing a full skirt with a peasant bodice that laced up her bosom. This new woman exchanged her fashionable clothes and Taos-style shawls for demure calico and gingham.[80]

What was at work here? Had these modern sophisticates sold out their big-city feminist notions when they moved to New Mexico? Why did they seem to seek to reclaim a vision of woman's role in the home that more closely resembled the BIA's hopes than Heterodoxy Club ambitions? Had the more conservative climate of the 1920s caused these women to reconsider their more radical views of gender relations? In actuality, the antimodern feminists' apparent longing for domestic bliss and the centrality of the home in women's lives had more to do with fundamental contradictions among their ideals. On the one hand, these feminists championed new opportunities for women (at least white women)—careers in the public sphere and greater sexual expressiveness. They recognized that many of these opportunities had opened up through industrialization and the modernization of the economy and society. And yet they also disliked modern, industrializing America and sought an agrarian, home-centered productive alternative to it.

In their portrayals of Pueblo women and their homes, the contradiction between their two major ideals—women's individual advancement in the modern world and antimodernism—came to a head. In the cases of Austin and Luhan, their antimodernism won out over their modern feminism. Pueblo society became a place where they could vicariously experience a preindustrial ideal, while in their own society they could live as "modern" women. As Luhan and Austin forged ahead into the "modern era," abandoning traditional roles in their own society in order to pursue and write about unladylike adventures in the Southwest, they often constructed Pueblo women as the repositories of tradition, of women who would keep alive the lifestyle that modern women had abandoned but nostalgically recalled. A class dynamic may have been at work here as well. As Linda Gordon has noted of welfare reformers, their feminism exhibited a class double standard. For educated middle-class women, these reformers supported careers, economic independence, and public activism, but for poor women, they "recommended domesticity and economic dependence on men."[81]

Although she generally stressed women's high status in Pueblo culture, Parsons rarely idealized the Pueblo home. While remarking that many Hopi women on First Mesa had never been to Second Mesa, only six to eight miles distant, Parsons commented that "truly Pueblo Indian women are home stayers!" Yet she did not claim this, as Austin and Luhan did, as a virtue. Nor did she celebrate the women's community that she observed. Rather she presented it more dispassionately.[82] As a social scientist who strove for objectivity, Parsons may have been less comfortable than Luhan or Austin in lauding Pueblo customs. But Parsons had also broken more decidedly with late-nineteenth-century gender norms regarding domesticity. Thus Parsons's brand of antimodernism did not lead her to suggest that women would find their greatest fulfillment in a productive household. Instead, antimodernism and modern gender standards coexisted more easily for Parsons than they did for Luhan and Austin.

Given their own celebration of female sexuality, many antimodern feminists also regarded Pueblo society as a feminist utopia because they believed the Pueblos held a healthy attitude toward sexuality. Influenced by Freud's views, these new feminists believed that civilized society had repressed its natural sexual instincts, while so-called primitives expressed their drives in a healthy manner.[83] Parsons claimed that the Zunis were "naturalistic, not reticent," about matters of sexual intercourse. Austin claimed that while "the most usual form of marriage was strict monogamy," the Pueblos allowed greater sexual experimentation before marriage than white culture, a custom of which she approved. Luhan asserted that Indians were comfortable with their bodies while whites were not. Describing the Taos Indians who came to dance at her house, she wrote, "[T]heir brown bodies are beautiful, for every inch of them has a gleaming awareness as though their flesh is wholly awake. . . . [O]ur bodies are deserted. We do not live in them and they are like abandoned houses."[84]

Ultimately, antimodern feminists differed in their assessment of male and female sexuality among the Pueblos, associating Pueblo masculinity with sexual uninhibitedness and holding more contradictory views of Pueblo women's sexuality. According to Luhan, the Pueblos still retained their true masculinity, a quality she found lacking in modern white America. As she watched her first Pueblo dance, Luhan asserted that "the sonorous drum fused the voices of the men and the volume of it all together was strong and good and very masculine."[85] When antimodern feminists turned to depicting Pueblo women, they revealed a great deal of confusion about what constituted women's healthy sexuality. While claiming in general that the Pueblos were sexually expressive, they often cast Pueblo women as "modest." Mary Roberts Coolidge wrote, "Indian women are extremely modest and reticent. They do not wish to converse with strange men nor to be questioned concerning the details of their domestic life." Coolidge contrasted modest Pueblo women with "white women in men's clothes," who are "especially incomprehensible to them, offending their primitive concepts of modesty." Parsons also contended that Pueblo Indian women are "shy and reticent."

When she acquired a shawl like those Pueblo and Mexican women wore, Luhan noted that "the Indian women were sheltered in their shawls, seeming so comfortable and encompassed within them, so that their whole being was contained, not escaping to be wasted in the air, but held close and protected from encroachments. How exposed we live, I thought, so revealed and open! I longed for the insulation of the shawl and wore mine whenever I could."[86] Luhan maintained that the Pueblos led "a well balanced, natural and usual sex life . . . in their family life. Furthermore they have not got sex on the brain like the missionaries and others whose religion has been given the purification of civilization. They never think sex—or talk sex. They all seem to be horrified at bringing it into speech, letter, and discussion as [the moral reformers] are doing here—they are ashamed to think 'their pueblo' could come under any such consideration. They have a strong natural modesty always. I have never seen a sign of sex exhibitionism in an Indian. They are . . . the purest people I know."[87] Here Luhan depicts Pueblo sexuality as "well balanced, natural and usual"— terms current among new women of the 1920s—and at the same time as "modest" and "pure," phrases more common to female moral reformers.

The antimodern feminists' view of Pueblo sexuality seems as riven with contradictions as their portrayals of Pueblo homes. Within their own society, Parsons, Luhan, and Austin had all broken with older Victorian traditions and championed women's sexuality. They seemed to disdain modesty and purity as outmoded concepts that inhibited women's sexuality. Yet upholding Pueblo culture as an idyllic model to be emulated by white society, these women characterized Pueblo sexuality in general as healthy and natural but described Pueblo women as modest and pure. Were these antimodern feminists hopelessly befuddled, a mass of contradictions? More likely, they struggled to create a model for themselves to be both sexually expressive and in control of their own sexuality. Despite their general support of sexual emancipation, new feminists sometimes suffered great ambivalence about emerging sexual mores.

After separating from Edwin Dodge, when anarchist Alexander Berkman tried to kiss her, Luhan protested, "I couldn't bear to have anyone think that my anomalous situation, that made me my own protector, was any augury of light behavior or undignified self-indulgence." When Maurice Sterne pressured her to have sex, Luhan wrote, "I felt very weary and emancipated. When he argued that it would interfere with his Work if I didn't let him make love to me, that old persuasion convinced me that I might as well be hospitable to him without stint and not be narrow-minded." Although Austin had found the "country of lost borders" liberating, she also recognized that the supposed breakdown of gender conventions in the West could exact a harsh toll on women. In tale after tale in *Stories from the Country of Lost Borders*, Austin featured a heterosexual couple who defied social conventions in some way, either through reversing gender roles, refusing to marry, or engaging in an interracial relationship. In every case, the man abandoned the woman, leaving her to fend (ultimately with success) for herself.[88] Austin intimated that "lost borders" could make a woman both emancipated and vulnerable.

What Luhan, Austin, and other new feminists had come up against was an unintended consequence of the new standards they helped to create. As other historians have noted, in the 1910s and 1920s, "emancipated" women were not just allowed to be sexually expressive, they were required to be. Women who held back sexually risked being labeled as sexually repressed. As Christina Simmons and Estelle Freedman have argued, the new sexual mores benefited men more than women. Victorian sexual standards had given precedence to women's control of sexual relationships. New sexual attitudes divested women of this control, "cast women as villains if they refused to respond to" male sexuality, and increased men's power in sexual relationships. Simmons has argued that the new rhetoric of sex expression in the 1920s was more an attack on "women's control over men's sexuality" than an assault on sexual repression.[89]

The process of articulating and living a new vision of womanhood was an often painful and difficult transition for antimodern feminists. In the end the new set of mores they helped to shape sometimes became as confining to them as had the Victorian strictures of their childhoods. When Mabel Dodge married Maurice Sterne, Marie Howe, suffragist and founder of the Heterodoxy Club, came to see her the next day. "You have counted so much for Women!" Howe exclaimed to Luhan. "Your Example has stood for courage and strength! . . . You had the nerve to live your own life openly and frankly—to take a lover if you wished, without hiding under the law. You have shown women they had the right to live as they chose to live. . . . But now! When I think of the disappointment in the whole woman's world today!" To Luhan, Howe's comments seemed a new form of pressure and conformity. "Everything seemed very tiresome and difficult," Luhan remarked.[90] In their depictions of the Pueblos, seemingly in contradiction to their own experiences, Luhan and Austin found an opportunity to create a model for a new type of sexuality, still controlled by women, yet more sexually expressive.

The new attitude of appreciation for Native Americans, and Pueblo Indians in particular, can be seen as emanating from both an antimodern perspective and, at least among white women, from changing views of sexuality and the questioning of women's supposed moral superiority. Luhan, Parsons, and Austin were not driven by the same need as moral reformers such as Clara True and Mary Dissette to proselytize and civilize Native Americans. They did not see it as women's mission to change other women, especially if those women seemed to have greater status and opportunities than they themselves enjoyed. Yet while Austin, Luhan, and Parsons had strayed far from the gendered and racial assumptions that underpinned the lives of True and Dissette, they shared with them a tendency to act out their struggles upon Pueblo Indian women. True and Dissette cast Pueblo women largely as victims of male lust, who must gain an education and an independent wage in order to uplift themselves. This view of Pueblo women closely paralleled their own struggles as women in American society. Education and income were not the defining issues for most antimodern feminists. Well-educated and often well-heeled, these women concerned themselves with a different set of questions—marriage, divorce, sexuality, and the relation of the home to modern women's lives. They, in turn, used their studies of and writings about the Pueblos as a means to articulate their emerging views on these issues. As the next chapter explores, antimodern feminists ultimately helped to define a new vision of the Pueblos, one that created both new benefits and new limitations for both white women and Native Americans.

CHAPTER FOUR

Antimodern Feminists' Redefinition
of Gender and Race

How alien I was in that Indian world. It is a separate world. The white man sees it, he touches it, some even have the temerity to try to break into it, to change it. But they cannot. For his is a world apart, a brown world of brown people. *Erna Fergusson*, Dancing Gods, *1931*

In portraying the Pueblos as an admirable society worthy of emulation, antimodern feminists participated in the growing intellectual movement that espoused cultural relativism over cultural evolution and the policy of assimilation. Elsie Clews Parsons contributed to the emerging anthropological theory of cultural relativism through her fieldwork and writings and by financing a generation of other anthropologists. Mary Austin and Mabel Dodge Luhan became popularizers of this new concept. On the surface, cultural relativism seemed to have little if anything in common with cultural evolution and assimilation. Moreover, the new vision of gender relations that antimodern feminists championed also seemed to represent a radical break from late-nineteenth-century gender notions.

According to many historians, transformations in ideas about both gender and race played important roles in shifting America from one cultural paradigm—Victorianism—to another—modernism. The terms "modernism" and "antimodernism" are slippery. A person such as Mabel Dodge Luhan, labeled a modernist by many because of her support of modern art and literature, could also be labeled an antimodernist because of her disdain for industrialization. I take modernism to mean a specific movement in art and literature that developed in the first decades of the twentieth century. I conceive of antimodernism as an aversion to modernization—the industrialization and commercialization of American society. Thus it was possible and quite common for "modernists" to be antimodern.[1] Some scholars have identified as a key hallmark of modernism its attack on binary oppositions and hierarchies.[2] According to some historians, during the Victorian era a civilized-savage dichotomy dominated the discourse about racial difference. Modernists allegedly replaced this dichotomy with a culturally relativist view that emphasized the "oneness" of humanity.[3] Some gender historians have asserted that a public-private dichotomy characterized Victorian gender notions but that modernists undermined this polarity by emphasizing women's similarity to men.[4]

At first glance, antimodern feminists appear to confirm these historians' analyses of the shifting meanings of race and gender from Victorianism to modernism. Antimodern feminists, however, did not so much shatter older gender and racial oppositions and hierarchies as recast them. Though many of these women defied notions that women were innately pure and domestic while men were inherently licentious and worldly, they nevertheless called for allowing "natural," as opposed to socially constructed, sex differences to guide gender relations. In addition, although by the 1920s many antimodern feminists no longer considered Indians savage or inferior to supposedly civilized white people, they rearticulated the difference between Indians and whites as that between primitive and modern peoples. Though they often privileged the primitive over the modern, some of these feminists created polarities that proved even more rigid, essentialized, and enduring than those the Victorian female reformers had erected.[5] Despite the rhetoric of cultural relativism, this new generation of Indian sympathizers appeared to be wedded to a vision of cultural difference that would reaffirm their own longings for a premodern past.

Antimodern feminists did not, of course, all view gender and race in the same way. Parsons, as a trained social scientist who conducted extensive field research, often eschewed a simplistic notion of gender and cultural differences. She did not represent the Pueblos as complete opposites of white Americans. In much of her sociological and anthropological work, she tried to convey the underlying similarities between cultures and between the sexes. Neither did Parsons generalize about the Pueblos; she reported on the diversity and variability of Pueblo cultures.[6] Austin and Luhan, on the other hand, wrote for a popular audience. They tended to present more stark polarities between men and women and between modern white Americans and so-called primitives. As they popularized the notion of cultural relativism, they transformed the theory into a concept for preserving, even enforcing, cultural difference rather than a belief in the "oneness of humanity." Reinforced by the work of their male peers and by advertising, fairs, and expositions, Austin's and Luhan's views gained wide currency in popular thought.

Despite their strong objections to the socially contrived gender differences of Victorianism, especially the equation of women with morality and sexual purity, many antimodern feminists believed that real differences did exist between the sexes. Austin held to a notion that there were fundamental natural differences between men and women. She characterized war as "an exhibition of masculinity run amuck [*sic*]" and argued that humans needed to learn to live in the world "femininely." In *The Young Woman Citizen*, a tract designed to encourage women to vote once suffrage was attained, Austin declared, "[T]he first thing the woman citizen must ask herself is whether she is coming to her new obligation [of political participation] as another, less experienced man, or whether she has anything to contribute as a woman." Austin had already answered the question for herself: "[T]he capacity for intuitive judgment is the best thing women have to bring to their new undertaking," and a woman's second greatest gift to politics is "her habit of centering the administration of her affairs around the production and nourishment of life."[7] To Austin, when women participated in politics, they would inevitably bring their "feminine" qualities to bear.

Austin believed it essential that women maintain their "feminine" side while engaging in traditionally male activities. She worried that the "mothering instinct" in women might be irreparably damaged or suppressed if not carefully protected. Thus, regarding working-class women, she wrote,

During the past one hundred years, . . . the freshness and vivacity of young girls has been valued as an industrial asset. The bubbling vitality of youth is set to turn machines. Natural coquetry, the love of beauty and soft enhancing fabrics, which is all part of the mothering instinct, has been suppressed because it interfered with labor values. Engaged as the woman worker has been in a desperate struggle to get her work recognized on the same wage and time basis as men, she could make no struggle at all for her potential mother-value. This is a battle which the non-working woman must fight for her, since mother-energy is even more a social than a personal asset.[8]

As for Luhan, she too believed that women had certain innate maternal qualities that made them fundamentally different from men. Describing her desire to plant a garden in the spring, Luhan commented that "this mid-wifery is latent in all women and we are, every one of us, always aching to deliver the unborn, if not in ourselves, then outside ourselves in some vicarious fashion." In 1938 Luhan revealed to a friend that she believed "the final, great, simple solution of life [for women] is to return to having children—only better one(s)."

Luhan had already expressed this sentiment in 1924 in a poem entitled "The Ballad of a Bad Girl." The poem tells the tale of a little girl who steals her father's walking stick and flies to heaven upon it. In heaven there was "no way to tell the boys from the girls; . . . they all wore dresses and they all wore curls." Continuing on, the girl pushed "past all barriers and beyond locked gates." When she finally met God, he pushed her out of heaven, but she was happy to return home where she "lay down in the pansy-bed and whispered: 'Mother! Mother me, / And Teach me how to mother and that's all, all, all!'"[9] Although both Luhan and Austin had questioned the notion that women, due to their moral superiority, were different from men, they seemed to believe that women's capacity to bear children conferred on them a unique distinction in society. While Austin never asserted that women should play only a domestic role, Luhan increasingly advocated that women (at least women other than herself) should return to their roles in the home.

Even Parsons believed in inherent differences between the sexes. She made a fine distinction between "natural" sex differences and those manufactured by society. As she phrased it,

Far from wishing to let the natural differences of sex count in life, [those in favor of sex taboos] seek to prescribe differences which may or may not correspond to fact, but which because they are arbitrary may be collectively and so comfortably encountered. In their great fear of sex they endeavour to make it a matter of collective habits, of dress, or manners, of occupations, of pastimes, particulars all subject to endless regulation. . . . Were we less afraid of the real heterogeneities of sex, would we not be less insistent upon the differences we have provoked, those differences which are but blinds for the real differences?

Parsons did not explain what constituted these "real" gender differences. But she made it clear that left to their own devices, unregulated by the government, and unrestricted by social conventions, men and women might discover their "natural" differences. In her unpublished "Journal of a Feminist," Parsons spoke of the "attribute of maleness" and the "woman nature." Although she believed that every individual combined both of these "natures," she believed in some identifiable male and female essences as well.[10]

The views of Austin, Luhan, and Parsons regarding gender call into question the dominant paradigms of both women historians and historians of modernism. These women, all new feminists of the 1920s, neither completely abandoned the notion of inherent gender differences nor adopted a late-twentieth-century postmodern notion of the social construction of gender and sexuality.[11] Instead, they sought to replace what they deemed "artificial" differences, those that the dominant culture imposed on women and that many "Victorian" feminists had turned to their advantage, with a new set of distinctions based on "natural" or "real" differences.[12] In this endeavor they did not radically differ from the Victorian female moral reformers they often chided. New feminists also sought their own measure of authority; yet rather than asserting that their authority derived from women's innate moral superiority over men, they based their claim to power on other factors.

For Parsons, this power emanated from her education and research in the social sciences. Scientists and trained social experts such as herself could help to identify the artificially contrived divisions in society and determine what constituted natural differences. Regina Kunzel has documented that in the first decades of the twentieth century, the basis of social work evolved from a notion of women's evangelical moral reform (not unlike that carried out by Mary Dissette and Clara True with the Pueblo Indians) to a new faith in science and professional social reform. New women social workers "aspired to the broader cultural authority of professional legitimacy."[13] A similar process appears to be at work in Parson's reconceptualization of gender differences. For Austin and Luhan, women's authority derived from their "potential mother-value" and the "midwifery latent in all women." Austin's and Luhan's conceptualization of gender differences proved no less essentialist than that espoused by female moral reformers; in fact, it was actually more biologically determinist. In the view of female moral reformers, women cultivated and achieved moral authority. In Austin's and Luhan's view, women inherited social authority simply by virtue of their capacity to bear children.

The views of many antimodern feminists toward other cultures proved no less essentialist than their perspectives on gender differences. Like many of their male peers in New Mexico, these women believed that Pueblo culture differed significantly from modern American culture. Indeed, there were striking differences between the cultures of the Pueblos and modern Americans. The Pueblos for the most part continued to farm their communally owned lands and expected each man to participate in the communal work of cleaning irrigation ditches. Still practicing their own unique religions, most Pueblos participated in a seasonal round of ritual dances. Some of the pueblos still organized themselves matrilineally and matrilocally.[14]

For all their significant differences from white Americans, the Pueblos also shared many similar problems, especially with rural Americans. As farming became less practicable, many Pueblos became wage earners as opposed to self-sufficient agriculturists. At the margins of the American economy, many Pueblos also were extremely poor, and they suffered from serious health problems, particularly tuberculosis and trachoma. With changes in work life as well as the assimilation policy of the BIA, some Pueblos began to favor adaptation to modern conditions and the selective adoption of new American values. Many pueblos became riven with conflict over how best to cope with modern America and the changes it wrought upon their culture. This conflict over how to adapt to modern life also permeated American culture at large in the first decades of the twentieth century.

Yet for all the complexities of Pueblo life at the turn of the century, and for all of its parallel dilemmas with the rest of America, most of the antimodern feminists who gathered in the Southwest represented Pueblo society as a culture wholly antithetical to white American culture. The women who wrote so profusely about the Pueblos selected certain aspects of their cultures to discuss and left out others. In portraying the Pueblos as the virtual opposite of modern American culture, antimodern feminist writers in the Southwest also defined what it meant to be modern. Their descriptions of the Pueblos were replete with negatives, signifying an absent subject of comparison—modern white Americans. While these women writers emphasized the communalism, artistry, and deep religiosity of the Pueblos, they implicitly and explicitly defined modern American life as individualistic, mechanized, materialistic, and divested of spiritual and artistic significance. And as these women praised Pueblo cultures as existing in consonance with the natural world, they condemned modern American culture for its separation from and abuse of nature.

The concept of Pueblo communalism formed the basis for much of the belief of these women in the vast cultural gap between Pueblos and white Americans. As anthropologists began to study the Pueblos in the late nineteenth and early twentieth centuries, they observed that "lack of individualization is a pronounced Pueblo trait." Instead, anthropologists asserted, the Pueblos emphasized conformity to communal standards and the subordination of individual desires to the community's needs. Pueblo standards also frowned upon many forms of individual expression; they regarded boastfulness, for example, as dangerous.

Several incidents in the life of Maria Martinez, the famous potter from San Ildefonso, illustrate the extent to which the Pueblos esteemed a communal ethic. At age ten, Martinez became ill. To help cure her, her father took her on a pilgrimage to the church in Chimayo, which made her feel special; but knowing that she would be chastised by her parents if she bragged to others about her pilgrimage, she only "told the Santo Nino about it privately, each night when she had finished her Rosary. It had to be private telling, for Mother was kneeling beside her, saying her Rosary, too. Maria knew what her mother thought about people who tried to be important, even to themselves." Later in life, after Maria had become a successful potter, a trader came to her requesting her pottery. She told him that her and her sisters' pottery all looked alike, and it all came from

San Ildefonso. While the trader persisted in wanting pottery made by her alone, Martinez insisted that "it's the pueblo that makes the difference, not the woman who makes the pottery."[15]

Anthropologists have long argued about whether the communal ethic described by Martinez served merely as a norm or whether it constituted a widely shared Pueblo practice. Many anthropologists, including Ruth Benedict, Ruth Bunzel, and Laura Thompson, contended that by promoting communalism the Pueblos had organized a utopian, peaceful society. Benedict, in fact, characterized the Pueblos as having an "Apollonian" society. By contrast, other anthropologists such as Esther Goldfrank and Dorothy Eggan have argued that the Pueblos were members of a conflict-ridden, deeply factionalized society that brutally tried to enforce social harmony.[16]

In either case, by the turn of the twentieth century the communal ethic was already under considerable strain as many Pueblo Indians came into contact with white traders, missionaries, and BIA employees who emphasized a different set of values. Some Indians contested the norms set by their pueblos. For example, the Melchor family, John Dixon of Cochiti Pueblo, and Edward Hunt of Acoma questioned whether they should have to participate in communal irrigation work.[17] Parsons noted that the degree of communalism varied from pueblo to pueblo. In Taos Pueblo she found communalism less pronounced than in other pueblos; moreover, Taos leaders seemed to rely to a greater extent on jail sentences, fines, and whipping to control their residents.[18]

Despite evidence that communal norms and practices among the Pueblos varied and were undergoing a transformation, women writers and activists in the 1920s represented the Pueblo communal ethic as a fixed racial essence at odds with modern American individualism. The residents of Taos Pueblo "all move as one . . . in the winter," Mabel Dodge Luhan remarked. "Like a flock, a tribe is actuated with a single impulse." Invariably, antimodern feminists contrasted this supposed communal trait with the perceived individualistic impulses of modern Americans. Mary Austin compared white society to Pueblo culture using the metaphor of bubbles. In white society, Austin wrote, individualized bubbles "crowd and coalesce and break into one another, until something of its neighbor's wall has become a portion of every filmed inclosure [*sic*]." Thus, "there are a million souls shut in the foam cloud, for whom the color and shape of the universe is the shell of their neighbor's thinking. Here and there great souls detach themselves and go sailing skyward in a lovely world of their own seeing, poets and prophets. But what happens in the pueblo is the gentle swelling of film into film until the whole community lies at the center of one great bubble of the Indian's universe, from which the personal factor seldom escapes into complete individuation." Similarly, Mabel Dodge Luhan contrasted white society to Pueblo culture by juxtaposing the Anglo-American section of Taos with Taos Pueblo. It seemed to Luhan that in the Anglo area, "there was never a place with less *esprit de corps,* or group spirit, . . . while out there [in the pueblo] it was only a tribal or group life."[19]

Luhan's and Austin's belief that the Pueblos practiced communalism led them to portray Pueblo men and women as lacking in any individual will. When Austin portrayed the Pueblos who left their villages and settled among hostile whites or Mexicans, she remarked, "Fear out of proportion to the occasion worked in them, and what could it work upon but the minds of men too long immersed in communality to be able to turn the sharp edges of decision against an enemy who fought out of a common impulse, each man for his own hand?" Believing that Pueblo Indians lacked individuality, and indeed homogenizing all Native Americans, some white women writers spoke of an "Indian mind." Implicitly contrasting Indian with white, writer Mary Roberts Coolidge generalized that "the Indian mind is not literal, specific, scientific—it is philosophical, vague, and poetic."[20]

Interestingly, while antimodern feminists shared with Greenwich Village radicals the belief in "the power of the individual to shape the self and the environment in terms of an inner vision," they extended no such power of individual determination to the Pueblos. In contrast to female reformers who acted on the credo of "Kill the Indian, save the man," Luhan, Austin, Coolidge, and other popular writers of the 1920s seem to have turned this phrase on its head, instead emphasizing "Save the Indian, kill the man." Interestingly, this tendency to deny the individual subjectivity of Indians paralleled a development in modern American gender roles and sexuality. Pamela Haag has documented the ways in which the dominant culture between 1920 and 1940 constructed women as irrational beings who lacked the subjectivity to control their sexuality.[21] Indeed, Luhan, Austin, and other antimodern feminists subscribed to new Freudian theories that conceived of women's sexuality as an irrational cluster of uncontrollable drives and instincts. Even as new ideologies developed that implicitly denied women their individual will, Luhan, Austin, and other antimodern feminists simultaneously refused Indians their own subjectivity. Female moral reformers in contrast believed that Indians could consciously choose whether to "improve" their lives or not: they were not lacking in individuality or will.

Often seeing themselves as unique individuals who had risen above the mass of conformity and conventionality, these feminists judged Pueblo communalism in different ways. Austin found it "an ideal state, but failing to produce freedom of thought." She believed that "the revolt of youth against the despotic communism of the pueblos—more strangling to individual genius than the less happy tyrannies of kings—must be led." Luhan also believed that in due time, through contact with individualistic white society, the Pueblos would lose their communal ethic. "These two extremes [of Taos and Taos Pueblo] so close together but not touching," Luhan commented, "were, perhaps, destined to exchange their modes some day, the Indians to individuate, the valley folk to unite in some new group form."[22] Unlike Austin, however, Luhan portrayed Pueblo group spirit as liberating, not despotic. As she listened to eighty or ninety Pueblo men singing around a great drum, she thought, "perhaps the only way to go free is to live as a group, and to be part and parcel of a living tribal organism, to share everything, joy, pain, food, land, life, and death and so lose the individual anguish and hunger." Luhan believed that white Americans had "individualized themselves up out of the collective mass" and become "lost souls," who had "broken out of the pattern of established life and [were] whisked about with no sense of either past or future." She asserted that white society would inevitably move toward "communal life at a new level," which she saw modeled among the Pueblos.[23]

Many antimodern feminists blamed the triumph of science and technology in modernizing America for fostering excessive individualism. As Luhan so dramatically expressed it:

Out of the endless breaking up and recombining of elements, the numberless taking-to-pieces of things, the examination and the observation—out of all that knowledge people had learned how to move faster, how to transmit electrical force, and how to be more physically comfortable. The practice of infinite divisibility had produced an enormous number of devices. Indeed, the whole world was cluttered up with devices. . . . Actually, the conquest of machinery was to promote the separation of the individual from the mass; and the by-product of scientific conquest was become the elaborate, unhappy, modern man, cut off from his source, powerful in mechanisms, but the living sacrifice of his scientific knowledge.

To Luhan, science and sophisticated technology did not bring progress but instead served as catalysts for creating the shattered and divided modern individual. In contrast, according to antimodern feminists, the Pueblo person was integrated with all life around him or her. He is "not an accumulator of material things," Mary Roberts Coolidge wrote, "but a man who enjoys what he has, endures what he must, does not fret, does not resist Nature, and adapts himself to whatever happens. He thinks of himself, not as an individual competing with others for place, but as a being one with his people, one with all animate life."[24]

The image of the agricultural Pueblo Indian was integral to the antimodern feminist vision of the Pueblos as a nonmechanized, communal society. Popular writers suggested that Pueblo society could only remain communally oriented by foregoing industrialization. Luhan suggested that a special foundation should be established to preserve Pueblo culture and to encourage Pueblo Indians "to be what they have been for so long—real farmers—with a farmer's poetic vision of the land." Luhan and other new champions of the Pueblos particularly admired traditional Pueblo farming methods because they eschewed mechanization. Luhan described with appreciation how the Indians had traditionally "harvested their crops by hand with scythe and sickle, threshed it with horses," and then the women cleaned and ground it. Although Taos Pueblo had one threshing machine, Luhan claimed that most Indians disliked it because they "felt instinctively that the old way was the best." Here again, Luhan obscured the changes and conflicts within the pueblos. In actuality, according to Parsons, many Indian men preferred to use the threshing machine, but it was frequently in disrepair. Many Indian women had grown weary of grinding their corn by hand. In her study of Taos Pueblo, Parsons contended that "grinding corn went out of fashion some time ago."[25]

Antimodern feminists and their male peers even upheld the Pueblo farmer as the quintessential yeoman farmer, an ideal so crucial to American self-images. In a 1927 leaflet published by the Santa Fe–based School of American Research, "The Pueblo Indians: A Suggestion to Those Who Visit Them," the author commented that "the most treasured of our American traditions, it is agreed, is respect for self-supporting men. This tradition has made America a free country. The Pueblo Indians were forerunners in this essentially American requirement." The pamphlet's author constructed the Pueblo Indian as the epitome of the "industrious, self-supporting farmer."[26] Interestingly, this new yeoman-farmer image did not emphasize the rugged individualism so inherent in the nineteenth-century ideal but instead countenanced both independence and communalism. By remaining communal, white primitivists believed, the Pueblos could avoid becoming dependent on machines and their owners. In turn, by eschewing machinery the Pueblos could supposedly preserve their unique communal ethic. Of course, even as antimodern feminists extolled the Pueblo man as the quintessential yeoman farmer, the Pueblos were struggling to maintain their subsistence economy in the face of ecological disasters and new economic and assimilation pressures. Yet what mattered to the antimodern feminists was not the complicated, changing reality of Pueblo Indians' lives but the antimodern ideal they were bent upon creating.

Human relationship to nature provided another critical part of antimodern feminists' ideal and a means to measure the relative modernity of a culture.

These women deemed the Pueblos as closer to nature than modern Americans. As Luhan commented, "Whatever comes in Nature, [Indians] meet it with acceptance as though it were right. They do not know how to resist natural things like drought or hail or cloudbursts with anger and hate because they are so much at one with all the elements. . . . We watch things happen in Nature as though they were outside and separate from us, but the Indians know they are that which they contemplate." A School of American Research leaflet asked its readers, "[B]ecause of our separation from nature . . . have we not lost much of the quiet dignity, the aspiration of thought, and the response to beauty of the American Indian?"[27] Crafting the Pueblo Indians as inseparable from nature while excoriating whites for becoming alienated from the natural world further differentiated the Pueblos from modern white Americans.

To antimodern feminists, the Pueblos' "at-oneness" with nature constituted the basis of their religion. Erna Fergusson stressed that the Pueblos "live close to the earth. . . . A religion of an idea, of an ideal, is foreign to them. Their religion is of earth and the things of earth." Fergusson and her peers particularly idealized Pueblo religion as the antithesis of modern institutionalized religion. Austin was fond of projecting an image of God extending his two hands down toward the Earth. "In the Days of the New," she explained, "all life was shaped as it flowed from the right hand to the left [of God], pulling the dust up through the corn to be man, pulling man down to the dust again." The Pueblos, "the only existing human society that ever found . . . the secret of spiritual organization," practiced a religion that recognized both hands of God, and "so long as the two hands were open, men experienced the one without boasting, and suffered the other without complaint. It was not until they fell into the clutch of this most Christian but un-Christlike civilization of ours, that with anguished certainty our Ancients felt close over them the Left Hand of God."[28]

Austin made clear that the "Left Hand of God" was simultaneously both the destructive force of Christianity and the modern force: "Robbed of his lands, wounded in his respect for himself, all the most colorful expression of his spiritual experience filched from him in the name of education, the great Left Hand of modernism closes over the Puebleño. But if the Holders of the Paths laugh at all, it is at us they are laughing. For we cannot put our weight on the Left Hand of God and not, ourselves, go down with it."[29] Unlike female moral reformers who sought to convert the Pueblos to Protestantism, the antimodern feminists vehemently condemned "this most Christian but un-Christlike civilization of ours," and characterized Pueblo religion as superior to Christianity.

As with their other depictions of the Pueblos, when these white women writers wrote of Pueblo religion, they simplified a complex composite of religious beliefs and practices. Many Pueblo Indians also practiced Catholicism and had been exposed for decades to Protestant proselytization through missions and American schools. Yet antimodern feminists almost wholly ignored Christianity among the Pueblos and instead characterized Pueblo religion as a purely indigenous religion. In addition, these white women writers conceived of religion as the most defining and important aspect of Pueblo life. As Coolidge phrased it, "[R]eligious conceptions are the key to [the Indian's] whole existence." Many male writers agreed, adding that Pueblo religion further promoted communalism and stifled individualism. As archaeologist Adolph Bandelier put it, "There is no greater slave than the Indian. Every motion of his is guided by superstition, every action of his neighbor suspiciously scrutinized. . . . He is not his own master. Nature, deified by him to the extent of innumerable personalities and principles, exacts from him the conduct which we blame. His religion . . . reduces him to utter helplessness, . . . making him a timid, fettered being, anxiously listening to the voice of nature for advice. These voices stifle the silent throbs of conscience."[30]

While many Pueblo Indians indeed placed a high value on their religion, and continue to do so, Bandelier and the white women writers of the 1920s and 1930s exaggerated the degree to which religion served as the key to their existence and as their "enslaver." Edward Dozier, an anthropologist from Santa Clara Pueblo, has remarked upon the variable importance of religion among the Pueblos. He argues that the Western Pueblos (the Hopis, Zunis, Acomas, and Lagunas) rely more on magical rites to deal with weather, illness, warfare, village harmony, hunting, and agriculture while the Rio Grande (or Eastern) Pueblos are "more practical" about these matters. Dozier attributes this difference to divergent agricultural methods; the Western Pueblos rely on dry and flood farming, while the Rio Grande Pueblos depend on irrigation. While Dozier observes that among the Western Pueblos "all activities are subordinated to religion," he makes no such claims for the Eastern Pueblos.[31] Yet in the view of Bandelier, Austin, and Luhan, religion takes on an independent role, further reducing or altogether eliminating the individual will of Indians.

The tendency to portray nonwhite peoples as slaves to their religions and their religions as the key to understanding their cultures was common to a number of white Americans and Europeans from the late eighteenth to the early twentieth centuries. Interestingly, British colonial administrators and cultural observers in India also depicted the people of India as lacking in all individualism and as mindless followers of their religions. Similarly, they regarded religion to be the center of Indian lives. Edward Said has identified such a practice as part of the "Orientalist" representation of peoples of Asia and the Middle East.

In "the Orient" and in the Southwest this representation had the effect of obscuring the diversity and contested nature of religious beliefs and practices and of further reinforcing the notion that nonwhite peoples acted as part of a collective mass and lacked individual will and subjectivity. Furthermore, by treating all aspects of Pueblo Indian life as emanating from religion, this image denied white culpability in fostering social inequities. Poverty and disease could be explained away as the inevitable consequences of a people devoted to their religion.[32]

Believing that a connection existed between spirituality and sexuality, antimodern feminists also extolled Pueblo religion for what they believed to be its sexual virility. Luhan asserted that there was an "incompatibility between those emasculated religions and the virile religion of the Indian that has retained its vigor and its life just because it has, symbolically, a sexual basis. Of course they worship creation and we know almost all their symbols are sexual as in all the ancient religions."[33] Interestingly, up until the 1920s female moral reformers had generally coded Pueblo Indian culture as feminine and had even identified with it in some sense. Mary Dissette and Clara True had drawn parallels between the situation of white women and that of the Indians: both white women and Indians were the innocent victims of evil white men who spread venereal disease. Until 1920 neither women nor Indians could vote. Defining Pueblo culture as feminine, Dissette and other moral reformers could imagine a sisterhood linking them with the entire Indian race.

In contrast, Luhan and other antimodern feminist writers reinscribed Pueblo culture as masculine and as sexually virile. Luhan seemed to envision Pueblo culture as a potent sexual partner that could metaphorically help to release her sexuality. This new gendering of Pueblo culture may have derived from a new emphasis in American culture at large on expressing sexuality in heterosexual relationships.[34] Luhan's "masculinization" of the Pueblos worked against what Barbara Babcock and Marta Weigle have identified as a tendency on the part of the Santa Fe Railroad and the Fred Harvey Company to stage the Southwest as "pueblocentric, domestic, and feminine." Babcock and Weigle assert that this "feminine" construction of the Southwest was "necessary to the anti-modernist" as an alternative "to masculine, industrialized production."[35] Luhan's characterization of Pueblo religion as virile points to an alternative vision of modernity as effete and to antimodern life as hypermasculine.

The antimodern feminist vision of the Pueblos as a communally oriented, deeply religious, sexually expressive premodern society that was "at one" with nature depended on seeing the Pueblos as an ageless, changeless people with a pure and pristine culture. Notwithstanding centuries of contact with Spain and

Mexico, antimodern feminists downplayed the role of change in Pueblo society, referring to the Pueblos as "our Ancients."[36] Austin asserted that "in its two and a half centuries of White contact, Taos has actually changed very little, except superficially." Despite the interference of the BIA and missionaries, Austin found Taos to be "sturdily unimpared [*sic*] of its essential primitiveness, its vital pagan quality."

The Pueblos existed, to Austin and other antimodern feminists, as a kind of paradisiacal, primitive island surrounded by a sea of modernism but unaffected by its tides. As Austin phrased it, "Always, for the most casual visitor at Taos, there is the appeal of strangeness, the dark people, the alien dress, the great house-heaps intricately blocked in squares of shadow and sunlight on tawny earthen walls. . . . Everywhere peace, impenetrable timelessness of peace, as though the pueblo and all it contains were shut in a glassy fourth dimension, near and at the same time inaccessibly remote."[37] Referring to the Pueblos in this manner set up another contrast with modern Americans, who in just a few generations had experienced a dramatic transformation of their society. Antimodern feminists represented the Pueblos as outside time and history and as holders of a treasured American heritage. While robbing the Pueblos of their history and erasing the effect of some four centuries of contact with Apaches, Navajos, Spanish, Mexicans, and Anglos, antimodern feminists used the Pueblos to create an ancient past for America, to provide a sense of rootedness and authenticity to white Americans in an era of seemingly rapid change.[38]

If these feminists portrayed Pueblo culture as ancient, timeless, and unchanging, they particularly selected Pueblo women as the bearers of tradition. For example, Erna Fergusson asserted that in ancient times as now "meal was ground by a kneeling woman who swung her body back and forth, bearing down on the mano which crushed the kernels into finer and finer meal. No doubt the prehistoric woman sang the very songs which still celebrate the wonder of the corn, for then as now the corn was the sacred mother, typical of all good, on whose bounty life depended." Though evidence revealed that many Pueblo women had given up the tedious labor of grinding corn by hand in favor of buying cornmeal ready-made, Fergusson and other white women writers invested Pueblo women with the timelessness and unchanging tradition they perceived in Pueblo culture at large.[39]

In their attempts to define and condemn modernity, antimodern feminists even set up a contrast between Pueblo women as dignified bearers of tradition and fickle, modern white women who seemed buffeted about by the whims of fashion and fads. Charles Lummis asserted that "no [Pueblo] woman . . . ever envied her neighbor's dress, nor feared her own was out of style. No Pueblo woman ever made her hair or her dress provocative, a challenge, a bait, a temptation." Unlike many feminists, Lummis, who had a reputation as a philanderer, looked askance at emerging sexual mores in American society. But even feminists could not quite reconcile their support for women's "sex expression" in modern America with their disdain for the consumerism and materialism that they believed had accompanied it. Feminists often feared that modern, white American sexual mores and their attendant consumerism would invade Pueblo country. At a Hopi dance Fergusson observed that young Hopi virgins, who used to wear their hair rolled up in "squash blossoms" as a sign of their virginity, "appear now in badly made calico dresses or sleazy silk ready-mades from the stores. . . . A couple of young Carmens, draped in flowered shawls, sat on roof-edges, dangling silks stockings and high heels and turning giggling away from the boys. The white woman's brand of coquetry is only beginning to supplant the more subtle quiet of the Indian maid."[40] Antimodern feminists seemed to prefer what they believed to be a more subtle, "natural" sexuality to the coquettish sexuality of modern American women that they believed had become manipulated by big business.

In representing the Pueblos as ancient and unchanging, these feminist writers tended to associate Pueblo culture with "Oriental" culture. The number of times antimodern feminist authors and their male counterparts compared Pueblo Indians to "Orientals" is striking. In an article meant to attract tourists to the Southwest, Fergusson asserted that "motorists crossing the Southwestern States are nearer to the primitive than anywhere else on the continent. They are crossing a land in which a foreign people, with foreign speech and foreign ways, offer them spectacles which can be equaled in very few Oriental lands."[41] Several scholars have remarked that the Southwest served as America's "Orient" and that American writers, artists, anthropologists, bureaucrats, and missionaries engaged in the same process of essentializing Southwestern native cultures as Europeans did in their colonies in Asia.[42]

The scientific theory that Native Americans originated in Asia and migrated to North America across the Bering Strait may have led these women to link Pueblo Indians with Asians. But this tendency to equate Pueblo Indians with Asians extended well beyond accepting demographic theories and noticing similarities of appearance. Luhan pondered the name "Taos": "Does it perhaps derive from the small band of devotees who followed Lao Tze westward out of China, imbued with his teachings of the Taos, the golden mean, the Middle Way? Are these Indians descended from these Taoes? Their religion closely resembles the non-aggressive, moderate politesse of the heart discernible in Lao Tze's few existent axioms."[43] Other white women writers of the 1920s portrayed the Pueblos as inscrutable, like the Asian stereotype. As Austin wrote, "[T]here is perhaps no such thing as an absolutely knowable Indian, any more than there is a completely individual Japanese." Fergusson called Pueblo peoples "enigmatic." Elizabeth DeHuff claimed, "The Indian is an Oriental. And the difference between the Oriental mind and the Occidental, is the difference between spiritual-mindedness and practical-mindedness." Luhan related her encounter with a man named Candelario who owned a curio shop in Santa Fe. When she told him she wanted to know the Indians, he replied curtly that "No one can know an Indian except an Indian."[44]

These feminists may have drawn such connections between "Orientals" and Pueblos because they had begun to create a vision of all nonwhite peoples as to some extent primitive. According to historian David L. Lewis, several white writers during the 1920s depicted and celebrated blacks as close to nature, sexually expressive and uninhibited, incapable of logic, and guided by their primeval instincts. White supporters of black primitivist writing and black culture believed that Western civilization had been ruined by industrialization. They rediscovered the African American as a "symbol of cultural innocence and regeneration," who could play a major role in destroying the old corrupt order and saving America. Furthermore, many white intellectuals believed that blacks "had retained a direct virility that the whites had lost through being overeducated." Many of the same white women who romanticized the supposed primitivism of the Pueblos also supported the Harlem Renaissance. Luhan, for example, patronized many "primitivist" black writers and reportedly had an affair with writer Jean Toomer in the 1920s.[45] The rich white woman primarily known for her patronage of Harlem Renaissance primitivist writers—Charlotte Osgood Mason—was also fascinated by "primitive" Indians and journeyed to the Southwest with ethnomusicologist Natalie Curtis Burlin to gather materials for Burlin's *The Indian Book*. Burlin, after collecting two hundred songs from eighteen tribes, turned to recording African American music. Like Burlin, after several years of research among the Pueblos, Elsie Clews Parsons began collecting African American folklore.[46]

Other white intellectuals looked to South Pacific Islanders or to Mexicans to find primitive models. When Luhan suggested that her then-husband Maurice Sterne go to the Southwest to paint the Indians, she hoped that he could "do something of the same kind as your Bali pictures." Sterne had already spent a year painting "natives" on Bali.[47] Austin and many of her friends in New Mexico also similarly primitivized Mexican-American peoples there, starting an organization to preserve and promote Spanish colonial arts. Austin hoped that farming and handicrafts could sustain the primitivism of the Mexicans and prevent them from becoming "average installment-plan, sub-rotarian middle-class Americans."[48] Although antimodern feminists tended to see all nonwhite peoples as primitive, they ranked them nevertheless in their own hierarchical order, placing those cultures they considered most "pristine" and untouched by modernity at the top, and ranking more "modern," industrialized cultures at the bottom. Thus in New Mexico they elevated Indian culture and land claims above those of Mexicans, especially in Taos.[49] Rather than eliminating the racial hierarchy of the nineteenth century, then, antimodern feminists redefined it.

While Luhan, Austin, and other white women who settled or sojourned in New Mexico after World War I had overturned the racial hierarchy that cast "savage" and "barbarian" peoples as inferior to civilized people, they did not abandon the view that each "race" inherited its own set of both biological and personality traits. They did not so much challenge the notion of inherent racial difference as they recast it in modern terms. Modernity became a racial essence. Whites were modern, Indians (and other "races") primitive. Luhan personified modernism in the form of her third husband, Maurice Sterne, and primitivism in Tony Luhan. While still married to Sterne but attracted to Tony Luhan, Mabel wrote, "I had a strange sense of dislocation, as though I were swinging like a pendulum over the gulf of the canyon, between the two poles of mankind, between Maurice and Tony; and Maurice seemed old and spent and tragic, while Tony was whole and young in the cells of his body, with his power unbroken and hard like the carved granite rock, yet older than the Germanic Russian whom the modern world had destroyed."[50]

Luhan and Austin actually accepted the most essentialist view of the source of racial difference—blood. In determining who was an Indian and therefore who should be granted an allotment of land, the federal government had introduced the system of "blood quantum level" into Indian communities. Rather than rejecting this view of culture as biologically determined, Luhan and other antimodern feminists embraced and extended it.[51] Luhan believed that Indian culture would evaporate if Indians intermarried with other races. She confessed to John Collier in 1933: "Although I married an Indian I did not do so when we were both young (and I don't believe in it for others). I cannot bring myself to change from my previous hope that the Indian culture may be saved as it cannot be if he [*sic*] becomes absorbed into the Mexican or the white races."

Austin asserted that she had inherited a "special grace" and been drawn to Indians in the first place due to "the persistence in [her], perhaps, of an uncorrupted strain of ancestral primitivism, a single isolated gene of that far-off and slightly mythical Indian ancestor of whose reality I am more convinced by what happened to me among Indians than by any objective evidence."[52] For both

Luhan and Austin it was "blood" that made the Indian, not culture and history. The more "pure" and "undiluted" the blood, the more authentically primitive the individual and the tribe. Forced modernization could lead Indians to ignore their blood instincts, but ultimately Indians would only lose their essential primitiveness through racial intermarriage. Thus, Mexican-Americans, a "racial mixture" of Spanish and Indian, seemed to antimodern feminists less primitive (and less interesting) than Pueblo Indians.

Antimodern feminists had not really exploded the racial concepts of the nineteenth century; they had instead exchanged the civilized-savage dichotomy for the modern-primitive duality and inverted the racial hierarchy.[53] The word "savage" all but disappeared from the lexicon of these feminist writers. Connoting cruelty and ferocity, "savagery" would not do for women who wished to exalt the Pueblos and other Indians. Instead, they turned to the term "primitive," which suggested a quality of being the first or earliest inhabitants of America and of being simple, unscathed by the excesses of modern life. This new term fit with their desire to find a new American identity, influenced by indigenous sources rather than European intellectual currents.[54] Similarly, antimodern feminists rarely used the term "civilized," except to critique it. They favored "modern," a term that they associated with rampant industrialization, bureaucratization, militarism, and consumerism. Ironically, by making modernity and primitivism racial essences, these feminists actually emphasized biological determinism more than had female moral reformers. Female moral reformers believed in cultural evolution; thus a person's racial status as a "savage" was not fixed but mutable. To antimodern feminists, a primitive individual could not change his or her racial status; only through intermarriage and producing "mixed-race" progeny could a race become less primitive.

Even Parsons did not hold to the view that race was purely a social or cultural construction. Although she abhorred the notion of state intervention in sexual relations between consenting adults, Parsons hoped that "more [would] be asked of parenthood . . . when based on eugenic facts than of merely juridical or proprietary parenthood," and "similarly eugenic ideas of mating [might] give a new and compelling significance to stock or race."[55] Parsons decried an artificial "sense of caste" but believed that "real" differences did exist between the races, differences that could be enhanced through eugenics. The language of "racial stock" was ubiquitous among early-twentieth-century Americans, from the liberal Parsons and the sexologist Havelock Ellis to the head of the Ku Klux Klan, Hiram Evans.[56] In a less formal moment, Parsons also admitted to her husband that "it may seem a queer taste, but Negroes and Indians [are] for me. The rest of the world grows duller and duller. But for you and the children I would cer-

tainly spend little time in this part of it."[57] Parsons clearly believed that at base
the so-called primitive races differed substantially from her own. Many scholars
have perhaps been too quick to embrace Parsons as an early-twentieth-century
woman who shared a thoroughly late-twentieth-century sensibility, defining
gender and race purely as social constructions.[58]

Of course there were some white women who resisted this tendency to dualize
white and Indian culture. They were, however, less likely to write lengthy
books and articles about their views. In fact, Ina Sizer Cassidy told an interviewer, "I wanted to write about the Indians . . . but was aware I knew too little
of them, so studied their ways of life. The more I learned of them, the more I
realized my store of knowledge was inadequate so just decided not to pursue it
further." Elizabeth DeHuff vacillated between a romantic view of the Pueblos as
innately poetic and artistic and a sense that the Pueblos were "neither savages
nor super-humans." Later in life, DeHuff made fun of her earlier tendency to
romanticize the Pueblos. In her unpublished "Pueblo Episodes," DeHuff recounted seeing an old Indian man standing in the pueblo: "Cloud-filmed, his
gray eyes stared into space . . . his thought filled with mysticism. 'Sitting in
deep mediation,' I mumbled as I neared to pass him, 'How truly venerable he
looks! They are a deeply spiritual people!' Then as I drew aside my skirt to pass
on the narrow ledge before him, he looked up swiftly and demanded, 'Gimme
cigarette!' "[59]

Another woman who eschewed an essentialist view of the Pueblos was Edith
Warner, who went to New Mexico temporarily in 1922 to recover from physical
stress. In 1928 she settled there for the rest of her life. Single and determined not
to ask for money from her family, Warner took a job as manager of a small freight
depot at Otowi Bridge, a station between San Ildefonso Pueblo and present-day
Los Alamos. The Indians helped Warner remodel her house. Warner had close
personal relationships with several San Ildefonso women, including a woman
named Quebi, whom she considered a sister, and the potter Maria Martinez,
from whom she often sought advice and on whose land she lived. Indian men
helped by bringing her wood, plowing her garden, and lending her horses. In
addition, an older San Ildefonso man, Tilano, went to live in Warner's home at
Otowi Bridge and became her lifelong companion. According to her biographer, Warner's Pueblo friends and neighbors did not feel patronized by her because she lived on the verge of poverty as they did.[60]

Although Warner commented, "[E]ach year I do less of the customary things
of our civilization," she refused to romanticize the lifestyle and culture of the
Pueblos she knew. According to Peggy Pond Church, "[O]nce someone asked
her if it were true that the Pueblos had developed a way of life that protected

them from the frustrations and tensions which the white world seemed to be facing. She smiled. 'These people are human beings like ourselves,' she told him, 'with their own full share of human good and ill.'" In the only published essay she wrote, Warner concluded about her interaction with the Pueblos, "It matters not that the color of skin be different, that language be not the same, that even the gods of our fathers be known by a different name. We are people, the same kind of human beings who live and love and go on, and I find myself ever forgetting that my friends are known as Indians and I am a white woman born."[61] Edith Warner's belief in the commonalities between her culture and that of the Pueblos was drowned out by the writings of women such as Luhan and Austin. Their view of Pueblo culture as the dualistic opposite of white American culture gained a much wider currency and popular following than did Warner's perspective.

Because they believed so strongly that Pueblo culture provided an absolute alternative to modern white culture, many antimodern feminists tried to become what they believed to be Indian. Today Indians would call them "wannabees." Luhan wished to purge herself of "her people." "Was it possible for me to get away from [my people]," she queried, "and wash away from myself the taint of them, the odor of their sickness and their death? . . . I hated them in myself and myself in them, and I longed to blot them out in this other."[62] Unattracted to organized Christianity but desirous of some form of spirituality, Luhan and Austin believed that they could freely borrow Pueblo religious beliefs. Luhan believed that she had found real spirituality among the Pueblos and through her relationship with Tony Luhan. As she put it, when "I came to Taos . . . I was offered and accepted a spiritual therapy that was cleansing, one that provided a difficult and painful method of curing me of my epoch and that finally rewarded me with a sense of reality." Luhan believed that Tony Luhan made it possible for her to "leave the world I had been so false in, where I had always been trying to play a part and always feeling unrelated, a world that was on a decline so rapid one could see people one knew dropping to pieces day by day, a dying world with no one appearing who would save it, a decadent unhappy world."[63]

Luhan, however, in her attempt to be like the Taos Indians, also played a part. She cut her hair in the fashion of Pueblo women and wore a shawl about her as the Pueblo women did. When she returned from one of her visits to Taos Pueblo, she "assumed a bright, noncommittal expression which I supposed was the way Indians looked. I wanted to be like them and felt, in an obscure way, that if I looked and acted the way they did, I would be."[64] Curiously, Luhan wanted Indians to be antithetically different from modern Americans, and yet at the same time she wanted to be able to become Indian. If there were permeability between what antimodern feminists believed to be the two separate worlds of whites and Pueblo Indians, it allowed for movement in only one direction. Indians could never become truly white and modern, but somehow whites could become Indians. Having an alleged drop of Indian blood allowed some whites to go Indian; sexual intimacy with Indians enabled other whites, such as Luhan, to believe they could become Indian.[65] As explored at length in chapter 6, collecting and becoming an "expert" on Indian objects served as another means whereby some white women believed they could enter the Indian world.

Parsons also attempted to become Indian for quite different reasons. When she traveled to the Hopi mesas, she hoped to collect material on their religion and culture; yet like all of the Pueblos, the Hopis were suspicious of anthropologists and unwilling to share their cultural secrets with outsiders. When Parsons stayed with a Hopi family, the "neighbors began to take notice" of her. Later, when "an evening visitor suggested . . . that it might be well, in order to disarm criticism of [Parsons's] presence on the mesa, for [her] to have [her] head washed and get a Hopi name, [she] concurred."[66] Thus Parsons did not "go primitive" for romantic reasons as Luhan and Austin did, but for pragmatic reasons, to further her anthropological aims.

Other white women who favored cultural relativism and the preservation of Indian culture nevertheless ridiculed their peers who "proceeded to 'go Indian.'" Referring to one white woman who went to live in a Hopi home, Elizabeth DeHuff wrote, "[S]he was willing to take all they had to offer of things spiritual and religious and willing to give nothing in exchange excepting her smiling, verbal thanks." DeHuff's view of this white woman as a cultural consumer is echoed by scholars today. As Leah Dilworth has noted, white practices of collecting Indian objects and playing Indian "induced a relationship between representer and represented based on consumption and appropriation rather than on communication between subjects."[67]

Antimodern feminists who played Indian seemed to also measure their own status within their subculture by who best "knew" the Pueblos and who wrote most authentically about them. Austin wrote to Ina Sizer Cassidy that "Elizabeth [DeHuff] is still unsuccessfully trying to dispose of her Indian stories. I think it bothers her to see me sell mine, when I am sure that she feels that hers are truer—which I doubt. It takes more years than Elizabeth has given to it to know Indians so that you can convince other people that you know them." Although ostensibly referring to anthropologists, Austin might have been writing about herself and her competitors when she quipped, "The desire on the part of the White to learn such details [of Indian ceremonials and practices] is usually motivated by the profound wish that there should be such mysteries, by possession of which the owner may aggrandize his own importance."[68]

More was involved and at stake than just creating a representation of Pueblo Indians that affirmed antimodern feminists' ideal and enhanced their social status. As some feminists sought to enforce their ideals, these representations had real consequences for Indians. While battling to "save" the Pueblos in the 1920s, these white women consciously manipulated the images they had created of the superior primitive. When the new activists brought delegations of Indians from Pueblo country to Washington DC, or on a national tour to raise money, they preferred to take the Indians who wore their traditional dress and long hair rather than those who appeared more Americanized. In fact, for the formal hearings in Washington, Elizabeth Shepley Sergeant insisted that "the older delegate must wear the beautiful Pueblo dress. If the younger delegate prefers to wear American clothes on the train he must surely bring Pueblo dress also— blanket, moccasins, etc." Interestingly, perhaps to conform to American expectations, white activists sometimes embellished the Pueblo delegates' traditional dress by posing them with feathered headdresses on, an accessory of the Plains Indians.[69] Luhan told John Collier that the new white activists must select the Indian delegates themselves. "They always vote that their smart short haired Americanised ones shall go: just the wrong ones."[70]

Austin grumpily wrote to Luhan that Collier needed Austin there to manage the Indians because Collier's interests in the Indians was "too philosophical and too largely economic to catch the popular interest. He doesn't know how to make them seem exciting and romantic figures, as the public likes to see them, and he does not know how to make them perform as I do. Everybody commented on the fact that they sang and danced better and the program was more varied when I managed them."[71] The new activists enjoyed great success by bringing traditionally dressed Pueblo Indian delegates to big cities. In New York City they took the Pueblo delegates to the stock exchange, which, according to Austin, "unbent." "When the Indians stood up in the gallery and sang the Morning Song," Austin marveled, "the Exchange simply got up on its hind legs and howled." Activists raised a hefty five hundred dollars a day from the stock exchange to fund the defense of the Pueblos.[72]

Because they set up the Pueblos as a model and as a social critique of white, middle-class American society, the new activists had little sympathy for Native Americans who did not conform to their image of the primitive. On a trip to Taos in 1919, Austin wrote that the Taos Indians were "all torn up . . . over a fight between the radicals, who wish to wear store clothes and cut their hair, and the conservatives who want nothing of the kind, and the friends I stopped with were so unfortunate, from my point of view, as to sympathize with the radicals." Later, when Austin collaborated with photographer Ansel Adams on a book about Taos Pueblo, she wrote of a "Radical" who "was touched by our American Protestant fetishism, which required that he testify to his faith by cutting his hair and discarding his blanket." After being ostracized by other villagers, however, the man finally returned to the customs of Taos. Austin made clear that such "radical" Indians would eventually see the error of their ways and would weaken "before the condition of being outcasted [sic] from the service of the *acequia madre*, from the community of loving service to the sacred water."[73] Such a privileging of the "traditional" Indian denied the "Indianness" of those Indians who engaged in nonfarming occupations or moved to the city, who challenged the leadership of the tribal officials, who desired an education, who wore American clothes or cut their hair, or who simply struggled to balance the claims of both Pueblo and modern American culture. This preference for "pure" and "traditional" Indians further denied the history of Pueblo Indians, including their contemporary interactions with women such as Austin.[74]

Despite these white women's criticism of "radical" Indians and their promotion of traditional Indians, some Pueblos resented the representation of them as the antithesis of all that was modern. At the end of World War II, veterans returning to Taos Pueblo wanted conveniences such as electricity and plumbing, while many older Pueblo officials objected. Luhan wrote a letter to the editor of the local newspaper that the old ways were best, and the Pueblos should stick to them. A young Indian responded to Luhan's letter by suggesting that Luhan try the old ways she advocated. She could trade houses with him and live without electric lights, running water, or a toilet.[75] For other Indians it was simply not an issue whether or not they conformed to white notions of primitive purity. When Elizabeth DeHuff went to a Pueblo wedding, which included the traditional custom of traveling to three houses—the home of the male attendant, of the groom, and of the bride—she noted that in the last house her hostesses served "a pineapple upside-down cake, with half a dozen other deserts [sic] and as many aspic salads, all works of art accurately copied from pictures in the women's magazines, cleverly fashioned and beautiful in their varied colorings, yet strangely discordant surrounding an Indian bowl of stew and piles of paper bread."[76] What DeHuff found "strangely discordant" could only be so if she imagined the Pueblos as a people petrified in time, who remained utterly impermeable to outside influences. Instead, DeHuff's observation reveals that the Pueblos creatively blended elements of white and Pueblo culture, rejecting an all-or-nothing approach to cultural exchange.

The ways in which many Pueblo Indians combined modern white ways with their own practices seem to have eluded or been ignored by most antimodern feminists. They preferred to cast the Pueblo Indians as a pure culture unto themselves. While they sought to overturn the moral reformers' assumptions that Native Americans were inferior peoples in need of uplift and assimilation, antimodern feminists of the 1920s did not simply destroy the civilized-savage dichotomy. Instead, they erected a whole new set of assumptions regarding the differences between a universal Pueblo culture and a white culture. Most antimodern feminists were not so much concerned with attempting to depict the Pueblos accurately as they were with defining and critiquing modernism. In particular, through the Pueblos, these women struggled to articulate and shape a new womanhood and a new sexuality. This becomes particularly apparent when we examine their role in defending Pueblo dances and in promoting Indian arts and crafts.

CHAPTER FIVE

The 1920s Controversy over Indian Dances

In 1920, as part of an extensive effort to gather information about the rumored immorality of Pueblo dances, an inspector from the U.S. government took sworn affidavits and written statements from about a dozen Hopi Indians and seven white observers. To prove her contention that "the Hopi dance is an evil influence in their lives, tending to keep alive all their traditional immorality as well as that which is natural to the flesh," witness Evelyn Bentley, a field matron on the Moqui Indian Reservation in Oraibi, Arizona, reported to the inspector the following scene:

> Two clowns dressed as women came into the court. Their skirts were very short, not over eleven inches long. The men clowns would go up to them and try to pull the skirts down a little. The clowns who stood behind the women would try to pull the skirts down in the back but while doing so the skirts would slip up in front. Then the clowns who stood in front would stoop down and look up under the skirt as if looking at a woman's private organs. Then the other clowns would come around and have a look, then all would make believe that they were trying to pull the skirts down, then stoop and look under to see how much they could see. All this brought forth much laughter and many yells from the crowd.[1]

Other witnesses charged Pueblo clowns with "imitating animals in the act of sexual intercourse," pretending to fondle and suck one another's sex organs, and "going through the motions of fornication." The inspector compiled about two hundred pages of this testimony into what came to be known in Indian reform circles as the "Secret Dance File."[2] It is important to view this document not as an accurate description of Pueblo sexual practices in the 1920s but as a primary source that reveals much about white moral reformers and their preoccupations, interpretations, and concerns.[3]

Having spent their careers trying to "uplift" Native Americans to the standards of white, middle-class American civilization through schools, missions, and home visits, female moral reformers and missionaries such as Bentley condemned Indian dances as impediments to their goal of assimilating Native Americans. Armed with the Secret Dance File, they hoped to pressure the government to ban Indian dances they deemed harmful to Indian progress. In the early 1920s Commissioner of Indian Affairs Charles Burke responded favorably to their concerns, issuing Circular 1665 and a subsequent supplement to all BIA superintendents that sought to restrict the number, kind, and frequency of dances, as well as the age of the participants. Burke's circular elicited a strong reaction from antimodern feminists and many of their male allies, and they became involved in a nationwide publicity campaign to protest the circular and to contest the reformers' view of Indian dances. Rather than seeing Bentley's statement as evidence of sexual depravity among the Hopis, antimodern feminists tended to view it as testimony to the Indians' "natural" and healthy sexuality. Circular 1665 and the Secret Dance File also became a contentious issue for Pueblo Indians. After all, several Hopi men had themselves testified that the dances of the Hopis were immoral, and some New Mexico Pueblo men also came out in favor of Commissioner Burke's dance circular. Many other Pueblo Indian men vehemently defended their dances.

Historians have generally characterized the dance controversy as a struggle over whether religious freedom should be extended to Native Americans.[4] Many Native Americans certainly viewed the threat to ban Indian dances as interference with their religious practices. Yet the controversy itself involved more than a constitutional debate on religious freedom. In their discourse regarding Indian dances, non-Indian, female participants revealed a greater concern with emerging sexual mores in American society at large than with the traditional religious practices of Native Americans. The 1920s witnessed a conflict between female moral reformers who sought to maintain the notion of female purity and new feminists who argued for women's self-fulfillment and expression of sexual desire.[5] Their debate on changing social and cultural mores did not always take place openly or consciously, however; often it showed up in arenas in which gender and sex were not explicitly being discussed.[6] Thus, from the perspective of the white women who participated in it, the dance controversy can be partly understood as a masked debate regarding gender and sexuality. Groping to understand the transformation of gender roles and the loosening of sexual standards going on around them, female moral reformers and antimodern feminists defined and redefined their own conceptions of womanhood and sexuality by attempting to superimpose their competing ideals onto Pueblo Indians, especially Pueblo women.

As for the Pueblo men who participated on both sides of the dance controversy, the perpetuation or elimination of traditional dances symbolized competing approaches to coping with new economic, social, and cultural forces. They highlighted a multitude of other interests, centered around land and water rights, deepening economic dependence on non-Indians, and interactions with Protestant missionaries, government bureaucrats, anthropologists, writers, and artists. Allying themselves with one side or the other of the two groups of white reformers, Pueblo men used the controversy to assert their own agendas. Those Indians who opposed the dances utilized white moral reformers in their bids to acquire or take back individual allotments of land, to avoid communal work, to avenge what they felt to be cruel punishment, to challenge the traditional leadership of their pueblos, and to push for adaptation and "improvement" in their pueblos. Indians who defended their dances used their white patrons' romantic representations of Pueblo life as a means to assert their right to practice their religion, to regain group lands and water rights, to increase badly needed tribal income, to punish recalcitrant "progressive" Indians, and to promote tribal autonomy.

Due to the Pueblo custom that only certain men, chosen by the religious hierarchy, should represent their pueblos to outsiders, no evidence of Pueblo women's direct participation in the dance controversy surfaces in the written record. Interestingly, however, Pueblo women became powerful symbols for all sides in the dance controversy. White women who debated Indian dances, depending on their orientation toward changes occurring in white society, invested Pueblo women with either their greatest fears of sexual degeneration or their greatest hopes for sexual liberation. Pueblo men on both sides of the debate insisted on Pueblo women's modesty yet divided over the role Pueblo women should play in the work of their villages and in the future of their pueblos.

Quoting from, describing, and writing about the debates over Pueblo dances in the 1920s risks reopening the controversy on the nature of Pueblo sexuality and exposing the Pueblos once again to the public scrutiny they so abhor. My intent here is neither to analyze the "true" nature of Pueblo sexuality nor to prove one side or the other right regarding Pueblo dances. Instead, I seek to examine why this issue was of such significance to white women in the 1920s and what implications this controversy had for Pueblo Indians.

Before the 1910s the reformers' discussions of Indian dances had centered more on the dances of the Plains Indians than on those of the Pueblos. The BIA worried that Indian dances promoted "savagery" and warlike behavior and prevented the Indians from becoming more industrious. In the 1880s the BIA targeted the emergence of the Ghost Dance and its incorporation by the Plains tribes, with whom the United States was still at war. In 1883 the BIA compiled a "List of Indian Offenses," for which offenders could be tried before Indian judges who presided over courts of Indian offenses. Rather than targeting criminal offenses or civil conflicts, the government's "list" aimed at eradicating the Ghost Dance, the Sun Dance, give-aways, and other ceremonials that the government believed led the Indians to be more warlike and less industrious.[7]

Before the 1910s, in fact, the government and most white observers held the Pueblo Indians' dances to be of little consequence. During this period, the U.S. government had not even classified the Pueblos as Indians. Courts ruled in several cases that "it would be improper to consign the Pueblo people to the same set of laws and trade 'made for wandering savages.'"[8] In replying to the inquiry of the U.S. Indian agent at the Pueblo agency in 1883 as to whether the "modest dances indulged in by the Pueblos" were intended to be discontinued under the recently released "Rules Governing the Court of Indian Offenses," Commissioner of Indian Affairs Hiram Price wrote:

> I have to advise you, that the dances, or feasts as they are sometimes called, which are provided for under the rules, are such as are intended and calculated to stimulate the warlike passions of the young warriors of the tribe, and, when the warrior recounts his deeds of daring, boasts of his inhumanity in the destruction of his enemies, and his treatment of the female captives in language that "ought to shock even a savage ear."
>
> The rules do not contemplate any interference with the social gatherings for the amusement of the Indians; neither is it intended to discountenance or discontinue anything in the nature of "modest dances."

The government virtually took no notice of the Pueblos' dances before 1915. In 1913 a lengthy report on the Pueblos contained nothing about their dances at all.[9]

In 1915, however, stirrings of concern over Pueblo dances and religious practices reached Washington DC. P. T. Lonergan, the superintendent of the Pueblo day schools, submitted a report entitled "Immoral Dances among the Pueblo Indians," which would later be incorporated into the Secret Dance File. In his report Lonergan asserted that the dances the Pueblos held in secret were "grossly immoral" and that "some of the most disgusting practices are indulged in, the particulars being so bestial as to prohibit their description." To substantiate his claims, Lonergan included six letters "from the everyday people living in the vicinity of the Indians, who have seen these dances, and not from occasional visitors or tourists." Reformer Mary Dissette claimed that Lonergan asked for her help in getting the Indian Rights Association (IRA) to work for the suppression of all such performances.[10] In that same year a syndicated article appeared in newspapers around the country, quoting Matilda Coxe Stevenson, an anthropologist who had begun working among the Pueblos in 1879, as saying that the Pueblos engaged in human sacrifice, keeping large snakes in captivity, to which they routinely fed babies.[11] The complaints regarding Pueblo dances and religion did not emanate only from white observers. Some Pueblo Indians contacted BIA officials to alert them to their displeasure at having to perform the dances. After twelve years in BIA schools, Rosendo Vargas did not wish to participate in the dances when he returned home to Picuris Pueblo. Although his father, the governor of the Pueblo, insisted that he dance, Vargas refused and hid in the woods. Like other Indians who refused to dance, Vargas claimed he was severely beaten.[12]

Despite these first signs that some whites and Indians found Pueblo dances problematic, it was not until the 1920s that an organized campaign against the dances erupted. In the meantime female moral reformers focused on the BIA as the hotbed of corruption and immorality. Even as Lonergan began his assault on what he deemed "grossly immoral practices among the Pueblo Indians," he and other BIA employees had become the subjects of an attack by female moral reformers who alleged sexual misconduct on their part. Clara True waged a campaign to have Lonergan, his assistant, Chavez, and other Indian Service employees removed from their positions because, she charged, Chavez had venereal disease, Lonergan knew about it, and they were corrupting the Indians. In the 1920s True would become one of the most vociferous opponents of Indian dances, but in 1915, she still reserved her moral condemnation more for the BIA than for the Indians.[13]

In the early 1920s the issue of Pueblo dances became more pronounced when Inspector E. M. Sweet compiled the Secret Dance File. According to Indian reformers, this file contained such indecent material that it was too obscene to be sent through the mails or published. But reformers "confidentially passed [the Dance File] from hand to hand for two years," and a great chain of gossip within Indian reform circles developed regarding its contents. As John Collier complained, "[I]t is . . . left to be inferred that horrible immoralities are a part of the Indian religious creed and observances; that the details cannot be given because they are too 'raw.' . . . Very large numbers of citizens have thus been impressed."[14] A furor built among reformers to condemn and restrict the dances they deemed most sexually offensive.[15]

Reformers saw their efforts come to fruition in 1921 when Commissioner of Indian Affairs Charles Burke issued Circular 1665. The circular began with very specific types of dances that should be banned—those involving "self-torture, immoral relations between the sexes, the sacrificial destruction of clothing or other useful articles, the reckless giving away of property, the use of injurious drugs or intoxicants, and frequent or prolonged periods of celebration which bring the Indians together from remote points to the neglect of their crops, live-stock, and home interests." It moved quickly, however, to very general conditions for restricting the dances—"any disorderly or plainly excessive performance that promotes superstitious cruelty, licentiousness, idleness, danger to health, and shiftless indifference to family welfare." As its opponents pointed out, the circular could be interpreted to cover almost any dance that a BIA employee deemed harmful.

In 1923 Burke issued a supplement to the circular that endorsed six recommendations made by a 1922 conference of missionaries. Concerned that Indians should adopt white conceptions of thrift and agricultural production, these recommendations prohibited give-aways, forbade anyone under age fifty from dancing, banned all dances between March and August, and limited dances to one a month in the daylight hours on a day in midweek at one center in each district between the months of September and February. They called for a "careful propaganda" to "educate public opinion against the dance and to provide a healthy substitute." Furthermore, Burke's supplement urged close cooperation between government employees and missionaries and called for an effort "to persuade the management of fairs and 'round-ups' in the towns adjoining the reservations not to commercialize the Indian by soliciting his attendance in large numbers for show purposes." Hoping to make use of moral influence, the circular suggested controlling the dances "by educational processes so far as possible" but threatened to take "punitive measures when [their] degrading tendencies persist." Burke requested a special report from each jurisdiction and declared that he would "take some other course" of action if the Indians did not voluntarily give up their dances within the year.[16]

Circular 1665 and its supplement bear the particular mark of female moral reformers, whose concerns for family and home are evident throughout its text. Not only did the circular condemn dances that led Indians to neglect their "home interests" and promoted "shiftless indifference to family welfare," but it also promoted alternatives to dances: "wholesome, educational entertainment that will tend to divert interest from objectionable native customs." Kathy Peiss has shown that progressive reformers tried to provide similar "wholesome" alternatives to working-class women who frequented dance halls. The circular recommended "the moral influence of our schools" and promoted cooperation between Indian Service field workers and missionaries in "fixing the standards of individual virtue and social purity that should prevail in all forms of amusement or symbolism" and in inculcating "a higher conception of home and family life."[17]

The supplement maintained that "the instinct of individual enterprise and devotion to the prosperity and elevation of family life should in some way be made paramount in every Indian household to the exclusion of idleness, waste of time at frequent gatherings of whatever nature, and neglect of physical resources upon which depend food, clothing, shelter, and the very beginnings of progress."[18] As Peggy Pascoe has observed, such rhetoric was ubiquitous among female moral reformers of the late nineteenth and early twentieth centuries. Indian reform organizations, the BIA, and moral reformers claimed that by rescuing or uplifting Indian women and promoting their adoption of Christian homes, the entire race of Indians could be brought along the road to progress and civilization. Furthermore, as Karen Anderson has pointed out, there were strong "ideological connections between notions of social order and sexual order in the construction of Indian policy."[19]

When word of Burke's circular and supplement reached the newly formed Indian reform organizations—the American Indian Defense Association (AIDA), the Eastern Association on Indian Affairs (EAIA), the New Mexico Association on Indian Affairs (NMAIA), and the Indian Welfare Committee of the General Federation of Women's Clubs (GFWC)—they quickly adopted a position in opposition to the dance circular of the "Bumbletonian Indian Bureau." They also claimed to have "started the Indians to protesting on their own account" through the All-Pueblo Council. These new groups had already successfully organized a nationwide campaign to defeat the Bursum Bill, legislation that might have forced the Pueblos to relinquish much of their land to their surrounding neighbors. By exchanging representatives between groups and by writing letters and articles, the new activists mobilized their members and other sympathetic Americans to protest against the dance order.[20] Mary Austin sent out a questionnaire to notable experts in Pueblo Indian affairs to ask their opinion of the dances. Elsie Clews Parsons, who was not a formal member of any of these organizations, also did her part; she encouraged the American Association for the Advancement of Science to oppose the circular and requested that the editor of the New York Tribune write an editorial against it.[21]

This new group of activists reacted to the charges of the Secret Dance File in numerous ways. Some defended Indian dances purely on what might be called an equal rights doctrine. Stella Atwood of the GFWC contended that "in the light of the fact that the Constitution of the United States guarantees religious liberty, [and] the treaty of Guadalupe Hidalgo asserted that none of [the Pueblo Indians'] religious ceremonies or religious life could be interfered with, . . . it seems impossible to think that the American people would stand by and see an injustice perpetrated." Atwood further called upon "all good people to sustain her in every effort toward bringing life and freedom to the wards of the Government." Atwood's position, and that of many other new Indian activists, revolved around what some historians might call "republicanism," calling for the extension of republican principles to the Indians.[22]

Other dance defenders argued against the circular on the grounds that it would destroy a valuable part of America's cultural treasure. The American Indian Defense Association characterized the circular as part of the government's efforts to destroy "an incalculable wealth of folklore, of beautiful customs and arts and moral values." Austin touted the Indian dances as the true American culture that Americans should appreciate rather than scorn. She compared Indian rituals to "dances such as Europe has not known since the great days of Homer." Erna Fergusson also supported the preservation of the dances because "of all these survivals of primitive ritual the Indian dance is probably the most interesting to be found anywhere in the world. . . . It is the genuine religious expression of a primitive people which has survived without serious interruption for thousands of years. . . . The Indian dance is a prayer, performed with the greatest reverence, and it is also a dramatic representation, as finished and as beautiful as a modern ballet." Like Austin, Fergusson believed that the Indians had a unique contribution to make to American society. Fergusson held that "if the heavy hand [of the government] could be lifted, imagine what a gorgeous contribution he might make to drama—this Indian with this gift for the grotesque, his sly sardonic humor, and his perception of human frailty which is witty without being bitter!"[23]

Many antimodern feminists also developed what might be called a "sexually relativist" position in defense of the dances. Elizabeth Shepley Sergeant railed against moral reformers' sexual mores when she wrote to Mabel Dodge Luhan, "Burke says he is going to suppress 'objectionable practices' of the [Hopi] Snake Dance and he likes the Indian girls to wear white dresses and do maypole dances. He told them 'white!' God save us." Mary Austin justified the dances on the grounds that they expressed a natural and healthy sexuality connected with Pueblo religion; she believed that only whites schooled in Victorian sexuality could find them "debauched." In *Land of Journey's Ending*, published in 1924, Austin directly attacked the moral reformers' views of the dances as sexually immoral:

> It is at Hopi that the association of fire with the idea of life-increase and the god of germination, takes most definitely the form which it naturally would take in a society where procreation is still associated with worship.

Not that it is the only ritual touched with the sense of the sacred function-
ing of the principle of male and female, but it is the one most recognizable
by our debauched sense of such things. That the objectionableness of phallic rites is chiefly in the mind of the observer, is proved by the fact that they
seldom appear objectionable unless we know that they are phallic, and we
never know except when they obviously violate our particular taboos.

When they lie, as many of the most enjoyed life-increasing ceremonies
do, outside our prepossessions, we are stirred and recreated by them.[24]

Rather than seeing Pueblo dances as sexually illicit, Austin questioned the Victorian standards she had grown up with and which she self-consciously worked
to shed throughout her adult life. In effect, Austin and other antimodern feminists accused moral reformers of wearing cultural blinders, of being so preju-
diced by their Christian upbringing that they could not appreciate a culture with
different sexual standards. In the ensuing dance controversy, these antimodern
feminists took female moral reformers to task for their sexual ethnocentrism.

The performance in the Pueblos' dances of ritual clowns, known as *koshare*,
chiffonettes, and *koyemshi*, and by other titles, elicited particular disagreement
between antimodern feminists and female moral reformers. Although Pueblo
dances were solemn occasions in which the participants prayed for rain, a fertile
and abundant crop, or a good hunt, the dances also involved intermittent inter-
ruptions by a group of clowns, supposedly spirits of the dead. As Fergusson explained it, "While the dancers, serious and intent, follow the rhythm of drum
and chant, the Koshare, each a free spirit in his own right, dash in and out, dar-
ing the dancers not to laugh, making wicked fun of the spectators, shouting im-
promptu lewdness. . . . Their fun is often coarse and vulgar, some observers
find it obscene."[25]

Female moral reformers did indeed find the clowns' antics obscene and immoral. Evelyn Bentley's description of the Hopi clowns' skit in which men
peeked up women's dresses epitomized the vulgarity of Indian dances to moral
reformers. Other testimony regarding the Indian dances made them seem even
more immoral to moral reformers. One of the witnesses who wrote to Superintendent Lonergan in 1915, L. R. McDonald, a BIA farmer at Jemez Pueblo,
claimed to have witnessed a dance on the plaza at Santo Domingo from a distance of 150 or 200 feet in which each clown "pulled his penis from under his
breech cloth," and "women marched by either kissing or taking a bite of the
clown's penis. The women, ranging in ages from 16 to 40 years, giggled and
laughed and some spit on the ground." A Mr. Mitchell, the Indian Service
farmer at Cochiti who attended this dance with McDonald, noted that the
women were "dressed in clownish attire." Mitchell also observed that this scene

elicited great laughter from the audience, who "would yell and clap their hands in delight." At a distance of 150 to 200 feet, McDonald and Mitchell were unable to distinguish that the "women" in the dances were actually male clowns dressed as women. Neither could they discern that the clowns' "penises" were probably gourds or other exaggerated imitation phalluses. Other witnesses accused the clowns of having sexual intercourse with animals, of acting as if they were copulating with animals, or of imitating animals having sex.[26]

The Secret Dance File also contained testimony regarding Hopi dances from Hopi converts to Christianity, who agreed that the practices of the clowns were obscene and immoral. Although the sentiments of the Hopi witnesses seem to be genuine, their written testimonies appear to be edited and embellished by their interviewers, much as white writers would do with as-told-to autobiographies by Indians. For example, Hopi witness Johnson Tuwaletstiwa, who testified that his life had been "unspeakably evil" before his conversion to Christianity, described to his interviewer a scene in a dance in which two male "katsinas," one dressed as a woman and one as a man, pretended to work in their fields in front of the clowns.

> The clowns pretended not to see them. These two katsinas at length pretended to grow tired of their work, and went over to a place representing their booth and rested. Then, while the whole crowd of spectators were looking on, men, women and children, the katsina man took hold of the katsina woman and went through the performance of the act of cohabitation. Upon its conclusion the clowns turned and appeared to discover them, and asked what they were doing, to which, feigning shame, they made no reply. Thereupon one of the clowns approached the katsina woman and solicited her to do the same act with him. This led to a quarrel between the katsina husband and wife, ending in the wife discarding her husband, who walked around the street feigning weeping and lamentation because he was thus divorced after the Hopi manner. . . . Thereupon one and each and all the clowns severally, five in all, went through the act of cohabitation with the katsina woman successively. . . . The whole scene was a dramatization of the act of Hopi life depicting adultery and prostitution; the crowd meanwhile laughing and apparently approving and enjoying it as a dramatic representation of Hopi life.[27]

As Tuwaletstiwa expressed here, through the filter of his white interviewers, moral reformers and witnesses who testified in the Secret Dance File understood the performances of the clowns to be actual representations of Pueblo life. The clown performances depicting frequent adultery, prostitution, and easy divorce, they insisted, both reflected and encouraged the very same practices in the daily lives of the Hopi.

To antimodern feminists, the Pueblo ritual clowns did not appear sexually immoral. Fergusson asserted that some of the clowns' sexual acts served as fertility rites; she wrote that their "prayers for rain often include appeals for all life, animal and human as well as plant." Antimodern feminists also believed that at times, rather than mirroring the common sexual behavior of the Pueblos, the clowns burlesqued inappropriate behavior. As Austin conceived of the issue,

> Between the intervals of the song-cycle [the clowns] enliven the dancers with buffoonery of a type often broader than our sort of society admits, but never so slimy.
>
> The social function of the Delight-makers is to keep the community in order, with whips of laughter. These humorous interludes often take the form of dramatic skits based upon the weakness or the misadventures of the villagers.

Fergusson also characterized the clowns as using "their privilege to correct the foibles of their people by salutary laughter."[28]

Fergusson, Austin, and other antimodern feminists interpreted the clowns' performances much as latter-day anthropologists would. According to Pueblo anthropologists Edward Dozier and Alfonso Ortiz, the clowns' skits serve in part to promote both agricultural and human fertility and to enforce community morals. Ortiz explains that the clowns' sexual lampoons, particularly those involving phallic jokes, are "intended for . . . cosmic regeneration and renewal." Dozier also asserts that the clown skits concern the "maintenance of flora and fauna"; "plant, animal, and human fertility is an objective of all ceremonies because fertility is so basic to Pueblo culture." Pueblo clowns also policed sexual and social behavior through making fun of inappropriate actions. As anthropologist Vera Laski put it, "[B]y discussing, publicly and jokingly, the most recent village gossip, especially that related to sex matters—ridiculing adultery and airing the gossip as to who sleeps with whom—they are the friendliest, gayest, and best liked moral squad any community ever had."[29] Far from reflecting Pueblo norms, many of the clowns' sexual skits served the opposite purpose.

In addition to advancing what became standard anthropological interpretations, however, antimodern feminists added another layer of meaning to the clowns' performances. They extolled Pueblo dances as reflections of a sexuality that was "more natural" than white American sexuality. As Fergusson put it, "To an Indian, human generation is no more obscene than is the fertilization and development of a plant." This view of Indian sexuality contrasted markedly with that of the BIA and moral reformers, as seen in the following exchange between Fergusson and a BIA employee. As she viewed an Indian dance, Fergusson "watched one beautiful young dancer, posed perfectly on the balls of his feet, his body slim and straight like an arrow, wild and fawn-like even under baggy . . . trousers." In dismay, Fergusson turned to an Indian Service man sitting near her. "Why, oh why, does he wear trousers?" Fergusson wailed. "His body is so beautiful." The Indian Service man told her sternly, "Young lady, . . . don't talk like that to me. I've spent the best years of my life trying to get these fellows into pants."[30] In lauding the "natural" sexuality the clowns supposedly expressed, antimodern feminists seemed to thumb their noses at the moral reformers' standards of acceptable sexuality.

Female moral reformers and antimodern feminists also were divided as to whether the dances served as occasions for unbridled sexual license. Reformers believed that the dances promoted premarital sex, adultery, and divorce. As Hopi witness Talasnimtiwa phrased it, "[A]ll the Hopi dances are a stimulus to the adulterous life." Hopi witness Kuwanwikvaya asserted that at Hopi dances, "young unmarried men and women . . . commit fornication, and the married ones commit adultery. These evils have their root in the dances, because they are the occasions of public gatherings, where flirtations among men and women are carried on, and end in these evil things."[31] Field matron Evelyn Bentley reported that an unfaithful Hopi husband, Otto, told her that "after the Hopi dance, the Cow-Kacheena, he was so 'worked up' over the things he saw at the dance that he 'did not know what to do.'" Both Otto's wife and his mistress allegedly told Bentley "that after a big dance many immoral acts took place." Reformers believed that such adulterous activity at dances resulted, lamentably, in more frequent divorces. One Hopi witness, Quoyawyma, testified that "divorces . . . often occur after these dances." Hopi witness Tuwaletstiwa recalled "six women . . . who have had five or six husbands, discarding one for another, and nearly always at these dances or growing out of these dances."[32]

Antimodern feminists responded to these charges in a variety of ways, as is evidenced in how they portrayed Taos Pueblo's annual August ceremony at Blue Lake in the mountains above the pueblo. Female moral reformers freely speculated that this ceremony, which no white person had ever witnessed, was merely a sexual orgy. Some of the white women who supported Pueblo dances agreed. Blanche Grant, a member of the Taos art colony, declared that the Blue Lake ceremony "is the one dance to which the so-called reformers have a right to object, in the name of fair play for the Indian woman." Adopting the familiar image of Indian women as the victims of male lust, Grant claimed that "girls and childless women are forced to go to the mountain. So thoroughly is this against the wish of the Indian women, though long used to the custom, that daughters of the pueblo, now and then, prefer exile to returning from the government schools and having to submit to this ceremony imposed upon them by the older men." Unlike the moral reformers, however, Grant refused to condone white interference with the dances. She wrote, "[I]t is only as it comes from within the tribe itself that any real change can be effected. The white man should keep his hands off and cease his prattle."[33]

Disagreeing with Grant, other antimodern feminists claimed that the alleged debauchery at Blue Lake was just a white fantasy. Austin tried to explain why the moral reformers would have developed such a fiction. She asserted that "the myth of the orgiastic ceremonial . . . has its source . . . in the inhibitions and repressions forced upon our pagan ancestry, particularly the inhibition of our inate [*sic*] wish to preserve for the sex impulse its pagan sanctity, its mystical connotations, of which Christianity has so utterly bereft it." Mabel Dodge Luhan shared Austin's view, arguing that "just because their religion is alive and because in their daily life they are not inhibited, they do not revert to orgiastic overcompensations, and in their ceremonials never, I believe, approach each other libidinously."[34] While claiming that Pueblo Indians expressed sexuality symbolically through their dances, Austin and Luhan challenged the notion that this sexual symbolism led to promiscuity. This stance reveals an acceptance of some of the moral reformers' terms of debate. Notably, Luhan and Austin did not argue that promiscuity was acceptable; instead they simply denied that the Indians practiced it.

At least one antimodern feminist—Elsie Clews Parsons—accepted the claim of moral reformers that the dances were, indeed, occasions for unrestrained sexual license, but she refused to judge this as indecent or degenerate. Parsons accepted the possibility that the Taos Blue Lake ceremony involved promiscuity; she quoted her informant as telling her it was "the time the girls get with their fellows." Although Parsons qualified this statement by declaring her uncertainty as to whether or not this involved complete sexual intimacy, she appeared comfortable with the idea that the Blue Lake ceremony might have involved some kind of "general promiscuity." In one of her essays Parsons matter-of-factly discussed a supposed Laguna custom that the night before the winter solstice celebration, "men were free 'to plant seeds' in any woman they met." In a footnote Parsons explained that her source was a Zuni informant, and "the practice was described to a company of Zuñi, and the description amused them just about as it would have amused a company of sophisticated whites."[35] Parsons may have accepted as fact what was meant to be a joke by the Zuni about Laguna Pueblo; yet she communicated that the Indians themselves were not disturbed by the supposed sexual promiscuity at the dances and that she, counting herself among a "company of sophisticated whites," was also unperturbed by such a possibility. Unlike Luhan and Austin, Parsons did not try to deny the charges of sexual promiscuity leveled at the Pueblos.

Parsons's and the Pueblos' seemingly nonchalant attitude toward openly discussing sexuality deeply disturbed female moral reformers, who expressed alarm that "sex subjects and sex functions are the subjects of common conversation between [Hopi] men and women, boys and girls, in the home, anywhere, without restraint." Again, moral reformers and their witnesses blamed the dances for cultivating this atmosphere. Hopi witness Talasnimtiwa testified that during the preparatory days before the men's rite, the men "carve out of watermelon or pumpkin rinds images representing the woman's sexual organs, and present them to women openly, accompanied by conversation of the vilest and most obscene character." Similarly, prior to the women's rite, "it is common for women to make, out of clay or other material, images in the likeness of men's sexual organs and present them to the men, accompanied with like obscene conversation."[36]

As this passage also reveals, moral reformers and their Hopi converts lamented that Indian women appeared to be active sexual beings. McDonald seemed surprised that the "women" depicted by male clowns at Santo Domingo enjoyed their part in the dance. "A man would chase a woman like a rooster chases a hen. The woman would not struggle to escape the man, but entered into the spirit of the game with as much zeal as the man." Tuwaletstiwa also expressed his disgust at the Hopi dance in which two kachinas went through the motions of sexual intercourse. He remarked that "the conclusion of the scene was that the man got up and went leaping and singing happily and thus disappeared, while the woman katsina, more quietly but with expressions indicating happiness, also disappeared."[37]

Antimodern feminists, by contrast, emphasized the Indian women themselves, who participated in other facets of some dances, rather than the male clowns' representations of women. They portrayed Indian women dancers as strong figures who played prominent roles in Pueblo culture. Fergusson described the Deer-dance at Taos:

Two women lead, dignified figures wrapped in white buckskin robes. . . . In one hand each woman carries pine twigs, in the other a gourd. At certain points in the dance each woman moves slowly down the line of waiting men, making sharp peremptory motions with the gourd. As she does this, each man drops to his knees. Returning, she makes a reverse gesture and the men rise. This perhaps typifies the call of the universal spirit of fertility, the usual significance of a woman figure in the Indian dances. They are treated with reverence, and during this figure the nonsense and the thieving of the Chiffonete are stopped.

Describing the same kind of dance, Luhan noted that the "power of the tribe was invested in the two women who gently danced before the helpless creatures, leading them to their doom. . . . The feminine principle is the strongest one in nature—and the wild animal must follow where it leads, must be sacrificed, assimilated, and converted into a new energy."[38] In their portrayals of Pueblo dances, antimodern feminists depicted Pueblo women as powerful figures who controlled not only themselves but also the men who appeared in the dances.

Thus the controversy over Pueblo dances involved conflicting depictions of Pueblo sexual practices and of Pueblo women. Given the cultural climate of the 1910s and 1920s, it is no coincidence that the furor over alleged sexual immorality in Indian dances erupted when it did. Although moral reformers such as Dissette and True had worked with the Pueblos since 1888 and 1902 respectively, neither seemed to express any concern about Pueblo sexual morality until after 1915. As sexual mores and gender expectations became hotly contested in the 1910s and 1920s, moral reformers suddenly discovered rampant sexual immorality among the Indians and attempted to curtail the very same indiscretions and immoralities that they condemned in white society. All the charges they brought against Pueblo Indians in the Secret Dance File and in many articles—the supposedly greater frequency of premarital sex, adultery, and divorce; a freer discussion of sexuality; and women's more outspoken interest in sex, all supposedly brought on by pornographic dances—disturbed moral reformers as dangerous trends in white society as well. As Paula Fass has illustrated, "traditionalists" in the 1920s lamented that white, middle-class American youth had supposedly become hedonistic, rejecting all sexual standards and engaging in unrestrained sexual license. Additionally, the "traditionalists" complained that young American men and women talked and joked openly about sex. Many moral reformers were also alarmed by the growing frequency of divorce: between 1867 and 1929 the divorce rate among Americans had risen 2,000 percent, and by the end of the 1920s one in six marriages ended in divorce.[39]

Before 1920, moral reformers had depicted Indian women as the innocent victims of Indian male lust and BIA corruption. In the 1920s, however, these reformers supplemented the earlier view with a new notion of Indian women as active sexual beings. These conflicted depictions of Indian women mirrored the new conceptions of womanhood put forward by moralists in the 1920s in which, as one historian explains, "the proverbial dark lady and fair maiden were fusing into the same woman."[40] Whereas Victorian female moral reformers blamed male lust for fallen women, moral reformers of the 1920s raised the specter of "the girl vamp" who corrupted young men.[41] Moral reformers worried about young white women's new definition of equality as the "right to self-expression, self-determination, and personal satisfaction." Young women's newfound expectation for sexual satisfaction, railed one critic, was likely to lead to "a pagan attitude toward love itself."[42]

Indeed, many moral reformers believed that the new dances championed by working-class youth and adopted by the middle class facilitated these changes in sexual mores. In the 1920s dancing proved to be the most popular pastime for both high school and college students. Irene Castle, one of the leaders in popularizing and sanitizing jazz dance forms, noted that "America had gone absolutely dance-mad," and "the whole nation seemed to be divided into equal forces, those who were for it and those who were against it."[43] Some moral reformers sought to police and to provide wholesome alternatives to youthful dances; the *Ladies' Home Journal* urged the legal prohibition of jazz dancing.[44] Some commentators even drew connections between Indian dances and the new jazz dances. As one critic put it, "One touch of jazz makes savages of us all."[45] Some of the moral reformers who opposed Indian dances also actively worked against other "moral evils" in the larger American culture. William "Pussyfoot" Johnson, who penned a vitriolic article against Indian dances, also campaigned for the worldwide prohibition of alcohol. Bishop Hare, an Episcopal minister who worked with the Sioux and who had mentored Clara True, successfully attacked South Dakota's liberal divorce laws, calling options to divorce and remarry "consecutive polygamy." Edith Dabb, who wrote several editorials against Indian dances, was active in other moral reform activities through the Young Women's Christian Association.[46]

Moral reformers and their Pueblo informers often used terminology current in debates on white sexual mores. Mary Dissette claimed, "[T]he Shalako dance at Zuni is followed by a week of other dances which are the occasion of a free for all sex orgy." Hopi witness Quoyawyma claimed about the Snake Dance: "[M]en and boys and women and girls mingle freely together—there is 'free love.'" Mary Dissette disparagingly termed Pueblo divorce at Zuni as "trial marriage."[47] Dissette's use of the phrases "free for all sex orgy" and "trial marriage," as well as Quoyawyma's usage—perhaps coached or edited by Inspector Sweet—of the term "free love," reveals to what extent those who opposed Indian dances projected their concerns about white sexual mores onto Pueblo Indians. The term "free love" gained wide exposure and censure in popular magazines in the 1910s and 1920s. Sexologist Havelock Ellis, Judge Ben Lindsey, and Elsie Clews Parsons all had advocated the notion of "trial marriage," a "legal marriage with birth control and with the right to divorce by mutual consent for a childless couple." Furthermore, moral reformers' and witnesses' depictions of Pueblo dances as occasions for a "free for all sex orgy" closely mirrored their concerns about new jazz dances in white American society.[48]

In the minds of female moral reformers Indian women became in essence "new women." Pueblo Indians and their dances provided a convenient object on which to displace moral reformers' anxieties about changes occurring in white culture. As Elaine Tyler May has shown, reformers' efforts to stem the tide of divorce in white society—over one hundred pieces of state legislation to restrict divorce between 1889 and 1906—had little effect. Though divorce did become more difficult to obtain in many states, couples continued to sever their marriages with greater frequency. Additionally, though physicians and reformers had succeeded in criminalizing abortion and in outlawing the dissemination of birth-control information through the mails, the fertility rate among middle-class Americans continued to plummet.[49] Reformers' efforts to enforce Victorian moral codes seemed to have little effect on preventing what they believed to be rampant social disorder. While ostensibly condemning the supposedly free and easy sexual customs among Pueblo Indians, moral reformers actually seem to have given voice to their anxieties over the social disorder they believed would result from changes in white sexual mores. Reformers' fears that free love and trial marriage were replacing their cherished notions of chastity and purity within their own culture led them to superimpose this view of unfettered sexuality upon the Indians. If this disorder and sexual immorality could be distanced from white culture and located within a "primitive" culture, perhaps it could be properly contained. If they could not control their own society, perhaps they could control a smaller culture within it.

Further evidence that moral reformers projected their concerns about white sexual mores onto the Indians emerges from the way in which witnesses and moral reformers embellished the contents of the Secret Dance File. Even though asked to report only what they had witnessed directly, many observers added innuendo and rumors to the record. Witness Blas Casaus, a mail carrier, accused the Indians at Jemez of forbidding him passage on the public road, "so that we might not see them dancing naked and going through the motions of fornication." Not really a witness to what went on beyond the barrier in the road, Casaus imagined that the Indians must be naked and dancing in a lascivious manner. Spying only for a moment on a Pueblo dance, government farmer McDonald asserted that "the Indians kept up the performance for hours" and speculated that "very likely the performance grew worse as the hours went by. For naturally such a performance could lead only up to a carnival of promiscuous carnal indulgence."[50] Although asked only to give an account of what he

Maria and Julian Martinez with second son, John, at San Ildefonso Pueblo, 1926. Courtesy Museum of New Mexico, neg. no. 26335.

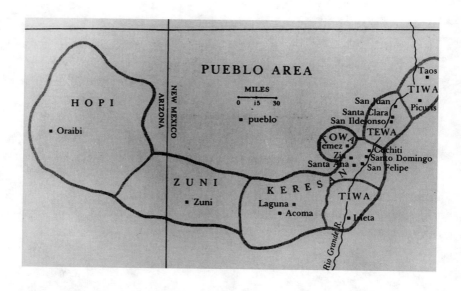

Map of the Pueblos' area. From John
Bierhorst, *The Mythology of North America*
(New York: William Morrow, 1985).

Mary Dissette. From *Home Mission
Monthly,* February 1895, courtesy
Menaul Historical Library.

(*Left*) Clara True. From Harry
Lawton, *Willie Boy: A Desert Manhunt* (Balboa Island CA: Paisano,
1960); used with permission.

(*Right*) Helen Sekaquaptewa. Photo
by Robert R. Lewis; reprinted with
permission.

(*Opposite above*) Polingaysi
Qoyawayma working with children
in her classroom at New Oraibi.
From Qoyawayma, *No Turning Back:
A Hopi Indian Woman's Struggle to
Live in Two Worlds*, as told to Vada
Carlson (Albuquerque: University of
New Mexico Press, 1962).

(*Opposite bottom*) Elsie Clews Parsons. Neg. 718; courtesy American
Philosophical Society.

Mary Austin and unidentified Pueblo
man, ca. 1923. Courtesy The
Huntington Library, San Marino,
California, album 296, fold. 03(56).

Mabel Dodge Luhan and Tony
Luhan in Taos, 1924. Courtesy The
Huntington Library, San Marino,
California, album 296, fold. 04(26).

(*Opposite above*) Tourists watching
Eagle Dance, Santa Clara Pueblo,
ca. 1930. Courtesy Museum of New
Mexico, neg. no. 46939.

(*Opposite bottom*) Tonita Peña,
Harvest Dance, undated. Courtesy
of Avanyu Publishing, Inc.

(*Above*) Indian Detour car and
tourists with Pueblo artists, Santa
Clara Pueblo, ca. 1930. Photo by
T. Harmon Parkhurst, courtesy
Museum of New Mexico, neg. no.
46936.

Tonita Peña (Quah Ah). Photo by
T. Harmon Parkhurst, courtesy
Museum of New Mexico, neg. no.
73945.

Pablita Velarde. Courtesy Museum
of New Mexico, neg. no. 16926.

himself had seen at Santo Domingo, McDonald also wrote to Lonergan that he was informed by Mr. Mitchell of Cochiti "that at one of their dances the men have the privilege of sucking any woman's teats, which they do in the most promiscuous fashion in the plaza and the streets of the pueblo." In his own letter Mitchell never mentioned having seen such an exhibition at Cochiti. Field matron Evelyn Bentley asserted that she had heard from another teacher that she had seen "a clown urinate down another clown's throat."[51]

Among female moral reformers, rumors also abounded regarding the contents of the Secret Dance File. For example, in a letter to "Miss Willard," Mary Dissette wrote that a Mrs. Robinson told Dissette that she overheard a quarrel between Mary Austin and a Mrs. Friedman regarding the dances. Evidently, Lonergan had described allegations in the Secret Dance File to Friedman's husband, who had then told Friedman, who had then confronted Austin. Robinson overheard the quarrel, then told Mary Dissette, who was now communicating this to Miss Willard. In the same letter, Dissette related that she was "told that Superintendent [Lonergan] concealed himself and a companion or two [during a ceremony at Santo Domingo] in the bushes near the river . . . and saw one or more old women instructing young girls in sex matters one of which was 'manipulating the penis.'"[52] No such report is actually in the Secret Dance File. This chain of gossip, however, reveals the way in which moral reformers projected their concerns about white, middle-class sexual mores onto Pueblo Indians. Further, it attests to an almost consuming passion on the part of moral reformers to imagine the Indians engaged in all sorts of sexual acts.

Ironically, the Secret Dance File, designed to document and condemn the alleged immorality of Pueblo dances, actually seemed to function as a form of sanctioned pornography for the reformers. Open discussions of sexuality were theoretically off-limits to female moral reformers as well as their male peers, but the Secret Dance File and rumors about it seemed to serve as a source of titillation for some reformers. As Elazar Barkan has remarked, "[W]hen it came to primitives, Victorians allowed themselves to transgress their own accepted morality." Susan Yohn's observations regarding Presbyterian missionaries in the Southwest who were simultaneously appalled and titillated by the Penitentes, a religious order of Hispanos who practiced rituals of self-flagellation, are also instructive. Filling the *Home Mission Monthly* with accounts of Penitente ceremonies, which were closed to outsiders, the missionaries' "act of telling the story became a ritual in and of itself."[53] The same could be said for the compilation, circulation, and reading of the Secret Dance File.

Like moral reformers, antimodern feminists used the Pueblos to articulate their views on changing sexual mores in white society. They sometimes even invented a reflection of themselves within Pueblo cultures, as, for example, when Parsons concluded that a Zuni woman who dressed and acted as a man was "a 'strong-minded woman,' a Zuñi 'new woman,' a large part of her male."[54] Much like the moral reformers, in fact, antimodern feminists envisioned Pueblo women as "new women." In their eyes, however, this merited admiration, not contempt. Yet antimodern feminists also harbored doubts about emerging sexual mores. When they set out to defend the Pueblos' dances on sexually relativist grounds, they came up against their own ambivalence about white sexual standards. At times, they argued that Pueblo Indians held more natural and healthy sexual standards than white, middle-class Americans. At other times, these feminists seemed to accept the terms of moral reformers and denied that the Pueblos were sexually immoral. This confusion over how best to meet the charges of moral reformers reveals itself in the policy statement shared by a number of the new organizations that emerged in the 1920s: "Indians should have religious and social freedom in all matters not directly contrary to public morals and any effort to break down the independence of Indian groups by interfering with their religion or dances, or customs, should be frowned upon. Questions of actual morality should be decided on the same basis as in white derelictions. It should not be assumed without proof that a ceremony is immoral or unsanitary without expert evidence to this effect." This policy statement left uninterpreted what matters would be "directly contrary to public morals" and who would determine "questions of actual morality."[55]

The dance controversy climaxed in 1924 at the biennial convention of the GFWC, where moral reformers provoked a showdown with dance defenders. The support of the GFWC seemed crucial to both moral reformers and antimodern feminists, not only because the GFWC was a large and powerful organization, but also because acceptance of either side's view of Native Americans meant tacit approval of that side's conception of white American womanhood and sexuality. In essence, the 1924 GFWC meeting was an important forum for debating and affirming appropriate sexual mores. While Stella Atwood, the head of the Indian Welfare Committee of the GFWC, sided and worked closely with John Collier in his call for the preservation of Indian cultures, Clara True sought to foment a mutiny against Atwood's position.

Hired by the IRA to raise funds in June 1924, True instead labored to organize a delegation of "progressive" Indians and moral reformers to attend the convention of the GFWC in Los Angeles "to speak for themselves if they could get a hearing" and to go to the "Christian women of the convention with a protest against the program of paganism . . . approved by Atwood." The BIA inspector and prominent Hispana civic leader Adelina "Nina" Otero-Warren accompanied

True. Even before she arrived in Los Angeles, True attempted to influence the women attending the convention. She intercepted thirty-seven carloads of women delegates en route to the convention and staged for them "a brilliant Indian dance," performed by "progressive" Indians. Since "the dancers were merely entertaining the visitors and were not observing any religious ceremony," True did not object to them. By staging a dance in which the clowns did not perform any of their sexual antics, True suggested that nothing would be lost if the dances were kept within the moral boundaries she upheld.

When True arrived in Los Angeles, she sized up the crowd of eight thousand women and decided it to be "nearly solidly hostile." "[W]e had to convert them," she realized. After much behind-the-scenes organizing, True succeeded in getting ten minutes on the program to make her case. During the allotted ten minutes, first Nina Otero-Warren made an appeal to the "Christian women of America." Then Ida May Adams, a member of the Indian Welfare League of California, spoke on behalf of the "progressive" Indians. Adams asked the "progressive" Indians to stand, and they "received vigorous applause." Then, according to True, "everybody knew there was a big fight on right then and there. It was no longer a one-sided game with Collier and the pagan issue getting all the support. There was a FIGHT on."[56]

In the meantime, hearing of True's planned attack, Atwood and her supporters had organized their own campaign to convince the women delegates of the need to preserve Indian dances. Charles Lummis, a renowned Southwestern writer and magazine editor, penned a pamphlet for the AIDA to be distributed at the door of the convention. In it he appealed to the GFWC women in the language of moral reformers. Since it "is Woman who has kept Religion and Home alive and fundamental," the pamphlet declared, she "realizes that without the Home, humanity would fall to pieces; and that without Reverence and Faith . . . Home itself must fall." Playing off the anxieties about the breakdown of the home and family that members of a mainstream women's organization in the 1920s were likely to have, Lummis argued that the GFWC must support Indian religion because "for milleniums [*sic*]" it "has made good husbands and good wives, good fathers and good mothers, obedient and filial children, good neighbors, and good citizens of that tiny Republic. The result of destroying that Faith would be to destroy that home life which no longer has general parallels among ourselves." Lummis further asserted that Pueblo dances were key elements of Pueblo religion, and that "no Pueblo dance was ever so provocative, so suggestive or so demoralizing as many—I fear I should say the majority—of the dances which our boys and girls witness and take part in."[57]

Lummis, Collier, and Atwood probably rightly calculated that in this setting, the sexually relativist argument of antimodern feminists would not do. Here, it was necessary to appeal to the GFWC women on the grounds that since home and religion were rapidly disappearing in white culture, where they still existed in Indian culture, they must be preserved. Yet Lummis, Collier, and Atwood were also more conservative when it came to sexual matters than antimodern feminists. Even though he was known for his promiscuous behavior, Lummis seems to have had very conservative views regarding women's roles and sexuality.[58] In Lummis's pamphlet the Pueblos became emblems of a premodern life where home and religion still mattered, rather than harbingers of a modern sexuality and a new gender order.

At the GFWC meeting and at other venues, both sides of the dance controversy brought their hand-selected group of Indians to confirm their views. In effect, opponents and defenders of Pueblo dances vied with one another to determine who might speak for the Indians. The moral reformers portrayed their group of Indians—the so-called progressives—as the victims both of a tradition-bound, virtual dictatorship of Pueblo officials and of romantic white propagandists who wanted to preserve the Indian in his "backward" state for the benefit of science and art.[59] By contrast, the new activists characterized the Pueblo Indians as inheritors of an ancient and beautiful religious tradition who were being victimized by overzealous moral reformers and a misguided Indian Bureau.[60] By posing these two virtually opposite portraits of the Pueblo Indian and by serving as patrons for one or the other, both sets of white activists set the terms of debate in which Pueblo Indians could argue for or against their dances. Despite their differences, both the whites who opposed and those who defended Pueblo dances conceived of the Indian as a homogeneous entity and a passive victim. Both constructions rendered Indians silent and tended to obscure the meanings that Pueblo Indians attached to the dances and to the controversy. Yet this is not the end of the story.

Pueblo Indian men did not accept their role as ventriloquists' dummies but sought instead to redefine the terms of debate. Both those Indians who opposed and those who defended Indian dances sought to make their voices audible above the din of white debaters. During an All-Pueblo Council in 1926, Pablo Abeita expressed frustration that whites left Indians out of debates about Indian matters. "They say: 'The Indians want this and the Indians want that,'" he observed of the recent hearings in Washington. "No Indian knows about it. They simply go ahead telling what they think the Indian wants. They ought to call the Indians there and ask what they want. It is not necessary to give him all he wants but it is necessary to listen to him. . . . [W]e ought to have a voice."[61] Indian men attempted to find a means to make their voices heard, but given the determination of white activists to control the image of the Indian, this proved difficult. When John Collier recommended that an upcoming Indian delegation to the East Coast should include mostly Pueblo singers, dancers, and drummers, Desiderio Naranjo of Santa Clara Pueblo interrupted to say, "It is all right to have two or three dancers and one drummer, and the rest of them ought to be good, intelligent men who will present the Indian question and the Indian trouble. . . . some good men that can talk."[62] While Collier wished to convey his image of the Indian through the performance of Indian ceremonials, many Indians, such as Naranjo and Abeita, wished to have a voice unfiltered through Collier or some other self-proclaimed "friend of the Indian."

When Pueblo men did make their opinions known to white audiences, it was a laborious process. At the end of a nine-page, single-spaced, typewritten letter, Joseph Tafoya, president of the Santa Clara Progressive Indians, admitted the difficulty the Pueblos had in articulating their views: "This letter had been a hard job. It takes about three languages to get out what my party and I think, into anything like a shape you will understand. We have to hammer along until we get something like we want, which we think clearly enough but can't say with force, then I sit up nights writing it all out in a rough pencil draft, then I take this home to the pueblo and we go over it, then I get a typist to put my letters into shape to read in Washington with some possibility of understanding."[63] Despite the challenge of articulating their positions, and the greater obstacle of getting their voices heard, Pueblo men did become engaged in the dance controversy on both sides of the debate.

Opposition to the dances originated from different sources among the Hopis of Arizona and the Pueblos of New Mexico. Within New Mexico, opposition to the dances developed mainly among some Pueblo men who had spent long years in boarding schools away from their pueblos. Whites called these Indians "progressives," and many Indians adopted this label for themselves. Among the Hopi, opposition to the dances derived from two diverse groups—older men of the tribe who considered themselves "traditional" and some younger Hopis who attended boarding school and converted to Christianity. Employees of the BIA and reformers labeled these Indians as "Friendlies," and again many Hopis came to identify themselves in this manner as well. Whites considered that "progressives" and "Friendlies" accepted the assimilation agenda: cutting their hair, wearing American-style dress, supporting white education, becoming Protestants, and renouncing all of their culture. Conversely, they imagined that the "conservatives," "traditionals," or "Hostiles" clung tenaciously to their old "pagan" ways and resisted all interaction with whites.

Unfortunately, the labels of "progressive" and "Friendly" and their counterparts—"traditional/conservative" and "Hostile"—have become accepted means of delineating differences within Indian communities. The dance controversy, in fact, contributed to rigidifying the lines between "progressives/Friendlies" and "conservatives/Hostiles." Female moral reformers like Clara True focused on promoting "progressive" Indians and dismissed other Indians as a "few old medicine men."[64] Viewing the traditional Pueblos as children of nature not yet encumbered with the neuroses of civilization, many antimodern feminists championed the so-called conservative Indians and marginalized "progressive" Indians as a few malcontents corrupted by BIA boarding schools.

These labels actually obscure the diversity of opinions and strategies Pueblo Indians developed for coping with new white influences. For example, at Taos Pueblo, many young men who attended boarding school embraced the new pan-Indian religion that used peyote as a sacrament. When they returned to the pueblo, they wore American dress and sometimes opposed the pueblos' dances. Taos Pueblo officials labeled these men as renegades and punished them severely, but white reformers certainly did not consider them "progressives."[65] At Santa Clara Pueblo, during a forty-year factional dispute between the "more progressively oriented" Winter Moiety and the more "conservative" Summer Moiety, both sides "professed 'to keep the custom' and each accused the other of noncooperation." The dissident Winter Moiety "did not abandon completely the basic cultural values of the pueblo, nor did it give up entirely the practice of native religion."[66] As Karen Anderson has pointed out, most Indian men and women have "felt compelled to appeal to the idea of tradition in support of contemporary goals" in an "attempt to construct a usable past." Thus, there is no easy way to categorize the variety of Indian perspectives.[67] Nevertheless, faced with the two stark visions of progressive and conservative, Pueblo Indians in the dance controversy manipulated these images for their own purposes—to secure land and water and to assert and enforce their respective visions of how Indians should best adapt to twentieth-century America.

Pueblo Indians who opposed the dances may have appeared on the surface to agree with the moral reformers that their dances were illicit occasions for "carnal indulgence" and that their cultures encouraged promiscuity, easy divorce, adultery, and an active sexual role for women. A closer look, however, reveals that the Indians opposed the dances for their own reasons; in fact, some of them actively countered the view of Pueblo society as sexually unrestrained. The Hopis who testified in the Secret Dance File often mentioned that they believed the dances were immoral and evil. They did not necessarily testify, however, for the reasons moral reformers hoped and expected: that they had become converts to Christianity and so had renounced their cultures. Instead, many of the Hopi witnesses explained their decision to testify as a wish to fulfill an ancient Hopi prophecy. For example, several years before the compilation of the Secret Dance File, the Hopi Indian Masawistiwa had written a letter to the commissioner of Indian affairs in which he complained about the immorality of the dances. Masawistiwa explained:

[T]he idea of reporting these matters to the Commissioner did not originate with me. Since the creation of the world, according to the traditions held by the Hopis, a revelation of these things was so ordained. The tradition tells us that when the Man-from-the-Sun-Rising brings the truth to us. . . , then he who dares to reveal these things or speak about them will find himself singled-handed against the multitude. . . .

I also remembered that Chief Loloma . . . came to our peach-drying house one night in peach-drying time, and, in talking with my father and myself, he said that the time was fast approaching when the traditions of the fathers must be fulfilled. He said also that when that time came, it would be like the completion of a circle, the circle of Hopi traditions and history, and that from that time a new history for the Hopis would begin.

So when we had been expelled from Oraibi Upper Village, I felt that we were standing alone against a multitude. According to the Hopi traditions, therefore, it seemed that the time had come for me to speak against the wrong things that I knew existed in Hopi ceremonies and Hopi life. I felt that the time had come for those things to end. That is why I wrote the letter to the Commissioner of Indian Affairs.[68]

Masawistiwa maintained that he reported on Hopi "immoralities" as retribution for his clan's expulsion from the Oraibi village and because he adhered to Hopi beliefs regarding the appearance of a "Man-from-the-Sun-Rising" who would bring the "truth." Interestingly, it was the "Hostiles," those Hopi who most opposed adaptation to white culture, who were expelled from Oraibi. The testimony of Masawistiwa, a Hostile, thus shows the fallacy of pigeonholing Indians into "progressive" and "conservative" positions. Other Hopis also accepted some white beliefs, because they interpreted the presence of whites who came from the East as the fulfillment of their prophecy. Rather than condemning Hopi customs because they had assimilated to white society, the Hopi informers testified because they adhered to their interpretation of traditional Hopi beliefs.[69]

The Pueblos in New Mexico who opposed the dances emerged from a group of boarding-school-educated Indians who had spent years away from their pueblos. For example, Joe Lujan of Taos Pueblo had been educated at a boarding school, fought in the Spanish-American War, married (and later divorced) a white woman, and lived for a number of years away from Taos. When he returned to Taos Pueblo, he resisted participation in the dances.[70] Refusal to dance and to conform to other Pueblo norms had painful consequences; Pueblo officials often fined or whipped individuals who wore American clothes, who cut their hair, or who failed to take part in dances or in communal agricultural work. During the dances, nonparticipants might find themselves doused in a cold river.[71] According to Joe Lujan, Taos Pueblo's governor and his officers tried to revoke Lujan's allotment of land and drive him away from the pueblo. Likewise, Edward Hunt of Acoma and Juan Melchor of Cochiti complained of similar treatment.[72] Alcario and Margarita Tafoya refused to participate in Santa Clara Pueblo ceremonies. According to them, the officials retaliated by building a fence through the middle of the site of their new home. Later, Tafoya and his wife alleged, when they tried to build on a different lot, the officials destroyed the foundation of the house and started to build an extension of their kiva on that site.[73]

When questioned by the IRA or the BIA, this group of Pueblos articulated different reasons for opposing the dances than the Hopis. They did not disapprove of the dances as sexually immoral. Instead, they had more "practical" reasons for opposing the dances, believing that they interfered with work and impeded the progress of the tribe. According to Antonio Montoya of Cochiti Pueblo,

> I myself think that the Indians are not doing the right, especially in the summer, some of these Indians they will be lock up in [the kivas] for four days, in one of the houses [for their societies' secret dance ceremonies]. . . . Each society takes his turn to be lock up for four days. . . .
>
> This is the thing that some of us men don't like, especially the men that don't dance don't like it, because there might be a ditch work to be done and only few of the men will be present the ones that don't take part in the secret dances or any kind dance, and the rest will have an easy time getting ready for a dance. . . .
>
> I wish this things be stopped so we will get to work all like brothers and not quarrel all the time.[74]

Montoya did not object to the dances on the grounds that they were sexually immoral but only because he thought they allowed some men to avoid communal agricultural work.

Other Rio Grande Pueblo Indians concurred with Montoya's assessment. Joe Lujan told the moral reformers who interviewed him that "the only thing is that [the dances] interfere with the progress of the children. I don't know of any immorality connected with them." Returned student Rosendo Vargas, who had been beaten for his refusal to take part in the dances at Picuris Pueblo, also did not object to their content: "As far as Indian dances are concern [*sic*], I do not have any thing against it, but I do not believe that the old Indians should make any school boy dress Indian and force him to dance. When the boy comes to school he is working towards education and preparing himself to make a better living after he leaves school, but if he should go back home and dress up in Indian dress, he would soon forget what he has learned in school and will be just like his father who has never been to school."[75] Like Montoya and Lujan, Vargas's complaint lay not with the supposedly illicit sexual content of the dances but with his sense of having grown beyond those traditions and his belief that the dances interfered with progress for his people.

Many other Pueblo Indians, by contrast, defended the dances. In 1924 the All-Pueblo Council protested Commissioner Burke's order against Indian dances by adopting a statement that read:

> We make as our first declaration the statement that our religion to us is sacred and is more important to us than anything else in our life. The religious beliefs and ceremonies and forms of prayer of each of our Pueblos are as old as the world, and they are holy.
>
> We denounce as untrue, shamefully untrue and without any basis of fact or appearance, and contrary to the abundant testimony of white scholars who have recorded our religious customs, this statement [that Pueblo dances are immoral], and we point out that the Commissioner's order . . . is an instrument of religious persecution. . . .
>
> We are but a few people, in the Pueblos. We have inherited and kept pure from many ages ago a religion which, we are told, is full of beauty even to white persons. To ourselves at least, our religion is more precious than even our lives.[76]

This statement, prepared in advance of the All-Pueblo Council meeting by John Collier, does not provide a direct window into Pueblo Indians' perspectives but rather is refracted through the lens of the new activists. While championing cultural pluralism, new white activists had developed a view of Pueblo Indians as the antithesis of modern Americans, including a belief that Pueblo Indians lived for and by their religion above all else. Many Pueblo Indians were willing to use the new activists' exaggerated, highly romanticized views to further their own cause.

To these Indians, the defense of their dances represented an immensely important cause. They worked to protect the dances for several reasons—because they perceived them as an essential part of their religion and economy, because the dances represented a powerful symbol of their vision of "Indianness," and because they provided a means by which Pueblos could mock whites, temporarily overturning power relationships and distancing themselves from white culture. From a religious standpoint, the dances were essential to the perpetuation of both Pueblo spiritual practices and related economic enterprises. Although the BIA, moral reformers, and some Indians characterized the dances as a diversion from farming, many Pueblos, particularly at Hopi and Zuni, believed that the ceremonies served such an integral role in their agricultural work that a failure to perform them would lead to crop failures and drought. As Dozier put it, many Pueblos believed that "rites and ceremonies properly performed keep the seasons moving, allow the sun to rise and set properly, bring rain and snow, quell the winds, and insure a well-ordered physical environment and society."[77]

The dances also became a powerful symbol of the maintenance of Pueblo Indian identity. By many accounts the dances had already lost some participants, due to economic dislocation, epidemics, and assimilation pressures. When crops failed at San Ildefonso, many Pueblo men had to move outside the village to find work. As a result, the dances suffered. To compound the problem, men who ventured away from the pueblo sometimes took to drinking. When they returned to the pueblo, if they continued to drink, they were not allowed to dance. Failures in farming, no matter how much they might be related to external pressures beyond the control of the Pueblos, might have led many Pueblos to doubt their religion. Since many of the ceremonies of the Eastern Pueblos centered on curing, it seems likely that the influenza, diphtheria, and smallpox epidemics that took so many lives in the pueblos at the turn of the century may have led many Indians to further question the efficacy of their ceremonies.[78] Pressures to assimilate only exacerbated these problems. Taught in boarding schools and day schools to view their cultures as backward and evil, many young Indians refused to participate in the dances.

Erna Fergusson observed that some Zuni dances used to feature four people who went among the young people to invite them to take part in the dance. "Now we see only one discouraged man who makes half-hearted efforts to interest these Indian school-children, all of whom refuse him. Finally he gives up with a hopeless gesture and sits down."[79] In this time of rapid change for the Pueblos, continuing to dance meant a commitment to one's Pueblo identity. Those who defended the dances may have freely (or reluctantly) adopted change in other arenas of life, but they still wanted to preserve a sense of their unique cultural identity.[80] Because to this group of Indians, failure to participate in dances signified a rejection of Pueblo identity, many Pueblo officials were willing to use harsh punishment against individual members who refused to dance.

First, officials punished individuals through fines and whippings. If these methods failed to bring recalcitrant members back into village ceremonies, Pueblo officials sometimes denied these individuals a right to use Pueblo land and water, apparently sending the message that they no longer regarded these renegades as true Pueblos.

Those Pueblos who defended the dances asserted their distinct "Indianness" and sought to fortify a cultural boundary around themselves. In addition to writing letters of protest, like that of the All-Pueblo Council, many Indians attempted to regulate the flow of information about the dances and other Indian practices. When white reformers charged the Pueblos with sexual immorality in their dances, many Pueblos tried to prevent whites from obtaining any information at all. A Hopi man, known as Poli, and his followers contested the testimony gathered by Inspector Sweet in the Secret Dance File. They accused Sweet of refusing to talk with the educated Indians. Sweet defended himself by saying that he could never get one of the educated Indians alone because the antimissionary Hopis "had organized a compact to prevent my talking with anyone alone. . . . [T]hey tried to organize a monopoly for the control of every word of testimony that reached the Inspectors."[81]

Clearly, some of the Pueblos wanted to control how they were represented and to contest images that had already circulated about them. The Pueblos particularly resented ethnographic probing into their ceremonies and kinship relationships. When anthropologist Alice Marriott conducted a series of interviews with Maria Martinez in the 1940s, "by order of the governor and the council of [San Ildefonso pueblo], Mrs. Martinez was forbidden to discuss certain topics," native religion being one of them. Laguna officials refused to allow anthropologists Elsie Clews Parsons and Franz Boas to attend a summer solstice ceremony, guarding the door of the house where they stayed to prevent their intrusion at the dance.[82] Many Pueblos also sought to control popular representations of themselves. Most Pueblos forbade outsiders from taking any pictures of their ceremonies, telling white observers that "our ways would lose their power if they were known." At Taos Pueblo a white film crew obtained permission to film part of the fiesta-day dance to be shown at the 1935 San Diego World's Fair, but "there was a part of the dance which the Indian negotiators asked to have omitted. Nevertheless it was taken." According to Parsons, "after the first performance at San Diego the taboo part of the film was missing." The Pueblo officials also sometimes restricted the content of Pueblo painters. At Taos in the 1920s and 1930s the officers restricted painters to painting rows of houses instead of dances.[83]

To maintain control of information, Pueblo officials severely punished Indians who gave out secret information to government inspectors, anthropologists, writers, or tourists. For example, one Acoma Pueblo man, Edward Hunt, spent a week in Albuquerque telling a government employee old-time stories, the songs of medicine men, and other details of Acoma ceremonies. Hunt asked for the protection of the federal government because he believed that if he was found out, his people would kill him. "Anybody might get a club and beat me in the head," he said.[84] Though Hunt may have exaggerated, the Pueblos nevertheless did beat, whip, and fine people for divulging secret information to outsiders. Anthropologists caused particular friction when they published what they observed or what their informants told them about the secrets of Pueblo ceremonies. Pueblo officials often ostracized named informants. When informants were not named, rumors about who might have divulged secret information led to deep conflicts within villages.[85]

Many scholars have noted that "by erecting a wall around their ceremonial life," the Pueblos had historically controlled surrounding pressures for change to a considerable degree. Dozier asserted, "[R]igid control mechanisms and equally rigid surveillance procedures have made it possible for the Pueblos to endure in spite of corrosive and divisive pressures, such as droughts, epidemics, and European-American contact." According to Dozier, the Pueblos devised this surveillance system of their own people under Spanish rule when the Franciscan friars attempted to root out native religion. Although Pueblos relaxed restrictions on secrecy during the late eighteenth century and during Mexican rule, they tightened them again in the early twentieth century when Pueblo dances became a target of moral reformers.[86]

In addition to trying to prevent information about the dances from seeping outside the pueblo, some Pueblos did portray the dances to whites but took pains to counter the images both moral reformers and the new activists had constructed of them. Though often chastised by their pueblos, an emerging group of so-called self-taught Pueblo artists painted Indian dances. Sponsored by white patrons who often tried to direct them to paint in what they regarded as a "primitive" style in which "environments disappeared and figures increasingly became firmly outlined," they produced paintings that suffused the dances with order and solemnity.[87] Tonita Peña of Cochiti Pueblo was the only Pueblo woman among this emerging group of artists. Her painting *Harvest Dance* represents a striking contrast to both moral reformers' and antimodern feminists' depictions of Pueblo dances. In this painting, two lines of dancers, one male and one female, dance parallel to one another, looking straight ahead. They dance in precise unison, each with his or her right foot raised to the same height. Peña presents little variation in the faces or bodies of the dancers. They all seem to concentrate intently on the dance.[88] Like other dance paintings by the "self-taught artists," *Harvest Dance* conveys communalism, dignity, contemplativeness, and order, not the sexual abandon and disorder that comes across in many white portrayals of the dances. While Peña and other Pueblo artists sometimes painted the clowns, they did not convey their sexually "risque" skits; instead they generally emphasized other parts of the dances.

Not only did they attempt to control images of the dances, but many Pueblo Indians used parts of the dances themselves as a form of protest against white encroachment and as a means to maintain some level of autonomy from white culture. In fact, the performance of the clowns that moral reformers found so objectionable comprised an integral element in how the Pueblos mitigated their increased interaction with whites. While moral reformers characterized the clowns' skits in Pueblo dances as immoral, and antimodern feminist reformers viewed them as "naturally" sexual, the Indians derived several altogether different meanings from them. The clowns' skits, along with the rest of the dances, served to promote both human and agricultural fertility. Furthermore, the clowns also served to regulate community behavior by making fun of inappropriate actions.[89] The clowns' skits and antics may also have served to create a carnival-like occasion. Louis Hieb explains that the "ritual clowns turn the world topsy-turvy, and their behavior is often described as involving inversion and reversal."[90] Like the carnivals of European peasants, the clowns' performances allowed villagers to temporarily subvert hierarchies and vicariously engage in behaviors deemed inappropriate by Pueblo cultures. As Dozier perceived it, "[T]ownspeople find release of emotions by watching clowns perform acts denied them by Pueblo mores or authorities."[91]

The clowns' performance must also be put in a historical context. Pueblo clowns had long designed skits to make sense of new historical events and actors. According to Alfonso Ortiz, "pueblo dramatizations, performed in their native languages, serve to transform what might have been unique and disruptive historical events into a part of the ongoing, internal, cultural dialogue of the people. They depict the first arrival of the Spaniards and encounters with government bureaucrats, missionaries, anthropologists, and others with whom they have recurrent encounters. What all these depictions have in common is that they make fun of outsiders, thereby reinforcing the community's own sense of self-worth and cultural continuity."[92] In the 1920s, when moral reformers attacked the dances and tourists started to inundate dance performances, the clowns' antics served in part as a parody of white behavior. This parody served as a lesson in how not to behave, a means to differentiate Pueblo from white culture, and a way for Pueblo Indians to at least temporarily overturn power differences with whites. As Erna Fergusson observed, The clowns "seem to embody the Indian's real attitude toward whites. The white man is usually the butt of the joke."[93] Thus, in some of the clowns' skits, what moral reformers (and to some extent antimodern feminists) thought they saw—reflections of actual Pueblo and Hopi sexuality—was actually a mirror held up for them, showing how the Pueblos represented white sexuality.

The clowns parodied whites in all their interactions with the Pueblos. For example, Erna Fergusson described one of the buffalo and deer dances at San Felipe Pueblo. The clowns, she wrote, "carry on their burlesque of the inept white hunter. They trip over their own guns, they frighten the game, they interfere with the Indian hunters, they make generally pestiferous nuisances of themselves and uproarious fun for the onlookers." The clowns also satirized American Protestantism. During one skit at Isleta, "one of them stood solemnly intoning from a mail-order-house catalogue, held upside down, while the others knelt in the dust before him. Then he closed the book and began to thunder in wrath, waving his arms and vociferating in tones that any European audience would have recognized as American. The angrier he got, the more sleepy grew his audience, until they finally fell over, overcome with sleep."[94] In this skit the clowns not only made fun of white evangelical religion but perhaps also critiqued American materialism by using a mail-order catalogue rather than a Bible.

In fact, the Pueblo clowns enacted other scenes that lampooned the perceived materialism of whites. Elizabeth DeHuff described one farce in which the clowns "rush into a house without a 'by your leave,' nose into every crack and corner, open closed doors, and then grab personal effects and exclaim, 'How much? How much you take for this?'" In another scene, the clowns rushed "around among the Indians rudely examining their beads, ear-rings, bracelets, and each item of their apparel, even peeping beneath skirts to examine the intricacies of wrapped leggings. Next they trade and cheat, insult Indian maidens by pinching their averted cheeks and act as real savages."[95] In other dances, the clowns carried "alarm clocks as a means of ridiculing the white man, the slave of time and the slave of worries." Mary Austin observed that sometimes the "presence of a white man is indicated by a pile of tin cans."[96]

Pueblo clowns also satirized the behavior of white women. "Ridiculous, beflowered women's hats were jauntily perched on one side of [the clowns'] heads," DeHuff observed at one dance. "They daintily grasped one side of their skirts and kept pulling these aside to keep them from touching Indians as they passed." Donning white ladies' hats and handbags, the clowns would strut through the plaza with a "switching walk, head thrown back, and toes turned out." On other occasions a "fat Indian man [would appear] adorned in an extremely low-cut evening gown, to sing and trill upon an improvised platform or to flirt with all the handsome braves."[97] At San Ildefonso one of the clowns "made a specialty of tourists. With parasol and handbag, [he poked] his way around the Indians like a member of the Podunk Woman's Club, gathering material for a lecture on aborigines. He patted the babies, fingered the women's jewelry, asked embarrassingly intimate questions, and made explanatory remarks over his shoulder. 'She says she does bathe her baby every day. . . . Yes, she wears underwear.'"[98] Given that the clown in this skit spoke in English, it seems that the clowns obviously aimed such lampoons at white observers.

The clowns also mocked white sexual behavior. Pueblo observations of white dances and loosening sexual mores often became fodder for Pueblo clowns. While attending a Pueblo dance in the 1920s, Elizabeth DeHuff watched a group of small Indian boys who were dressed in the "cast-off garments of white neighbors" perform in a "dance closely related to the 'Charleston.'" Though she expected the dancers to sing their own chants, instead "they sang something strangely familiar in tune. . . . Suddenly as it was repeated the true song flashed upon me—'Any old rags any bones any bottles to-day!'"—a popular song of the era.[99] Even one witness in the Secret Dance File realized that the Pueblo clowns imitated white dances. As the BIA farmer L. R. McDonald observed, "[I]t seemed to me that the dancers were imitating Americans or Mexicans and wished to convey the impression among their people that they were imitating Americans and Mexicans because some of the women bowed and scraped and strutted and attempted to waltz a little, all of which seemed to me to be an attempt to parody an American or Mexican woman at a dance."[100]

For the most part, however, white observers, especially those who allied with the moral reformers, failed to comprehend that much of what they observed was intended to satirize white observers, not to reflect Pueblo daily life. What one shocked white woman deemed an indecent performance in the scene described below was more likely another attempt by Pueblo clowns to parody current 1920s white dances.

> One very large woman got out of the dance group and she came up to some of the spectators and made, I would not say immoral gestures, but one of the men dancers came up to keep her company, . . . and all of a sudden the Indian woman stuck her tongue out to the Indian man that was standing opposite her, and he stuck his tongue out at her, and then she went through the performance of a hula-hula dance, and Mrs. Y—— said, "Look, she is going to shimmie," and then they approached each other and embraced and went through a very indecent performance. The woman was a big fat

woman; it lasted only a few seconds, but it was very indecent while it lasted and mortified us to death. It was so indecent that it is impossible to describe. . . . [T]hey went through the movements of sexual intercourse in pantomime.[101]

Although pantomiming sexual intercourse might have served as a fertility rite, in this instance, the clowns' performance also suggests a parody of American dance crazes—particularly the shimmy, which became popular among middle-class youth during World War I—and white sexual mores.[102]

The Pueblos also spoofed the very conflict over new gender roles and sexual mores that pitted moral reformers against rebellious 1920s youth. What field matron Evelyn Bentley testified to in the Secret Dance File as gross sexual immorality can be seen from the Pueblos' point of view as a mocking of white sexual behavior. Bentley had testified that she witnessed a scene in a Hopi dance in which several male clowns tried to pull down the very short skirts of several "female" clowns. In so doing, their skirts would slip up in the front, and the male clowns would then sneak a peek up their skirts. The male clowns continued to alternate between trying to pull the skirts down and looking up the skirts.[103] As Pueblo women did not wear short skirts, it seems quite likely that the clowns in this scene spoofed new fashions (and the new notions of sexuality they symbolized) in American society at large. The clowns also suggested that moral reformers, while condemning new sexual mores, seemed to be secretly titillated by them. Though claiming to be repulsed and shocked by the alleged sexual immorality of Pueblo dances, moral reformers seemed to take a voyeuristic interest in attending the dances and in collecting ever more testimony about them. This phenomenon was not lost upon the Indians.

Their increasing contact with moral reformers, as well as with tourists, may have led Pueblo clowns to step up their ridicule of whites in the 1920s. Citing testimony like that of Evelyn Bentley, the moral reformers constantly emphasized that the dances had become more debauched over the years and lamented that many of the most-educated Indians took part in them. The Hopi witness Siventiwa asserted that "the dramatization of the act of cohabitation as between man and wife was not so common in the plaza in former days; this has become quite common in recent years. I think I was about grown when I first saw such an act dramatized in public. But such acts became so popular among the Hopis that the crowds would not be satisfied with anything else, and in recent years such acts have become very common."[104]

Neither the inspector nor most witnesses gave an explanation for why these acts had supposedly become more popular. One would expect that, given the government's and reformers' forty-year efforts to teach the Indians that their dances were evil, the Indians might have, in fact, deemphasized the sexual antics of the clowns. The reformers seemed unaware of any contradiction between their belief that they were helping to assimilate the Indians and their view that the dances had become increasingly sexually immoral. If indeed the dances seemed more sexual in the 1910s and 1920s, it may have been because the clowns had increased the number of skits designed to parody observed white sexual behavior. Through boarding-school education, the Pueblos had experienced an increased opportunity in the 1910s and 1920s to observe white culture. In fact, some Hopi witnesses and moral reformers charged the most-educated Indians with being "among the foremost in defending these Hopi ceremonies and denying the immorality associated" with them. If they were correct that "the returned students are the backbone of these immoralities," perhaps it was these returned students who supplied the clowns with new material for their acts.[105]

The clowns' mocking of white behavior served many purposes: to temporarily overturn power relationships between whites and Indians, to critique white culture, and to differentiate Pueblo from white culture. The clowns' skits afforded the Pueblos one arena in which they momentarily had power over whites. Pueblos had become increasingly dependent on whites for their economic livelihoods in the 1920s, and the government had succeeded in forcing many of their children into schools. Moral reformers repeatedly stressed to the Indians that their cultures were inferior to white civilization. Overpowered by whites in many aspects of their lives, the Pueblos found in the dances a much-needed opportunity to reverse hierarchies, to feel superior to whites. At the same time, the clowns' parody of white behavior provided another lesson in how good Pueblos should not behave. Given that some Pueblos had become interested in adopting white ways, the clowns may have increased their ridicule of white lifestyles in order to deter individuals from choosing to abandon Pueblo ways. By constructing a caricature of "the Whiteman" (or in many cases "the Whitewoman"), the Pueblo clowns found a means, as Keith Basso has put it in regard to the Apache, "to confer order and intelligibility upon their experience with Anglo-Americans." Further, Basso argues, "'[T]he Whiteman' serves as a conspicuous vehicle for conceptions that define and characterize what 'the Indian' is not."[106] By vividly illustrating how not to behave, the clown performances provided many Pueblo Indians with a humorous means of asserting their autonomy and strengthening a cultural boundary around themselves.[107]

Despite their differences, both Pueblo defenders and opponents of Indian dances shared several important perspectives. Neither group, for example, accepted the moral reformers' views that their daily lives were riven with unrestrained sexuality. Many Pueblos who opposed the dances rejected the notion that Pueblo women were either victims of male lust or had themselves become active perpetrators of sexual misconduct; instead they stressed the great modesty of Indian women and contrasted them favorably with white women. Hopi Otto Lomavitu, a contributor to the Secret Dance File who opposed the Hopi Snake Dance, wrote to the editor of the Flagstaff, Arizona, newspaper, "I wish to say that I am proud of my poor benight [*sic*] people that though they lack education, they have enough decency to mark out a woman clothed in nudity, ever admiring herself in a glass, twisting her head like a reptile, ever powdering her nose and painting her lips and eyelids, as absolute shamelessness."[108]

Pueblos who defended the dances similarly emphasized the great modesty of Pueblo women and the strict sexual standards of their communities. They did not respond in the sexually relativist way that antimodern feminists did, by claiming that their culture had a healthier and more natural sexual standard than whites. Turning moral reformers' judgments of sexual immorality against whites, many Pueblo Indians contended that it was really white dances that were sexually illicit. As Martin Vigil of Tesuque Pueblo phrased it, people call our dances "wicked" but "you hug and dance around, before you know it there might be a fight. . . . [W]hy[? B]ecause they dance with ladies, maybe someone would get jealous." Vigil added that "our dances are not wicked like you people. . . . You come down to any Pueblo, visit our dances, we don't hug each other when we dance. . . . [We] dance about five feet apart, not like you people." In an article written in 1916, Pablo Abeita of Isleta Pueblo contrasted the infrequent ritual dances of the Pueblos with those of white Americans, who "dance at least every Saturday night, and in most cases for the benefit of one person and the perdition of a dozen others. I have seen balls of the worst kind conducted by Americans, more scandalous and immodest than the worst savage dance ever held by Indians in New Mexico."[109]

Pueblo Indians on both sides of the controversy blamed deviation from Pueblo sexual norms on white influences. Although the Hopi witnesses in the Secret Dance File agreed with the moral reformers that Hopi dances were immoral, they often fixed the blame for this alleged immorality on different parties than did the moral reformers. The reformers blamed "traditional Hopis" and vehemently opposed the dances because of their concern that federally sponsored education for Indian children would be a waste of money if the children were then reexposed to traditional dances. Some Hopi observers, however, believed that the returned students were the cause, not the victims, of the supposed sexual immorality of the dances. Judge Hooker Hongeva contended that "the returned students are the backbone of these immoralities. They have gone off to school and learned enough of the white man's ways to give them a puffed-up mind, or the 'big head,' and they come back and plunge into these ways, with adultery as their bait, and become leaders in these gross wrong things." Some Hopis believed that it was white educators who violated the Hopis' strict sexual standards and corrupted young people. Helen Sekaquaptewa claimed that in her Keams Canyon boarding-school class, "when the class came up to 'read,' [the teacher] always called one of the girls to stand by him. . . . He would put his arms around and fondle the girls, sometimes taking them on his lap." Seka-quaptewa screamed when the teacher tried to fondle her.[110] At least to some Hopis who opposed the dances, boarding-school education, not tribal tradition, was to blame for the supposed immorality in Hopi dances.

Like Indians on the other side of the dance controversy, Pueblo dance sup-porters were particularly troubled by boarding schools and the new types of so-cial interaction to which they exposed Pueblo children. The Santa Fe Indian School held a dance every other month. Although boys and girls were not al-lowed to sit together and were strictly supervised, American-style dancing brought Indian children into closer physical contact than they would ever have experienced at home. Former students at Santa Fe Indian School remembered much covert flirting—passing notes, exchanging glances. Boarding-school stu-dents found other occasions as well to break both BIA rules and tribal mores. A Jemez woman remembered that as a girl she and her friends snuck out of the girls' dormitory at the Santa Fe Indian School to go to a carnival in town, where they stayed out all night.[111] Many Pueblos objected to these new opportunities for heterosocial interaction. Blanche Grant reported that one young Pueblo man "who went without his bride to the pueblo school parties and became known soon as a flirt was recently sent home by order of the council and told that he could no longer go to the [school] dances."[112] Here was a point of agreement among both groups of Indians in the dance controversy. Both Pueblos who op-posed and those who supported the dances represented "traditional" Pueblo life as a culture with strict sexual standards and portrayed Pueblo women as the em-bodiments of modesty. If some Pueblo women no longer appeared modest, and if some Pueblos seemed to be behaving in a sexually immoral way, then it was white contact, both sides seemed to agree, not indigenous tradition, that was to blame.

Later, in the 1940s, Don Talayesva would present a very different portrait of Hopi sexuality to anthropologist Leo Simmons, who recorded his autobiogra-phy. According to Talayesva, aunts routinely chased their young nephews and pretended to have intercourse with them, men joked together and told stories about sex, couples who were engaged were permitted to have intercourse, and sex was not seen as dirty or sinful. After years away at boarding school and a brush with death, Talayesva concluded, "I wanted to become a real Hopi again, to sing the good old Katcina songs, and to feel free to make love without fear of sin or a rawhide."[113] Though, according to Talayesva, the Hopis did not attempt to contain or punish sexuality in the same way that whites did, they still had developed their own set of standards. For example, it was permissible for older women to tease young boys about sex, but actual intercourse between them was not tolerated. Premarital sex was accepted, according to Talayesva, but only when the two parties involved were engaged to be married.[114]

Juxtaposed against the insistence of Pueblo Indians during the dance controversy that the Pueblos were more moral by white, middle-class standards than most whites, Talayesva's autobiography presents something of a puzzle. His frequent discussions of sexuality may have reflected in part the questioning and editing of his interviewer, Leo Simmons. Further, as Frederick Dockstader points out, a small number of Hopis served as informants to white anthropologists over the course of the twentieth century. Talayesva, according to Dockstader, had a virtual monopoly on supplying white scholars with information. "We must guard against judging the group," cautions Dockstader, "by the opinions or reactions of a very few of its members, many of whom may deliberately or unconsciously mislead."[115]

When it came to sexual norms for Pueblo girls and women, Talayesva's autobiography appears to confirm the ideal espoused by Pueblo Indians during the dance controversy. Several sources reveal that Hopi sexual norms at the turn of the twentieth century may have been stricter for girls than for boys. Talayesva suggests that parents were more protective of their daughters' sexuality. Sekaquaptewa's mother had advised her as a girl, "Never sleep away from me, even in the same house with your father and brothers. If I am away overnight you sleep in the bed with your grandmother." As girls reached puberty, Sekaquaptewa related, their mothers taught them the "Hopi moral code, which is that [a girl] is to keep herself a virgin until she is married." Anthropologist Alice Schlegel concurs, asserting that for Hopi girls "chastity [was] the ideal." Yet Schlegel also found an "ambivalent attitude toward [girls'] sexuality," as Hopi parents "expected that there [would] be attempts at youthful experimentation" and fully accepted any children born out of wedlock.[116] As for other pueblos, anthropologist Sophie Aberle, who took a special interest in researching gender and sexuality, found no stigma against premarital sex at San Juan Pueblo, although she and Parsons both mentioned that Pueblo communities protected girls and gave them few opportunities to mix with boys.[117]

Talayesva's autobiography also suggests the probability that at the turn of the twentieth century, after centuries of Spanish contact and decades of Anglo proselytization, sexual norms and practices within each pueblo were highly contested and unstable. Talayesva provides some insight into the way that sexual norms and practices among the Hopis may have been undergoing a dramatic transformation during this time. After attending boarding school for two years, Talayesva returned home for the summer. After a heavy rain, he happened upon four Hopi girls skinny-dipping in a pool. Although they asked him to join them, Talayesva "declined because [he] had learned at school that boys should not swim with girls." Nevertheless, Talayesva watched the girls till sunset and then snuck off with one of them to engage in sexual experimentation in a chicken house.[118] As this episode indicates, some Pueblos had learned to regard sexual activity outside a Christian marriage as sinful. Some Indians attempted to impose these norms on themselves and other Pueblos. And yet other standards and practices persisted, creating a complex notion of appropriate sexual conduct. That Pueblo men on both sides of the dance controversy defended Pueblo sexual standards as morally superior to white norms suggests that Pueblo men were willing to close ranks in the 1920s to prevent white outsiders from prying into and judging the sexual practices of their culture.

These two opposing groups, however, did not always agree on the ideal role of Pueblo women. When it came to the appropriate sexual division of labor, the two Indian sides in the dance controversy presented competing visions of Pueblo women. In the 1920s, as white women had superimposed their view of womanhood onto Pueblo women, Pueblo Indian men also invoked Pueblo women to symbolize their respective interpretations of Anglo-induced change. The dispute in the late 1920s at Santa Clara Pueblo illustrates this point. When representatives from both the "progressive" and "conservative" parties in the pueblo met with Assistant Commissioner of Indian Affairs Edgar Merritt to resolve their differences over who should govern the pueblo, the issue of whether Pueblo women should work only in the home or still participate in the customary cleaning of the entire village proved particularly contentious. Desiderio Naranjo, the governor from the Progressive Party, listed as one of his grievances the way in which the village was cleaned:

Now according to the regulation of this village, sweeping the village is just once a year. We are not opposed to any affairs of the village. What we don't agree with is for all us to get out, women, children; the men are sweeping the village and the women carrying the dirt out on their backs and that doesn't suit us very well. It may be all right a hundred years ago the time when we didn't have no wagons or teams to throw the trash out. But now we have teams and wagons to haul the trash out of the village. It is not necessary for the women to get out and sweep the village, they have plenty to do at home.[119]

Naranjo objected especially when his own daughter, a teacher for the BIA, was compelled to carry dirt on her back. Naranjo voiced his beliefs: "[T]here are lots of us males to [throw the trash away] and the women ought to do the house work such as cooking."[120] Other members of the Progressive Party at Santa Clara also linked women's work roles to their vision of "progress." Joseph Tafoya boasted, "[M]y wife makes the very finest pottery but she is raising our babies right and doesn't have much time to do anything else."[121] Apparently, the so-called progressives had imbibed some of the BIA's stated goals of inculcating domesticity among Indian women. In contrast, so-called conservatives argued that Pueblo women should maintain their customary work roles in and out of the home. Juan Jose Gutierrez, governor for the Conservative Party, insisted that women should still dispose of the trash in the village.[122]

Since the BIA had also bound Indian women's work roles to the notion of Indian "progress," it was not surprising that Merritt agreed with Naranjo, using the occasion to preach, "We men in America pride ourselves upon our generosity to our women folks. It is said that the American husband is the best husband in the world because he is always generous to his wife and children and he protects them in every way possible. I am sure that you want to be just as good to your women folks as any other man in America." Merritt ruled that on cleaning days, the women be required to work in their homes but not to haul the trash away.[123] Thus, to all participants in the dance controversy, Pueblo women took on symbolic significance but did not seem to take part directly in the debate. To white moral reformers and to antimodern feminists, Pueblo women functioned as "new women" and thus as either threatening or liberating figures. To Pueblo men on both sides of the controversy, Pueblo women symbolized their competing approaches to white contact. Defenders of dances portrayed the ideal Pueblo woman as resistant to change and determined to maintain the Pueblo way of life. Dance opponents portrayed their ideal as a woman who had taken on the trappings of American domesticity and had thus acceded to white American norms. In both cases, Pueblo women were "modest," never sexually "free," as in the images of white women.

Though they often contested the images whites projected of Pueblo women and Pueblo sexuality, both Indian sides in the controversy learned to use their white allies for their own purposes. In their efforts to fight what they perceived to be the injustices meted out to them by their leaders, the Indians who opposed the dances fostered support from moral reformers. For example, after writing to the IRA to ask for their assistance in recovering tourist earnings, Joseph Tafoya carefully articulated his loyalties to Clara True, a reformer who had long worked with Santa Clara Indians, and to Samuel Brosius of the IRA: "What are we going to do when Miss True dies? This is what I am thinking constantly. I want to get our affairs in good shape while she is still with us. I might add also, where shall we find a man to take your place when you go to your reward? Where would be our help at this hard time without you? This is why I am trying so hard to get a better condition before we lose all of our strong friends who are not afraid to stand for us."[124]

Once allied with the moral reformers, however, this group of Pueblo Indians did not passively accept their agenda. Instead they used the moral reformers' concern as a vehicle through which they made known their other grievances. To some extent, they diverted the moral reformers from their original purposes. What moral reformers initiated as a campaign to eradicate the "immoral" dances of the Pueblos evolved instead into a defense of those Indians who did not wish to dance or to clean the pueblo's community irrigation ditch. In the late 1920s these Indians turned their attention, and that of the moral reformers, to challenging the old leadership of their pueblos. After the dance controversy died down, for example, the Progressive Pueblo Council at Santa Clara Pueblo and its primary white sponsor, Clara True, sought to challenge the existing leadership structures among the pueblos, calling essentially for a separation of civil from religious affairs by disempowering the religious leader of the pueblo, the cacique.[125] Ultimately, the Indians who opposed Pueblo dances were more concerned with retaining their individual land and water rights within their pueblos and breaking the power of religious leaders over the governance of their pueblos than they were with the alleged sexual immorality of their dances. By allying with moral reformers over the issue of dances, they eventually reframed the reform agenda.

Just as Joseph Tafoya had assured the IRA of his loyalty and devotion to Clara True and Samuel Brosius, so too did the "conservative" Pueblos similarly cultivate their white allies. Antonio Abeita, an Isleta Pueblo man active on the All-Pueblo Council, wrote Mary Austin that he supported her and the "Collier crowd" over the "Santa Fe crowd." He told a reporter, "I knew Mr. Collier, Mrs. Atwood, and Mrs. Austin wouldn't do anything but what was best for the Pueblos. I will personally stand by the Collier crowd come what may." Another All-Pueblo Council activist, Sotero Ortiz of San Juan Pueblo, wrote Austin, "[W]e always think of our Friends those who are working with . . . Pueblo land legislation." If white activists often portrayed them in romantic terms, the Indians realized that such visions could help further their primary interests—the return of land and water rights. Many Pueblos wrote letters to the NMAIA asking for help in procuring more land or protecting their existing land and water rights. Their letters also requested assistance in preventing the excavation of burial sites.[126]

During the dance controversy, new white activists had developed images of the profoundly religious traditional Pueblo Indians who had kept pure their ancient, nature-based creed against all odds. So-called conservative Pueblo Indians turned this white fascination with their religion to work for them in their battles to regain land. If claims to the land based on precontact sovereignty had little impact in courts, perhaps claims based on the sacredness of certain land sites and on religious freedom would resonate among white activists and policy makers. As Sylvia Rodriguez has pointed out for Taos Pueblo, by using the emerging white romantic view of them in the 1920s, the Indians eventually regained the Blue Lake area in the mountains above the pueblo—land they had once used freely.[127]

In addition, individual Pueblo Indians used the piqued interest in the "traditional" Indian to their financial benefit. One Pueblo woman recalled that a white man "offered her five dollars to tell him if they watched the sun from the housetop." When Elsie Clews Parsons walked into a house at Laguna where eight women were grinding corn together, they told her that if she paid each woman a dollar, she could enter and observe them. Often desperate for money, even Indians who felt uncomfortable about revealing the secrets of their pueblos sometimes relented to the pressure of white anthropologists. An Isleta Indian painted one hundred watercolors of Indian dances at five dollars each for Elsie Clews Parsons. (Later he was severely punished by his pueblo.)[128] As Dockstader has mentioned, "a thriving business has been built up in the supplying of ethnological information."[129]

Who won the dance controversy? Clara True believed that the GFWC meeting in Los Angeles vindicated the moral reformers. At the end of the meeting, True declared that the "rout of enemy seems complete." No resolution calling for the preservation of Indian dances had been passed. Instead, the convention had merely passed a vague resolution calling for the president of the United States to appoint a commission to investigate the Indian Bureau to insure justice for all Indians. True had also succeeded in postponing the election of the Indian Welfare Committee chair. After the meeting she continued her efforts to undermine Stella Atwood.[130] True believed she had achieved victory at the Los Angeles meeting, writing to Matthew Sniffen of the IRA that the organization "may well congratulate itself upon its recent services in forming and conducting a small world court in which paganism was tried and found wanting."[131]

Yet True may have declared victory too soon. After publishing a debate in 1924 between Mary Austin and reformer Flora Seymour in *Forum*, the editors received many more letters favoring the preservation of Indian dances.[132] In the aftermath of the climactic events of 1924, Stella Atwood won back her position as chair of the Indian Welfare Committee. Later, Atwood left the GFWC to work full-time for the AIDA. Though she continued to organize the Pueblo progressives, True had not carried out her assignment to raise funds for the IRA, and in early 1925, threatened with being fired, she resigned her position with the IRA.[133] In that same year, in a case brought against the governor and council of Taos for allegedly beating two returned Indian students who did not wish to wear Indian costumes during their dance, the judge found that the Pueblos should be allowed to regulate their own affairs. The BIA also allowed Taos Pueblo to pull two boys from boarding school for eighteen months in order to train them in the Taos religion.[134]

By 1927 the BIA had developed a compromise between the two sides in the dance controversy. When Edgar Merritt met with the Santa Clara Indians in 1927, he revealed, "[I]t is not the intention of the Federal Government at Washington to interfere with your ceremonials or dances or your customs so long as they do not violate the law." The government only stipulated that "each member of the pueblo should be free to decide whether he wants to participate in the dances" and that officers of the pueblo could not compel anyone to dance.[135] Although the BIA continued to use Circular 1665 to suppress native religion among some tribes, by the late 1920s the issue of Indian dances had all but faded from public debate.[136] The new Indian reform organizations turned their attention to questions of public health, water rights, and the preservation of Indian arts and crafts.[137] Notwithstanding the dance controversy and predictions that the dances as well as the rest of their cultures were dying out, the Pueblos continued their dances unabated.

At the same time, it is not clear who "won" the subtextual battle over white sexual mores. True believed that "pagan" sexual immorality, with all of its parallels to emerging modern sexual mores in America, had been on trial at the GFWC meeting. She was convinced that it had been convicted and given a death sentence. She may have been right. Though the dance controversy was settled in favor of the Pueblos, those who defended the dances at the GFWC meeting did so on the terms of the moral reformers. No one stood up to argue that Pueblo dances should not be outlawed because the Pueblos had more "natural" sexual standards than white Americans. Instead, Charles Lummis's elevation of the Pueblos as the epitome of "Home" and "Reverence and Faith"—values that moral reformers had long upheld—became the major argument in favor of the dances.

By the late 1920s white women concerned with preserving Indian culture seemed to revive the mission of the BIA and of moral reformers that white women should assist Indian women in "establishing an American home." Vera Connolly, who wrote an impassioned series of articles for *Good Housekeeping* in the late 1920s on the need to transform the BIA and its policy toward Indians, ended one of her articles by calling upon white American women to push for change in the BIA. Connolly asserted that "the righteous wrath of American womanhood—of home women, consecrated women, aroused to deep indignation and banded together in a crusade"—could obtain justice for Indians.[138] Mrs. Wiegel, chair of the GFWC's Indian Welfare Committee in Colorado, believed that righteous American women should turn their attention to helping Indian women make better homes. "Now, if all other matters are forgotten, legislative matters," Wiegel explained, "everything is forgotten, except establishing the Indian women in an American home, we will have solved the great Indian question."[139] Antimodern feminists, themselves ambivalent about emerging sexual mores in white America, seemed to retreat from their sexually relativist stance. Increasingly, they became more involved in promoting the arts and crafts movement, an effort they also defined as helping Pueblo women to retain their premodern role in the home.

As for the Pueblos, if defenders of the dances won the actual battle, it is not clear whether they and their white allies realized their symbolic goals. Although they equated the defense of their dances with the maintenance of autonomy and the prevention of integration into white culture, the Pueblos' dire economic straits forced them to develop some means of earning income. Increasingly, they commercialized their public dances as well as their traditional crafts. In essence, they marketed their ethnic identity for tourists in order to cope with the exigencies of dependency. Would such a strategy break down the very cultural boundary many Pueblos had sought to strengthen? Would Pueblo Indians lose the autonomy they fought so arduously to maintain? White women, again, played a major role in trying to determine the answer to that question. Both women who supported assimilation and those who favored "preservation" of Indian culture participated in the Indian arts and crafts movement and in the commodification of Pueblo culture. Each group sought through this movement either to insulate the Pueblos from modern America or to integrate them fully into American society. But as in the dance controversy, the Pueblos had other ideas. This time, however, Pueblo women played an active as well as a symbolic role in the arts and crafts movement. They not only molded the *ollas* and other pieces of pottery that became so appealing to white women, but they also shaped the contours of this new movement.

CHAPTER SIX

Women and the Indian Arts
and Crafts Movement

This isn't an Art Form. . . . It's a living religion. . . . If people come in here—don't you see?—they'd grab all this and commercialize it somehow. As soon as religion is commercialized, it has turned into an Art Form! Commercial value is the standardized, accepted foundation of acknowledged Art. It is Recognition! I'd *hate* to have these Indians get recognition! Why, it would be the end of them! *Mabel Dodge Luhan, speaking of a Santo Domingo Pueblo dance*

So, we've saved the Pueblos for Fred Harvey. *Alice Corbin Henderson*

By the late 1920s the controversy among white women over Indian dances had quieted. Antimodern feminists who had defended Pueblo dances turned more of their attention toward bettering health care and promoting arts and crafts among the Pueblos. Likewise, female moral reformers, who had vehemently opposed Pueblo dances and worked for the erasure of Pueblo culture, became engaged in the same movement to promote Indian arts and crafts. The Indian arts and crafts movement can be seen, in part, as a branch of the larger movement to revive handicrafts in Britain and America at the turn of the century. Historians have explained this movement as a reaction against industrialization and a related search for authenticity. Believing that industrialization had produced a mass culture of imitation, destroyed communal bonds, and divested work of its inherent worth, supporters of the arts and craft movement sought "authentic" objects and experience in preindustrial cultures and modes of production. Other scholars have argued that the white elites who patronized Indian arts in the Southwest consciously attempted to redefine the Southwestern identity and economy—to transform it from an area known primarily for ranching, agriculture, and extractive industries to a region known for its picturesque scenery and people.[1] These studies have contributed greatly to understanding the advent of modernism, its concomitant search for "the real thing," and the role of the Southwest in this quest for authenticity. For all their insights, these explanations neglect two significant aspects of the Indian arts and crafts movement among the Pueblo Indians of New Mexico—its gendered nature and its heterogeneity.[2]

Although several men played key roles within it, the Indian arts and crafts movement functioned largely as a women's phenomenon. Many white women claimed credit for initiating the movement. They also constituted a large number of the members of the Indian Arts Fund (IAF) and the Arts and Crafts Committee of the New Mexico Association on Indian Affairs (NMAIA). Moreover, most of those who purchased Indian arts and crafts were white women. Kenneth Chapman, an anthropologist who took a leading role in the arts and crafts movement, estimated that "fully 75 percent of all purchases of Indian crafts were by women, and for Navajo and Pueblo silver jewelry no doubt the figure would be nearly 90 percent." Because so much of the movement focused on pottery, a woman's craft among the Pueblos, it also involved many more Indian women than men as producers.[3]

Women who participated in the arts and crafts movement, however, did not share a consensual view of its nature and purpose. Their competing perspectives led to a diverse and contentious campaign. Scholars have tended to treat the arts and crafts movement as a homogeneous entity, ignoring or conflating differences among its members; yet it encompassed a wide variety of participants who competed with one another in attempting to establish the ground rules and purposes of Indian art. Those most commonly associated with the movement were preservationists who sought to revive "high-quality," "traditional" Indian art as a means to insulate the Pueblos from modern America. Many antimodern feminists participated in this endeavor. As seen in Mabel Dodge Luhan's remark that recognition would be the end of Indian religion and Alice Corbin Henderson's sarcastic observation that the new activists had saved the Pueblos for Fred Harvey (a foremost promoter of Southwest tourism), antimodern feminists feared that mass tourism acted as a corrupting force on the Pueblos and their art. Instead, they sought a small, elite market for Indian art.[4]

Another group of white women figured in the Indian arts and crafts movement as well. This wing of the movement included moral reformers such as Clara True, who conceived of Indian art as uplift, as a means to better the conditions and morals of Indians through integrating them into the American economy. Curiously, these women who had once deemed the Indians' ethnic identity as a barrier to their progress now believed that the marketing of Indian ethnicity and art could accomplish what the policy of assimilation had not. To them, tourism would help uplift the Pueblos. They tended to be less concerned with authenticity and the expression of a "traditional" style than with promoting financial gain for both Indians and themselves. Antimodernism alone does not explain why so many women of different ideological persuasions participated in this movement. As with the dance controversy, the arts and crafts movement functioned for many white women as a means to articulate their competing approaches to womanhood and sexuality. It also served as a new arena in which women could gain a measure of cultural authority and fashion a new vision of womanhood.

White women in both wings of the movement transformed Indian women artists into powerful symbols of their own competing notions of women's roles in modern America. While the assimilationist wing of the movement saw pottery production as a means to achieve the uplift of Indian women, antimodern feminists conceived of art as a means to preserve what they believed to be idyllic gender relations among the Pueblos. Despite their idealization of Pueblo women artists, white women generally perceived them as passive producers of pots and paintings. In contrast, these white women conceived of themselves as the active agents who created the meaning and value associated with Indian arts and crafts. Most scholars, too, have focused largely on the ways in which white preservationists, according to their notions of Indian authenticity, defined and even limited Indian art.[5] We should not neglect, however, the part that Native American women themselves played in shaping the Indian arts and crafts movement and in developing new roles for themselves, roles that neither conformed to antimodern feminists' nor uplifters' ideals. In the dance controversy, even as all the different participants invoked Indian women to support their perspectives, Indian women seemed to be silent. In the arts and crafts movement, however, Pueblo women became vocal participants. Although white women may have framed the struggle of Native Americans as one between preservation of culture and assimilation, Pueblo women artists did not necessarily view their world in such stark terms. Instead, they utilized time-honored strategies to turn the arts and crafts movement and tourism to their own ends.

Among the Pueblos, white patrons evinced the greatest interest in painting and pottery. Pueblo painting originally functioned as "essential elements of ritual, as a form of prayer." Pueblos destroyed ritual paintings once completed and did not have a tradition of decorating with paintings. The Pueblos had used pottery primarily to carry water and store grain. Occasionally, Pueblo Indians incorporated pottery making into their sacred ceremonies.[6] At the turn of the twentieth century, white patrons "discovered" and became involved in movements to "revive" the supposedly dying arts of Pueblo painting and pottery.

Standard accounts of the Indian arts and crafts movement have focused primarily on men's roles within it. In 1895, according to many scholars, anthropologist J. Walter Fewkes, concerned with the supposed decline in the quality of Hopi pottery, initiated the so-called Hopi pottery revival. Conducting an excavation at Sikyatki on First Mesa, Fewkes encouraged the potter Nampeyo, wife of one of his Hopi workmen, to imitate the designs found on old pottery shards. Nampeyo's pottery became famous, and the renaissance of pottery production she began at Hopi came to be known as the Sikyatki Revival. In the early 1900s Fewkes also promoted the painting of kachina dancers by several Hopi men. Some scholars have also given credit to trader Thomas Keam for initiating the pottery "revival" among the Hopis by suggesting to Indian women potters that they copy "prehistoric" designs to increase the value and marketability of their pottery.[7]

In New Mexico, historians have highlighted the role of Edgar Hewett, a self-trained archaeologist and the first director of the School of American Research in Santa Fe. According to many scholars, in 1907 and 1908, while excavating near San Ildefonso Pueblo in New Mexico, Hewett urged Maria Martinez, the wife of one of his Indian employees, to craft a pot based on an old pottery shard and to use old pottery stones found in the excavation to polish the pottery. Eventually, Martinez's pottery, on which her husband Julian painted designs, became world-famous and commanded high prices. Hewett also took credit for initiating "self-taught" painting among the Pueblo Indians in 1917–18 by commissioning a San Ildefonso Indian, Crescencio Martinez, to paint a series of dances.[8] Kenneth Chapman, an anthropologist and the first director of Santa Fe's Laboratory of Anthropology, and John Collier have also been accorded much influence in the Indian arts and crafts movement. Together with physician Harry Mera, Chapman founded and headed the IAF, an organization dedicated primarily to Pueblo pottery preservation. Collier promoted the Indian Arts and Crafts Board, a governmental effort aimed at promoting Indian handicraft.[9]

A focus on these men has overshadowed white women in the Indian arts and crafts movement. Around 1905 a renegade San Ildefonso Day School teacher first encouraged Crescencio Martinez to paint his dance ceremonials. This was almost a decade before Hewett met Martinez. "Self-taught" painter Tonita Peña told her biographer that she learned to paint when her day-school teacher at San Ildefonso, Esther Hoyt, gave her watercolors and encouraged her to paint. Edgar Hewett subsequently "discovered" Peña at the day school and supplied her with paints and paper thereafter. Peña's cousin at Cochiti, Romando Vigil, who also became a renowned artist, first learned to paint in day school from his teacher Elizabeth Robbins.[10] Elizabeth DeHuff, writer and wife of a superintendent of the Santa Fe Indian School, insisted that the "real awakening" of Southwest Indian painting occurred not as a result of Hewett's efforts but through her own endeavors. Beginning in May 1918 DeHuff brought seven boys from the Santa Fe Indian School to her house in the afternoons to paint. Among them were Fred Kabotie and Otis Polelonema, both Hopi, and Velino Herrera (or Shije) of Zia Pueblo, all of whom became well known and respected painters.[11]

White women seem to have taken an even greater part in promoting Indian pottery. In 1917 Madame Verra von Blumenthal and Rose Dougan from Pasadena arrived at San Ildefonso Pueblo to promote a "better grade of ceramics . . . that could be sold in greater quantity throughout the country." To some pottery patrons, a "better grade of ceramics" could best be found in the works of Nampeyo and Maria Martinez. As anthropologist Ruth Bunzel noted of Nampeyo, "[S]he makes no modern white forms, no worthless trifles. She makes only dignified pieces in the best traditional style."[12] In the 1920s white women helped to initiate the IAF, originally to promote the preservation and revival of "high-quality" Pueblo pottery.[13] Mary Austin and her friend Ina Sizer Cassidy contended that they came up with the idea for the IAF in the winter of 1915–16 at the National Arts Club in New York City. Supposedly, Austin, Cassidy, and Cassidy's husband, Gerald, discussed the need to preserve Indian arts and crafts. In February 1917 they reportedly set up an Indian booth at the Actor's Fund Fair in New York City, where they sold Indian-made wares from around the United States. Cassidy and some of her friends staged what they called a "Hopi masked dance." In the early 1920s Mary Austin wrote to Mabel Dodge Luhan of her plan "for helping the Pueblos to be self-sustaining by reviving Indian arts." At this point, however, Austin's plan differed substantially from the eventual goals and tactics of the IAF, for she recommended that the Pueblos make turquoise beads and wampum out of shells, crafts unknown among the Pueblos.[14]

The official "Story of the Indian Arts Fund" asserts that the idea for the fund originated at a 1922 dinner party at the home of Elizabeth Shepley Sergeant, another of the feminists who had come to New Mexico after World War I and had become involved in "saving" the Pueblos. According to one account, just before the party Sergeant broke one of her prized Zuni pots. When she told her guests, one of them, Harry Mera, expressed a desire to piece it back together and to preserve other pottery. Kenneth Chapman concurred. Mera and Chapman proved to be the central leaders of the IAF, but the original Board of Trustees included many women who had long been interested in the preservation of Indian culture: writers Mary Austin, Mabel Dodge Luhan, Elizabeth Shepley Sergeant, and Alice Corbin Henderson; Margaret McKittrick, the chair of the NMAIA and its Arts and Crafts Committee; and Amelia Elizabeth White, head of the Eastern Association on Indian Affairs (EAIA). Except for Austin, who died in 1934, all of these women served for more than twenty years on the IAF board. White served for forty years. White also opened a store in New York City called ISHAUU to market Indian wares, and she helped to organize the Exposition of Tribal Arts in the early 1930s.[15]

White women also figured significantly in the eventual efforts of the BIA to promote Indian arts. Until the late 1920s the BIA officially disapproved of teaching Indian art in Indian schools. As the early experiences of many "self-taught" artists reveal, however, many female day-school teachers defied official policy and encouraged Indian artists to paint in an emerging Indian style. In 1928 the Meriam Report, based on the investigations of the Meriam Commission, condemned the BIA policy of prohibiting the instruction of Indian culture and art in school curricula and recommended that these subjects be introduced into the schools. In 1932 the BIA hired Dorothy Dunn to teach Indian art and Mabel Morrow to instruct in Indian crafts at the Santa Fe Indian School. When John Collier became the commissioner of Indian affairs in 1933, the Studio of the Santa Fe Indian School, under Dunn's direction until 1937, became the centerpiece of his administration's commitment to Indian arts and a model for other Indian schools across the country. From 1937 until 1962 Geronima Cruz Montoya of San Juan Pueblo directed the studio.[16]

Many of the women who became involved in efforts to "preserve" and "revive" Indian arts could be characterized as antimodern feminists. Combining a disdain for the modernization of American society with a quest for women's self-fulfillment and sexual expression, these feminists admired and romanticized Pueblo culture as the utopian antithesis of modern American culture. The arts and crafts movement became a primary vehicle through which they articulated and even enforced their view of Pueblo culture. Whereas these antimodern feminists portrayed modern white Americans as rational and scientific, they characterized the Pueblos and their artistry as irrational, intuitive, and mystic. In Indian art, anthropologist Ruth Bunzel maintained, "[S]ensation and intuition play a larger role than intellect in the creation of design." Bunzel also asserted that the Pueblo potter's "appreciation of form and surface is non-intellectual and non-analytical." In the minds of these feminists Pueblo artistry was inseparable from Pueblo religion. Mary Austin contended that Indian art "is the only art in America which arises directly from the perfect interaction of the spirit and the hand; when there is nothing left but the hand, when the spirit goes out of the suave designs of the pottery, the bright hues and subtle weft of the textiles, there will be little left that the machine cannot supply." Just as Pueblo religion emanated from nature, as antimodern feminists saw it, so too did Pueblo art. An article on Tonita Peña declared that "she learned [to paint] from the corn, the rain, the eagle, the butterfly, and the buffalo."[17]

Reinforcing their view that the Pueblos represented and must remain a preindustrial society, new feminist preservationists insisted that Indian arts and crafts be completely handmade. Mary Austin condemned the federal government for the "amputation of [the] capacity in the Indian [to make useful and desirable articles with his hands]." She hoped that "our present deep distrust of the Machine as the chief idol of our own culture has come in time to save the aboriginal from being offered up to it." In their portrayals of Indian art, preservationists also emphasized the antiquity and timelessness of the Pueblos. "For thousands of years," Dorothy Dunn asserted, "[the Pueblo peoples] have woven and modeled, carved and painted, sung songs and made dances, until art and their daily life have become one."[18]

The preservationists discovered an innate artistic ability in all Pueblo Indians. Elizabeth DeHuff claimed that they are "racially artistic." According to the IAF, "[c]raft instinct and artistic sense are inherent and permanent" among Pueblo women. Dolly Sloan, art patron and wife of the artist John Sloan, declared that the Indian race was "the only race whose every member is an artist."[19] Furthermore, preservationists believed Pueblo art to be the expression of their communal society. The Collier administration's publication *Indians at Work* posited that Maria Martinez's work was her own, "yet it is so much a part of the life of the pueblo that one can seldom tell where individual creation ends and community participation begins." A *New Republic* article insisted that "primitive art—and above all American Indian art—is communal art."[20] Preservationists linked the Pueblos' art to all other so-called primitive art. Mary Austin believed "primitive peoples have always been artists—superb natural craftsmen." One journalist asserted that "in his fidelity to tribal convention, the Indian artist seems closer to the Far East than to the Occident." Further, he maintained that both "African Negro" and "Indian art are potently associated with religious observance and the legion fetishes of tribe superstition."[21]

Antimodern feminists sought through a variety of means to preserve the style that they believed best expressed the vision of the Pueblos and the lifestyle that produced such artistry. Preservationists believed that a twofold effort was needed to preserve authentic Indian arts. They must educate the Indians to produce the "best" art and instruct the public in good taste. *Indians at Work* "question[ed] whether the Indian himself is aware of his vast store of priceless culture." The Indian, they concluded, "has not been taught to value his own genius." In painting, preservationists emphasized that Indians should practice a "primitive" style and adhere to painting religious and ceremonial activities. Elizabeth DeHuff instructed her Indian pupils that they must not imitate the paintings of white artists, "but they must visualize a whole dance movement and paint as if the participants were dancing." DeHuff also believed that in "true Indian art, . . . the figures should not be three-dimensional, but should be painted . . . as they were painted on kiva walls." When writing to Dorothy Dunn about her efforts, DeHuff further asserted that the paintings of so-called self-taught painter Crescencio Martinez were not real Indian art because he used backgrounds. Neither did she consider the paintings of another self-taught artist, Alfredo Montoya, to be authentic Indian painting because supposedly he imitated white artists. "The painting I saw showed a deer among trees," DeHuff wrote disparagingly of Montoya's realism.[22]

Dorothy Dunn's art studio in the Santa Fe Indian School played a prominent role in defining "the Indian way" of painting. Dunn, who had been educated at the Art Institute of Chicago and had worked as a teacher at Santo Domingo Pueblo and on the northern Navajo Reservation from 1928 to 1931, stressed that she would teach "no European traditions of painting such as light and shade, perspective, anatomy, [or] the use of models." She also insisted that "advertising art, cartooning, landscape and portrait painting have no place in the schools' course because they are not in keeping with the precedents of Indian Art." Like DeHuff, Dunn emphasized that dances and dancers constituted the proper subject of Indian painting. Furthermore, Dunn only allowed the use of "earth colors" extracted from natural clays, sandstones, and plants.[23] Clearly, Dunn and other preservationists had created their own standard of traditional and authentic Indian painting, a process that has led scholar Dean MacCannell to call Dunn's approach "coloniality tagged as 'authentic traditional' art." Furthermore, as J. J. Brody points out, by dictating the subjects of Indian painting, Dunn and other preservationists prevented Indian artists from using their art to portray poverty or social criticism of any kind. On the other hand, art historian Bruce Bernstein argues that Dunn's students remembered her fondly and that she gave them a sense of pride and achievement.[24]

As with patrons of Indian painting, the IAF stressed that pottery produced by Indians must be "authentic." This meant, as Edgar Hewett told Maria Martinez, "the old kind of pottery with the old tools." As one means to educate Indians "to study, appreciate and reproduce the art of their own pueblos," the IAF and the NMAIA collaborated to "place technical books on Indian crafts . . . in the various boarding schools for the Indian children." Many preservationists also treated Indian adults as children who had to be guided and directed by white patrons. Ruth Bunzel believed that in the case of Nampeyo and Maria Martinez, their innovation and artistic brilliance had "been the result of an outside influence—the encouragement of white people interested in reviving aboriginal arts—working upon an individual endowed with technical equipment and creative imagination."[25] The preservationists believed that it was white attention that evoked true artistic brilliance from Indian artists.

In their efforts to instruct Indians in the "right" way to make pottery, the IAF also carried out the curious practice of searching pueblos for their oldest pots, purchasing them, and then installing them in a museum. In museums white instructors of Indian arts could bring their Indian students to view "high-quality, authentic" pieces of Indian artwork. The IAF believed their collections were "not dead and shelved away," as in other museums, but alive and vital to the Indian communities.[26] White patrons saw no contradiction between collecting art from the pueblos and lamenting that Indians were losing their innate sense of art. A paternalistic attitude is apparent in one woman who went to collect pots at Acoma Pueblo, a pueblo that sits atop a mesa. Despite the hardship of climbing the mesa in sweltering heat, the woman took great satisfaction in obtaining some pots. "After all these years they are safe," she proclaimed. As this woman made clear, preservationists seemed to believe that Indians could not be trusted with their own objects.[27] Likewise, Indians could not teach themselves the art of pottery making but had to be instructed by white experts.

Preservationists did not just seek to instruct Indians to produce what they deemed the most "authentic, traditional" Indian arts and crafts. They also believed that the purchasers of Indian art—mostly white women—must be educated away from buying "trinkets" and "curios." Mary Austin spoke of the necessity of "the re-education of the American public in taste and in the technical appreciation of handcraft." Austin identified this appreciation as a particular ability of women. "There is nothing inately [sic] improbable in the descendants of women who could name and discriminate between forty and fifty designs of handpieced quilts," Austin wrote, "learning to evaluate at sight the fifteen or twenty types of Indian pottery made in their country, the four or five types of blanket." To accomplish this education of consumers, some Indian art patrons, such as Amelia Elizabeth White, opened their own stores to compete with the traders who more likely featured "curios" and "trinkets."[28] Eileen Boris has commented that two segments existed within the broader arts and crafts movement in America—one focused on transforming the nature of labor and attacking commercialization and the factory system, the other intent on improving taste. In New Mexico, preservationists in the Indian arts and crafts movement, though disdainful of modernization, became almost solely focused on the latter intent.[29]

The two-fold effort of preservationists to dictate both authenticity and taste can be seen in a letter written in 1940 by three women of the NMAIA to their fellow members, decrying "a digression from the traditional style of Indian painting." The women accompanied their letter with "visual graphic proof," a collection of paintings done by Indian artists as evidence that "Indian painting is being led to conform to other standards than its own." The women juxtaposed "examples of good and bad Indian artwork" by the same artist on each page. Featuring two paintings by Ma-Pe-Wi, a Zia Pueblo Indian, the NMAIA women wrote that "the upper picture [of a dance ceremonial] was painted without outside suggestions or guidance. Its beauty is due to the artist's natural feeling for space and design." The lower picture by Ma-Pe-Wi, painted for the Education Division of the U.S. Office of Indian Affairs for "The Papago Indians of Arizona," offended the women's aesthetic sensibilities because "we see realism, perspective, shading. We see billowing clouds in place of sacred cloud symbols. . . . It lacks beauty . . . because [the artist] has tried to imitate a 'school' of painting in which he is not at home."[30]

In contrasting the good and bad Indian artwork of two Navajo painters, the NMAIA women asserted that "Indians paint naturally from memory not from models or landscape" and that Indians have a "natural and intuitive feeling for dignity and grace and rhythm [that is] attained in contradiction to the white man's method. There is no perspective and some of the figures are out of scale, but the result is beautiful, and good art, and good Indian Art." Further, the women asserted that Indians have an "instinct for fine spacing and composition." They objected to teachers of Indian arts and government bureaucrats who had "insufficient appreciation of the subtle difference between true and mongrel Indian art" and who made "no allowance for the differences between Indians and white men in thinking and traditional concepts." The women of the NMAIA hoped to remedy this "tragedy" of mongrelized Indian art by both educating the BIA and the public about "true" Indian art and by promoting those artists who remained true to their "racial talents."[31] The purpose of their letter, in fact, was to raise money to prevent the "mongrelization" of Indian art.

The dual purposes of preservationists to educate both Indians and white Americans also merged in their sponsorship of Indian fairs. Here white judges gave prizes for the best Indian products, alerting both the Indians and their white customers to "high-quality" art. The fairs reinforced the hierarchy of authenticity that preservationists had established. "Prizes are offered in all classes for traditional forms," the Arts and Crafts Committee of the NMAIA advertised. "In addition, smaller prizes are offered for adaptations of Indian material and handicraft to modern usage. But strictly non-Indian designs such as flags, lodge emblems, etc. will not be considered."[32] Judges also awarded cash prizes to "the Indian woman wearing the most attractive and complete costume characteristic of her Pueblo" and granted free admission to the fair to "Indians wearing something characteristically Indian."[33] Through this type of offer, the preservationists made a mighty effort to make sure the fairs only featured "authentic" Indians. Amelia White wrote to Mike Kirk, a trader who organized the Gallup Inter-Tribal Ceremonial each year: "[L]ast year I thought [the Ceremonial] one of the most beautiful and interesting things I had ever seen. Do confine it to primitive Indians. The so-called educated ones, like the Princess and Pablo Abeita get to be rather tiresome."[34]

As can be seen in the organizing and judging of fairs, the Indian arts and crafts movement proved to be one means whereby those women who had come to New Mexico after World War I attempted to enforce their vision of Indianness. White interest in Indian art paralleled white patronage of Harlem Renaissance writers. As David Levering Lewis has written, the white presence served as a "benevolent censor, politely but pervasively setting the outer limits of creative boundaries." Dean MacCannell argues that a white value on authenticity may have a very negative effect on native cultures. With such a value, one "can only conclude that most art is not authentic and that most formerly traditional people live inauthentic lives." White tourists thus dismissed most native peoples as "victims" of development and modernization.[35]

Preservationists in the arts and crafts movement have gained all the attention, but another wing also existed in the movement, against whom the preservationists constantly fought. This group conceived of art production as a means of fully assimilating Native Americans, providing them with the income that would "uplift" them out of their "degraded," "backward" lives and allow them to live as modern Americans. Such a view is evident in the title of an address by a BIA agent at the opening of the First Annual Southwest Indian Fair and Indian Arts and Crafts Exhibit in 1922. The agent called his speech "Story of Indian Is Story of Unparalleled Progress Upward." Many assimilationists in the arts and crafts movement shared the belief of one anthropologist of the cultural evolutionary strain who observed that the "making of pottery [is] the stepping-stone from savagery to barbarism."[36]

This new belief in promoting Indian art as uplift represented a significant departure from the past. In the late nineteenth century, although the BIA tentatively approved efforts to promote Indian arts and crafts as a means to industrialize Indians, it quickly shelved this solution to the so-called Indian problem, believing that it would encourage Indians to remain savage. The BIA had also opposed Indian participation in entertainment enterprises, such as Buffalo Bill's

Wild West Show, in which they reenacted their "traditional" way of life.[37] By the mid-1920s, however, many female moral reformers came to believe that promoting Indian art could elevate the Indians to "civilization." For example, in 1925 Clara True attempted to uplift Pueblo girls by "reviving" Indian embroidery, a craft Pueblo women had never pursued. As a means of "bettering" their condition, True also attempted to get Pueblo men to build old Spanish furniture that "carries out Indian design and decoration."[38]

As can be seen by True's efforts, "uplifters" in the arts and crafts movement were not so much concerned with reviving a "traditional" and "authentic" craft as with supplying the Pueblos with a viable means of making a living. They differed from the preservationists in that they supported the use of Indian designs on non-Indian items. Many of these women worked for the BIA, which promoted "embroidery of house furnishings and dress accessories as well as . . . native handicrafts." In a BIA report on "The Use of Indian Design in Government Schools," the author explained to BIA home-economics teachers that "geometric Indian designs offer effective motifs for dress trimmings, pocketbooks embroidered in wool, hooked rugs, and for hand-woven squares and bags." The author added that "for place cards, greeting and announcement cards, lamp shades, bedspreads, pillows, book covers, and in countless other ways the Indian designs may be used to give pleasure to the girls and their friends and to . . . make a contribution to the cultural life of the Indian child."[39] Preservationists in the movement deemed such items "atrocities."

Although the uplifters were not concerned that Indians should make only traditional Indian forms with traditional Indian designs, they did insist that only Indians should make Indian arts and crafts. For example, T. F. McCormick, superintendent of the Northern Pueblos Agency, made it known to Cleto Tafoya, a Santa Clara Indian who opened a curio shop at the Puyé Cliff Dwellings, that he could only sell "strictly Indian made articles and no imitation, whatever, as such business as this would ruin the Indians." The assimilationists did not care if Indians produced ashtrays, candlesticks, and other "curios" for tourists as long as Indians, not nonnative peoples, produced them. Their concern was not for enforcing some notion of authentic tradition but for ensuring that Indians benefited from producing their own goods.[40]

Although some promoters of Indian arts and crafts fell strictly into one wing or another of the movement, many members wavered between support for preservation of "Indianness" and a desire to see Indians assimilate. Stella Atwood of the General Federation of Women's Clubs (GFWC), for example, had defended Pueblo dances, but she nevertheless conceived of arts and crafts as a means of uplift. "If we do not help [Indians on reservations] to help themselves they will

be a race of paupers and derelicts," Atwood asserted. As much as she tried to enforce her notion of Indian tradition on the young painters in her studio, Dorothy
Dunn and the Santa Fe Indian School conceived of art that would both preserve
and uplift Indian culture. The school's 1935–36 Annual Announcement declared that "the school seeks to . . . show [the children] that [their] culture is appreciated, valued, respected and honored. Then, it is hoped, the students will
build their lives upon what they or their people have, rather than to abandon it
without first securing an adequate substitute. At the same time, it is desired that
they will borrow from white civilization those things which offer improvement,
and which can be adapted to their lives after leaving school."⁴¹

Elizabeth DeHuff, for all her belief in an authentic style of Indian painting
and an innate artistic sensibility in Indians, also believed that art could serve as
uplift. In her 1926 portrayal of Maria Martinez, DeHuff depicted pottery as the
salvation of Martinez: "A few years ago Marie [sic] Martinez and her husband,
Julian, were living embodiments of 'Lo, the poor Injun.'" At that time the Martinezes lived in a "two-room adobe hut"; but "now they are living in a modern
four-room house" with furniture and driving a Dodge sedan. "Ceramics
wrought the fairy tale transformation," DeHuff believed. DeHuff remarked
that Maria Martinez, "by her skill, has raised herself above the level of her
Pueblo sisters. She is an Oriental aristocrat of quiet dignity, modest and gra-
cious, and possessed of childlike reticence."⁴² DeHuff's portrayal of Martinez
conveys both the romanticism with which antimodern feminists often imbued
Pueblo women and the commitment to the uplift of Indian women more common to female moral reformers.

Given their opposing views of Pueblo artists and the purpose of promoting
arts and crafts, preservationists and uplifters in the Indian arts and crafts movement often clashed with one another. This was most apparent in 1933 at the Indian Fair in Shiprock, New Mexico, when a "serious conflict" erupted between
the two judges of the fair. The Southwest Indian Fair Committee (which became
the Arts and Crafts Committee of the NMAIA in 1934) appointed one judge; the
BIA appointed the other. "The result of the natural disagreement between the
two groups of judges is confusing to the Indians," wrote the Southwest Committee. "The first prize for a native wool pillow top was given to a realistic reproduction of Shiprock with the words 'Shiprock, N.M. 1933.'" To prevent a repeat of
what the preservationists considered an appalling event, the Southwest Committee desired to have complete control of the judging in the future. The division between those who saw art as uplift and those who saw it as preservation
even split the IAF, an organization more identified with preservation than uplift.
Apparently, according to Kenneth Chapman, some "progressive" members,

much to the dismay of "conservatives," desired more art education, fieldwork, and sales rather than the pure collecting and displaying of pottery and other artwork. Interestingly, Chapman posed the conflict as one between "progressives" and "conservatives," the same terms white patrons used for factions within the pueblos.[43]

Two main issues divided the feminist preservationists from the moral uplifters in the Indian arts and crafts movement—tourism and their respective views of Indian women. Preservationists concluded that pottery production in many pueblos had "degenerated [due] to the production of cheap souvenirs for tourists." When "the Indian potter makes what the trader tells her the white man wants," Bunzel asserted, "she makes abominations like candle-sticks and contorted vases." Catering to white tourists had led to what preservationists dreaded most: "factory methods" that produced the "worst possible workmanship."[44] Art patrons lamented that many art critics did not even know that Indian art existed, because they had only seen "the endless array of ash trays, candle sticks, swastikas, pillow tops, and other atrocities . . . which confront the average traveler in Indian country." As Mabel Dodge Luhan declared, "I'd hate to have these Indians get recognition! Why, it would be the end of them!"[45] "So, we've saved the Pueblos for Fred Harvey," commented Alice Corbin Henderson wryly. These women and others believed that tourism would irrevocably alter the religious life of the Pueblos. Anthropologist Elsie Clews Parsons predicted that religious kiva groups would "become mere clubs—vaudeville dance groups perhaps."[46]

Though members of the preservationist wing of the Indian arts and crafts movement purported to detest tourism, they did countenance and even encourage some commercialization of Indian art. Bunzel believed she would find the most "authentic" pottery in pueblos such as Zuni, where it was still made "primarily for household use within the village." Nevertheless, Bunzel asserted, "the stagnation and inferiority of the art [at Zuni] has made it advisable to include surveys of villages where commercial success has stimulated new and interesting developments." Bunzel maintained that among the Hopis, the old style was "cramped" and "sterile." She believed that "through some such [commercial] stimulus it may yet be possible to revive ceramic art in those villages where it is nearing extinction through its own barrenness."[47] Bunzel reveals here that she and other preservationists did not reject all commercialization so much as they sought to control and direct it away from "cheap souvenirs" to tasteful art objects. In her use of the sexual metaphors of sterility and barrenness, Bunzel also suggested a correlation between the loss of pottery skill and the loss of women's reproductive power. In supporting a pottery "revival," she reinforced the notion that pottery production could preserve women's traditional role in Pueblo society.

Other preservationists seemed to be unaware of the contradictions between their disdain for mass tourism and participation in the commercialization of Indian art. When Mabel and Tony Luhan visited a Mexican home, Mabel spotted an old chest and wanted to buy it. She wrote that Tony could not understand why she wanted the old chest; he wanted a new one, as did other Indians and Mexicans. Mabel commented that "that is how, here in this valley, we are shifting things around, and exchanging values." Interestingly, Mabel saw the desire of Indians and Mexicans who wanted new chests as part of their developing materialism, a white value. She saw her own desire for an old Mexican chest and her ability to purchase it not as materialism and as a step toward the commercialization of folk cultures, but as a value associated with Indianness.[48] In the 1930s promoters of Indian arts and crafts managed to market Indian goods successfully at Macys in New York City and Marshall Fields in Chicago. They saw their efforts, however, as separate from and above "cheap" tourism. Supposedly, Macys handled "Southwest Indian crafts in such a manner [that] it will meet the approval of lovers of the Indian arts and all those who deplore the present cheapening trend in the manufacture of these products which has been brought about by the tourist market and other urges toward standardization and quantity production."[49]

Preservationists insisted on what they believed to be the tasteful display and marketing of Indian wares. They wished not only to promote what they thought were authentic Indian arts but also to preserve for themselves the special possession of Indian arts and crafts. They seemed to believe that owning expensive, handmade Indian arts heightened their status in an increasingly standardized society. Cheap imitations would mean that any person, no matter of what social class, could masquerade as a member of the elite. Mary Austin captured this sentiment best when she declared, "[E]ven the people who come to stare [at Taos Pueblo] . . . remain to retrieve their own subtly emphasized unimportance, if by no better means than the purchase of innumerable badly chosen souvenirs."[50] As antimodernists, feminists in the Indian arts and crafts movement might have developed a critique of work and the factory system in modern society. Instead, their support for Indian arts and crafts took more the form of fetishism and the commodification of Indian objects for an elite market. Unwittingly, antimodern feminists in this movement promoted the very modernization of society that they condemned.[51]

Despite their desire to prevent, or at least control, tourism, the preservationists could not stem the tide that engulfed the Southwest. Business enterprises as well as individual promoters in the Southwest also contributed immensely to increasing interest in the region and its "exotic" peoples. As explored in chapter 1, Charles Lummis and Edgar Hewett served as boosters for the region while the Santa Fe Railway and the Fred Harvey Company accelerated the growing romanticization of the region through their advertising campaigns, tours of Indian sites, and establishment of an Indian department to market Indian arts and crafts. Even the efforts of preservationists to tell the world about the Pueblos and to promote Indian arts and crafts had raised nationwide interest in the Pueblos. When Mary Austin returned from Santa Fe to New York with Indian wares, she found, "[E]verybody is crazy about my things, and already they have 'pried' . . . most of my rings off me. I gave away two jars I brought with me last time, and could give away a barrel full."[52]

Even before arts and crafts aficionados consciously sought to distribute Indian arts and crafts in Macys and Marshall Fields, department stores in big cities helped to fuel interest in the Southwest and its "exotic" inhabitants. Historian William Leach has found that in the first two decades after the turn of the century New York department stores capitalized on the growing vogue of the Indian and other "primitives" to sell new fashions and home furnishings. Before World War I an Oriental theme proved to be the most popular merchandising theme. Between 1915 and 1920 Rodman Wanamaker peddled a Mayan motif in purses, hats, cushions, and parasols. Wanamaker's fashion show in New York City included framed pictures that showed the treasures of Mayan civilization and posed "real" Indian women near the pictures.

Leach also notes the significant degree of cooperation between merchandisers and museum collectors. Stewart Culin, the curator of the Brooklyn Museum and a collector of Indian artifacts throughout the Southwest and northern California, routinely supplied fashion shows with folk artifacts from around the world. In 1925 he acted as an art consultant to the Palace of Fashion Exhibit.[53] Around 1920 Mary Austin told Mabel Dodge that she was collaborating on a book on Indian design with a woman from Tiffany's, an expert in "Oriental" goods.[54] The department store's efforts met with success. In 1931, as part of the promotion for the Indian Tribal Arts Exposition, a journalist observed, "[T]here is a growing vogue for the use of all-American, or Indian, tribal art products for interior decorations in American homes." The reporter continued, "Certainly you can achieve a most picturesque study, play room, living room, children's den or the coziest kind of a collegiate bedroom by using Indian rugs, pottery, baskets and wall hangings."[55]

Other parts of the country wanted not merely to bring Indian objects to their department stores but also to display the Indians themselves. Beginning in the

1880s, national and international fairs sought "real" Indians to lure visitors. The BIA and fair promoters often differed over the best representation of the Indian. Desirous of justifying their mission, the BIA wished to depict the Americanized, boarding-school-educated Indian who had "risen" out of his condition. Fair promoters, by contrast, wanted to portray the adventurous "savage." At the World's Columbian Exposition held in Chicago in 1893, the BIA assumed responsibility for presenting "civilized Indians" in a model Indian school while promoters hired anthropologists to develop ethnological and archaeological presentations. The anthropological exhibit included a camp where representatives of various Indian tribes demonstrated their aboriginal lifestyles. In 1904 the Louisiana Purchase Exposition in St. Louis further institutionalized this "before and after" approach to Indians. Congress appropriated forty thousand dollars for the construction of an Indian building, one side of which contained "old Indians" demonstrating their traditional crafts, while the other part housed Indian schoolchildren. In the "old" section, Maria and Julian Martinez demonstrated their pottery-making techniques; Geronimo himself signed autographs for a fee and sold bows and arrows. Despite the BIA's intentions, the "traditional" side of the Indian building proved more alluring to fair visitors than did the school.[56]

Both antimodern feminists and female moral reformers also participated in promoting tourism. In the 1930s Clara True wrote a series of articles detailing New Mexico's many wonders. Although she had once berated "traditional" Pueblo culture, now she celebrated it as picturesque and quaint. True remarked that tourists "never forget the peace of the artistic community" of San Ildefonso and declared that the Puyé Cliff Dwellings just outside Santa Clara Pueblo offered "a spiritual experience." In a 1938 article True described her Santa Clara Indian guide as a "faithful old chap who had learned the mountains like a book during twenty-five years of sheepherding. His kind is rapidly passing out of the Indian picture, giving way to supposedly superior tribesmen brought up in classrooms." Ironically, True, who had once served as a BIA schoolteacher, now seemed to ridicule the assimilation endeavor. In the poem "Toast for New Mexico" True even adopted her arch enemies' romantic viewpoint toward the Indians. In one stanza, she toasted

> To Red Men unhurried,
> To broncos uncurried,
> To peasants unworried
> In youth or in age.

Despite her disdain for the sexual antics of the clowns, or *koshare*, during Pueblo dances, by 1925 Clara True was collaborating on a book about New Mex-

ico to be called "Koshare Land," the cover of which featured an old Indian ceremonial. True hoped to have Fred Harvey distribute it. When it came to promoting tourism in the region, True was not above using the very symbols of Indian
religion she had professed to abhor.[57] Had True's hard-line assimilationist
stance mellowed with age, or had she become less averse to Pueblo religion and
culture once she realized the profits to be made from marketing the region and
its people? Perhaps True saw no contradiction between "uplifting" Pueblo Indians and commodifying Pueblo tradition; by capitalizing on their ethnicity, she
reasoned, Pueblo Indians might uplift themselves.

In 1921 antimodern feminist Erna Fergusson and her friend Ethel Hickey, a
former University of New Mexico professor, profited from and reinforced the
new interest in the Southwest through the formation of a company called Koshare Tours. Born and raised in New Mexico, Fergusson had received her bach-
elor of arts degree at the University of New Mexico and her master's degree in
history at Columbia before traveling in Europe. During World War I she served
as the field director for the Red Cross in New Mexico. Koshare Tours brought
tourists (Fergusson called them "dudes") in seven-passenger sedans from the
Santa Fe Railway to points of interest in New Mexico, mainly Pueblo villages
and old Indian ruins. In 1926, due to Fergusson's great success, the Fred Harvey
Company purchased her company, renaming the venture Indian Detours.[58]

Young women served as the guides, or "couriers," for Fergusson's dudes.
Fergusson's brand of tourism offered a new career opportunity to women in the
West. In contrast to the image of the Harvey Girl, who "dressed in black shoes
and stockings, plain black dresses. . . , and a heavily starched white apron,"
Erna Fergusson's couriers cultivated more of an adventurous, autonomous style
as "new women" of the West. Early couriers wore riding britches, men's shirts,
ties, cowboy hats, leather gloves, and high, laced-up boots. Since this attire
shocked some of her dudes, Fergusson later changed the courier uniform to a
skirt with a walking pleat, Navajo-style velveteen shirts with a silver concho
belt, a squash-blossom necklace, tan stockings, and walking shoes or boots. Fergusson insisted that her couriers be intelligent, well-educated, knowledgeable
of New Mexico, capable of speaking Spanish, and socially graceful.[59] Although
Fergusson carved out a niche for the new woman in New Mexico, she advertised
her business by touting traditional feminine traits associated with domesticity.
Fergusson claimed to give her guests a "personal touch." "That is why I think
such a business as ours is more successful conducted by women than by men,"
Fergusson asserted. "Women make more of the little things which mean so
much than men do."[60] Even Mabel Dodge Luhan, who longed for the days when
the San Geronimo Feast Day at Taos Pueblo had not yet been "taken up by the

'Lions Club' in Taos village for purposes of commerce and exploitation," got in on the tourist craze. In the late 1920s she and Tony Luhan set up their adobe home as a "dude ranch" and hired Fergusson to run it. In the spring of 1929 Tony Luhan hired himself and his Cadillac out to take tourists through pueblos and Hispano villages.[61]

Department stores, fairs and expositions, the Santa Fe Railway, the Fred Harvey Company, and Indian Detours all created markets for Indian arts and crafts. The new portrayal of the exotic in New Mexico and the ethnic tourism it fueled also brought more white Americans to Pueblo dances. The Snake Dance of the Hopis, for example, became one of the most famous tourist attractions in the Southwest in the late 1920s, attracting thousands of visitors a year to witness the ceremony in which dancers carried live rattlesnakes in their mouths. Fergusson captured the way in which white tourists had transformed the Snake Dance:

> The mob gathering slowly, crushingly, in the little plaza, bulging against the inadequate rope which has been strung along the edge; small boys squirming through, fat women sweating unpleasantly, men coatless, fanning themselves with straw hats, Hopis selling the same roof-space again and again, collecting before delivery, and then calmly disappearing when rival parties of swearing, jangling whites arrive to claim their "reserved space." Men boosting fat old ladies on to roofs, occasional prehistoric beams giving way and tumbling a struggling mass of human beings into dusty debris, unpleasant, but soft enough to prevent broken bones. Movie stars in white veils, women novelists picturesquely distributing peacock-feathers among good-looking young Hopis, tall drivers in international costumes of English riding-boots and breeches, cowboy hats, and Russian blouses. Bitter complaint from women without parasols against women with parasols. So the white man comes to see the Snake-dance.

Once spectators of the "erotic exotic," whites had become part of the spectacle itself. Formerly haunted by only a few curious moral reformers, anthropologists, or writers, the Pueblo dances now attracted hordes of tourists. As one travel writer observed, "[I]ncreasing travel throughout the Southwest from April to October now ensures an audience for almost any public ceremonial in any village."[62]

Though some white women, such as Mabel Dodge Luhan and Alice Corbin Henderson, lamented the commercialization of Indian dances, many others supported Indian dancing as a commercial endeavor. Ironically, although Clara True and other opponents of Indian dances objected to dances when they were performed in the context of secret religious ceremonies, they wholeheartedly supported them when performed under their auspices for commercial purposes. In 1924 True sponsored a dance by so-called progressive Indians to raise money for their trip to the GFWC meeting in Los Angeles, where, ironically, they planned to challenge the support of the GFWC for the preservation of Pueblo dances. In 1925 the progressives gave another dance—"the most beautiful old Indian dance ever given here." True asserted approvingly, however, that "the Indians gave the dance not as a ceremony in which they participated from religious motives, but as a 'show,' just as we would give a Martha Washington ball."[63] Assimilationists had departed radically from their earlier stance against the commercialization of Indian culture. Rather than preventing the Indians from progressing, Indian participation in reenacting Indian customs could now further the "uplift" of the race.

By the late 1920s many antimodern feminists had also begun to support the commercialization of Indian dances. In her book on the ceremonials of Southwest Indians, Fergusson described the way in which Indian dances were being commercialized: "Various shows in New Mexico are featuring Indian dances. At first the old men of all the tribes were opposed to having their ceremonials presented away from the pueblos or off the reservations. They quite naturally dread to see the commercializing of their religious rituals, they hate the effect of applause on their young men, and they resent all change. . . . Their resistance is slowly breaking down, however, and it may be that giving the dances for white audiences will prove the means of perpetuating them as an art form when their significance as a religious form has unhappily passed away." Though Fergusson bemoaned the "passing away" of the religious significance of Indian dances, she nevertheless saw a future for Indian dances as a tourist attraction. Perhaps rationalizing her own role as a tourist promoter, Fergusson emphasized, "[I]t is important that interested white people should help [the Indians] to preserve their dances as an art form when they no longer serve as a religious form." Further, Fergusson posited, "[L]ately, with the increasing interest in Indian affairs, white people are showing a disposition to assist the Indian to preserve his dances in their purity."[64] Commercializing the dances, in Fergusson's view, served as a means to preserve the dances "in their purity." Fergusson's comments reveal that for some antimodern feminists and their male peers, it was the form of Indian dancing, and not its meaning, that mattered.

Indeed, these feminists encouraged the performance of dances as a means to enhance the fairs and ceremonials where Indians sold their arts and crafts. In a 1931 letter to all the Pueblo governors, Margaret McKittrick of the NMAIA informed them: "[W]e will have a place [at the upcoming Indian Fair] where the Indians can dance, and we will have places where people can sit and watch. We will take tickets at the gate and the money that people pay at the door will be divided among all the Indians that dance, but we will not pay anybody to come in and dance. They must come in and dance, and if they put on good dances people will pay a lot of money to come and see them." Charitably, McKittrick added, "We will not charge anything for helping the Indians put on their dances like this." At this same annual fair, white organizers offered prizes "for perfection of dance form, and for traditional accuracy of costume."[65] Here was a conception of Indian dances upon which both female moral reformers and antimodern feminists could agree and from which they could both benefit—as an art form commercialized for its entertainment value for white tourists. Although uplifters and some antimodern feminists had initially divided over the issue of tourism, the two sides eventually seem to have reached an accommodation. Although antimodern feminists still sought to promote "high-quality" Indian art, they also began to participate more actively in the tourist trade.

The two wings of the movement also divided over the nature of Pueblo women artists. Feminist preservationists promoted Indian arts and crafts, in part, because they saw artistic production as a means to preserve what they believed to be women's ideal role in Pueblo society. Many feminists who came to New Mexico after World War I nostalgically idealized the Pueblo home as a place where women still wielded power and engaged in meaningful productive work with one another. This can be seen in Ruth Bunzel's portrait of the Pueblo potter. "'Pottery bees' are a common feature of Hopi life," wrote Bunzel. "If a woman sits down in her front room to decorate pottery it generally follows that a relative or neighbor who also has pottery to decorate will bring over her work and join her. Three or four women will frequently gather in this way and gossip merrily over their work."[66] Bunzel's choice of the phrase "pottery bee" suggests that she associated Pueblo women's work with a time in white American culture when women also engaged in shared home production through participation in quilting bees. Other observers also celebrated the Pueblo woman artist's productive role in the home. A subheading in an early 1930s article on Maria Martinez marveled that "Women Work in Own Homes." The same article featured a portrait of Tonita Peña: "She is surrounded by children. The youngest one was strapped to Tonita's back most of last summer while she was painting. . . . She works at a tiny table by a window. Her paints and paper are there, and she goes to it when she is not busy with other things, just as our mothers pick up the socks that have to be darned." Antimodern feminists idealized the life of a Pueblo woman artist, a life that combined domesticity with creativity and a career.[67]

Modern women, antimodern feminists believed, had lost the possibility and the inclination to seamlessly blend home, art, and work. Mabel Morrow contrasted the Indian woman artist with the modern white woman. "With the Indian woman, we find a true art situation," Morrow wrote, "where art is interwoven with her life and every activity of her life, and not something superficial." With a not-so-subtle dig at modern women, Morrow added, "It is truly a wonder that the primitive Indian woman found time for the consideration of the beautiful, since she had no electric mixers, gas ranges, or canned tomatoes."[68] As Morrow's comment reveals, antimodernists believed that modern women had unfortunately turned from productive work in the home—quilting bees, perhaps—to the consumption of new labor-saving devices and products. In so doing they had lost the artistry that supposedly accompanied home production.

Antimodern feminists hoped that such a transformation would not occur in the pueblos. Bunzel and other white women lamented that at many pueblos, few Indian women would "now take the trouble to make what is required for their household needs." Instead, they either bought manufactured tins or purchased pottery from one of the few Pueblo women who engaged in this occupation on a "semi-professional basis." Bunzel and many other arts and crafts aficionados believed that boarding schools' Americanization programs had stifled young women's interest in pottery. As Bunzel stated, "Younger women whose command of English was satisfactory were mostly too completely Americanized to practice native arts."[69] Thus, Bunzel and other preservationists located the perpetuation of pottery production in the most traditional, least Americanized Pueblo women.

In contrast, female moral reformers characterized the Pueblo artist as a morally upright pioneer among her people, who through her industry would "uplift" herself and eventually the rest of her people. Clara True encouraged Pueblo Superintendent Crandall to send several potters "of good character and with skill in clay working" from Santa Clara Pueblo to the Louisiana Purchase Exposition in St. Louis in 1904. True equated "skill in clay working" with "good character." Conversely, in True's view, Pueblo women who did not live up to her moral standards also failed to make good pottery. She told Crandall, "[T]here are plenty of women who would go [to St. Louis] but they are not needed here nor elsewhere, as they are idle, dirty loafers who wouldn't make pottery worth the name."[70] It is worth noting that True's image of Pueblo women artists did not put them in the context of home, but rather in the commercial arena of the 1904 exposition. To uplifters, Pueblo women artists were thus women who were moving into the modern era.

As in the dance controversy, white women seem to have used the arts and crafts movement as a forum for articulating and debating their competing visions of gender and sexuality in modern America. Women in both wings of the movement endowed Indian women artists with their rival visions. Uplifters' image of the Pueblo artist mirrored their own ideal of womanhood and their own desires for inclusion in American society. They saw Indian women (and men) as unfairly segregated from modern America. Arts and crafts could help Indian women, indeed all Indians, to become full members of American society. Morally upstanding, the gifted Indian woman artist could, according to female uplifters, overcome her supposed "backwardness" to uplift herself into modern American society. Not coincidentally, female moral reformers also saw themselves as segregated from the mainstream of modern American life but able perhaps to attain integration within that society through their work for moral uplift.[71] It was small wonder that women such as True and Dissette identified assimilation into modern American life as their goal for Native Americans; it was also their own ambition for white women.

In contrast to uplifters, white women in the preservationist wing represented Indian women artists not as morally upstanding pioneers who sought to assimilate into modern America, but as the most traditional members of their villages who found satisfaction in the home and in the daily round of domestic duties. Preservationists' veneration of Pueblo women's domesticity reveals the tension that developed for these women between their antimodernism and their vision of womanhood. Although they invented public roles for themselves in modern America, they condemned the very society from which they sought recognition. In their portrayals of Pueblo culture, preservationists sought to reconcile their competing values. While they envisioned powerful roles for women, they also looked back to a time when the center of power and influence supposedly rested with women in the home and not with men in the office or the assembly hall. In their idealizations of what they believed to be Pueblo women's traditional roles, Austin, Luhan, and other preservationist women seemed to want to recover a period in which women supposedly gained power through their roles in the home. Many white women who sojourned or settled in New Mexico after World War I promoted Indian arts and crafts in part because they saw artistic production as a means to preserve what they believed to be women's ideal role in Pueblo society.

White women in the arts and crafts movement also sought to establish a new public space in which to operate and gain social mastery. Through their own quest for moral authority at the turn of the century, female reformers had hoped to (and to some extent did) participate more readily in the public life of the nation. In the first decades of the twentieth century, however, moral reformers found themselves and their quest for female moral authority increasingly under attack by people such as Austin and Luhan. The promotion of Indian arts and crafts constituted a new way for white women to gain some measure of public authority in modern America. This time that authority would be based on other supposedly "feminine" attributes—women's increasing association with consumerism and their experience in the decoration of their own homes.[72] To moral reformers, arts and crafts would serve not only to integrate Indian women into public life but also to grant white women a new form of cultural authority. The movement may also have served a similar purpose for antimodern feminists, who found little in the new ideology of women's sex expressiveness to grant them any cultural dominion.

To understand the ways that Pueblo women may have perceived their participation in the arts and crafts movement, we often must rely on the same sources that provide such ideal images of Pueblo women—the correspondence and promotional material that white patrons produced regarding Indian arts and crafts. Once in a while a Pueblo woman's own words surface in the historical record, but more often than not, Pueblo women's viewpoints and actions are filtered through white women's (and men's) writing. It is possible nevertheless to piece together some sense of how Indian women may have interpreted white women's efforts to promote Indian arts and crafts.

Indian women seem to have been quite indignant about many of the assumptions that white women brought to the arts and crafts movement. Some Pueblo potters objected to the preservationists' portrayal of pottery production as a dying or lost art that needed to be revived by whites. Maria Martinez made clear to her biographer, Alice Marriott, that making pots was alive and well at San Ildefonso long before whites became interested in reviving it. In a 1939 article Elizabeth DeHuff quoted a Pueblo woman as exclaiming, "I do not need nobody to teach me about pottery! . . . My grandmother teach me long ago!"[73] In an unpublished essay DeHuff also recounted an incident in which one summer a young white woman who had studied ceramics in the East came to live in a Pueblo village. She intended to teach Pueblo women how to make pots that would hold water without seepage. All summer long she gathered together the potters of the pueblo and taught them how to glaze their pots. According to De-Huff, "[T]he Indian women watched, followed instructions and made the glazed pottery." When the young ceramic artist left at the end of the summer, she congratulated herself on her "successful philanthropy." But "the Indian women—one and all—walked to the edge of the mesa and, with a cluck of disgust, hurled all of the glazed pots they had made over the precipice, breaking them into bits."[74] While outwardly seeming to accommodate the white woman,

Indian women appear to have resented deeply the white woman's assumptions that she knew better than they how to make pots.

Other native women artists contested preservationists' notions that they should avoid the tourist trade and make only the "highest quality" objects for an elite white market. Many white women art enthusiasts had also become involved in promoting "high-quality" Navajo rug making. After attending a conference on Navajo rug making sponsored by the Santa Fe Laboratory of Anthropology, Sarah Smith, a Navajo weaver, objected to the conference's suggestion that only very fine spinning yarn be used for weaving blankets. "It's this way," Smith explained. "[T]he Indians weave blankets only for their eats especially, than for their clothing. It will be very hard on those that live far away from the trading stores, they say it takes a year or two to finish one blanket like that. What if they run out of coffee or sugar and if they get hungry for meat what could they do, get to work and weave a blanket quick so they can sell it and get some coffee and sugar and meat or maybe a sack of flour and something else."[75] To the artists, the production of arts and crafts was more than a hobby. In an era in which farming was becoming increasingly difficult, it represented a primary means whereby Pueblo women helped to support their families and villages. In 1930 the sale of Indian arts and crafts accounted for about a quarter of the total income of Indians of the Southwest. In San Ildefonso Pueblo, home of Maria Martinez, income from arts and crafts was three times the income of all other sources combined.[76] Producing only for an elite market did not meet the needs of most Pueblo artists.

Many Indians also seem to have resented the practice of the IAF of collecting pots from their pueblos. As one patron recalled, "Some of them, some of the time, refused to sell some of their pottery." Even then, IAF collectors persisted in seeing Indians as irrational and childlike. "Argue with them? Tell them it was for their own good? Arguments are nothing when they fall against turquoise stopped ears." Other Indians drove hard bargains, attempting to get as high a price as they could for their pots when the IAF came collecting.[77] Some artists made subtle but pointed critiques of the IAF. When Kenneth Chapman asked Maria Martinez whether he could learn the designs of Pueblo pots and put them together in new ways, Martinez supposedly replied, "Why, Mr. Chapman, . . . you ought to do better than we can, because you have been taking all our old pottery away from us and making pictures of it, and then sending it away, and we can't remember any of the old designs."[78]

Rather than openly revealing their resentment of white patrons, some Indian artists found ways both to accommodate and to mock the value preservationists placed on authenticity and tradition. The black-on-black pottery that came to be identified as the authentic, traditional style of Maria Martinez and the San Il-defonso Indians originated in a disaster for Maria and her husband Julian. Maria told interviewer Alice Marriott that one day Julian put too much manure on the open fire where they fired their pottery. All the pots turned black. Disappointed that they had expended all this effort and ruined every pot, Julian and Maria stored the pots away. Soon, a trader came by, desiring more pots. Maria and Julian had not produced any new ones. When the trader persisted, Julian told him they did have some stored in the back, but they were very special. Maria added that they cost more. The trader liked the pottery, sold it immediately, and asked for more. Thereafter, Maria and Julian produced almost exclusively their black-on-black ware. Soon the Martinezes taught other San Il-defonso potters their secret. As revealed in the following conversation between Julian, Maria, and Maria's father, the Martinezes manipulated preservationists' desires for oldness, tradition, and authenticity. Maria told Julian that she wanted to make "some more of the new kind of bowls." He replied, "You mean the old kind." Maria's father quipped, "The new old kind." Maria concluded, "The kind the white people want."[79]

Martinez and other Pueblo artists seem also to have been skillful in appearing to embody preservationists' image of the home-staying, tradition-bound, Pueblo woman artist while turning the movement to their own ends and altering their own roles in Pueblo society. Feminist preservationists believed that traditional Pueblo gender norms accorded Pueblo women a degree of power and authority unknown in modern American culture. The Pueblo woman artist would thus conform to and reinforce these norms. By the turn of the twentieth century, gender norms and relations varied enormously from pueblo to pueblo. And within some pueblos, the role of women had become a contentious issue, as witnessed by the debate at Santa Clara in the 1920s over what type of work women should do. As in the larger American society, Pueblo gender roles and practices in the first several decades of the twentieth century were in flux.

Indian women who became potters or painters actually helped to create new notions of appropriate gender roles among their pueblos. In every pueblo it had been expected that girls would center their lives around domestic affairs. Through fulfilling this role, in fact, many Pueblo women had gained respect and a measure of authority.[80] Antimodern feminists saw art as an extension of Pueblo women's role in the home; yet some artists seemed to have eschewed a domestic role and used their art as an escape from, rather than as a complement to, their household duties. When Martinez became successful, she did not maintain her traditional ways of cooking over a fire. Instead, she purchased an iron cooking stove. Vital to both her own household economy and that of the pueblo, Martinez no longer had time for her customary household duties. Instead, she hired Mexican-American women to help her with her children and housework.[81] Neither did Tonita Peña view domestic responsibilities in the romantic light that antimodern feminists did. When asked why she liked to paint during all her spare moments, Peña replied, "Well, it's better than washing clothes, or taking care of children, or fighting with my husband."[82] Rather than helping them to preserve their supposedly fulfilling domestic roles, Martinez's and Peña's artistic careers liberated them to some extent from household chores.

Although Pueblo Indian women rarely ventured far from home, women who became artists were more likely to travel than their peers. Martinez, Peña, and other native women artists traveled extensively to fairs, expositions, and exhibits. The Navajo weaver Sarah Smith offers a view of what travel might have meant to women who were accustomed to staying in their villages all of their lives. After attending the Laboratory of Anthropology's conference on rug making in Santa Fe with other Navajo women, Smith wrote, "[W]e enjoyed our trip seeing places we never had seen before. . . . And also we like to look around in town, and I wish very much to look inside of the capital, I never seen it in my life, I just see the picture of it, I like to see it while we are near it, now."[83]

Traditionally, Pueblo women had also refrained from dealing with outsiders; this was men's assigned role. However, rather than relying on Pueblo men to market their pots, Pueblo women did it themselves. This may have been a result of the expectations of pottery consumers, who sought, after all, not just to buy a pot but to purchase a piece of ethnicity. Buying pottery from its supposed actual maker allowed consumers to feel a sense of authenticity and enhanced the value of Pueblo arts. In this process Pueblo women created a new role for themselves. Pueblo men's roles may have also shifted during this period. Some men, following Julian Martinez's lead, began to paint their wives' pottery, even though, up to that point, "men [hadn't] very often decorate[d] pottery."[84]

Rather than being resistant to change in their pueblos' gender norms, then, at least some women artists may have consciously reshaped these norms to suit the changing conditions of their lives. We have already seen how Maria Martinez subtly shifted away from a life centered around domesticity to a life that revolved around her vibrant artistic career. Martinez had exhibited a desire to break with female traditions from an early age. At age five, after selling and trading her mother's cheese to other villagers, her mother asked her if she liked to trade. Maria responded "yes" enthusiastically. "When I grow up," she told her mother, "I'm going to have a trading post of my own and sell things all the time." Her mother admonished her that she had better have a man to help her with that.[85] Martinez did pursue marriage and domesticity within the pueblo's norms as well as the woman's craft of pottery making, but she turned this craft into a lucrative enterprise that sustained her family and other pueblo families through difficult years.

The lives of Tonita Peña and Pablita Velarde also illustrate how some women who became artists may have reshaped Pueblo gender relations. Tonita Peña (or Quah Ah) was born in 1893 at San Ildefonso Pueblo, about ten years after Martinez. In day school at San Ildefonso, Peña first found encouragement to paint from her teacher. Peña's mother and younger sister died of the flu when she was twelve, and she was sent to live with her aunt, Martina Montoya, at Cochiti Pueblo. Her aunt taught her to make pottery while her uncle taught her to paint designs on it. Like Martinez, Peña attended St. Catherine's Indian School in Santa Fe. When she reached age fifteen, the Pueblo elders arranged for her marriage to Juan Chavez. After Peña bore two children, Chavez died. Rather than staying in the pueblo and looking immediately for a new husband, Peña left her children with one of their aunts so that she could return to St. Catherine's to finish her schooling.[86]

In 1913 the Pueblo elders again arranged a marriage for Peña, to Felipe Herrera, who worked in an iron oxide mine. While married to Herrera, Peña bore one son, finished her schooling, and continued painting. In 1920 her second husband died in a mining accident. In 1922 Peña married Epitacio Arquero, a farmer, and bore five more children from 1923 to 1935. Peña relied on supportive husbands and older children to shoulder some of the responsibilities of household work and child care while she pursued her artistic career. One white man who had lived with Peña's family off and on as a child remembered that "Tonita spent every bit of her free time painting . . . painting was her life."[87] In the 1920s her artwork became increasingly well known. She sold many of her works to art collectors and to the La Fonda Hotel in Santa Fe. In the 1930s she also taught art at the Santa Fe and Albuquerque Indian Schools.[88] While ostensibly fulfilling her expected role, Peña also generated new possibilities for herself and other Pueblo women.

Peña, in fact, inspired Pablita Velarde (or Tse Tsan) to take up painting as well. Velarde was born in 1918 at Santa Clara Pueblo. Her mother died at a young age from tuberculosis. Like Martinez and Peña, Velarde also attended St. Catherine's but later transferred to the Santa Fe Indian School in 1929 and graduated in 1935. She first met Peña at the Santa Fe Indian School, where Peña and other artists were painting murals on the school walls.[89] From a young age, Velarde preferred boys' chores to girls' domestic tasks and "sensed that the traditional women's role in the pueblo might be confining for her." When she attended the Santa Fe Indian School, she found her aversion to women's work reinforced by the school's domestic training programs. The examples of Tonita Peña and Maria Martinez, as well as art classes with Dorothy Dunn, gave her the courage to defy her pueblo's norms. According to Velarde, Peña's example and friendship gave Velarde "the inner strength" she needed "to dare the men to put me in my own place or let me go."[90] When Velarde was the only girl in Dunn's studio classes, she resented that the boys made fun of her and that "all they drew were boys and men horseback riding and dancing. They never showed women." With Dunn's encouragement, Velarde "drew nothing but women's activities." By Velarde's own account she remained an "independent woman" all her life. She married a white man and bore a daughter whom she named Helen, who also became an artist. According to Velarde, however, she never found the supportive husband that Peña had.[91] Velarde stayed away from Santa Clara for twenty years, only moving back in the 1960s.

Veering from the established path of one's culture is not without its difficulties for anyone, and for Martinez, Peña, and Velarde, it may have carried particularly painful consequences. At San Ildefonso, Martinez's success brought jealousy and spite from other women artists and may have even contributed to a split in the pueblo between the north and south sides. Martinez sought to mend relations with other women, in some instances signing their pottery so that they might sell it more readily to tourists seeking the famous Martinez ware. In the 1940s several members of Cochiti Pueblo objected to Tonita Peña's artwork, believing she had divulged tribal secrets through her paintings. But the governor of the Pueblo, Peña's husband Epitacio Arquero, successfully defended his wife, arguing that her paintings only depicted dancers and dances that could be seen by outsiders. Despite the quieting of protest, Peña thereafter painted only scenes that could not be construed as revealing tribal secrets. As for Velarde, once she returned to Santa Clara Pueblo, she found, according to Sally Hyer, that the "quick wit, gregariousness, and strong-willed personality that had helped her survive in the outside world were generally not viewed as appropriate female behavior at Santa Clara." Velarde also chafed at the Santa Clara rule that the children of Pueblo women and non-Pueblo men were not considered full members of the pueblo.[92]

By reshaping their pueblos' notions of women's place, these three Pueblo women artists did appear to conform more to the image of modern pioneers extolled by uplifters in the arts and crafts movement. Yet while Martinez, Peña, and Velarde adopted many of the trappings of modern America, they did not see themselves as uplifters or assimilationists. Instead, they integrated elements from both Pueblo and Anglo cultures (as well as Mexican culture). Martinez, for example, sought to incorporate new material acquisitions into her own system of cultural values. When she and Julian bought a new car, Julian painted Indian pottery designs on it. Maria told one of her interviewers, "That was the first car in the pueblo! . . . It was a black car, all black. I can see the designs Julian put on that car. He painted it all around just like pots. You be surprised what I do with that car. We take everybody who is sick. And we get food. We help everybody with that car."[93] Rather than conveying modernity and individual achievement with her new car, Martinez and her husband instead imbued their vehicle with values more associated with their pueblo. Likewise, Peña did not ultimately regard her work in the same manner as whites valued art. When she died, "her husband Epitacio gathered all of Tonita's personal things, including paintings, from the home and placed them in an old shed nearby on their property and set fire to the building and destroyed all of the contents."[94]

Scholars who study the effect of cultural contact on the gender relations of Native Americans often conclude that European and American influence undermined Indian women's power and authority within their tribes. These scholars argue persuasively that missionaries' efforts to replace the pantheon of male and female deities with a patriarchal God may also have corroded women's status in Native American societies. They also assert that drawing Indians out of their subsistence economies into a European and American cash economy often undermined women's control of resources within the tribe.[95] The effect of the arts and crafts movement on Pueblo women, however, reveals a more complex scenario. Whites in the movement, particularly preservationists, did try to define and control the production of and market for Indian arts and crafts to fit their own cultural needs. Yet Pueblo women artists did not sit idly by, passively producing pots; they, too, shaped the movement to accord with their own needs. Martinez especially seemed to artfully manipulate white desires for authenticity while fulfilling her own interests.

Prior to contact with Europeans, Pueblos had set their own standards of worth and esteem. First the Spanish and then Anglo-Americans introduced new ways of measuring status that added new layers to Pueblo society. As the Pueblos' traditional activities of subsistence farming became less viable, wage earning became an important source of authority within Pueblo society, in some cases undermining the status of those who did not earn wages. As men began to earn wages, women's roles may have declined in status;[96] but through their participation in the arts and crafts movement, women could also earn wages, oftentimes more than their menfolk, and could thus tap into new sources of power and authority.

Thus, for both Indian and white women, the arts and crafts movement fostered new possibilities for expanded roles and influence. Ironically, new feminist preservationists believed that promoting art production among Indian women would strengthen their roles in the home. Instead, arts and crafts undermined the Pueblo gendered division of labor and the meaning attached to that division. Antimodern feminists often wistfully emphasized the stark differences between Indian and modern white women. To them, Indian women still occupied an enviable position in the home, a place where their nonindustrial labor empowered them. White women, these feminists believed, had lost this power. Yet the arts and crafts movement actually served to blunt differences between Indian and white women. Through the movement and the tourism that accompanied it, more Indian women began to create a public, nondomestic role for themselves. Far from assimilating them, however, the commercialization of Pueblo culture fostered new cultural forms and a set of fresh strategies for both maintaining ethnic identity and integrating into the American economy.

Conclusion

In just a few decades the Pueblos had witnessed a remarkable reversal in the attitudes of many of the white women whom they encountered. Once seen by white, female moral reformers as backward, dirty, pagan, and in dire need of uplift, by the 1920s the Pueblos found themselves the objects of antimodern feminists' intense curiosity and admiration. Pueblo women, whom moral reformers had characterized as degraded by their men and by tradition, suddenly became elevated by antimodern feminists to the status of powerful women whose traditions embodied ideal gender relations. This metamorphosis in white women's attitudes was integrally linked to changes in white women's gender roles and relations. Many middle-class white women in the first decades of the twentieth century began to question women's quest for moral authority and its basis in the notion of female sexual purity. Instead, they called for female "sex expressiveness" and individual self-fulfillment. Some of these women also developed a critique of the technological modernization of American society. Many of these antimodern feminists came to settle in New Mexico during and after World War I and there became involved in transforming the image of the Pueblos, in defending their lands and religion, and in challenging the federal Indian policy of assimilation.

The attention of antimodern feminists yielded some real benefits to the Pueblos. Feminist concern helped some Pueblo Indians to recover land and water and to protect their existing resources. These white women also battled the government in order to protect Indian religious freedom and to improve the health care of the Pueblos. Their efforts contributed to the Indian New Deal, which, despite its shortcomings, reversed the land losses of the Dawes Act, institutionalized Indian self-government, and promoted Indian languages and arts and crafts in government schools. In particular, antimodern feminists' leadership and participation in the Indian arts and crafts movement opened up a valuable new means of earning a living for Pueblo artists, most of whom were women. Though not without problems, the attention of antimodern feminists, their male peers, and the tourist industry, as Alfonso Ortiz remarked, was "preferable to racial hate and genocide" and promoted Pueblo cultural survival.[1] Casting Indian culture as the dichotomous opposite of white American culture also afforded antimodern feminists (and, increasingly, Native Americans) a critical perspective on modern America.

The new romantic images that antimodern feminists helped to create, however, also proved to be problematic for the Pueblos. Antimodern feminists' desire to create an alternative to modern America led to a new reification of cultural difference. Through the Indian arts and crafts movement, they sought to freeze in time their notion of the "authentic," "traditional" Indian. By the 1930s these images became the predominant view of the public. The tourist industry deserves partial credit (or blame) for advancing this view. Despite antimodern feminists' distaste for tourism, tourist promoters designed their advertising campaigns around feminist notions of Pueblo Indians as ageless, changeless, primitive people. One tour brochure characterized New Mexico as "the home of the one unspoiled primitive people remaining in North America."[2] Another brochure declared that the Southwest "is at once the Last Frontier and the home of an ageless antiquity. In it the American reads his history in a few raw decades. . . . The rush of the 20th century disturbs little the slumberous content of the old Spanish-American towns. The Indian lives much as he did when Columbus sailed."[3]

Tourist promoters and travel magazines also built on antimodern feminist images of the traditional, domestic, home-staying, and modest Indian woman and juxtaposed her against the modern white American woman. Photographs for a 1938 *National Geographic* article on New Mexico illustrated this contrast. The article's photos posed young white women as coeds on the University of New Mexico campus, interspersed with young men, and as bathing beauties on the sands of Alamogordo. Its only pictures of nonwhite women showed Maria Martinez making pottery; Navajo women weaving rugs; a young Pueblo woman in her customary dress, standing on a ladder before an adobe building; two other traditionally dressed Pueblo women, one of whom carried a basket of provisions on her head; and a trio of Mexican women wearing their traditional garb.[4] This article perpetuated the antimodern feminists' notion that white women were modern, while nonwhite women were primitive. Interestingly, these photographs also portrayed white women in sexual terms as emblems of the new sexual mores but depicted nonwhite women as "traditional" and nonsexual. Antimodern feminists, as they celebrated the liberating potential of the new sexual mores, had once cast Pueblo Indian women as sexually emancipated models for the American new women. But their sexual relativism seemed to fade through the 1920s as they wrestled with the consequences of women's "sex expressiveness" without female control. Already by the end of the dance controversy in 1924, feminists had recast Pueblo Indian women as "modest" and "pure." Promotional articles for the Southwest thus reinforced antimodern feminists' images of Pueblo women and Pueblo life.

Such images could be confining and limiting, particularly to some Pueblo women. For example, under John Collier's Indian New Deal, which had so dramatically reversed the direction of education for Indian children, the program of education for Indian girls did not radically change. As Sally Hyer has noted, home economics "continued to be the cornerstone in the education of Indian girls." This situation led one former student at the Santa Fe Indian School to complain that she was not educated enough to find a good job. The only thing available to her was housework. When he framed his new agenda for Indian education, Collier may have relied on his former feminist colleagues' notions that Pueblo women's traditional role in the home conferred power and authority on them. Thus, Indian education during the New Deal, designed to celebrate and build upon native cultures, continued to stress a domestic role for women.[5]

The abundance and accessibility of antimodern feminists' writings about the Pueblos also tended to mute the voices of Pueblo women who sought to forge their own complex identities. At the turn of the century, these voices were barely audible, at least to whites, and few Pueblo women at the time left their written words as a record of their own perceptions. Occasionally, a Pueblo woman wrote a letter that has been preserved within the archives, or a white activist seems to have transcribed verbatim the words of a Pueblo woman. It was not until after World War II, however, that Pueblo women's perspectives became somewhat more accessible. These perspectives, of course, have been varied and contradictory. Polingaysi Qoyawayma believed the expected domestic role of a Hopi woman to be restrictive and unsatisfying. Helen Sekaquaptewa seemed to fulfill Hopi gender expectations happily but supplemented them with wage work. On the surface Maria Martinez appeared to conform to Pueblo domesticity but actually avoided domesticity and pursued a stimulating artistic career, as did Tonita Peña.

Some Pueblo women today emphasize that they do enjoy an enviable position in relation to other, non-Pueblo women and to Pueblo men. Rina Swentzell, an architect and member of Santa Clara Pueblo, remarks, "[T]he women in [Pueblo] communities are really strong because they are still part of the home, and the home has really never disintegrated in the communities. It is still a vital center of activity. The mother, the grandmother, the great aunt, all of these people are still milling around their places, making their pots, watching the kids. They are in context. Meanwhile, the men have really been uprooted from the fields, from the mountains, from that whole thing that gave them meaning thirty years ago."[6] Other Pueblo women, measuring women's status in other ways, present a less rosy picture of Pueblo gender relations. Maria Martinez's great-granddaughter, Barbara Gonzalez, complains that "Pueblo life is harsh on women. [The San Ildefonso] political structure is male oriented. This has been difficult for me to accept, especially since I have been to college. Women are useful in our dance ceremonials, to which the public is invited, but other than that we are ignored. We are not allowed to voice our opinion on matters that affect both men and women at the pueblo."[7] Gonzalez was particularly irritated that women were not allowed to vote in San Ildefonso Pueblo elections. In contrast to the one-dimensional, static, and idealized picture of Pueblo gender relations that antimodern feminists projected, these myriad perspectives reveal that gender relations among the Pueblos were and are as fluctuating and contested as they are in the larger American culture.

It is the antimodern feminists' image, however, and not this complex reality that continues to capture the imagination of white Americans. In the late twentieth century, writers often unquestioningly repeat notions the antimodern feminists first popularized almost a century ago. For example, Mabel Dodge Luhan's biographer, Lois Rudnick, writes, "Over a thousand years old, Pueblo culture was one of timeless and stable values."[8] Taos author Claire Morrill declares, "[T]he [people of] Taos [Pueblo] are wise with an old wisdom, rooted in the earth, magnanimous through integration with the natural world around them; they draw from sources we cannot tap."[9] Indeed, by the late twentieth century, many of the assumptions that white women writers made about the Pueblo Indians in the 1920s have become accepted as truths about all Native Americans. The belief that Native Americans are "at one with nature," deeply spiritual, mystical, and feminist-oriented have become virtual clichés in the late twentieth century. The New Age movement particularly has exploited these concepts.[10] Like antimodern feminists, many late-twentieth-century observers declare that all "authentic" Indians think and act with one perspective and that a great chasm exists between the worlds of whites and Indians. As Morrill puts it, she had "never been so rash as to think [she had] gained more than a faint glimmer of insight into the Indian tribal mind."[11] Due in part to women such as Luhan and Austin, we seem to have established rigid cultural boundaries, to have accentuated the differences, between whites and Indians.

In many ways, however, the Pueblos' problems at the turn of the century were not unlike those faced by other Americans. All agricultural Americans, including the Pueblos, confronted a modernizing economy that increasingly valued industrialization and found less and less use for subsistence farming. Like immigrants from Mexico, Asia, and eastern and southern Europe, the Pueblos also faced harsh attempts to "Americanize" them. Pueblo women, like other American women, also struggled to invent new roles for themselves that could accommodate rapid changes in the economy. Ironically, the arts and crafts movement, by creating new economic opportunities for Pueblo women and often elevating them to the status of primary breadwinners within their families and pueblos, increasingly eroded the antimodern feminists' vision of "authentic Indianness" and idyllic gender relations.

New feminists and female moral reformers presented Pueblo Indians with two stark choices—become just like us or stay just the way you are (or, more accurately, the way we imagine you to be). Pueblo Indians instead sought a means to maintain a sense of cultural uniqueness while adapting in other ways to modern America. As the All-Pueblo Council, the all-male group that antimodern feminists considered to be "traditional," stated, "We are not facing backward, and we are not unchangeable. We are living in the present day, and our struggle is the struggle of present-day men."[12] It was also the struggle of present-day Pueblo women, even of antimodern feminists. This common struggle, although it took different forms for Indians and whites, can be seen as a dance between two enigmatic partners—one seeking, perhaps nostalgically, to hold on to a nonindustrialized, simpler past, the other seeking to grasp a piece of modernizing America. Locked in this dance together, the partners fumble clumsily along, each partner trying to lead and set the tempo. For the Pueblos, dances literally did embody this struggle and helped them to make sense of new events and actors in their world. In 1957, for example, after the launching of Sputnik, Zuni clowns "added space burlesque to their repertoire," dressing as satellites, rockets, and astronauts. Hopi clowns incorporated Jesse Jackson into the pantheon of their characters soon after his visit to their reservation in the 1980s. They also began to spoof the new health trend of aerobics.[13]

As much as they tried to partake in Pueblo culture, antimodern feminists lacked the Pueblos' ritualized and playful means of making sense of the changes occurring so rapidly around them. These women seemed unaware of the part they had played, through the arts and crafts movement and through their own writing, in bringing about the modernization of the Southwest. They began to accept modernity, but as with the Pueblos, this acceptance was tinged with melancholy. As Elizabeth Shepley Sergeant wrote to Mabel Dodge Luhan in 1954, "I long to go back Southwest [*sic*] once more to see you and my Indian friends, and the land, the New Mexican mountains and mesas. Yes, in spite of the travellers and the dreadful industrialisation following Los Alamos changes. I must live in my times, as I think you do, Mabel."[14]

Living in our own times, we are still haunted by the interactions between white women and Pueblo Indians at the turn of the century. Imagining ourselves in another dance, this time between Indians and whites, it is easy to fall back into the familiar steps, to request the same old tunes. How daunting but necessary the task of inventing a new choreography, set to new music, with new composers.

Notes

ABBREVIATIONS OF ARCHIVAL SOURCES

Aberle papers Sophie Aberle papers, Center for Southwest Research, General Library, University of New Mexico, Albuquerque.

Austin papers–BANC Mary Austin papers, Banc Mss C-H 48, Bancroft Library, University of California, Berkeley.

Austin papers–CSR Mary Austin papers, Center for Southwest Research, General Library, University of New Mexico, Albuquerque.

Austin papers–HUNT Mary Austin papers, The Huntington Library, San Marino, California.

Austin papers–UCLA Mary Austin papers, Department of Special Collections, University Research Library, University of California, Los Angeles.

CLAI papers California League for American Indians papers, Banc Mss C-A 360, Bancroft Library, University of California, Berkeley.

Cassidy papers Ina Sizer Cassidy papers, Archives of the Laboratory of Anthropology/Museum of Indian Arts and Culture, Santa Fe, New Mexico.

Chapman papers–IARC Kenneth Chapman papers, School of American Research, Indian Arts Research Center, Santa Fe, New Mexico.

Chapman papers–LAB Kenneth Chapman papers, Archives of the Laboratory of Anthropology/Museum of Indian Arts and Culture, Santa Fe, New Mexico.

Collier papers John Collier papers, Manuscripts and Archives, Yale University Library, New Haven, Connecticut. Microfilm edition, Sanford NC: Microfilming Corporation of America, 1980.

DeHuff papers DeHuff Family papers, Center for Southwest Research, General Library, University of New Mexico, Albuquerque.

Dunn papers Dorothy Dunn Kramer papers, Archives of the Laboratory of Anthropology/Museum of Indian Arts and Culture, Santa Fe, New Mexico.

Duke collection Doris Duke American Indian Oral History Collection, Center for Southwest Research, General Library, University of New Mexico, Albuquerque.

Fall papers Albert B. Fall papers, The Huntington Library, San Marino, California.

Fergusson papers Erna Fergusson papers. Center for Southwest Research, General Library, University of New Mexico, Albuquerque.

GFWC papers General Federation of Women's Clubs papers, General Federation of Women's Clubs International, Washington DC.

IAF papers Indian Arts Fund papers, School of American Research, Indian Arts Research Center, Santa Fe, New Mexico.

IRA papers Indian Rights Association papers, Historical Society of Pennsylvania, Philadelphia. Microfilm edition, Glen Rock NJ: Microfilming Corporation of America, 1975.

Levien papers Sonya Levien papers, The Huntington Library, San Marino, California.

Luhan papers Mabel Dodge Luhan papers, Yale Collection of American Literature, Beinecke Rare Book and Manuscript Library, Yale University, New Haven, Connecticut.

Morrow papers Mabel Morrow papers, Archives of the Laboratory of Anthropology/ Museum of Indian Arts and Culture, Santa Fe, New Mexico.

NMAIA papers New Mexico Association on Indian Affairs papers, absorbed by Southwest Association on Indian Affairs papers, New Mexico State Records Center and Archives, Santa Fe.

Parsons papers Elsie Clews Parsons papers, American Philosophical Society, Philadelphia, Pennsylvania.

Pearce papers T. M. Pearce papers, Center for Southwest Research, General Library, University of New Mexico, Albuquerque.

Pueblo Records, NARA Pueblo Records, Bureau of Indian Affairs, Record Group 75, National Archives and Records Administration, Rocky Mountain Branch, Denver, Colorado.

Sweet collection E. M. Sweet Jr. collection, National Anthropological Archives, Smithsonian Institution, Washington DC.

White papers Amelia Elizabeth White papers, Catherine McElvain Library, School of American Research, Santa Fe, New Mexico.

Wickes papers Frances G. Wickes papers, Library of Congress, Washington DC.

Women of New Mexico collection Women of New Mexico collection, Center for Southwest Research, General Library, University of New Mexico, Albuquerque.

I. WHITE WOMEN, PUEBLO INDIANS, AND FEDERAL INDIAN POLICY

1. Amelia Stone Quinton, "Care of the Indian," in *Woman's Work in America*, ed. Annie Nathan Meyer (New York: Henry Holt, 1891), 383.
2. Mary Dissette to Superintendent Coggeshall, 10 May 1914, Santa Fe Indian School Superintendent's Correspondence with Day School Employees, 1900–16 (Entry 40),

Box 9, Folder: Santo Domingo 1914, May 1–Dec 29, Pueblo Records, NARA; Valerie Sherer Mathes, "Nineteenth-Century Women and Reform: The Women's National Indian Association," *American Indian Quarterly* 14 (winter 1990): 1–18; Helen M. Wanken, "'Woman's Sphere' and Indian Reform: The Women's National Indian Association, 1879–1901" (Ph.D. diss., Marquette University, 1981), 1, 7–38; Peggy Pascoe, *Relations of Rescue: The Search for Female Moral Authority in the American West, 1874–1939* (New York: Oxford University Press, 1990), 7–10.

3. Mary Austin, *Land of Journey's Ending* (New York: Century, 1924), 244.

4. Mary Roberts Coolidge, *The Rain-Makers: Indians of Arizona and New Mexico* (Boston: Houghton Mifflin, 1929), 45–46; Mary Austin, *Taos Pueblo*, photographs by Ansel Easton Adams (San Francisco: Grabhorn, 1930). This oversized book that includes no page numbers was hand-bound and signed by the author and photographer. Only 108 copies were printed. I am indebted to Michael Harrison for allowing me to look at this volume and other works on the Southwest in the Michael and Margaret B. Harrison Western Research Center in Sacramento.

5. Kenneth R. Philp, *John Collier's Crusade for Indian Reform, 1920–1954* (Tucson: University of Arizona Press, 1977); Lawrence C. Kelly, *The Assault on Assimilation: John Collier and the Origins of Indian Policy Reform* (Albuquerque: University of New Mexico Press, 1983).

6. Alice Marriott, *María: The Potter of San Ildefonso* (Norman: University of Oklahoma Press, 1948), provides basic biographical information on Martinez. On the Louisiana Purchase Exposition, see Robert A. Trennert, "Fairs, Expositions, and the Changing Image of Southwestern Indians, 1876–1904," *New Mexico Historical Review* 62 (April 1987): 144–45.

7. Marriott, *María*, 261. For more antimachine rhetoric in depictions of Indian arts and crafts, see Mabel Morrow, "Arts and Crafts among Indian Women," *Indians at Work* 3 (1 December 1935): 19.

8. Robert F. Berkhofer Jr., *The White Man's Indian: Images of the American Indian from Columbus to the Present* (New York: Knopf, 1978), 67; Leah Dilworth, *Imagining Indians in the Southwest: Persistent Visions of a Primitive Past* (Washington DC: Smithsonian Institution Press, 1996), 187.

9. Gretchen M. Bataille and Kathleen Mullen Sands, *American Indian Women: Telling Their Lives* (Lincoln: University of Nebraska Press, 1984), 51–52.

10. Edward P. Dozier, *The Pueblo Indians of North America* (New York: Holt, Rinehart and Winston, 1970), 121, 142. Throughout this book, the term "Pueblo" refers to a person who is a member of the Pueblo Native American group. The term "pueblo" denotes the village in which a Pueblo person lives.

11. Alfonso Ortiz, "The Dynamics of Pueblo Cultural Survival," in *North American*

Indian Anthropology: Essays on Society and Culture, ed. Raymond DeMallie and Alfonso Ortiz (Norman: University of Oklahoma Press, 1994), 297.

12. Polly Schaafsma, ed., *Kachinas in the Pueblo World* (Albuquerque: University of New Mexico Press, 1994), 2; Ramón A. Gutiérrez, *When Jesus Came, the Corn Mothers Went Away: Marriage, Sexuality, and Power in New Mexico, 1500–1846* (Stanford CA: Stanford University Press, 1991), xxii–xxiii.

13. M. Jane Young, "Women, Reproduction, and Religion in Western Puebloan Society," *Journal of American Folklore* 100 (October–December 1987): 441; Alice Schlegel, "Male and Female in Hopi Thought and Action," in *Sexual Stratification: A Cross-Cultural View*, ed. Alice Schlegel (New York: Columbia University Press, 1977), 250–53; Sue Ellen Jacobs, "Continuity and Change in Gender Roles at San Juan Pueblo," in *Women and Power in Native North America*, ed. Laura F. Klein and Lillian A. Ackerman (Norman: University of Oklahoma Press, 1995), 191.

14. For earlier theories that a strict sexual division of labor meant women's subordination, see Michelle Zimbalist Rosaldo, "Woman, Culture, and Society: A Theoretical Overview," in *Woman, Culture, and Society*, ed. Michelle Zimbalist Rosaldo and Louise Lamphere (Stanford CA: Stanford University Press, 1972), 17–42. For more on recent challenges to earlier theories, see Nancy Shoemaker, introduction to *Negotiators of Change: Historical Perspectives on Native American Women* (New York: Routledge, 1995), 1–25; Ramona Ford, "Native American Women: Changing Statuses, Changing Interpretations," in *Writing the Range: Race, Class, and Culture in the Women's West*, ed. Elizabeth Jameson and Susan Armitage (Norman: University of Oklahoma Press, 1997), 42–68; Daniel Maltz and JoAllyn Archambault, "Gender and Power in Native North America: Concluding Remarks," in *Women and Power*, 230–49.

15. Elsie Clews Parsons, "Journal of a Feminist, 1913–14," 34, unpublished manuscript, Parsons papers; Elsie Clews Parsons, "Waiyautitsa of Zuñi, New Mexico," in *Pueblo Mothers and Children: Essays by Elsie Clews Parsons, 1915–1924*, ed. Barbara A. Babcock (Santa Fe: Ancient City, 1991), 104; Elsie Clews Parsons, "The Zuni La'mana," in *Pueblo Mothers and Children*, 39–47; Young, "Women," 441, 444; Schlegel, "Male and Female," 264; S. E. Jacobs, "Continuity and Change," 181–82.

16. Gutiérrez, *When Jesus Came*, 14, 79.

17. Ford, "Native American Women," 47–50; Dozier, *Pueblo Indians*, 133–34, 137–38, 145–48, 163–66.

18. Schlegel, "Male and Female," 246–50; Alice Schlegel, "The Adolescent Socialization of the Hopi Girl," *Ethnology* 12 (1973): 451–53; Young, "Women," 440–42.

19. Gutiérrez, *When Jesus Came*, 39–130, passim. Gutiérrez's book has elicited harsh criticism from many Pueblos who believe that he accepts Spanish characterizations of Pueblo promiscuity as factual rather than biased observations. See "Commen-

taries on *When Jesus Came, the Corn Mothers Went Away: Marriage, Sex, and Power in New Mexico, 1500–1846*, by Ramón A. Gutiérrez," compiled by the Native American Studies Center, University of New Mexico, *American Indian Culture and Research Journal* 17:3 (1993): 141–77.

20. Marc Simmons, "History of Pueblo-Spanish Relations to 1821," in *Southwest*, ed. Alfonso Ortiz, vol. 9 of *Handbook of North American Indians*, ed. William C. Sturtevant (Washington DC: Smithsonian Institution Press, 1979), 182.

21. Edward H. Spicer, *Cycles of Conquest: The Impact of Spain, Mexico, and the United States on the Indians of the Southwest, 1533–1960* (Tucson: University of Arizona Press, 1962), 379–82, 388–95; Gutiérrez, *When Jesus Came*, 157–60; Dozier, *Pueblo Indians*, 187–91.

22. Dozier, *Pueblo Indians*, 4, 24, 75; Gutiérrez, *When Jesus Came*, 39–175; Joe S. Sando, "The Pueblo Revolt," in *Handbook of North American Indians*, 9:194–97; Frederick J. Dockstader, *The Kachina and the White Man: The Influences of White Culture on the Hopi Kachina Religion*, rev. ed. (Albuquerque: University of New Mexico Press, 1985), 71–73; Harry C. James, *Pages from Hopi History* (Tucson: University of Arizona Press, 1974), 44–70.

23. Marc Simmons, "History of the Pueblos since 1821," in *Handbook of North American Indians*, 9:206–7.

24. Dozier, *Pueblo Indians*, 106–9, 114–15; M. Simmons, "History since 1821," 210, 214; T. C. McLuhan, *Dream Tracks: The Railroad and the American Indian, 1890–1930* (New York: Harry Abrams, 1985).

25. Spicer, *Cycles of Conquest*, 202, 205; Dockstader, *Kachina*, 82; James, *Pages*, 100–116; John D. Loftin, *Religion and Hopi Life in the Twentieth Century* (Bloomington: Indiana University Press, 1991), xiii, 72; Barbara Tedlock, *The Beautiful and the Dangerous: Dialogues with the Zuni Indians* (New York: Penguin, 1992), 24. Until the early twentieth century, the government referred to the Hopis by the Spanish name "the Moqui," a term that the Hopi considered derogatory. See James, *Pages*, xii.

26. Dozier, *Pueblo Indians*, 9–14, 109–18; Sylvia Rodríguez, "Land, Water, and Ethnic Identity in Taos," in *Land, Water, and Culture: New Perspectives on Hispanic Land Grants*, ed. Charles L. Briggs and John R. Van Ness (Albuquerque: University of New Mexico Press, 1987), 338.

27. Joseph Filario Tafoya to Samuel Brosius, 6 November 1929, IRA papers, Reel 45; Marriott, *María*, 132–33; Spicer, *Cycles of Conquest*, 540–46; *American Indian Life*, Bulletin No. 2 (July–August 1925), Collier papers, Reel 9.

28. Loftin, *Religion and Hopi Life*, 70–71; Spicer, *Cycles of Conquest*, 175–76. Due to their greater isolation, the transition from an agricultural to a wage-earning economy seems to have occurred somewhat more slowly among the Hopi villages.

29. S. E. Jacobs, "Continuity and Change," 204; Young, "Women," 443; Schlegel, "Male and Female," 265.

30. Schlegel, "Male and Female," 265; Spicer, *Cycles of Conquest*, 176–77, 558–61; Edwin L. Wade, "Straddling the Cultural Fence: The Conflict for Ethnic Artists within Pueblo Societies," in *The Arts of the North American Indian: Native Traditions in Evolution*, ed. Edwin L. Wade (New York: Hudson Hills Press, 1986), 243–54; Barbara Babcock, "Marketing Maria: The Tribal Artist in the Age of Mechanical Reproduction," in *Looking High and Low: Art and Cultural Identity*, ed. Brenda Jo Bright and Liza Blakewell (Tucson: University of Arizona Press, 1995), 124–50; Tessie Naranjo, "Cultural Changes: The Effect of Foreign Systems at Santa Clara Pueblo," in *The Great Southwest of the Fred Harvey Company and the Santa Fe Railway*, ed. Marta Weigle and Barbara Babcock (Phoenix: Heard Museum, 1996), 187–96; Terry R. Reynolds, "Women, Pottery, and Economics at Acoma Pueblo," in *New Mexico Women: Intercultural Perspectives*, ed. Joan Jensen and Darlis Miller (Albuquerque: University of New Mexico Press, 1986), 279–300.

31. Spicer, *Cycles of Conquest*, 199; Dockstader, *Kachina*, 82–83; Loftin, *Religion and Hopi Life*, 68–69; Robert E. Cleaves, "The American Road to Freedom and Enlightenment," in *Hopis, Tewas and the American Road*, ed. Willard Walker and Lydia L. Wyckoff (Middletown CT: Wesleyan University Press, 1983), 39–56; Francis Paul Prucha, "Indian Policy Reform and American Protestantism, 1880–1900," in *People of the Plains and Mountains: Essays in the History of the West*, ed. Ray Allen Billington (Westport CT: Greenwood, 1973), 120–45.

32. Lewis Henry Morgan, *Ancient Society: Researches in the Lines of Human Progress from Savagery through Barbarism to Civilization* (Chicago: Charles H. Kerr, 1877); Brian W. Dippie, *The Vanishing American: White Attitudes and U.S. Indian Policy* (Middletown CT: Wesleyan University Press, 1982), 82–83, 98–106; Curtis M. Hinsley Jr., *Savages and Scientists: The Smithsonian Institution and the Development of American Anthropology, 1846–1910* (Washington DC: Smithsonian Institution Press, 1981); Robert Bieder, *Science Encounters the Indian, 1820–1880: The Early Years of American Ethnology* (Norman: University of Oklahoma Press, 1986); George Stocking Jr., *Race, Culture, and Evolution: Essays in the History of Anthropology* (New York: Free Press, 1968); George Stocking Jr., *Victorian Anthropology* (New York: Free Press, 1987); Audrey Smedley, *Race in North America: Origin and Evolution of a Worldview* (Boulder CO: Westview Press, 1993), 234–44; John S. Haller Jr., *Outcasts from Evolution: Scientific Attitudes of Racial Inferiority, 1859–1900* (Urbana: University of Illinois Press, 1971).

33. Dippie, *Vanishing American*, 156–159; Hazel W. Hertzberg, *The Search for an American Indian Identity: Modern Pan-Indian Movements* (Syracuse NY: Syracuse University Press, 1971), 20–21; Frederick Hoxie, "The Curious Story of Reformers and the

American Indians," in *Indians in American History*, ed. Frederick Hoxie (Arlington Heights IL: Harlan Davidson, 1988), 212; Francis Paul Prucha, *American Indian Policy in Crisis: Christian Reformers and the Indian, 1865–1900* (Norman: University of Oklahoma Press, 1975), 103–68; Philip Weeks, *Farewell, My Nation: The American Indian and the United States, 1820–1890* (Arlington Heights IL: Harlan Davidson, 1990), 217–33.

34. Mary Dissette to Miss Willard, 3 March 1924, IRA papers, Reel 40.
35. Hoxie, "Curious Story," 213; Dippie, *Vanishing American*, 108–11, 139–76; Lisa Emmerich, "'To respect and love and seek the ways of white women': Field Matrons, the Office of Indian Affairs, and Civilization Policy, 1890–1938," (Ph.D. diss., University of Maryland, 1987), 12–13; Prucha, *Policy in Crisis*, 169–401. Prucha's *The Churches and the Indian Schools, 1888–1912* (Lincoln: University of Nebraska Press, 1979) details the conflict between Protestants and Catholics over Indian education.
36. Dozier, *Pueblo Indians*, 133–34, 137–38, 145–48, 163–66; Gutiérrez, *When Jesus Came*, 161.
37. L. H. Morgan, *Ancient Society*, 66–67, 353–67, 476–99, quotes, 507, 512. For a description of Morgan's views, see David D. Smits, "The 'Squaw Drudge': A Prime Index of Savagism," *Ethnohistory* 29 (1982): 300.
38. Superintendent of Santa Fe Indian School to Mr. H. A. Larson, Chief Special Officer, 10 December 1913, Santa Fe Indian Day School Correspondence, 1913–14 (Entry 42), Box 1, Folder: L, Pueblo Records, NARA. Some other early anthropologists also echoed this view; see A. J. Fynn, *The American Indian as a Product of Environment with Special Reference to the Pueblo* (Boston: Little, Brown, 1908), who explained that there is not "such a family bond as we find in civilization" in a matrilineal society and that "marriage was . . . in a chaotic state" (124). Fynn believed, however, that the Pueblos were in transition from a "mother-right society" to a patrilineal society by the time the Spanish came (125).
39. Parsons, "Waiyautitsa," 96–98, 104, quote, 98; Elsie Clews Parsons, *Taos Pueblo*, General Series in Anthropology, no. 2 (Menasha WI: American Anthropological Association, 1936), 49–51, quote, 39.
40. Nancy J. Parezo, "Matilda Coxe Stevenson: Pioneer Ethnologist," in *Hidden Scholars: Women Anthropologists and the Native American Southwest*, ed. Nancy J. Parezo (Albuquerque: University of New Mexico Press, 1993), 46, 49. Stevenson and True knew each other and became involved in a long, drawn-out struggle over land. Parezo contends that True swindled Stevenson (52). Stevenson also studied several other pueblos. The Taos Pueblo Council expelled her from their pueblo because they believed she was making their secrets known to outsiders and causing disease. They also disliked her orders for a house to be prepared for her. See Parsons, *Taos Pueblo*, 15, and Parezo, "Matilda," 52. On Cushing, see Curtis M. Hinsley,

"Zunis and Brahmins: Cultural Ambivalence in the Gilded Age," in *Romantic Motives: Essays on Anthropological Sensibility*, ed. George W. Stocking Jr., History of Anthropology, vol. 6, (Madison: University of Wisconsin Press, 1989), 169–207; Curtis M. Hinsley, "Ethnographic Charisma and Scientific Routine: Cushing and Fewkes in the American Southwest, 1879–1893," in *Observers Observed: Essays on Ethnographic Fieldwork*, ed. George W. Stocking Jr., History of Anthropology, vol. 1 (Madison: University of Wisconsin Press, 1983), 53–69; Hinsley, *Savages and Scientists*, 196–200. The Zuni mistrusted both Stevenson and Cushing despite their varied approaches. See Tedlock, *Beautiful and the Dangerous*, 176–78; Phil Hughte, *A Zuni Artist Looks at Frank Hamilton Cushing* (Zuni NM: Pueblo of Zuni Arts and Crafts, 1994).

41. Barbara Tedlock, "Aesthetics and Politics: Zuni War God Repatriation and Kachina Representation," in *Looking High and Low*, 151–72.

42. Quoted in Rosalind Rosenberg, *Beyond Separate Spheres: Intellectual Roots of Modern Feminism* (New Haven: Yale University Press, 1982), 164–65.

43. Stocking, *Race, Culture*; Rosenberg, *Beyond Separate Spheres*, 162–69; Elazar Barkan, *The Retreat of Scientific Racism: Changing Concepts of Race in Britain and the U.S. Between the World Wars* (New York: Cambridge University Press, 1992); Julia E. Liss, "Patterns of Strangeness: Franz Boas, Modernism, and the Origins of Anthropology," in *Prehistories of the Future: The Primitivist Project and the Culture of Modernism*, ed. Elazar Barkan and Ronald Bush (Stanford CA: Stanford University Press, 1995), 114–30.

44. Ruth Benedict, *Patterns of Culture* (Boston: Houghton Mifflin, 1934), 5–6, 16. For more on Benedict, see Barbara A. Babcock, "'Not in the Absolute Singular': Rereading Ruth Benedict" in *Hidden Scholars*, 107–28; Judith Schachter Modell, *Ruth Benedict: Patterns of a Life* (Philadelphia: University of Pennsylvania Press, 1983); Margaret M. Caffrey, *Ruth Benedict: Stranger in This Land* (Austin: University of Texas Press, 1989); and George W. Stocking Jr., "The Ethnographic Sensibility of the 1920s and the Dualism of the Anthropological Tradition," in *Romantic Motives*, 208–76.

45. For more on the large numbers of white women anthropologists in the Southwest, see Barbara Babcock and Nancy Parezo, eds., *Daughters of the Desert: Women Anthropologists and the Native American Southwest, 1880–1980*, an illustrated catalogue (Albuquerque: University of New Mexico Press, 1988) and Parezo, *Hidden Scholars*.

46. Quoted in Rosemary Lévy Zumwalt, *Wealth and Rebellion: Elsie Clews Parsons, Anthropologist and Folklorist* (Urbana: University of Illinois Press, 1992), 129. For more on cultural pluralism, see David A. Hollinger, "Cultural Pluralism and Multiculturalism," in *A Companion to American Thought*, ed. Richard Wrightman Fox and James T. Kloppenberg (Cambridge MA: Blackwell, 1995), 162–66.

47. Charles F. Lummis, *Bullying the Moqui*, ed. Robert Easton and Mackenzie Brown (Prescott AZ: Prescott College Press, 1968), 1–12; Charles F. Lummis, *Mesa, Cañon, and Pueblo* (New York: Century, 1925); Richard H. Frost, "The Romantic Inflation of Pueblo Culture," *The American West* 17 (January/February 1980): 9, 56–57. Another popular writer who agreed with Lummis was Charles Francis Saunders, who wrote *The Indians of the Terraced Houses* (New York: G. P. Putnam's, 1912).

48. McLuhan, *Dream Tracks*, 9, 19–20, 28–33. For more on connections between the Santa Fe Railroad and artists, see Van Deren Coke, *Taos and Santa Fe: The Artists' Environment, 1882–1942* (Albuquerque: University of New Mexico Press, 1963), 59.

49. D. H. Thomas, *The Southwestern Indian Detours: The Story of the Fred Harvey/Santa Fe Railway Experiment in "Detourism"* (Phoenix: Hunter, 1978), 10–12, 13–40. For more on the role of the Santa Fe Railway, the Fred Harvey Company, and the Indian Detours in promoting tourism, see Dilworth, *Imagining Indians*, 77–124; and Weigle and Babcock, *Great Southwest*.

50. Spicer, *Cycles of Conquest*, 177–79, 496–501. Many scholars, including Spicer, Dozier, and Gutiérrez, assert that the Pueblos had always been riven with divisions. But Spicer and Dozier also grant that economic and social pressures from both the Spanish and the Americans exacerbated these divisions.

51. Loftin, *Religion and Hopi Life*, 72–79; Dockstader, *Kachina*, 83–84, 88; Spicer, *Cycles of Conquest*, 202–5; James, *Pages*, 13; Helen Sekaquaptewa, *Me and Mine: The Life Story of Helen Sekaquaptewa*, as told to Louise Udall (Tucson: University of Arizona Press, 1969), 63–84; Scott Rushforth and Steadman Upham, *A Hopi Social History: Anthropological Perspectives on Sociocultural Persistence and Change* (Austin: University of Texas Press, 1992), 123–48; Polingaysi Qoyawayma (Elizabeth Q. White), *No Turning Back: A Hopi Indian Woman's Struggle to Live in Two Worlds*, as told to Vada F. Carlson (Albuquerque: University of New Mexico Press, 1964), 42–46.

52. See Edward P. Dozier, "Factionalism at Santa Clara Pueblo," *Ethnology* 5 (April 1966): 172–85.

53. Florence Hawley Ellis, "Laguna Pueblo," in *Handbook of North American Indians*, 9:447; M. Simmons, "History since 1821," 218.

54. Philp, *John Collier's Crusade*, 1–91; Kelly, *Assault on Assimilation*, 124–348; John Collier, *From Every Zenith: A Memoir* (Denver: Sage, 1963); Elizabeth Shepley Sergeant, "The Red Man's Burden," *New Republic* 37 (16 January 1924): 199–201.

55. Dozier, *Pueblo Indians*, 108–9; M. Simmons, "History since 1821," 214–15.

56. Clara True to Herbert Welsh, 9 December 1924, IRA papers, Reel 41.

57. Lewis Meriam et al., *The Problem of Indian Administration*, Brookings Institute for Government Research, Studies in Administration (Baltimore: Johns Hopkins Press, 1928). For an analysis of the Meriam Report by a defender of Indian culture, see Vera

L. Connolly, "The End of the Road," *Good Housekeeping* 88 (May 1929): 44–45, 153–70.

58. Philp, *John Collier's Crusade*, 92–186.

59. Philp, *John Collier's Crusade*; Kelly, *Assault on Assimilation*.

60. Hinsley, *Savages and Scientists*; Stocking, *Race, Culture*; Stocking, "Ethnographic Sensibility," 208–76; George Cotkin, *Reluctant Modernism: American Thought and Culture, 1880–1900* (New York: Twayne, 1992), 51–73; Stanley Coben, *Rebellion against Victorianism: The Impetus for Cultural Change in 1920s America* (New York: Oxford University Press, 1991), 55–59; Barkan, *Retreat of Scientific Racism*.

61. Trennert, "Fairs," 127–50; McLuhan, *Dream Tracks*; Marta Weigle, "From Desert to Disney World: The Santa Fe Railway and the Fred Harvey Company Display the Indian Southwest," *Journal of Anthropological Research* 45 (spring 1989): 115–37; Weigle and Babcock, *Great Southwest*.

62. Dilworth, *Imagining Indians*, 2. Curtis M. Hinsley Jr. argues in "Authoring Authenticity" (*Journal of the Southwest* 32 [winter 1990]: 462–78) that the growing fascination with the "primitive" in the Southwest among some male authors in the 1890s was related to a crisis in masculinity. See also Barkan and Bush, *Prehistories of the Future*, 19.

63. Devon Mihesuah, *Cultivating the Rosebuds: The Education of Women at the Cherokee Female Seminary, 1851–1909* (Urbana: University of Illinois Press, 1993); K. Tsianina Lomawaima, *They Called It Prairie Light: The Story of Chilocco Indian School* (Lincoln: University of Nebraska Press, 1994); Hertzberg, *Search for Identity*.

64. Barbara Leslie Epstein, *The Politics of Domesticity: Women, Evangelism, and Temperance in Nineteenth-Century America* (Middletown CT: Wesleyan University Press, 1981); David J. Pivar, *Purity Crusade: Sexual Morality and Social Control, 1868–1900* (Westport CT: Greenwood Press, 1973); Pascoe, *Relations of Rescue*; Ruth Rosen, *The Lost Sisterhood: Prostitution in America, 1900–1918* (Baltimore: Johns Hopkins University Press, 1982), 51–68; Ellen K. Rothman, *Hands and Hearts: A History of Courtship in America* (New York: Basic, 1984), 186–200; Carroll Smith-Rosenberg, "A Richer and a Gentler Sex," *Social Research* 53 (summer 1986): 297.

65. Peter Gabriel Filene, *Him/Her/Self: Sex Roles in Modern America* (New York: Harcourt, Brace, & Jovanovich, 1974), 1–168; John D'Emilio and Estelle B. Freedman, *Intimate Matters: A History of Sexuality in America* (New York: Harper & Row, 1988), 171–274; Elaine Tyler May, *Great Expectations: Marriage and Divorce in Post-Victorian America* (Chicago: University of Chicago Press, 1980); Paula S. Fass, *The Damned and the Beautiful: American Youth in the 1920s* (New York: Oxford University Press, 1977); Paul A. Robinson, *The Modernization of Sex: Havelock Ellis, Alfred Kinsey, William Masters and Virginia Johnson* (New York: Harper & Row, 1976), 1–

41; William L. O'Neill, *Divorce in the Progressive Era* (New Haven: Yale University Press, 1967); Kathy Peiss, *Cheap Amusements: Working Women and Leisure in Turn-of-the-Century New York* (Philadelphia: Temple University Press, 1986); Carroll Smith-Rosenberg, "The New Woman as Androgyne: Social Disorder and Gender Crisis, 1870–1936," in *Disorderly Conduct: Visions of Gender in Victorian America* (New York: Alfred A. Knopf, 1985), 245–96; Lois Rudnick, "The New Woman," in *1915: The Cultural Moment: The New Politics, the New Woman, the New Psychology, the New Art and the New Theatre in America*, ed. Adele Heller and Lois Rudnick (New Brunswick NJ: Rutgers University Press, 1991), 69–81; Kathy Peiss and Christina Simmons, introduction to *Passion and Power: Sexuality in History*, ed. Kathy Peiss and Christina Simmons (Philadelphia: Temple University Press, 1989), 3–13; Christina Simmons, "Modern Sexuality and the Myth of Victorian Repression," in *Passion and Power*, 157–77; George Chauncey Jr., "From Sexual Inversion to Homosexuality: The Changing Medical Conceptualization of Female 'Deviance,'" in *Passion and Power*, 87–117.

66. Epstein, *Politics of Domesticity*; J. Stanley Lemons, *The Woman Citizen: Social Feminism in the 1920s* (Urbana: University of Illinois Press, 1973); Smith-Rosenberg, "New Woman as Androgyne"; Nancy Cott, *The Grounding of Modern Feminism* (New Haven: Yale University Press, 1987); William Leach, *True Love and Perfect Union: The Feminist Reform of Sex and Society* (New York: Basic, 1980).

67. Rothman, *Hands and Hearts*; O'Neill, *Divorce*; James R. McGovern, "The American Woman's Pre–World War I Freedom in Manners and Morals," in *Our American Sisters: Women in American Thought and Life*, ed. Jean E. Friedman and William G. Shade (Boston: Allyn and Bacon, 1973), 237–59.

68. In a path-breaking article published in 1974, Carl Degler argued that there was actually no consensus on female sexuality in nineteenth-century proscriptive literature. Furthermore, Degler contended that this literature could not be construed as representing actual female sexuality. See "What Ought to Be and What Was: Women's Sexuality in the Nineteenth Century," *American Historical Review* 79 (December 1974): 1467–90. Daniel Scott Smith's "The Dating of the American Sexual Revolution: Evidence and Interpretation," in *The American Family in Social-Historical Perspective*, 2d ed., ed. Michael Gordon (New York: St. Martin's Press, 1978), 426–38, also challenges the notion of Victorian passionlessness and asserts that the take-off for the "sexual revolution" of the 1920s really occurred in the last third of the nineteenth century. Carroll Smith-Rosenberg, on the other hand, argues for a close correlation between prescriptive literature in the late nineteenth century and women's actual sexual beliefs. She argues that women adopted beliefs about women's passionlessness to obtain a greater degree of control and power in their relationships with men (see "Richer and a Gentler Sex"). For an excellent overview of historical

debates on sexuality in the nineteenth century, see Estelle B. Freedman, "Sexuality in Nineteenth-Century America: Behavior, Ideology, and Politics," *Reviews in American History* 10 (December 1982): 196–215. Freedman argues for moving beyond the debate on norms versus behavior to examine "sexual politics" and "whether and how the growing importance of non-procreative sexuality influenced sexual ideas and politics" (197). See also C. Simmons, "Modern Sexuality"; Chauncey, "From Sexual Inversion"; and Pamela S. Haag, "In Search of 'The Real Thing': Ideologies of Love, Modern Romance, and Women's Sexual Subjectivity in the United States, 1920–40," *Journal of the History of Sexuality* 2 (1992): 547–77.

69. Pascoe, *Relations of Rescue*; Mihesuah, *Cultivating the Rosebuds*; Lomawaima, *They Called It Prairie Light*; Emmerich, "To respect and love"; Vicki L. Ruiz, "Dead Ends or Gold Mines: Using Missionary Records in Mexican-American Women's History," *Frontiers: A Journal of Women Studies* 12 (1991): 33–56; George J. Sanchez, "'Go After the Women': Americanization and the Mexican Immigrant Woman, 1915–1929," in *Unequal Sisters: A Multicultural Reader in U.S. Women's History*, ed. Ellen Carol DuBois and Vicki L. Ruiz (New York: Routledge, 1990), 250–63; Evelyn Brooks Higginbotham, *Righteous Discontent: The Women's Movement in the Black Baptist Church, 1880–1920* (Cambridge MA: Harvard University Press, 1993), particularly 14, 19, 88–119.

70. Some scholars have taken steps in this direction. See Elizabeth Ammons, "The New Woman as Cultural Symbol and Social Reality: Six Women Writers' Perspectives," in *1915*, 82–97; Vicki L. Ruiz, "'Star Struck': Acculturation, Adolescence, and Mexican American Women, 1920–1950," in *Small Worlds: Children and Adolescents in America, 1850–1950*, ed. Elliott West and Paula Petrik (Lawrence: University of Kansas Press, 1992), 61–80; Rosenberg, *Beyond Separate Spheres*.

71. Ellen Carol DuBois and Vicki L. Ruiz, introduction to *Unequal Sisters*, xii.

2. UPLIFTING INDIAN WOMEN

1. For the classic sources on the cult of true womanhood, see Barbara Welter, "The Cult of True Womanhood, 1820–1860," *American Quarterly* 18 (summer 1966): 151–74; Gerda Lerner, "The Lady and the Mill Girl: Changes in the Status of Women in the Age of Jackson, 1800–1840," *Midcontinent American Studies Journal* 10 (spring 1969): 5–14; Nancy F. Cott, *The Bonds of Womanhood: "Woman's Sphere" in New England, 1780–1835* (New Haven: Yale University Press, 1977); Kathryn Kish Sklar, *Catherine Beecher: A Study in American Domesticity* (New Haven: Yale University Press, 1973); Carroll Smith-Rosenberg, "Female World of Love and Ritual: Relations between Women in Nineteenth-Century America," in *Disorderly Conduct*, 53–76. For the ways in which the ideology of "true womanhood" or "separate spheres" served to bolster middle-class identities and norms, see Mary P. Ryan, *Cradle of the*

Middle Class: The Family in Oneida County, New York, 1790–1865 (New York: Cambridge University Press, 1981) and Christine Stansell, *City of Women: Sex and Class in New York, 1789–1860* (Urbana: University of Illinois Press, 1987). For a critique of the use of the concept of "separate spheres" by historians, see Linda K. Kerber, "Separate Spheres, Female Worlds, Woman's Place: The Rhetoric of Women's History," *Journal of American History* 75 (June 1988): 9–39; and Linda K. Kerber, Nancy F. Cott, Robert Gross, Lynn Hunt, Carroll Smith-Rosenberg, and Christine M. Stansell, "Beyond Roles, Beyond Spheres: Thinking about Gender in the Early Republic," *William and Mary Quarterly* 46 (July 1989): 565–85.

2. Epstein, *The Politics of Domesticity*; Pivar, *Purity Crusade*; Rosen, *Lost Sisterhood*; D'Emilio and Freedman, *Intimate Matters*, 139–67.

3. Mathes, "Nineteenth-Century Women," 1–18; Wanken, "Woman's Sphere," 7–38; Pascoe, *Relations of Rescue*, 7–10; Quinton, "Care of the Indian," 373–91; Dolores Janiewski, "Learning to Live 'Just Like White Folks': Gender, Ethnicity, and the State in the Inland Northwest," in *Gendered Domains: Rethinking Public and Private in Women's History*, ed. Dorothy O. Helly and Susan M. Reverby (Ithaca NY: Cornell University Press, 1992).

4. "Report of Field Matron," form # 5–055, 1895, *Letters Received and Other Records, 1894–1900* (Entry 14), Box 1, Folder: Letters Received 1895, Pueblo Records, NARA; Emmerich, "To respect and love," 16–36; Helen Bannan, *"True Womanhood" on the Reservation: Field Matrons in the U.S. Indian Service*, Southwest Institute for Research on Women, Working Paper #18 (Tucson: Women's Studies, 1984), 5–6.

5. Emmerich, "To respect and love," 40, 96, 98–99, quote, 46.

6. Epstein, *Politics of Domesticity*; Pascoe, *Relations of Rescue*, 36–37.

7. Smith-Rosenberg, "Female World," "New Woman as Androgyne," and "Richer and a Gentler Sex"; Blanche Wiesen Cook, "Female Support Networks and Political Activism: Lillian Wald, Crystal Eastman, Emma Goldman," in *A Heritage of Her Own: Toward a New Social History of American Women*, ed. Nancy F. Cott and Elizabeth H. Pleck (New York: Simon and Schuster, 1979), 412–44; D'Emilio and Freedman, *Intimate Matters*, 125–27, 173–80, 191–94; Michael Gordon, "From an Unfortunate Necessity to a Cult of Mutual Orgasm: Sex in American Marital Education Literature, 1830–1940," in *The Sociology of Sex: An Introductory Reader*, ed. James M. Henslin and Edward Sagarin (New York: Schocken, 1978), 59–83; Ronald G. Walters, *Primers for Prudery: Sexual Advice to Victorian America* (Englewood Cliffs NJ: Prentice-Hall, 1974); Leach, *True Love*; Degler, "What Ought to Be," 1467–90; Freedman, "Sexuality," 196–215.

8. "Report of Field Matron."

9. Bannan, "True Womanhood," 15–18; and Emmerich, "To respect and love," 137, 183–84, 190–91, 244–45, 255–56, 282–84. Other evidence exists that the BIA still

touted the field matron program as a means of uplifting Indian women. See Hubert Work, "Our American Indians," *The Saturday Evening Post* (31 May 1924): 94, 98.

10. Pascoe, *Relations of Rescue*, 134–35, 139–45; Margaret D. Jacobs, "Resistance to Rescue: The Indians of Bahapki and Mrs. Annie E. K. Bidwell," in *Writing the Range*, 230–51.

11. Mihesuah, *Cultivating the Rosebuds*, 3, 37–40; Lomawaima, *They Called It Prairie Light*, 81.

12. Francis Paul Prucha has written that it is possible to characterize reformers who sought the assimilation of Indians as a "single entity," "united in outlook and in goals." See Prucha, *Policy in Crisis*, vi. A more in-depth analysis along gender lines reveals the oversimplification of Prucha's view.

13. Joan Jacobs Brumberg, "Zenanas and Girlless Villages: The Ethnology of American Evangelical Women, 1870–1910," *Journal of American History* 69 (September 1982): 347–71; Susan Peterson, "'Holy Women' and Housekeepers: Women Teachers on South Dakota Reservations, 1885–1910," *South Dakota History* 13 (fall 1983): 245–60; and Pascoe, *Relations of Rescue*, 31, 39–40, 56, 211, all argue that female moral reformers' focus on non-middle-class women's supposedly degraded condition precluded them from questioning male dominance in their own society. Peterson asserts that the female teachers on the South Dakota Indian reservations "were not feminists interested in women's rights," nor did they resent male supervision and masculine authority (257). Further, Peterson remarks that "these women were neither innovators nor rebels" (260) and "they never questioned the value of their work or the superiority of their Anglo-European culture" (247). A recent article by Patricia A. Carter, "'Completely Discouraged': Women Teachers' Resistance in the Bureau of Indian Affairs Schools, 1900–1910," *Frontiers* 15 (1995): 53–86, argues that some white women teachers resisted the mission set forth for them.

14. Mary Dissette to Herbert Welsh, IRA papers, 18 June 1894, and Mary Dissette to Mrs. Miller, 14 March 1894, IRA papers, Reel 11. In 1894, acting on Dissette's recommendations, the Presbyterian Board established the Zuni Industrial School and appointed Dissette its superintendent. The Presbyterian Mission at Zuni consisted of two buildings, one belonging to the Presbyterian Board, the other to the U.S. government. According to Dissette, the board made many improvements in the government building and tried to acquire it from the government. See Dissette to "Friend," 7 April 1894, IRA papers, Reel 11. The Presbyterian Board became increasingly indebted, however, and eventually had to transfer their industrial school to the U.S. government in 1896. See Dissette to Welsh, 5 February 1896, IRA papers, Reel 12; Dissette to Miss Willard, 3 March 1924, IRA papers, Reel 40. From 1896 to 1898 Dissette worked as a BIA schoolteacher. See Dissette to D. R. James, 4 June 1895, IRA papers, Reel 12; Dissette to Welsh, 25 April 1898, IRA papers, Reel 13. For

the period after her work at Zuni, see Superintendent's Correspondence with Day School Employees (Entry 40), Box 5, Folder: Paguate 1914, and Box 8, Folders: Santo Domingo 1914, Pueblo Records, NARA; "Dissette Collection of Indian Photographs," *El Palacio* 51 (March 1944): 60; and Fred Kabotie with Bill Belknap, *Fred Kabotie: Hopi Indian Artist* (Flagstaff: Museum of Northern Arizona, 1977), 29. Dissette died in 1944.

15. Clara True to Matthew Sniffen, 29 January 1912, IRA papers, Reel 25; True to Samuel Brosius, 22 March 1913, IRA papers, Reel 27; True to Matthew Sniffen, 16 June 1919, IRA papers, Reel 34; True to Herbert Welsh, 19 April 1922, IRA papers, Reel 38; True to Superintendent Crandall, 29 August 1902, Santa Fe Indian School, Letters Received from Day School Teacher Clara D. True, 1902–7 (Entry 38), Box 1, Pueblo Records, NARA; "History of Schools in Santa Clara," n.d., Collier papers, Reel 29; Clara D. True, "The Experiences of a Woman Indian Agent," *Outlook* 92 (5 June 1909): 331–36. During her time at Morongo, True oversaw the legendary hunt for "Willie Boy," an Indian man accused of killing his Indian lover and her father. See Harry Lawton, *Willie Boy: A Desert Manhunt* (Balboa Island CA: Paisano, 1960), and James A. Sandos and Larry E. Burgess, *The Hunt for Willie Boy: Indian-Hating and Popular Culture* (Norman: University of Oklahoma Press, 1994). According to Sandos and Burgess, a movie made about the incident, *Tell Them Willie Boy Is Here*, made True into a "leggy and handsome," emancipated new woman, who had a torrid affair with the character played by Robert Redford (57, 66).

16. Dissette to Mrs. Miller, 14 March 1894, and Dissette to Herbert Welsh, 18 June 1894, IRA papers, Reel 11; Dissette to Herbert Welsh, 3 May 1895, IRA papers, Reel 12; True to Superintendent Crandall, 21 November 1902, Entry 38, Box 1, Pueblo Records, NARA.

17. Dissette to Captain Bullis, 23 November 1896, Entry 14, Box 3, Folder: Letters received, 1896 Zuni, Pueblo Records, NARA; Clara True to Superintendent Crandall, 31 December 1903, Entry 38, Box 1, Pueblo Records, NARA; D. D. Graham to Major Bullis, 23 February 1897, and Dissette to Major Bullis, 1 March 1897, Entry 14, Box 5, Folder: Letters Received, 1897, Pueblo Records, NARA; Mary Dissette to Captain Nordstrom, 13 October 1897, Entry 14, Box 4, Folder: Letters Received 1897, Pueblo Records, NARA; Dissette to Welsh, 25 April 1898, IRA papers, Reel 13.

18. Charles Burton, Supervising Teacher, to U.S. Indian Agent, Santa Fe, 31 March 1899, Press Copies of Letters Sent Concerning Day Schools (Entry 8) and "Zuni statistics, 1899," Entry 14, Box 15, Folder: Zuni, Pueblo Records, NARA. Emmerich devotes almost an entire chapter to the problems field matrons faced in trying to fight epidemics while confronting traditional tribal doctors ("To respect and love," 200–18).

19. Dissette to Welsh, 4 and 5 January 1899, IRA papers, Reel 14.

20. Dissette to Major Walpole, 3 March 1899, Entry 14, Box 16, Folder: Zuni, Pueblo Records, NARA. For a day-to-day account of Dissette's labors at Zuni during the epidemic, see Dissette's letters to Major Walpole, 16, 17, 18, 19, 20, 21, and 22 January 1899, IRA papers, Reel 14.

21. Parsons, "Waiyautitsa," 91.

22. Elmira Greason to U.S. Indian Agent, 9 March 1899, Entry 14, Box 16, Folder: Letters Received 1899, Zuni, Pueblo Records, NARA; Petition of Zuni officers to U.S. Indian Agent, Pueblos, 22 April 1899, Entry 14, Box 16, Letters Received, 1899, Folder: Zuni, Pueblo Records, NARA.

23. True to Francis McCormick, Clerk, Santa Fe Indian School, 20 and 21 January 1903; True to Crandall, 26 January 1902 and 28 January 1903; all letters, Entry 38, Box 1, Pueblo Records, NARA.

24. True to Crandall, 30 January 1903, Entry 38, Box 1, Pueblo Records, NARA.

25. True to Crandall, 30 January 1903 and 9 February 1903, Entry 38, Box 1, Pueblo Records, NARA.

26. Petition of Zuni officers to U.S. Indian Agent, Pueblos, 22 April 1899, Entry 14, Box 16, Folder: Letters Received, 1899, Zuni, Pueblo Records, NARA. In this letter the nice field matron was May Faurote, and one of the kind women in the school was Elmira Greason.

27. Dissette to Captain Bullis, 5 February 1896, Entry 14, Box 3, Folder: Letters Received 1896, Zuni, Pueblo Records, NARA.

28. Dissette to Welsh, 3 May 1895, IRA papers, Reel 12; Dissette to Captain Bullis, 17 June 1895 and 23 May 1895, Entry 14, Box 1, Folder: Letters Received 1895, Zuni, Pueblo Records, NARA; Dissette to Mrs. Miller, 14 March 1894, IRA papers, Reel 11.

29. Quoted in James S. Olson and Raymond Wilson, *Native Americans in the Twentieth Century* (Urbana: University of Illinois Press, 1984), 71–72.

30. Quinton, "Care of the Indian," 388; Mathes, "Nineteenth-Century Women," 7–8; Wanken, "Woman's Sphere," 4–5; Peterson, "Holy Women," 245–46; Barbara Welter, "She Hath Done What She Could: Protestant Women's Missionary Careers in Nineteenth-Century America," *American Quarterly* 30 (winter 1978): 630–32; Pascoe, *Relations of Rescue*, 9–10, 50–51; Emmerich, "To respect and love," 7; Bannan, "True Womanhood," 4.

31. Quoted in Emmerich, "To respect and love," 24.

32. Quinton, "Care of the Indian," 383.

33. Dissette to Captain Bullis, 4 November 1896, Entry 14, Box 3, Folder: Letters Received 1896, Zuni, Pueblo Records, NARA. For more of Dissette's disdain for Zuni mothering, see Dissette to "Friend," 14 March 1896, IRA papers, Reel 12.

34. Dissette to Miss Willard, 3 March 1924, IRA papers, Reel 40; Dissette to Superinten-

dent Coggeshall, 10 May 1914, Entry 40, Box 9, Folder: Santo Domingo 1914, May 1–Dec 29, Pueblo Records, NARA.

35. Dissette to Miss Willard, 3 March 1924, IRA papers, Reel 40.

36. Bannan, "True Womanhood," 3; Emmerich, "To respect and love," 18–19, 166–67; Pascoe, *Relations of Rescue*, 56–59; Smits, "Squaw Drudge," 281–306.

37. Welter, "She Hath Done What She Could," 630–31; Brumberg, "Zenanas," 368. See also Marjorie King, "Exporting Femininity, Not Feminism: Nineteenth-Century U.S. Missionary Women's Efforts to Emancipate Chinese Women," in *Women's Work for Women: Missionaries and Social Change in Asia*, ed. Leslie A. Flemming (Boulder CO: Westview, 1989), 118–20; Leslie A. Flemming, "A New Humanity: American Missionaries' Ideals for Women in North India, 1870–1930," in *Western Women and Imperialism*, ed. Nupur Chaudhuri and Margaret Strobel (Bloomington: Indiana University Press, 1992), 191–206; Pascoe, *Relations of Rescue*, 31, 51–56, 59–68.

38. Vron Ware, *Beyond the Pale: White Women, Racism and History* (London: Verso, 1992); Antoinette Burton, "The White Woman's Burden: British Feminists and 'The Indian Woman,' 1865–1915," in *Western Women and Imperialism*, 137–57; and Antoinette Burton, *Burdens of History: British Feminists, Indian Women, and Imperial Culture, 1865–1915* (Chapel Hill: University of North Carolina Press, 1994) point out the ways in which British feminists, in their desire to uplift Indian women, collaborated with the British imperialist project. Like white, middle-class female moral reformers in the United States, British feminists also invoked an ideology of global sisterhood that rarely allowed Indian women an opportunity to speak and represent themselves. Chandra Talpade Mohanty, "Under Western Eyes: Feminist Scholarship and Colonial Discourses," in *Colonial Discourse and Postcolonial Theory: A Reader*, ed. Patrick Williams and Laura Chrisman (New York: Columbia University Press, 1994), 196–220, argues that this process is still very much alive today as "First World" feminists represent themselves as emancipated subjects while they represent "Third World" women as universally oppressed objects. Pascoe similarly faults contemporary feminists for continuing this practice (*Relations of Rescue*, 208–12).

39. Dissette to Miss Willard, 3 March 1924, IRA papers, Reel 40; Dissette to Mrs. Miller, 14 March 1894, IRA papers, Reel 11. See also Dissette to "Friend," 7 April 1894, IRA papers, Reel 11. White women reformers proposed similar educational programs for Mexican women. See Ruiz, "Dead Ends," 33–56; Sanchez, "Go After the Women," 250–63; and Sarah Deutsch, *No Separate Refuge: Culture, Class, and Gender on an Anglo-Hispanic Frontier in the American Southwest, 1880–1940* (New York: Oxford University Press, 1987), 63–86.

40. True to Welsh, 9 December 1924, IRA papers, Reel 41. See also True, "Experiences of a Woman Indian Agent."

41. True to Brosius, 30 October 1919 and 1 November 1919, IRA papers, Reel 34; True to Superintendent Coggeshall, 13 September 1913, Day-School Correspondence (Entry 42), Box 2, Folder: T, Pueblo Records, NARA. For another case in which True attempted to defend the virtue of a young Indian woman from the alleged sexual depravity of Indian men, see True to Herbert Welsh, 19 April 1922, IRA papers, Reel 38.

42. True to Crandall, 28 November 1902, 30 November 1903, 24 February 1904, 7 March 1904, and Cora Marie Arnold to Clara True, 3 March 1904, Entry 38, Box 1, Pueblo Records, NARA. Cora Arnold found True's letter "insulting" and expected an apology. True to Brosius, 16 December 1926, IRA papers, Reel 43.

43. Dissette to Welsh, 18 June 1894 and 23 July 1894, IRA papers, Reel 11; Dissette to Welsh, 28 August 1895, IRA papers, Reel 12; Dissette to "Friend," 14 March 1896, IRA papers, Reel 12.

44. Dissette to Superintendent Coggeshall, 5 October 1913, Entry 40, Box 5, Folder: Paguate, 1913, Pueblo Records, NARA; Indian Arts Fund Report, 30 June 1932, IAF papers.

45. Dissette to Matthew Sniffen, 4 August 1914, IRA papers, Reel 29. When the Indian girls who lived with Dissette in the summer attended Santa Fe Indian School in the winter, Dissette regularly sent them packages of clothing and other goods. See, for example, Dissette to Superintendent Coggeshall, 1 October 1913, Entry 40, Box 5, Folder: Paguate, 1913, Pueblo Records, NARA.

46. True to Welsh, 9 December 1924, IRA papers, Reel 41.

47. See Brumberg, "Zenanas"; King, "Exporting Femininity"; Welter, "She Hath Done What She Could"; Peterson, "Holy Women"; and Pascoe, *Relations of Rescue*.

48. Dissette to Captain Bullis, 3 July 1896, Entry 14, Box 3, Folder: Letters Received, 1896, Zuni, Pueblo Records, NARA; Dissette to Captain Nordstrom, 13 October 1897, Entry 14, Box 4, Folder: Letters Received 1897, Pueblo Records, NARA.

49. Dissette to Herbert Welsh, 12 October 1894, IRA papers, Reel 11.

50. "Report of Field Matron," Mrs. Ellen Stahl, 16 August to 30 September, 1895, Entry 14, Box 1, Folder: Letters Received 1895, Zuni, Pueblo Records, NARA. Emmerich, "To respect and love," lists Stahl as one of the initial group of twenty-five field matrons who served during the period from 1890 to 1896 (96). Unlike most of her peers, Stahl worked for less than a year (102).

51. True to Crandall, 29 August 1902, Entry 38, Box 1, Pueblo Records, NARA.

52. Epstein, *Politics of Domesticity*, 127, 141.

53. Dissette to Matthew Sniffen, 4 August 1914, IRA papers, Reel 29; True to Sniffen, 29 January 1912, IRA papers, Reel 25; True to Brosius, 22 March 1913, IRA papers, Reel 27.

54. Pascoe, *Relations of Rescue*, 37.

55. Dissette to Captain Nordstrom, 13 October 1897, Entry 14, Box 4, Pueblo Records, NARA.
56. Dissette to Welsh, 5 January 1899, IRA papers, Reel 14; other field matron quoted in Emmerich, "To respect and love," 160
57. True to Herbert Welsh, 19 April 1922, IRA papers, Reel 38.
58. Epstein, *Politics of Domesticity*.
59. Dissette to Mrs. Miller, 14 March 1894, and Dissette to "Friend," 7 April 1894, IRA papers, Reel 11; Dissette to Samuel Brosius, 11 June 1921, IRA papers, Reel 37.
60. Smith-Rosenberg, "Female World" and "New Woman as Androgyne"; Cook, "Female Support Networks"; D'Emilio and Freedman, *Intimate Matters*, 125–27, 191–94.
61. True to Sniffen, 21 January 1912, IRA papers, Reel 25; Dissette to Welsh, 1 July 1897, IRA papers, Reel 13.
62. Dissette to Welsh, two letters, 5 January 1899, IRA papers, Reel 14. Dissette enlisted Herbert Welsh, president of the IRA, in her cause.
63. True to Brosius, 22 March 1913, and Dissette to Brosius, 18 April 1913, IRA papers, Reel 27; True to Sniffen, 31 August 1919, IRA papers, Reel 34.
64. Samuel Brosius to Matthew Sniffen, 22 and 23 March 1919, IRA papers, Reel 34; True to Herbert Welsh, 19 April 1922, IRA papers, Reel 38; Sniffen to True, 27 August 1924, IRA papers, Reel 41. See also correspondence between True and Brosius, Sniffen, and Welsh throughout 1924 and 1925, IRA papers, Reels 41 and 42.
65. True to Brosius, 6 December 1920, IRA papers, Reel 35; True to Brosius, 22 March 1913, IRA papers, Reel 27.
66. True to Brosius, 16 December 1926; True to Welsh, 17 December 1926, 27 January 1927, and 19 April 1927; telegram from True to Welsh, 20 January 1927, all in IRA papers, Reel 43; True to Sniffen, 12 January 1928, IRA papers, Reel 44.
67. Epstein, *Politics of Domesticity*; D'Emilio and Freedman, *Intimate Matters*, 139–67; Pivar, *Purity Crusade*.
68. Dissette to Brosius, 3 December 1910, and True to Brosius, 1 December 1910, IRA papers, Reel 23; Dissette to Brosius, 18 April 1913, IRA papers, Reel 27; True to Sniffen, 2 June 1919, and True to Brosius, 18 October 1919, IRA papers, Reel 34.
69. True to Sniffen, 2 June 1919, IRA papers, Reel 34; True to Brosius, 16 August 1920, IRA papers, Reel 41.
70. Allan M. Brandt, *No Magic Bullet: A Social History of Venereal Disease in the United States since 1880* (New York: Oxford University Press, 1985), 5, 15–16, 21–28, 31–33, 37–38.
71. True to Dissette, 27 April 1919, IRA papers, Reel 34.
72. True to Brosius, 1 December 1910, IRA papers, Reel 23.
73. Mary Dissette to Herbert Welsh, 10 February 1906, IRA papers, Reel 18.

74. True to Sniffen, 31 August 1919, IRA papers, Reel 34.

75. Emmerich also finds that ultimately, field matrons worked with both men and women. To teach women their "proper" domestic roles, it was also necessary to instruct Indian men that they should do the heavier labor and respect women ("To respect and love," 166–67).

76. True to J. F. Tafoya, 4 June 1929, IRA papers, Reel 45.

77. Dissette to "Friend," 14 March 1896, IRA papers, Reel 12.

78. Qoyawayma, *No Turning Back*; Sekaquaptewa, *Me and Mine*; Marriott, *María*. For more on the framing of Sekaquaptewa's autobiography, see Gretchen M. Bataille and Kathleen Mullen Sands, "Two Women in Transition: Separate Perspectives," in *American Indian Women*, 83–112. For a critical assessment of Marriott's biography, see Deborah Gordon, "Among Women: Gender and Ethnographic Authority of the Southwest, 1930–1980," in *Hidden Scholars*, 129–45.

79. Qoyawayma did not know her birth date. She was born before the Hopis had adopted a western calendar and before they kept records of births by date (*No Turning Back*, 104).

80. Sekaquaptewa, *Me and Mine*, 63–90; Qoyawayma, *No Turning Back*, 27–48.

81. Qoyawayma, *No Turning Back*, 22–26. Qoyawayma describes the coercive methods that white officials used to make the Hopi children attend school and the division that this caused in her village of Oraibi (17–21).

82. Sekaquaptewa, *Me and Mine*, 91–92, 132–33; Qoyawayma, *No Turning Back*, 53–54.

83. Qoyawayma, *No Turning Back*, 74–75, 79–80.

84. Sekaquaptewa, *Me and Mine*, 153–244.

85. Qoyawayma, *No Turning Back*, 77–180.

86. Marriott, *María*. A more critical assessment of Maria's life can be found in Wade, "Straddling the Cultural Fence," 243–54.

87. Marriott, *María*, 82.

88. Sekaquaptewa, *Me and Mine*, 145–46.

89. Marriott, *María*, 82–83.

90. Marriott, *María*, 85, 88, 91. Sekaquaptewa, *Me and Mine*, 128–29.

91. Sekaquaptewa, *Me and Mine*, 138; Qoyawayma, *No Turning Back*, 116.

92. Marriott, *María*, 92–93, 95, 97.

93. Qoyawayma, *No Turning Back*, 62, 64, 116.

94. Sekaquaptewa, *Me and Mine*, 138.

95. Marriott, *María*, 19 and passim.

96. Qoyawayma, *No Turning Back*, 69–70, 103, 149.

97. Mary Dissette to Captain Nordstrom, 13 October 1897, Entry 14, Box 4, Letters Received 1897, Folder: Pueblo Records, NARA.

98. Jane Hunter, in "The Home and the World: The Missionary Message of U.S. Domesticity," in *Women's Work for Women*, 159–66, finds, too, that female missionaries in China had an unintentional effect on Chinese women. As Hunter writes, "[I]n China, . . . the message of Christian domesticity preached by missionary women was less transformative than the force of their own example" (164). As a result, some Chinese girls adopted the missionary model over the domestic ideal; they chose to remain single (165). See also Hunter, *The Gospel of Gentility: American Women Missionaries in Turn-of-the-Century China* (New Haven CT: Yale University Press, 1984), 248–50.

99. Schlegel, "Male and Female," 245–69; Young, "Women," 436–45.

100. Sekaquaptewa, *Me and Mine*, 117–18.

101. Saunders, *Indians of the Terraced Houses*, 264.

102. May Faurote to Herbert Welsh, 22 April 1898, IRA papers, Reel 13.

103. Mary Ellicott Arnold and Mabel Reed, *In the Land of the Grasshopper Song: Two Women in the Klamath River Indian Country in 1908–09* (New York: Vantage Press, 1957; reprint, Lincoln: University of Nebraska Press, 1980), 212. See also Emmerich, "To respect and love," 138, 179, 181.

3. FEMINISTS AND CULTURAL RELATIVISM

1. Elsie Clews Parsons, "The Accident of the Forester," chapter in unpublished manuscript, "In the Southwest," excerpted in Peter H. Hare, *A Woman's Quest for Science: Portrait of Anthropologist Elsie Clews Parsons* (Buffalo NY: Prometheus, 1985), 127–28; Zumwalt, *Wealth and Rebellion*, 147–48; True to Parsons, 18 October 1912, Parsons papers.

2. Zumwalt, *Wealth and Rebellion*, 88, 150–51; correspondence from True to Parsons, 6 April [1911], 15 June 1911, 18 August [1912], fall 1912, 18 October 1912, 20 October 1912, 5 April 1913, 2 May 1914, 25 August 1915, 14 June 1916, 12 November 1920, in Parsons papers.

3. See True to Parsons, 2 May 1914, 30 November 1915, and 30 March 1919; "Final Judgment and Decree," Elsie Clews Parsons, Plaintiff vs. Clara True, Defendant, 18 June 1921, which transferred True's land to Parsons, and increasingly bitter correspondence from True to Parsons, 3 March 1922, 4 May 1922, 12 May 1922, 13 May 1922, and 4 July 1922, Parsons papers; and Zumwalt, *Wealth and Rebellion*, 159 n.7.

4. Arrell Morgan Gibson, *The Santa Fe and Taos Colonies: Age of the Muses, 1900–1942* (Norman: University of Oklahoma Press, 1983), includes a little on each of these women except Sergeant; Molly Mullin, "'Bryn Mawrters' Go West: 'Politicized Consumption' and the Gendered Geography of National Identity," chap. 2, "Consuming the American Southwest: Culture, Art, and Difference," (Ph.D. diss., Duke University, 1993), focuses on Sergeant and White. See also Elizabeth Shepley

Sergeant, "The Journal of a Mud House," serialized in four parts in *Harper's Magazine* 144 (March 1922): 409–22; 144 (April 1922): 585–98; 144 (May 1922): 774–82; and 145 (June 1922): 56–67. Sergeant's papers are housed at the Beinecke Rare Book and Manuscript Library, Yale University, New Haven, Connecticut, and much of her correspondence can also be found in the Collier papers. White's papers are accessible at the School of American Research in Santa Fe, New Mexico. For more on Ina Cassidy, see her papers at the Archives, Laboratory of Anthropology/Museum of Indian Arts and Culture, Santa Fe; T. M. Pearce, "Ina Sizer Cassidy: A Tribute," speech given 25 January 1925 at Presentation of the Gerald Cassidy Memorial Art Library, University of New Mexico, in Box 2, Folder 26, T. M. Pearce papers, Center for Southwest Research, General Library, University of New Mexico, Albuquerque; and "Ina Sizer Cassidy—Lady of Contrasts," *The Santa Fe Scene*, 13 December 1958, Austin papers–BANC. Alice Corbin Henderson's papers are at the University of Texas at Austin. For more on Erna Fergusson, see her papers at the Center for Southwest Research, General Library, University of New Mexico, Albuquerque, especially "Interesting Westerners," *Sunset Magazine* (January 1925), and "Here Is Our Only Woman Dude Wrangler: She Guides Tourists to the Wild Spots to see Picturesque Indian Rites," *Philadelphia Record*, 3 January 1926, both clippings in Box 15, Scrapbook 1, Erna Fergusson papers; her many books, especially *Dancing Gods: Indian Ceremonials of New Mexico and Arizona* (New York: Alfred A. Knopf, 1931); and Robert Franklin Gish, *Beautiful Swift Fox: Erna Fergusson and the Modern Southwest* (College Station: Texas A & M University Press, 1996).

5. Erna Fergusson, "Crusade from Santa Fé," *The North American Review* 242 (winter 1936–37): 377; Clara True to Matthew Sniffen, 15 January 1932, IRA papers, Reel 48.
6. George W. Stocking Jr. also makes a similar point about feminist anthropologists such as Margaret Mead and Ruth Benedict in the 1920s. See "Ethnographic Sensibility," 208–76.
7. I have come across one other reference to the term "antimodern feminist," in Mary W. Blanchard, "Anglo-American Aesthetes and Native Indian Corn: Candace Wheeler and the Revision of American Nationalism," *Journal of American Studies* 27 (1993): 377–97. Blanchard, however, uses the term to describe Wheeler's philosophy in the late nineteenth century.
8. Mabel Dodge Luhan, *Edge of Taos Desert: An Escape to Reality*, vol. 4 of *Intimate Memories* (New York: Harcourt, Brace, 1937), 64; Lois Palken Rudnick, *Mabel Dodge Luhan: New Woman, New Worlds* (Albuquerque: University of New Mexico Press, 1984), 193; Mabel Dodge Luhan, *Lorenzo in Taos* (New York: Alfred A. Knopf, 1932). Austin's published works and letters are full of the view that the Pueblos and other Native American tribes represent America's unique heritage. See,

for example, Austin to Luhan, 9 November, no year (but ca. 1920), and 26 July 1922, Luhan papers.

9. Luhan, *Edge of Taos Desert*, 197, 66–67. John Collier characterized the Pueblos in similar terms. See "The Red Atlantis," *Survey Graphic* 2 (October 1922): 16. At other times, Luhan was more pessimistic, believing that the Pueblos were "by some kind of predilection, and by the destiny that has been determined for them by the influence of the Indian Bureau Schools, headed for Progress, a mechanical civilization and an undermined racial stock." See Mabel Dodge Luhan, *Winter in Taos* (Denver: Sage, 1935), 48.

10. "Indian Welfare Work Will Be Undertaken," *General Federation News* 2 (August 1921): 1, 9.

11. Peter Nabokov, "Present Memories, Past History," in *The American Indian and the Problem of History*, ed. Calvin Martin (New York: Oxford University Press, 1987), 151; Philp, *John Collier's Crusade*; and Kelly, *Assault on Assimilation*, particularly explain the Indian reform movement of the 1920s in these terms. See also T. J. Jackson Lears, *No Place of Grace: Antimodernism and the Transformation of American Culture, 1880–1920* (New York: Pantheon Books, 1981).

12. Saunders, *Indians of the Terraced Houses*, 8–9.

13. Zumwalt, *Wealth and Rebellion*, 139; Rosenberg, *Beyond Separate Spheres*, 168–69; Rudnick, introduction to Mabel Dodge Luhan, *Movers and Shakers*, vol. 3 of *Intimate Memories* (New York: Harcourt, Brace, 1936; reprint, Albuquerque: University of New Mexico Press, 1985), x. Though all three women associated with anarchists and radicals, none of the women completely supported anarchism or labor radicalism. For example, both Luhan and Parsons expressed their ambivalence about the use of violence by radicals; in a letter to IWW organizer Elizabeth Gurley Flynn, Parsons informed her that she did not support labor sabotage nor did she believe war derived solely from capitalism (10 December 1917, Parsons papers). In *Movers and Shakers*, Luhan expressed great discomfort about the violent Direct Action tactics of anarchists Emma Goldman and Alexander Berkman, whom she befriended despite her misgivings (57–58).

14. Austin to Luhan, 10 May [1923 or 1924], Luhan papers. Luhan, *Movers and Shakers*, 506.

15. Austin, *Taos Pueblo*, no page numbers.

16. Sally Price, *Primitive Art in Civilized Places* (Chicago: University of Chicago Press, 1989), 45–48.

17. Stella Atwood to Mabel Dodge Sterne [Luhan], 21 December 1922, Luhan papers; Stella Atwood, "The Case for the Indian," *Survey* 49 (October 1922): 7–11, 57, especially 10 and 57; "Indian Welfare."

18. Smith-Rosenberg's important essay "The New Woman as Androgyne" reinforces the media's stereotype of the young woman as "new" woman. Elaine Showalter refutes this stereotype in her edited collection *These Modern Women: Autobiographical Essays from the Twenties* (New York: Feminist Press, 1989), 3.

19. Rudnick, "New Woman," in 1915, 73, 78, 80–81; Heller and Rudnick, introduction to 1915, 4; Showalter, *These Modern Women*, 4; Fass, *Damned and the Beautiful*, 23, 72; Filene, *Him/Her/Self*, 69.

20. Luhan, *Movers and Shakers*, 215–16.

21. Quoted in Zumwalt, *Wealth and Rebellion*, 112.

22. Mary Austin, *Earth Horizon: Autobiography* (Boston: Houghton Mifflin, 1932), 325. For more on Gilman, see Mary A. Hill, *Charlotte Perkins Gilman: The Making of a Radical Feminist, 1860–1896* (Philadelphia: Temple University Press, 1980). Some scholars have characterized Austin in quite different terms. Richard Drinnon paints Austin as a sexually repressed woman who favored the conquest of Native Americans. See "The American Rhythm: Mary Austin," in *Facing West: The Metaphysics of Indian Hating and Empire Building* (New York: Schocken, 1980), 219–31. A full examination of Austin's life and work yields little evidence to support Drinnon's contention, however.

23. The biographical information that follows is based on these sources: Austin, *Earth Horizon*; Esther Lanigan Stineman, *Mary Austin: Song of a Maverick* (New Haven: Yale University Press, 1989); Gibson, *Santa Fe and Taos Colonies*, 199–217; Augusta Fink, *I-Mary: A Biography of Mary Austin* (Tucson: University of Arizona Press, 1983); Helen MacKnight Doyle, *Mary Austin: Woman of Genius* (New York: Gotham House, 1939); T. M. Pearce, *The Beloved House* (Caldwell ID: Caxton, 1940); Willard Hougland, ed., *Mary Austin: A Memorial* (Santa Fe: Laboratory of Anthropology, 1944); T. M. Pearce, ed., *Literary America, 1903–1934: The Mary Austin Letters* (Westport CT: Greenwood, 1979); Peggy Pond Church, *Wind's Trail: The Early Life of Mary Austin*, ed. Shelley Armitage (Santa Fe: Museum of New Mexico Press, 1990).

24. Mary Austin, "The Land," in *Stories from the Country of Lost Borders*, ed. Marjorie Pryse (New Brunswick NJ: Rutgers University Press, 1987), 156; Austin, *Earth Horizon*, 115.

25. Mary Austin, "Sex Emancipation through War," *Forum* 49 (May 1918): 611.

26. Mary Austin, "Woman Alone," *Nation* (2 March 1927): 228–30; also reprinted in Showalter, *These Modern Women*, 82–83.

27. Doyle, *Mary Austin*, 195.

28. May, *Great Expectations*, 2–5; O'Neill, *Divorce*.

29. Austin to Luhan, 9 November, no year (ca. 1920), and 26 July 1922, Luhan papers.

30. Austin to Luhan 9 November, no year (ca. 1920), Luhan papers; Austin, "Sex Emancipation through War," 620.

31. May, *Great Expectations*, 68, 92, 95; Robinson, *Modernization of Sex*, 1–41; Fass, *Damned and the Beautiful*, 32–33, 72, 74, 262–68; Peiss, *Cheap Amusements*; Rothman, *Hands and Hearts*, 260–61.

32. Austin, *Earth Horizon*, 351; Austin, "The Forward Turn," *Nation* (20 July 1927): 57.

33. Austin to Luhan, 28 September [1920], Luhan papers; May, *Great Expectations*, 101, 114; Fass, *Damned and the Beautiful*, 31.

34. Mary Austin, "A Child Must Have Some Kind of Religion," *Pictorial Review* (August 1928), no page numbers, reprint available in Austin papers–CSR. For correspondence between Luhan and Austin regarding their spiritual practices, see, for example, Austin to Luhan, 25 November 1930, 5 March [1920], "Monday morning" [1922?], 31 December [1923], 10 May [1923], Luhan papers. Luhan experimented with "mind cure," mysticism, Eastern religions, and the Christian Science religion. Luhan, *Movers and Shakers*, 18–22, 123–39, 465–73, 533; Rudnick, *Mabel Dodge Luhan*, 129, 134. Also see correspondence from Mabel Dodge Luhan to Sonya Levien, Levien papers. For more on these movements, see William Leach, *Land of Desire: Merchants, Power, and the Rise of a New American Culture* (New York: Pantheon, 1993), 225–60; Donald Meyers, *The Positive Thinkers: A Study of the American Quest for Health, Wealth and Personal Power from Mary Baker Eddy to Norman Vincent Peale* (Garden City NY: Doubleday, 1965); and Ann Douglas, *Terrible Honesty: Mongrel Manhattan in the 1920s* (New York: Farrar, Straus, and Giroux, 1995), 32–33, 130–31, 155, 161–62.

35. Austin, *Earth Horizon*, 157; Mary Austin, "American Women and the Intellectual Life," *The Bookman* 53 (August 1921), 482.

36. Biographical information on Luhan can be found in Rudnick, *Mabel Dodge Luhan*; Luhan, *Movers and Shakers*; and Gibson, *Santa Fe and Taos Colonies*, 218–29.

37. Luhan, *Movers and Shakers*, 40. For more on her account of the 1913 International Exhibition of Modern Art at the Armory, see Luhan, *Movers and Shakers*, 25–38.

38. For Luhan's interest in psychoanalysis and Freudianism, see Luhan, *Movers and Shakers*, 23–24, 142, 439–57, 505–12; Rudnick, *Mabel Dodge Luhan*, 130–31. See also Elsie Sergeant to Luhan, 21 August 1929, Luhan papers. Elizabeth "Elsie" Shepley Sergeant, another feminist who worked among the Pueblos, told Luhan, "In this half analysed state so much libido is underneath that you just have to decide to leave half of the rest of your life untouched while that is done!" In letters from Sergeant to Luhan (ca. 1925) and 14 April [1927], Sergeant further discusses psychoanalysis. See also the article entitled "Mabel Dodge Talks on Mothers of Men," n.d., correspondence of Elsie Sergeant with Luhan, Luhan papers. For more on Freud's influence on "modern" Americans, see Douglas, *Terrible Honesty*; and San-

ford Gifford, "The American Reception of Psychoanalysis, 1908–1922," in *1915*, 128–45.

39. Luhan, *Movers and Shakers*, 247.

40. Quoted in Susan Ware, *Still Missing: Amelia Earhart and the Search for Modern Feminism* (New York: W. W. Norton, 1993), 126.

41. Leonard Abbot, Free Speech League of New York, to Mabel Dodge, 3 and 5 February 1915; William Sanger to Luhan, 28 February 1915, Luhan papers; Luhan, *Movers and Shakers*, 143.

42. Quoted in Judith Schwarz, *Radical Feminists of Heterodoxy: Greenwich Village, 1912–1940* (Norwich VT: New Victoria, 1986), 108; see also a copy in Parsons papers; and see Showalter, *These Modern Women*, 7.

43. Rudnick, introduction to Luhan, *Movers and Shakers*, xiii.

44. Luhan, *Movers and Shakers*, 69–71, passim.

45. Luhan, *Movers and Shakers*, 168–69, 263. As Fass in *The Damned and the Beautiful* has shown, many young Americans in the 1920s shared Luhan's qualified view that "love made sex right" (273).

46. Luhan, *Movers and Shakers*, 533–34.

47. Austin, *Earth Horizon*, 340; Austin to Luhan, 29 April [1923], Luhan papers. See also Stella Atwood to Mabel Dodge Sterne, 8 January 1923, and Austin to Luhan, 4 April [1923], regarding a "determined effort to push [Mabel] into newspaper publicity" because of her unorthodox relationship with Tony. Both in Luhan papers. Mabel paid Tony's former wife, Candelaria, thirty-five dollars a month for the rest of her life. When Mabel married Tony in 1923, Taos Pueblo barred Tony from participation in kiva ceremonies. In 1935 the Taos religious head, the cacique, publicly reversed Tony's prohibition from Pueblo ceremonies, and Tony reinvolved himself in the religious ceremonies of his pueblo. Rudnick, *Mabel Dodge Luhan*, 155, 251.

48. For more on Mabel's marital problems with Tony, see correspondence from Luhan to Frances G. Wickes, a Jungian therapist, in which Luhan alluded to Tony's affairs with other women, including Georgia O'Keefe. This correspondence can be found in the Wickes papers. See also Ellen Kay Trimberger, "The New Woman and the New Sexuality: Conflict and Contradiction in the Writings of Mabel Dodge and Neith Boyce," in *1915*, 98–115.

49. Hare, *A Woman's Quest*, 139.

50. Zumwalt, *Wealth and Rebellion*, 29; Rosenberg, *Beyond Separate Spheres*, 147–54. See also Desley Deacon, *Elsie Clews Parsons: Inventing Modern Life* (Chicago: University of Chicago Press, 1997).

51. Elsie Clews Parsons, *The Old-Fashioned Woman: Primitive Fancies about the Sex* (New York: G. P. Putnam's, 1913), 148; Elsie Clews Parsons, *Fear and Conventionality* (New York: G. P. Putnam's, 1914), 122.

52. Rosenberg, *Beyond Separate Spheres*, 156–62; Hare, *A Woman's Quest*, 11–12; Zumwalt, *Wealth and Rebellion*, 46–49. For others who experimented with and advocated trial marriage, see Robinson, *Modernization of Sex*, 30; Filene, *Him/Her/Self*, 70, 166; and Fass, *Damned and the Beautiful*, 38–39.

53. Parsons, *Fear and Conventionality*, 211; Zumwalt, *Wealth and Rebellion*, 78–81, 91.

54. Parsons, *Old-Fashioned Woman*, 157; Zumwalt, *Wealth and Rebellion*, 75.

55. Parsons, "Journal of a Feminist, 1913–14," unpublished manuscript, 106, 116, Parsons papers. For more on Parsons's views on women's sexuality, see her "Sex and the Elders" [1915], and "Sexual Taboo," n.d., unpublished manuscripts, Parsons papers.

56. Parsons, *Fear and Conventionality*, 102. See also Parsons, "Journal of a Feminist," 18–19.

57. Parsons, *Old-Fashioned Woman*; Zumwalt, *Wealth and Rebellion*, 98–99; Rosenberg, *Beyond Separate Spheres*, 163, 167, 169–70.

58. Rosenberg, *Beyond Separate Spheres*, 162–69. Also see Desley Deacon, "The Republic of the Spirit: Fieldwork in Elsie Clews Parsons's Turn to Anthropology," *Frontiers* 12 (1992): 13–38. Rosenberg points out that at this time there was little distinction between the disciplines of anthropology and sociology (163).

59. Zumwalt, *Wealth and Rebellion*, 124–25; Rosenberg, *Beyond Separate Spheres*, 168–69, 176–77. For other material on Parsons, see Barbara A. Babcock, "Taking Liberties, Writing from the Margins, and Doing It with a Difference," *Journal of American Folklore* 100 (October–December 1987): 390–411; Babcock, *Pueblo Mothers and Children*; entry in Babcock and Parezo, *Daughters of the Desert*, 14–19; and Louis A. Hieb, "Elsie Clews Parsons in the Southwest," in *Hidden Scholars*, 63–75.

60. Hare, *A Woman's Quest*, 141. In the introduction to *Pueblo Mothers and Children*, Barbara Babcock claims Parsons was fascinated by the "feminist nature" of Pueblo culture (9). At other times in American history, white women have also crafted Indian culture as a feminist utopia. Gail H. Landsman's "The 'Other' as Political Symbol: Images of Indians in the Woman Suffrage Movement," *Ethnohistory* 39 (summer 1992): 247–84, provides an excellent analysis of how feminists in the nineteenth century constructed Indian history, both to show an alternative to American patriarchy among the matrilineal Iroquois and to validate the need for white women to civilize Native American women. Deborah Gordon's "Among Women" also examines how gender ideology for three different historical periods influenced women anthropologists' representations of Native American women.

61. Parsons, "Waiyautitsa," 89; Coolidge, *Rain-Makers*, 45–46.

62. Quoted in Coolidge, *Rain-Makers*, 38. See also Saunders, *Indians of the Terraced Houses*, 249.

63. Dozier, *Pueblo Indians*, 133–34, 137–38, 145–48, 163–66.

64. Morgan, *Ancient Society*, 66–67, 353–67, 476–99, 507, 512; Fynn, *American Indian*, 124–25; Superintendent of Santa Fe Indian School to Mr. H. A. Larson, Chief Special Officer, 10 December 1913, Santa Fe Indian Day School Correspondence, 1913–14, Entry 42, Box 1, Folder: L, Pueblo Records, NARA.

65. Austin, *Taos Pueblo*. See also Parsons, "Waiyautitsa," 95; Marriott, *María*, 8.

66. Austin, *Land of Journey's Ending*, 73–74; Austin, *Taos Pueblo*.

67. Austin, *Taos Pueblo*; Lummis, *Mesa, Cañon, and Pueblo*, 353.

68. For example, Alice Marriott, the anthropologist who interviewed Maria Martinez, claimed that at San Ildefonso Pueblo there had been a rule against divorce, "established by custom and reinforced by the [Catholic] church," but that it had been abandoned at the turn of the twentieth century. See Marriott, *María*, 11. For more on divorce practices at Taos and Zuni, see chapter 1.

69. Margaret Lewis to Parsons, n.d. [ca. 1917], Parsons papers.

70. Austin, *Land of Journey's Ending*, 244. See also Parsons, "Waiyautitsa," 96, and *Taos Pueblo*, 49; and Sophie Aberle, "Pueblo of San Juan," 28, manuscript, Box 2, Folder 1, Aberle papers.

71. Parsons, "Journal of a Feminist," 34. Parsons herself mentioned the differentiation of the sexes in both labor and religion in Pueblo society. The primary difference in religious roles was that boys were initiated into secret societies and men managed sacred ceremonies while females played a less central role in religion. See Parsons, "Waiyautitsa," 89–92, 103. Dozier also outlines the differentiation of sex roles in the religious area (*Pueblo Indians*, 169). See also Schlegel, "Male and Female," 245–69; Young, "Women," 436–45; and S. E. Jacobs, "Continuity and Change," 77–213.

72. Parsons, "Zuñi La'mana," 43, and "Waiyautitsa," 104. For more on the famous Zuni berdache We-Wha, see Will Roscoe, *The Zuni Man-Woman* (Albuquerque: University of New Mexico Press, 1991).

73. Quoted in Zumwalt, *Wealth and Rebellion*, 154.

74. Austin, *Land of Journey's Ending*, 239, 242. Lummis also notes Pueblo men's part in caring for children. See *Mesa, Cañon, and Pueblo*, 311–12.

75. Luhan, *Winter in Taos*, 30, 231, 232. Many white women writers tended to present the Pueblos as a society in which the home occupied a central position, for both men and women. Artist and writer Blanche Grant declared that the Taos Indians "live on quite happily together in their pueblos, 'monuments to human love of home.'" See Blanche C. Grant, *Taos Indians* (Taos: Santa Fe New Mexican Publishing Corp., 1925), 121. See also Collier, "Red Atlantis," 16–17, for another romanticization of the Pueblo home. Interestingly, even tourist promoters reinforced this emerging image. According to Barbara Babcock, in their publication *American Indians: First Families of the Southwest*, the Fred Harvey Company portrayed the Pueblos as "set-

tled, domestic, agrarian, aesthetic, and peaceful." See Babcock, "First Families, Gender, Reproduction, and the Mythic Southwest," in *The Great Southwest*, 210.

76. Luhan, *Edge of Taos Desert*, 57; Luhan, *Winter in Taos*, 46.
77. Luhan, *Lorenzo in Taos*, 74; Luhan, *Winter in Taos*, 97.
78. Luhan, *Winter in Taos*, 78–79, 84–85.
79. Luhan, *Winter in Taos*, 106, 108, 234–35.
80. Luhan, *Edge of Taos Desert*, 227; Luhan, *Lorenzo in Taos*, 73–74. See also Luhan, *Winter in Taos*, 42.
81. Linda Gordon, *Pitied but Not Entitled: Single Mothers and the History of Welfare, 1890–1935* (New York: Free Press, 1994), 107.
82. Elsie Clews Parsons, "Hopi Mothers and Children," in *Pueblo Mothers and Children*, 108. Parsons dryly presented the ways in which a newborn baby's mother, the mother's aunt, and the head of the household, an elderly lady, presented a child to the gods in "Mothers and Children at Laguna," in *Pueblo Mothers and Children*, 70.
83. Dippie, *Vanishing American*, 290; Marianna Torgovnick, *Gone Primitive: Savage Intellects, Modern Lives* (Chicago: University of Chicago Press, 1990), 228; Douglas, *Terrible Honesty*, 44.
84. Parsons, "Zuñi La'mana," 44; Mary Austin, "Where We Get Tammany Hall and Carnegie Libraries," *World Outlook* 4 (January 1918), reprint available in Austin papers–CSR, no page numbers given; Luhan, *Lorenzo in Taos*, 193.
85. Mabel Dodge Luhan to Elizabeth Shepley Sergeant, 10 June [1925], Collier papers, Reel 5; Luhan, *Edge of Taos Desert*, 64. In his article "Red Atlantis," John Collier similarly casts the Pueblos as masculine and virile (17).
86. Coolidge, *Rain-Makers*, xii; Parsons, "A Hopi Ceremonial," *Century* 101 (December 1920): 177; Luhan, *Edge of Taos Desert*, 179.
87. Mabel Dodge Luhan to Elizabeth Shepley Sergeant, 10 June [1925], Collier papers, Reel 5.
88. Luhan, *Movers and Shakers*, 58, 375, 494.
89. C. Simmons, "Modern Sexuality," 158, 164, 169–70; See also Estelle Freedman, "'Uncontrolled Desires': The Response to the Sexual Psychopath, 1920–1960," in *Passion and Power*, 199–225, which argues that women paid a high price "for recognition of their sexual desire and the removal of female purity as a restraint on male sexuality" (212). Women who were victims of rape or sexual assault were thereafter portrayed as willing participants. Pamela Haag makes a complementary point. She argues that the so-called sexual liberalization that occurred in the 1920s was still based on older gendered assumptions that associated men with self-mastery and rationality and women with irrationality. In this scenario women were still not in control of their sexuality. See Haag, "In Search of 'The Real Thing.'"
90. Luhan, *Movers and Shakers*, 526–27.

4. FEMINISTS' REDEFINITION OF GENDER AND RACE

1. Daniel Singal, introduction to *Modernist Culture in America* (Belmont CA: Wadsworth, 1991), 2; and T. J. Jackson Lears, "Uneasy Courtship: Modern Art and Modern Advertising," in *Modernist Culture in America*, 176.

2. See, for example, Heller and Rudnick, 1915; Daniel Joseph Singal, *The War Within: From Victorian to Modernist Thought in the South, 1919–1945* (Chapel Hill: University of North Carolina Press, 1982); and Singal, introduction to *Modernist Culture in America*, 4–5, 8, 10, 17.

3. Hinsley, *Savages and Scientists*; Stocking, *Race, Culture*; Dippie, *Vanishing American*; Coben, *Rebellion against Victorianism*, 55–57; Rosenberg, *Beyond Separate Spheres*, 163–66; Douglas, *Terrible Honesty*, 49–50; Cotkin, *Reluctant Modernism*.

4. Rosenberg, *Beyond Separate Spheres*; Smith-Rosenberg, "New Woman as Androgyne," 245–96; Heller and Rudnick, *1915*, 3–4; Pascoe, *Relations of Rescue*, 192–96.

5. Ironically, the tendency to view the world in terms of polar opposites was not limited to nineteenth-century or early-twentieth-century Americans. According to anthropologist Alfonso Ortiz and Santa Clara Pueblo architect Rina Swentzell, the Tewa Pueblo people organize society into dual "moieties," and they believe that they live in a world of polarities. See Alfonso Ortiz, *The Tewa World: Space, Time, Being, and Becoming in a Pueblo Society* (Chicago: University of Chicago Press, 1969), and Jane Brown Gillette, quoting Swentzell in "On Her Own Terms," *Historic Preservation* 44 (November/December 1992): 33, 84, 86. Thus, "moderns" shared more with the "primitives" than they were aware. For more on primitivism, see Helen Carr, *Inventing the American Primitive: Politics, Gender and the Representation of Native American Literary Traditions, 1789–1936* (New York: New York University Press, 1996).

6. Parsons did, however, develop problematic relations with many of her subjects. Zumwalt, *Wealth and Rebellion*, 248–57, explores in depth Parsons's conflicts with Jemez and Taos Pueblos, who were aghast both that she had revealed many of their ceremonial secrets and that someone within their pueblos had told her of them. Parsons's publications on Taos and Jemez caused intensified division at the pueblos and made tribal members suspicious of one another. According to Zumwalt, however, Parsons believed that no matter what the repercussions of her research, the pursuit of "science" justified her violation of the Pueblos' desire to maintain their privacy and secrecy. For more on Taos Pueblo conflict with Parsons, see letter from Sophie Aberle to Elsie Clews Parsons, 18 January 1939; Parsons to Aberle, 9 January 1939; John Collier to Antonio Mirabal, 11 January 1939; E. B. Jensen to Governor Albert Martinez, 25 July 1937; Star Road Gomez, Taos, to Superintendent Sophie Aberle, 6 April 1939; and Report from Emil J. Sady to Parsons, 13 March 1939, all in Box 4, Folder 2, Aberle papers. At Parsons's request, the first edition of her book *Taos*

Pueblo also included a note that the owner should not permit the copy to be seen by any Indian. See, for example, copy owned by Michael Harrison in his private library of Western history, Sacramento, California. See also Hare, *A Woman's Quest*, 145–62.

7. Austin, "Sex Emancipation through War," 609–10; Mary Austin, *The Young Woman Citizen* (New York: Woman's Press, 1918), 16, 19, 22.

8. Austin, *Young Woman Citizen*, 136.

9. Luhan, *Winter in Taos*, 112–13; Mabel Dodge Luhan to Carl Hovey, HM56356, 12 September (c. 1938), Levien papers; "The Ballad of a Bad Girl," first published in *Laughing Horse* (May 1924), then reprinted in Luhan, *Lorenzo in Taos*, 95–97.

10. Parsons, *Fear and Conventionality*, 134; Parsons, "Journal of a Feminist," 117.

11. Barbara A. Babcock has tried to argue that Parsons "challenged the naturalizing and essentializing which is the basis of racist and sexist ideologies," ignoring evidence that Parsons actually did believe in essential "natural" differences, as opposed to artificial differences. See Babcock, introduction to *Pueblo Mothers and Children*, 20.

12. Paul A. Robinson also notes that sexologist Havelock Ellis developed a similar analysis. Although he believed in women's sexual equality to men, he also contended that women were inherently different from men. Women had an essential tendency to be confined in the home; motherhood was their destiny. See Robinson's *Modernization of Sex*, 35–37.

13. Regina G. Kunzel, *Fallen Women, Problem Girls: Unmarried Mothers and the Professionalization of Social Work, 1890–1945* (New Haven CT: Yale University Press, 1993), 2–3, 9–35, 63.

14. Dozier, *Pueblo Indians*; Joe S. Sando, *Pueblo Nations: Eight Centuries of Pueblo Indian History* (Santa Fe: Clear Light, 1982).

15. Parsons, *Taos Pueblo*, 117; Marriott, *María*, 32, 200.

16. See Charles H. Lange, "The Contributions of Esther S. Goldfrank," in *Hidden Scholars*, 221–32; Benedict, *Patterns of Culture*, 57–129.

17. Interrogation of Joseph Melchor by Inspector Adelina Otero-Warren, 3 January 1925, IRA papers, Reel 42. This same report contains interviews with other members of the Melchor family and with John Dixon. In a letter from Clara True to Matthew Sniffen of the IRA, 1 July 1924, IRA papers, Reel 41, True describes some of her efforts to publicize the plight of the Melchors and Dixon. For a description of the Hunt case in the 1920s and 1930s, see the report from C. U. Finley to George Stevens, Field Representative to the Commissioner of Indian Affairs, 22 May 1936, Box 6, Folder 48, Sophie Aberle papers.

18. Parsons, *Taos Pueblo*, 101, 117.

19. Luhan, *Winter in Taos*, 53; Austin, *Land of Journey's Ending*, 246–47; Luhan, *Edge*

of Taos Desert, 241. See also Collier, "Red Atlantis," 15–16, for another example of comparing the communal Pueblos to individualistic Anglos.

20. Austin, *Land of Journey's Ending*, 116; Coolidge, *Rain-Makers*, 114.

21. Rudnick, introduction to Luhan, *Movers and Shakers*, xi; Haag, "In Search of 'The Real Thing.'"

22. Mary Austin to Mabel Dodge Luhan, 28 September [1920], Luhan papers; Austin, *Land of Journey's Ending*, 9; Luhan, *Edge of Taos Desert*, 241–42.

23. Luhan, *Edge of Taos Desert*, 110; Luhan, *Movers and Shakers*, 64–65.

24. Luhan, *Edge of Taos Desert*, 63; Coolidge, *Rain-Makers*, 13.

25. Mabel Dodge Sterne to Mary Austin, 28 November [1922], AU 3581, Box 95, Austin papers–HUNT; Luhan, *Winter in Taos*, 30; Parsons, *Taos Pueblo*, 24. In a letter to Elsie Clews Parsons, 28 November [1922], Parsons papers, Luhan also expresses the desire to set up a special foundation to preserve Pueblo Indians as real farmers.

26. E. F. Estabrook, "The Pueblo Indians: A Suggestion to Those Who Visit Them," School of American Research leaflet, 1927, U.S.I.S. #1 folder, Dunn papers.

27. Luhan, *Winter in Taos*, 195–96; Estabrook, "The Pueblo Indians."

28. Fergusson, *Dancing Gods*, 276.

29. Austin, *Land of Journey's Ending*, 235, 238, 264–65.

30. Coolidge, *Rain-Makers*, 198; Bandelier quoted in Leo Crane, *Desert Drums: The Pueblo Indians of New Mexico, 1540–1928* (Boston: Little, Brown, 1928), 234–35. For another example of new feminists who stressed the centrality of religion in Pueblo life, see Fergusson, *Dancing Gods*, 27.

31. Dozier, *Pueblo Indians*, 133. As a member of Santa Clara Pueblo, among the Eastern Pueblos, Dozier may be "Otherizing" the Western Pueblos in the same way that many whites did to the Pueblos in general. Importantly, though, it is clear from his remarks that Dozier does not believe that religion is the only or chief concern of all Pueblo Indians.

32. Edward W. Said, *Orientalism* (New York: Pantheon, 1978). For an excellent analysis of the ways in which the British constructed Indians as driven by their religion, see Lata Mani, "The Production of an Official Discourse on Sati in Early Nineteenth-Century Bengal," *Economic and Political Weekly* 11 (26 April 1986): 32–40.

33. Mabel Dodge Luhan to Elizabeth Shepley Sergeant, 10 June [1925], Collier papers, Reel 5.

34. For more on the reorientation toward heterosexuality and heterosociality after World War I, see Peiss, *Cheap Amusements*; C. Simmons, "Modern Sexuality"; Freedman, "Uncontrolled Desires"; and Haag, "In Search of 'The Real Thing.'"

35. Weigle and Babcock, *Great Southwest*, 157.

36. In her book on modern primitivism, Marianna Torgovnick finds that a belief that existing primitive societies are outside of linear time is one of the most persistent as-

pects of primitivism (*Gone Primitive*, 46). See also Deborah Root, *Cannibal Culture: Art, Appropriation, and the Commodification of Difference* (Boulder CO: Westview, 1996), 37; and Hinsley, "Authoring Authenticity," 469–70.

37. Austin, *Taos Pueblo*.

38. For more on Americans' desire for authenticity and for a sense of their past during this era of rapid modernization, see Lears, *No Place of Grace*, and Miles Orvell, *The Real Thing: Imitation and Authenticity in American Culture, 1880–1940* (Chapel Hill: University of North Carolina Press, 1989).

39. Fergusson, *Dancing Gods*, 10. Barbara A. Babcock has also noted how white writers invested Pueblo Indian women with tradition, valuing them because they thought them "outside history, outside industrial capitalism" ("'A New Mexican Rebecca': Imaging Pueblo Women," *Journal of the Southwest* 32 [winter 1990]: 404).

40. Lummis, *Mesa, Cañon, and Pueblo*, 158; Fergusson, *Dancing Gods*, 141–42. In an informal interview with Michael Harrison, Harrison claimed that Lummis had a reputation as a philanderer.

41. Quoted in Thomas, *Southwestern Indian Detours*, 196. For other examples, see Saunders, *Indians of the Terraced Houses*, 5; Coolidge, *Rain-Makers*, frontispiece; Lummis, *Mesa, Cañon, and Pueblo*, 202–3; Luhan, *Winter in Taos*, 211.

42. Babcock, "A New Mexican Rebecca," 406; Marta Weigle, "Selling the Southwest: Santa Fe in Sites," in *Discovered Country: Tourism and Survival in the American West*, ed. Scott Norris (Albuquerque: Stone Ladder, 1994), 211–14. For the classic work on Orientalism, see Said, *Orientalism*.

43. Luhan quoted in Claire Morrill, *A Taos Mosaic: Portrait of a New Mexico Village* (Albuquerque: University of New Mexico Press, 1973), 5. See also Grant, *Taos Indians*, 14. Grant and Luhan seem to forget that the only element linking the words "Taos" and "Tao" is English spelling. Both are transliterations of Chinese and Tanoan pronunciations. The two words are pronounced utterly differently.

44. Austin, *Land of Journey's Ending*, 246; Fergusson, *Dancing Gods*, 3; Elizabeth DeHuff, "Indian Is Far from Dull or Stupid, Says DeHuff," *New Mexican*, 16 April 1927, clipping in DeHuff papers, addition; Luhan, *Edge of Taos Desert*, 20.

45. David Levering Lewis, *When Harlem Was in Vogue* (New York: Oxford University Press, 1979), 73, 91–92, 99, 188–89. Dippie, in *The Vanishing American*, has also made similar observations (290–91). See also Douglas, *Terrible Honesty*, on modern dance pioneer Martha Graham's interest in "savage choreography," in which she studied and incorporated elements of both Indian and Negro dance into her choreography (51).

46. Luhan, *Movers and Shakers*, 535; Lewis, *When Harlem Was in Vogue*, 151; Douglas, *Terrible Honesty*, 282; entries for Burlin and Parsons are found in *Daughters of the Desert*, 94–97, 14–19 respectively.

47. Luhan, *Movers and Shakers*, 351–53, 532.

48. Quoted in María E. Montoya, "The Roots of Economic and Ethnic Divisions in Northern New Mexico: The Case of the Civilian Conservation Corps," *Western Historical Quarterly* 26 (spring 1995): 20. For more on the movement to promote arts and crafts for Mexican-Americans, see Deutsch, *No Separate Refuge*, 187–99.

49. Dozier, *Pueblo Indians*, 109–14; Sylvia Rodríguez, "Art, Tourism, and Race Relations in Taos: Toward a Sociology of the Art Colony," *Journal of Anthropological Research* 45 (spring 1989): 77–99; Rodríguez, "Land, Water," 313–403.

50. Luhan, *Edge of Taos Desert*, 193. In *The White Man's Indian*, Berkhofer has argued that creating a "paradigm of polarity" between whites and Indians has been persistent throughout American history (xvi).

51. In "Playing Indian: Otherness and Authenticity in the Assumption of American Indian Identity" (Ph.D. diss., Yale University, 1994), Philip Joseph Deloria finds that post–World War II hobbyists engaged in a similar process of maintaining the rhetoric of cultural relativism while reaffirming "the difference and 'authenticity' of the Indian Other by privileging race—constructed around the idea of Indian 'blood'" (366). Deloria has also found that "'culture' and 'race' coexisted in American culture, paired in a doubled consciousness" (365); see also pp. 352–54.

52. Luhan to Collier, 30 November 1933, Collier papers, Reel 15; Austin, *Earth Horizon*, 267.

53. New feminists were not the only Americans who reconceived of race in modern versus antimodern terms. Ernest Thompson Seton, a cofounder of the Boy Scouts of America, also viewed Indians "as the perfect manifestations of a dialogic modern/ anti-modern identity" (Deloria, "Playing Indian," 280).

54. For more on the connotations of the words "primitive" versus "savage," see Carr, *Inventing the American Primitive*, 208. Mary Austin often called for redefining American literature and identity around Native Americans, especially the Pueblos, rather than Europeans. For an example, see *The American Rhythm: Studies and Reexpressions of Amerindian Songs* (Boston: Houghton Mifflin, 1930) and also Austin to Luhan 9 November, ca. 1920, and 26 July 1922, Luhan papers. Ann Douglas, in *Terrible Honesty*, has found this effort to break away from European influences to be a hallmark of modernist intellectuals.

55. Parsons, *Fear and Conventionality*, 214. Havelock Ellis shared similar ideas—that marriage should be based on sexual passion and psychological affinity but that parenthood should be based on racial fitness and eugenics. See Robinson, *Modernization of Sex*, 34. Ellis also asserted that the morality of art, whatever he meant by that, would replace the old moralities. But the quality of the population was not good enough to effect such a transformation. It needed to be improved through eugenics. See Havelock Ellis, *The Dance of Life* (New York: Houghton Mifflin, 1923), 349, 357–58.

56. Kathleen M. Blee, *Women of the Klan: Racism and Gender in the 1920s* (Berkeley: University of California Press, 1991), 23. Evans and the KKK opposed immigration because they believed in the need to develop a "good stock of Americans." Austin and Luhan also used this phrase frequently, though they all may have defined "good stock" differently. See, for example, Luhan, *Winter in Taos*, 48. John Collier and other prominent anthropologists and educators were also active in putting together a "graphic display of the Native Races of America" for the Third International Congress on Eugenics. See *Report of the International Committee on the Graphic Display of the Native Races of America*, 17 May 1932, Collier papers, Reel 9. See also Barkan, *Retreat of Scientific Racism*, who contends that many prominent cultural-relativist anthropologists, such as Boas and Parsons, participated in the eugenics movement (67, 108). Thanks to Laura Lovett for pointing out the ubiquity of "good stock" rhetoric at the turn of the century.

57. Quoted in Deacon, "The Republic of the Spirit," 27.

58. For the view of Parsons as a person wholly committed to race as a social construction, see Babcock, *Pueblo Mothers*, 20; Rosenberg, *Beyond Separate Spheres*, 147–77. Information regarding Lummis's alleged promiscuity derives from a personal conversation with Michael Harrison.

59. "Ina Sizer Cassidy—Lady of Contrasts" (*The Santa Fe Scene*, 13 December 1958, p. 7), clipping in the Austin papers–BANC; Elizabeth DeHuff, fragment of letter, 19 February 1932, Box 10, Folder 27, DeHuff papers; and "Pueblo Episodes," unpublished manuscript, 18, Box 6, Folder 48, DeHuff papers.

60. Peggy Pond Church, *The House at Otowi Bridge* (Albuquerque: University of New Mexico Press, 1959), 39, 45–49, 58.

61. Church, *House at Otowi Bridge*, 41, 106–7, and quote from Warner's essay in *Neighborhood, A Settlement Quarterly* (June 1931), reprinted in Church, *House at Otowi Bridge*, 49.

62. Luhan, *Edge of Taos Desert*, 222.

63. For correspondence between Luhan and Austin regarding their spiritual practices, see, for example, Austin to Luhan, 25 November 1930, 5 March [1920]; n.d. Monday morning [1922?]; 31 December [1923]; 10 May [1923], Luhan papers. Luhan, *Edge of Taos Desert*, 298. In *No Place of Grace*, T. J. Jackson Lears asserts that "antimodern impulses reinforced the shift from a Protestant ethos of salvation through self-denial to a therapeutic ideal of self-fulfillment" (xvi).

64. Luhan, *Edge of Taos Desert*, 178, 179, 221.

65. As Philip Deloria, "Playing Indian," has noted, "The dilemma of modernity . . . centered on finding ways to preserve the integrity of the boundaries that demarked exterior authentic Indians, and yet somehow gaining access to an organic Indian purity in order to make it one's own" (310). For more on "playing Indian," see Rayna

Green, "The Tribe Called Wannabee: Playing Indian in America and Europe," *Folklore* 99 (1988): 30–55.

66. Parsons, "Hopi Ceremonial," 178.
67. DeHuff, "Pueblo Episodes," 4, 6; Dilworth, *Imagining Indians*, 8.
68. Austin to Cassidy, 18 March [1926], Austin papers–BANC; Austin, *Taos Pueblo*. For other examples of competition between writers, see Austin to Cassidy, 12 December 1922, Austin papers–BANC; and Frank Applegate to Mary Austin, 6 March [1929], AU 1009, Austin papers–HUNT.
69. See photos of Santiago Naranjo of Santa Clara Pueblo and Pueblo delegates at Bolinas Bay and Montalvo, all looking like Sioux warriors with their elaborate feathered headdresses, in *American Indian Life*, Bulletin no. 3 (September–December 1925), Collier papers, Reel 9. For more on attempts by primitivists to impose paternalistic control over native peoples, see Carr, *Inventing the American Primitive*, 203.
70. Elizabeth Shepley Sergeant to Lorenzo Chaves, Interpreter to the Zuni Tribe, 4 January 1923, Collier papers, Reel 5; Mabel Dodge Sterne to John Collier, 21 November [1922], Collier papers, Reel 3. For other examples of occasions on which Luhan tried to manipulate delegations of Indians and the media, see Mabel Dodge Luhan to Collier, 13 October [1922?], Carton 1, Pueblo Indian Misc. Correspondence, prior to 1926, CLAI papers; and Mabel Dodge Luhan to Mary Austin, n.d., circa 1923, AU 3586, Box 95, Austin papers–HUNT.
71. Austin to Luhan, 1 February [1923], Luhan papers.
72. Austin to Luhan, 27 January, 1 February [1923], Luhan papers.
73. Austin to Gerald Cassidy, 7 April [1919], Austin papers–BANC, and Austin, *Taos Pueblo*. An *acequia madre* refers to the community's irrigation ditch. For John Collier's similar chastisement of an Indian "radical," see Jimmie Lujan to John Collier, 31 January 1935, and John Collier to Jimmie Lujan, 16 February 1935, Collier papers, Reel 15.
74. In "Playing Indian," Philip Deloria also finds that hobbyists who dabbled in Native American culture after World War II also dismissed Indian people who did not match their primitive ideal as "tragic, 'degraded' figures" (354).
75. Morrill, *Taos Mosaic*, 110. Luhan also received criticism from other whites. When her memoirs appeared in the 1930s, Marxist radicals accused her of romanticizing poverty. See Rudnick, *Mabel Dodge Luhan*, 256–57.
76. Elizabeth DeHuff, "A Pueblo Indian Wedding," *New Mexico Highway Journal* (October 1932): 23.

5. THE 1920S CONTROVERSY OVER INDIAN DANCES

1. Statement of Evelyn Bentley, 30 September 1920, Exhibit C, Sweet collection. The Bureau of Indian Affairs (BIA) referred to the Hopis as the Moqui, a derogatory Spanish term, until the 1930s.

2. Exhibits A, B, C, D, and E, Sweet collection. Reformers called the compilation of testimony the "Secret Dance File" because they believed that the dances described therein were held in secret by the Pueblos.

3. Unfortunately, the only other historian I know of who has made use of the so-called Secret Dance File treated it as a transparent source that reveals the nature of Pueblo sexuality at the turn of the century. See Martin Bauml Duberman, "Documents in Hopi Indian Sexuality: Imperialism, Culture, and Resistance," *Radical History Review* 20 (spring/summer 1979): 99–130.

4. Kelly, *Assault on Assimilation*, 295–348; Philp, *John Collier's Crusade*, 55–70; David M. Strausfeld, "Reformers in Conflict: The Pueblo Dance Controversy," in *The Aggressions of Civilization: Federal Indian Policy since the 1880s*, ed. Sandra Cadwalader and Vine Deloria Jr. (Philadelphia: Temple University Press, 1984), 19–43.

5. Fass, *Damned and the Beautiful*; Robinson, *Modernization of Sex*, 1–41; Coben, *Rebellion against Victorianism*; May, *Great Expectations*; Filene, *Him/Her/Self*, 1–168; Rothman, *Hands and Hearts*, 179–311; D'Emilio and Freedman, *Intimate Matters*, 171–274; O'Neill, *Divorce*; Peiss, *Cheap Amusements*, especially 163–84; Smith-Rosenberg, "New Woman as Androgyne," 245–96.

6. While historians Joan Wallach Scott and Carroll Smith-Rosenberg have argued in several essays about ways in which discourses use gender, sexuality, and the body as metaphors for other political and economic conflicts, this chapter argues that the reverse can be true as well. Discourses about other conflicts can also be used for debating matters of gender and sexuality. See Joan Wallach Scott, "Gender: A Useful Category of Historical Analysis" in *Gender and the Politics of History* (New York: Columbia University Press, 1988), 28–50; and Carroll Smith-Rosenberg, "Hearing Women's Words: A Feminist Reconstruction of History," in *Disorderly Conduct*, 11–52.

7. Robert M. Utley, *The Indian Frontier of the American West, 1846–1890* (Albuquerque: University of New Mexico Press, 1984), 220, 243. The Ghost Dance movement, which started among the Paiutes in Nevada, promised that God would kill off all the whites, bring dead Indians and buffalo back to life, and return the earth to the Indians. The Sun Dance is a dance practiced by many Plains tribes that involves a painful ritual designed to induce a trance. Reformers believed it was a savage form of self-torture. Give-aways were and still are practiced primarily among some Plains and Northwest tribes; in give-aways hosts display their status by giving away most of their possessions. Reformers believed such a practice discouraged thrift and industry. Weeks, *Farewell, My Nation*, 232; Hertzberg, *Search for Identity*, 10–14.

8. Sando, *Pueblo Nations*, 88. Sando points out that though a positive image of the Pueblos, this failure to bring the Pueblos under the guardianship of the federal government led to massive trespasses on Pueblo land. In the Sandoval case in 1913 the

223

Pueblos finally became classified as Indians, subject to the rules but also afforded the protection of the federal government (114).

9. Commissioner Price to Pedro Sanchez, U.S. Indian Agent, Pueblo Agency, 27 June 1883, Northern Pueblos, Miscellaneous Reports and Correspondence, 1868–1934 (Entry 83), Box 5, Folder 103, Pueblo Records, NARA; Superintendent, Santa Fe Indian School, "Memorandum for Supervisor Rosenkranz," 26 December 1913, Santa Fe Indian School Day School Correspondence, 1913–14 (Entry 42), Box 2, Folder s, Pueblo Records, NARA. In *The Pueblo Indians of North America*, Edward P. Dozier writes that up until 1900, Protestant missionaries did not "apparently object to the ceremonies of the Pueblos" (105–6). I have not found evidence of concern about Pueblo dances until 1915.

10. "Exhibit D," Sweet collection; Mary Dissette to Miss Willard, 3 March 1924, IRA papers, Reel 40.

11. For letters describing and protesting this article, see Francis Wilson to Cato Sells, 23 April 1915; Superintendent of Indian School, Santa Fe, to Commissioner Sells, 15 May 1915; and C. J. Crandall, Superintendent at Pierre SD Indian School to Cato Sells, 19 April 1915 in Entry 83, Box 17, Folder 070, Pueblo Records, NARA. For a Pueblo explanation of the snake, see Samuel L. Gray, *Tonita Peña: Quah Ah, 1893–1949* (Albuquerque: Avanyu, 1990), 42–44.

12. Rosendo Vargas to Santa Fe Indian School, 20 November 1915, enclosed in Frederic Snyder to Superintendent Lonergan, Pueblo Day Schools, 23 November 1915, Southern Pueblos Agency, General Correspondence Files, 1911–35 (Entry 90), Box 21, Folder 070, Pueblo Records, NARA.

13. A circular issued by Commissioner of Indian Affairs W. A. Jones in 1902, entitled "Long Hair Prohibited," mentions briefly at the end that Indian dances should be prohibited. This circular, however, did not specify which dances it found in need of prohibition, and it did not discuss sexual immorality as a reason for banning dances as Circular 1665 did. Neither did this circular seem to be concerned with Pueblo dances. See Circular, 13 January 1920, Special Collections, Knight Library, University of Oregon, Eugene. Thanks to Annette Reed-Crum for bringing this document to my attention.

14. John Collier railed against the Secret Dance File as "subterranean propaganda." See untitled manuscript, undated [ca. 1923], "For two years, the public has heard," and John Collier to editor of the *New York Times*, typed letter, 14 November 1924, Carton 1, Folder: "Collier, Pueblos and Religious Persecution," CLAI papers. In addition to the alleged sexual immorality connected with Pueblo dances, reformers were appalled by the Hopis' Snake Dance in which they took live rattlesnakes into their mouths. The Secret Dance File (Exhibits A, B, C, and E, Sweet Collection) contains much testimony regarding how this dance was carried out. For more on white fas-

cination with and representation of the Hopi Snake Dance, see Dilworth, *Imagining Indians*, 21–75.

15. For some of the publicity that reformers wrote in condemnation of the dances, see Flora Warren Seymour, "Our Indian Problem—The Delusion of the Sentimentalists," *Forum* 71 (March 1924), 273–80; William E. Johnson, "Those Sacred Indian Ceremonials," *The Native American* 24 (20 September 1924): 173–77; William E. Johnson, "Civilizing Indian Dances and White Writers," typewritten manuscript, Carton 1, Folder: "Pueblo Indian Religious Persecution Re. 'Pussyfoot,'" CLAI papers; Herbert Welsh, letters to the editor of the *Herald* and the *New York Times*, 22 August 1924 and 15 October 1924 respectively, clippings in Collier papers, Reel 9; "Indian Dances Degrading, Says Y.W.C.A. Leader," *New York Times*, 25 November 1923, clipping in Collier papers, Reel 9; Work, "Our American Indians," 92; Letter from Secretary of the Interior Hubert Work to San Ildefonso Pueblo, reprinted in *Indian Truth* 1 (March 1924): 4; and commentaries in *Indian Truth* 1 (April 1924): 4; *Indian Truth* 1 (June 1924): 1–2. *Indian Truth* was an official publication of the Indian Rights Association. See also G.E.E. Lindquist, *The Red Man in the United States: An Intimate Study of the Social, Economic and Religious Life of the American Indian* (New York: George H. Doran, 1923), 68–69, 267–68, 273, 287. This book published the results of an American Indian Survey begun in 1919 by the Interchurch World Movement. Moral reformers and missionaries, however, were not monolithic in their opposition to the dances nor in their support for federal intervention. Upon receiving information regarding the supposed immoralities of Pueblo dances, Bishop Howden of Albuquerque went to investigate and found the claims to be exaggerated. He called for better understanding of the meaning of the alleged immoralities in Indian dances. See Howden to Charles Burke, 12 March 1925, Entry 83, Box 17, Folder: Indian Customs, 1916–34, Pueblo Records, NARA. See also "Statement of Reverend and Mrs. H. Freyling," missionaries at Zuni, who opposed efforts to force Indians to give up their dances, 9 May 1924, IRA papers, Reel 40. Howden and the Freylings, however, were in the minority among missionaries.

16. Circular 1665, 26 April 1921, and Supplement to Circular 1665, 14 February 1923, Collier papers, Reel 5. The circular and its supplement were directed not just at the Pueblo Indians but at all Native American tribes, with dire consequences for some. Using the circular, the BIA stopped the Midewiwin dance of the Menominees and prohibited all dances on the Sac and Fox Reservation in 1924. See J. P. Harrington to Miss Brown, 10 September 1924, Carton 1, "Pueblo Indian Religious Persecution Correspondence, Collier" folder, CLAI papers. As late as 1932, the BIA cited the circular when they broke up a dance among the Tolowa/Hush people of northern California. See Annette Reed-Crum, "Tolowa 'Hush': Native Response to Circular 1665,"

paper presented at Western History Association conference, Denver, Colorado, October 1995.

17. Circular 1665 and Supplement, Collier papers, Reel 5.

18. Circular 1665 and Supplement, Collier papers, Reel 5; Peiss, *Cheap Amusements*, 163–84.

19. Pascoe, *Relations of Rescue*, 32–69; Karen Anderson, *Changing Woman: A History of Racial Ethnic Women in Modern America* (New York: Oxford University Press, 1996), 55.

20. "Bumbletonian Indian Bureau" was Mary Austin's name for the BIA; *Land of Journey's Ending*, 444. For some of the letters to the editor and articles written by defenders of Pueblo dances, see typewritten letter to the editor, *New York Times*, probably from Charles Lummis, 18 September 1924, Carton 1, Folder: "Collier, Pueblos and Religious Persecution," CLAI papers; "Society's Millions Behind Wild Indian Dances," clipping with no author, publication, or date in Collier papers [ca. 1924], Reel 9; "Religious Persecution of Indians Charged by Defense League Official," *Sacramento Bee* (28 August 1924), clipping in Collier papers, Reel 9; Collier to *New York Times*, written 2 December 1923, clipping in Collier papers, Reel 9; John Collier, "Do Indians Have Rights of Conscience?" *Christian Century* (12 March 1924): 346–49, clipping in Collier papers, Reel 10; Elizabeth Shepley Sergeant, "The Principales Speak," *New Republic* 33 (7 February 1923): 273–75; Mary Austin, "Our Indian Problem—The Folly of the Officials," *Forum* 71 (March 1924): 281–88.

21. See letter from F. W. Hodge to Austin with filled-out questionnaire, 28 August 1923, AU 2767, Box 82, Austin papers–HUNT; also letter from Austin's secretary to Elizabeth Shepley Sergeant, 5 January 1924, Collier papers, Reel 5; Mary Austin to Robert Brown, 23 March 1923, Box 2A, White papers; Cash Asher to Elizabeth Shepley Sergeant, 29 May 1924, Collier papers, Reel 5; Zumwalt, *Wealth and Rebellion*, 265.

22. Stella Atwood speech, 10 June 1924, at Seventeenth Biennial Convention, General Federation of Women's Clubs, Los Angeles, GFWC papers. For other examples of how historians have used the concept of republicanism, see Sean Wilentz, *Chants Democratic: New York City and the Rise of the American Working Class, 1788–1850* (New York: Oxford University Press, 1984); Thomas Dublin, *Women at Work: The Transformation of Work and Community in Lowell, Massachusetts, 1826–1860* (New York: Columbia University Press, 1979); and Linda K. Kerber, *Women of the Republic: Intellect and Ideology in Revolutionary America* (New York: Norton, 1980).

23. Statement of "The American Indian Policies Association" (later the AIDA), 14 February 1923, Box 2A, White papers; Erna Fergusson, *Dancing Gods*, xvi, 32. See also Ina Sizer Cassidy to Hubert Work, Secretary of the Interior, 23 March 1923, Cassidy papers.

24. Elsie Sergeant to Luhan, 1 June [1923], Luhan papers; Austin, *Land of Journey's Ending*, 255–56.
25. Erna Fergusson, "Laughing Priests," *Theatre Arts Monthly* 17 (August 1933): 657.
26. L. R. McDonald to P. T. Lonergan, 11 May 1915; L. H. Mitchell to P. T. Lonergan, 7 May 1915; Lyman Darnold to Lonergan, 19 May 1915; Macario Garcia to P. T. Lonergan, 28 October 1915; and Blas Casaus to Lonergan, 7 November 1915, Exhibit D, Sweet collection. Only men were clowns, and clowns often dressed as women. See Alfonso Ortiz, "Ritual Drama and the Pueblo World View," in *New Perspectives on the Pueblos*, ed. Alfonso Ortiz (Albuquerque: University of New Mexico Press, 1972), 135–61, and Ortiz, *Tewa World*, 36; Schlegel, "Male and Female," 255; Dozier, *Pueblo Indians*, 140.
27. Statement of Johnson Tuwaletstiwa, 14 August 1920, Exhibit A, Sweet collection. *Katsinas*, more commonly spelled *kachinas*, are supernatural beings who live in sacred areas near some of the pueblos. They are believed to have once visited the pueblos at certain times of year for religious ceremonies. Kachinas also refer to the masked impersonators of the supernatural beings who perform at some Pueblo ceremonies. Sometimes the kachinas entertain the crowd alongside the clowns. Kachina dolls representing the masked impersonators of the spirits have become a major tourist item for sale in the Southwest. See Dockstader, *Kachina*; Ortiz, *Tewa World*, 18; Jill D. Sweet, *Dances of the Tewa Indians: Expressions of New Life* (Santa Fe NM: School of American Research Press, 1985), 9–10; Schaafsma, *Kachinas*.
28. Fergusson, *Dancing Gods*, xiv, 31; Austin, *Land of Journey's Ending*, 258.
29. Ortiz, "Ritual Drama," 152; Dozier, *Pueblo Indians*, 151; Vera Laski, *Seeking Life*, Memoirs of the American Folklore Society, vol. 50 (Philadelphia PA: American Folklore Society, 1958), 14. See also Young, "Women," 436–38; Dockstader, *Kachina*, 9–10, 19, 123–24; and Emory Sekaquaptewa, "One More Smile for a Hopi Clown," in *The South Corner of Time: Hopi, Navajo, Papago, Yaqui Tribal Literature*, ed. Larry Evers (Tucson: Sun Tracks, 1980), 14–17.
30. Fergusson, *Dancing Gods*, xv, 246–47.
31. Statement of Talasnimtiwa, 12 August 1920, and statement of Kuwanwikvaya, 26 August 1920, Exhibit A, Sweet collection.
32. Statements of Evelyn Bentley, 30 September 1920, Exhibit C; Quoyawayma, 16 April 1921, Exhibit E; Johnson Tuwaletstiwa, 14 August 1920, Exhibit A; all in Sweet collection. Quoyawyma was Polingaysi Qoyawayma's father. The distinct spellings of their names are due to differences in transcription by white interviewers.
33. Grant, *Taos Indians*, 103–4.
34. Austin, *Taos Pueblo*; Mabel Dodge Luhan to Elizabeth Shepley Sergeant, 10 June [1925], Collier papers, Reel 5.
35. Parsons, *Taos Pueblo*, 99; Elsie Clews Parsons, "Nativity Myth at Laguna and Zuni," in *Pueblo Mothers and Children*, 57 n.22.

36. Statement of Johnson Tuwaletstiwa, 14 August 1920, Exhibit A, and statement of Talasnimtiwa, 12 August 1920, both in Exhibit A, Sweet collection.
37. L. R. McDonald to P. T. Lonergan, 11 May 1915, Exhibit D, and statement of Johnson Tuwaletstiwa, 14 August 1920, Exhibit A, both in Sweet collection.
38. Fergusson, *Dancing Gods*, 39; Luhan, *Edge of Taos Desert*, 100. Among the Pueblos, there are many dances in which male clowns impersonate women. There are also some dances—the Deer Dance, Corn Dance, and Rainbow Dance—in which women themselves dance. Furthermore, there are a few dances in which female clowns perform burlesques and parodies, particularly of the Navajos. Among the Hopis and at San Ildefonso and Santo Domingo Pueblos, there are even dances in which women parody men of their pueblo. See Schlegel, "Male and Female," 257; Charlotte J. Frisbie, "Epilogue," in *Southwestern Indian Ritual Drama*, ed. Charlotte Frisbie (Albuquerque: University of New Mexico Press, 1980), 319–20; Donald N. Brown, "Dance as Experience: The Deer Dance of Picuris Pueblo," in *Southwestern Indian Ritual Drama*, 71–92.
39. Fass, *Damned and the Beautiful*, 18–21; May, *Great Expectations*, 2; Filene, *Him/Her/Self*, 42–44; O'Neill, *Divorce*, 31, 33–88; Pascoe, *Relations of Rescue*, 37–38.
40. Filene, *Him/Her/Self*, 165.
41. Filene, *Him/Her/Self*, 149–50; Joanne J. Meyerowitz, *Women Adrift: Independent Wage Earners in Chicago, 1880–1930* (Chicago: University of Chicago Press, 1988); Kunzel, *Fallen Women*.
42. Quoted in Fass, *Damned and the Beautiful*, 23.
43. Quoted in Lewis, *When Harlem Was in Vogue*, 32. See also Rothman, *Hands and Hearts*, 292.
44. Peiss, *Cheap Amusements*, 163–84; Fass, *Damned and the Beautiful*, 22–23, 300–303. Interestingly, before becoming involved in Indian affairs, John Collier had conducted antivice activities in New York City, policing dance halls and contributing to the organization of the National Board of Censorship of Motion Pictures in 1909. See Pivar, *Purity Crusade*, 270. Evelyn Brooks Higginbotham has also found that an emergent class of black women in the black Baptist Church also disapproved of jazz music and dance halls. See *Righteous Discontent*, 200.
45. Quoted in Coben, *Rebellion against Victorianism*, 76.
46. For brief mention of Johnson's role in the prohibition crusade see Fass, *Damned and the Beautiful*, 359; for more on his job to break up liquor traffic among Indians, see Hertzberg, *Search for Identity*, 93–94. See also William E. Johnson to Matthew Sniffen, 4 April 1914, IRA papers, Reel 29. For more on Bishop Hare, see O'Neill, *Divorce*, 232–34, and on Dabb, see her correspondence throughout the IRA papers.
47. Mary Dissette to Miss Willard, 3 March 1924, IRA papers, Reel 40; Statement of Quoyawyma, 16 April 1921, Exhibit E, Sweet collection.

48. See Robinson, *Modernization of Sex*, 30; Filene, *Him/Her/Self*, 70, 166; Zumwalt, *Wealth and Rebellion*, 46; Fass, *Damned and the Beautiful*, 22–23, 300–303; Peiss, *Cheap Amusements*, 163–84.

49. May, *Great Expectations*, 4–5; D'Emilio and Freedman, *Intimate Matters*, 174.

50. Blas Casaus to P. T. Lonergan, 7 November 1915, and L. R. McDonald to P. T. Lonergan, 11 May 1915, both in Exhibit D, Sweet collection.

51. Letters from L. R. McDonald and L. H. Mitchell to P. T. Lonergan, 11 May and 7 May 1915, Exhibit D; statement of Evelyn Bentley, 30 September 1920, Exhibit C; all in Sweet collection.

52. Mary Dissette to Miss Willard, 3 March 1924, IRA papers, Reel 40.

53. Elazar Barkan, "Victorian Promiscuity: Greek Ethics and Primitive Exemplars," in *Prehistories of the Future*, 91; Susan Yohn, *Contest of Faiths: Missionary Women and Pluralism in the American Southwest* (Ithaca NY: Cornell University Press, 1995), 127.

54. Parsons, "Zuñi La'mana," 43.

55. Policy statement in brochure of Eastern Association on Indian Affairs (EAIA), 10 October 1923, also reprinted in American Indian Defense Association (AIDA) Announcement of Purposes, both in Box 2A, White papers. Interestingly, just as some of the new feminists attempted to wrest cultural authority away from moral reformers by espousing a need for a new scientific authority, so too did these new activists. Throughout the dance controversy, defenders of the dances complained that reformers had not sought the "expert" opinion of anthropologists and others who had made scientific study of the Indians. "Those who know the facts as to Indian religious morality are the anthropologists," Collier stated. See "The Defense of the Persecution," in Carton 1, "Pueblo Indian Religious Persecution Correspondence, Collier" folder, CLAI papers. See also Collier to Mrs. John D. Sherman, President, GFWC, 16 September 1924, Carton 1, Folder: "Pueblo Indian Religious Persecution Re. 'Pussyfoot,'" CLAI papers.

56. See *Indian Truth* 1 (June 1924): 2, 6; Matthew Sniffen to Clara True, telegram and letter, 24 May 1924; Samuel Brosius to Matthew Sniffen, 29 May 1924; and telegram from Clara True to Matthew Sniffen, 31 May 1924, IRA papers, Reel 40; letters from True to Sniffen, 1 and 23 July 1924; telegrams, True to Sniffen, 9 and 10 June 1924, IRA papers, Reel 41. Of Spanish descent, Nina Otero married Captain Warren of the U.S. Army in 1904. In addition to working as an inspector for the BIA, she was the chair of the New Mexico Federation of Women's Clubs, the state chair of the women's Republican organization, and from 1917 to 1929 she served as county superintendent of schools in Santa Fe County. During the 1930s, she directed a literacy project for the WPA. See Box 2, Folder 40, Women of New Mexico collection; Ruth Laughlin, *Caballeros*, 2d ed. (Caldwell ID: Caxton Printers, 1945), 393; and Char-

lotte Whaley, *Nina Otero-Warren of Santa Fe* (Albuquerque: University of New Mexico Press, 1994).

57. Charles Lummis, "To the Women of the United States in Biennial Convention Assembled," 6 June 1924, Indian Defense Association of Central and Northern California, private collection, Michael and Margaret B. Harrison Western Research Center, Sacramento. Lummis often repeated this sentiment. See Lummis, *Mesa, Cañon, and Pueblo*, 158; and Lummis's typewritten letter to the editor of the *New York Times*, 18 September 1924, CLAI papers, for just a few examples. Collier also frequently echoed this view; see "Do Indians Have Rights of Conscience?" 348.

58. Atwood once wrote to Mabel Dodge Luhan that she herself was a conservative and was not always comfortable with the radicalism of those with whom she worked in Indian affairs. See Atwood to Mabel Dodge Sterne [Luhan], 21 December 1922, Luhan papers. John Collier and many other male defenders of Pueblo dances commonly accepted the moral reformers' notions of appropriate sexuality and merely argued that the Pueblos were as moral, if not more so, than white Americans. See Collier's "Do Indians Have Rights of Conscience?" 348; Collier's "Regarding Misrepresentations," memo to the Directors and Friends of the Indian Defense Associations of California, 20 October 1924, Cassidy papers; and Mason Green, letter to the editor of the *Herald*, written 24 August 1924, clipping in Collier papers, Reel 9. For an example of Lummis's conservative attitude toward women and sexuality and his disapproving attitude toward divorce, see Lummis, *Mesa, Cañon, and Pueblo*, 158, 353.

59. See, for example, Clara True to Samuel Brosius, 28 October 1929 and 27 November 1929, IRA papers, Reel 45; and Clara True to Matthew Sniffen, 12 January 1928, IRA papers, Reel 44; and Seymour, "The Delusion of the Sentimentalists."

60. See, for example, Austin, "The Folly of the Officials"; Sergeant, "Principales Speak"; and Collier, "Do Indians Have Rights of Conscience?"

61. "Transcript of Proceedings of All-Pueblo Council," Santo Domingo Pueblo, 6 October 1926, Collier papers, Reel 8.

62. "Proceedings of Pueblo Indian Council," Santo Domingo Pueblo, 17 January 1924, Collier papers, Reel 8. After Naranjo's brief comment, Collier proceeded at length to explain his belief that singers and dancers had more effect on white opinion in the East than did Indian speakers. The Indians eventually approved Collier's delegation.

63. Joseph Filario Tafoya to Samuel Brosius, 6 November 1929, IRA papers, Reel 45.

64. True to Matthew Sniffen, 12 January 1928, IRA papers, Reel 44. See also True to Samuel Brosius, 27 November 1929, IRA papers, Reel 45.

65. Parsons, *Taos Pueblo*, 6, 62–66, 67, 118–19; Grant, *Taos Indians*, 104–6; Kelly, *As-*

sault on Assimilation, 339–40. Other material on the controversy surrounding peyotists at Taos can be found in Box 4, Folder 1, Aberle papers.

66. Dozier, "Factionalism," 177, 178.

67. Anderson, Changing Woman, 25. See also Richard O. Clemmer, "The Hopi Traditionalist Movement," *American Indian Culture and Research Journal* 18 (1994): 125–66, which argues that from the Hopi viewpoint, tradition "reflects a distinct political ideology that is not opposed to modernity but is part of it" (127). Further, Clemmer points out that the terms "traditional" and "progressive" among the Hopis "represent two broad metaphors rather than actual behavior patterns" (131). In *Righteous Discontent*, Higginbotham also notes how blacks have been divided into "accommodationists" (akin to "progressives") versus "resisters" (as in "conservatives" or "traditionals"). She also points out how this division denies the complexity of black perspectives. She shows how black women in the black Baptist Church reconciled these two polarities (18).

68. Statement of Masawistiwa, 11 December 1920, Exhibit A, Sweet collection.

69. See also statements of Judge Hooker Hongeva, 9 December 1920; Salako, 9 December 1920; and Siventiwa, 10 December 1920, all in Exhibit B; and Kuwanwikvaya, 26 August 1920, Exhibit A, all in Sweet collection. For firsthand accounts of the Oraibi split, see H. Sekaquaptewa, *Me and Mine*, 63–84, and Qoyawayma, *No Turning Back*, 31–48. See also James, *Pages*, 130–45; Rushforth and Upham, *A Hopi Social History*, 123–48; Loftin, *Religion and Hopi Life*, 75–79. Loftin argues similarly that "Friendlies" based their actions on what they believed to be Hopi prophecy (xix–xxi, 78). Spellings of key players in the Oraibi split vary. For example, although the transcriber of Masawistiwa's statement referred to Loloma, Qoyawayma and Loftin spell his name Lololoma; Rushforth and Upham call him Loololma; James refers to him as Lololomai.

70. Statement of Joe Lujan, 15 May 1924, IRA papers, Reel 40.

71. See, for example, Statement of Don Mondragon, 14 May 1924, IRA papers, Reel 40; Emory Marks to Superintendent Crandall, 26 September 1924, and Affidavits from Joe Sandoval, April 1925, and John Gomez, 9 April 1925, Entry 83, Box 17, Folder 070, Pueblo Records, NARA. See also Grant, *Taos Indians*, 88–89.

72. For more on Joe Lujan's case, see Statement of Joe Lujan, 15 May 1924, IRA papers, Reel 40. For Juan Melchor, see Luella Gallup to Superintendent Coggeshall, 12 September 1913, Santa Fe Indian School Day School Correspondence, 1913–14 (Entry 42), Box 1, Folder "G," Pueblo Records, NARA. For the case of Edward Hunt, see Statement of Mrs. Edward Hunt, 3 May 1924, IRA papers, Reel 40; C. U. Finley to George F. Stevens, 22 May 1936, Box 6, Folder 48, Aberle papers.

73. "The State of the Progressive Pueblo Indians," [1929], IRA papers, Reel 45. Letter from Clara True to Samuel Brosius, 27 November 1929, IRA papers, Reel 45, also al-

leges many penalties inflicted on progressive Indians. For more on confiscation of property of a family at Santo Domingo, see Mary Dissette to Superintendent Coggeshall, 11 and 25 February 1914, 9 and 29 March 1914, and 21 and 25 April 1914, Superintendent's Correspondence with Day School Employees (Entry 40), Box 8, Folder: Santo Domingo, 1914, January 22 to April 29, Pueblo Records, NARA. For more on the controversies that divided the Pueblo Indians, see "The Pueblo Indians and Constitutional Government," Carton 1, Folder: "Indian Religious Persecution Correspondence," CLAI papers; and *Indian Truth* 1 (April 1924 and May 1924).

74. Antonio Montoya to Samuel Beahm, 9 February 1923, Southern Pueblos Agency, General Correspondence Files, 1911–35 (Entry 90), Box 231, Folder 070, Pueblo Records, NARA. Montoya probably referred to a kiva as a house, and he noted that there are four societies with about twenty-five men in each.

75. Statement of Joe Lujan, 15 May 1924, IRA papers, Reel 40; Rosendo Vargas to Santa Fe Indian School, 20 November 1915, enclosed in Frederic Snyder, Supt. of Santa Fe Ind. School, to Supt. Lonergan, Pueblo Day Schools, 23 November 1914, Entry 90, Box 21, Folder 070, Pueblo Records, NARA.

76. Declaration of Council of All the New Mexico Pueblos, 5 May 1924, IRA papers, Reel 40. Also available in Carton 1, CLAI papers. Given the similarity of the text of the statement to a speech made by John Collier at the meeting, it is evident that Collier had already drafted the statement in advance for the Pueblos to adopt at the meeting.

77. Dozier, *Pueblo Indians*, 151.

78. Marriott, *María*, 10–11, 132–33, 135–36, 189–90. For more on the effect of epidemics on the Pueblos, see chapter 2.

79. Fergusson, *Dancing Gods*, 82.

80. Jill Sweet makes a similar point in *Dances of the Tewa*, 76–77. Because the clown's performances "neutralize history," turning disruptive events and outsiders into a permanent, unharmful part of Pueblo existence, Alfonso Ortiz has argued that the Pueblos' dramatic performances and ceremonies may be the most important element in Pueblo cultural survival. See Ortiz, "Dynamics," 303–4.

81. E. M. Sweet to William Layne, 6 February 1921, Sweet collection. Even before the 1921 Circular was issued, Poli had started a movement to expel the missionaries from Hopi villages.

82. Marriott, *María*, xii; Zumwalt, *Wealth and Rebellion*, 236–37.

83. Parsons, *Taos Pueblo*, 6, 14. For an analysis of the controversy generated by Pueblo artists, see Wade, "Straddling the Cultural Fence," 243–54. Wade notes that "conservatives" have often seen the painting of ceremonial dances as an "affront to the supernaturals." Sometimes they have condemned or ostracized painters. For example, the Hopi painters who illustrated Jesse Walter Fewkes's 1903 book on Hopi kachinas were labeled witches (244). For another story regarding Pueblo prohibition against

picture taking, see D. H. Lawrence, "Taos," reprinted in Marta Weigle and Kyle Fiore, *Santa Fe and Taos: The Writer's Era, 1916–1941* (Santa Fe: Ancient City, 1982), 91. Also see Luhan, *Edge of Taos Desert*, 280, for more on the Pueblo belief that their secret ways would lose their power if divulged.

84. Statement of Edward Hunt to Matthew Sniffen, 3 May 1924, IRA papers, Reel 40.

85. Parsons, *Taos Pueblo*, 14–15. For an excellent critical account of the internecine conflict caused by the publication of Parsons's *Taos Pueblo*, see Zumwalt, *Wealth and Rebellion*, 248–57.

86. Fred Eggan, introduction to *Pueblo Indians*, ix; Dozier, *Pueblo Indians*, xi, 115–17. Elizabeth Brandt has characterized the intense secretiveness of the Pueblos regarding their ceremonies not as an attempt to keep this information from non-Pueblos, but as a means to maintain internal secrecy. According to Brandt, "internal secrecy is primary; external secrecy is maintained to prevent information from going back into pueblo communities from the outside where it might have disruptive effects if the wrong individuals possessed it." Because each organization, clan, society, and kiva group within Pueblo society has its own secret knowledge, and "since governing systems are linked in important ways with these small-group cultures, the establishment of status hierarchies based on secret information in the possession of one group rather than another can have important political consequences." See Elizabeth Brandt, "On Secrecy and the Control of Knowledge: Taos Pueblo," in *Secrecy: A Cross-Cultural Perspective*, ed. Stanton K. Tefft (New York: Human Sciences, 1980), 126, 130.

87. J. J. Brody, *Indian Painters and White Patrons* (Albuquerque: University of New Mexico Press, 1971), 85–117. Brody also discusses the conflicts artists' renditions of dances caused in their villages (79–80, 112). See also Dockstader, *Kachina*, 134.

88. Gray, *Tonita Peña*, 31.

89. Ortiz, "Ritual Drama," 152; Dozier, Pueblo Indians, 151, 157–58; Young, "Women," 436–38; Barbara Babcock, "Arrange Me into Disorder: Fragments and Reflections on Ritual Clowning," in *Rite, Drama, Festival, Spectacle: Rehearsals toward a Theory of Cultural Performance*, ed. John J. MacAloon (Philadelphia: Institute for the Study of Human Issues, 1984), 112; E. Sekaquaptewa, "One More Smile," 14–17; Laski, *Seeking Life*, 14. See also Ekkehart Malotki, ed., *The Bedbugs' Night Dance and Other Hopi Sexual Tales* (Flagstaff: Northern Arizona University Press, 1995), vii, regarding two important Hopi kachinas—Mastopkatsina and Kookopölö—who, with their exaggerated phalluses, embodied human and plant fecundity.

90. Louis A. Hieb, "Meaning and Mismeaning: Toward an Understanding of the Ritual Clown," in *New Perspectives on the Pueblo*, 164; Ortiz, "Ritual Drama," 148–49; J. Sweet, *Dances of the Tewa*, 10, 32. Some Pueblo dances even involved an inversion of

men's and women's roles when women staged the dances. The Hopi Women's Society conducted Marau dances in which "three nights of burlesque plaza performance are included . . . with women mocking the men's kachina dances and singing obscene or humorous songs about their 'brothers.'" See Schlegel, "Male and Female," 257. In a letter to Superintendent Crandall, 25 December 1902, True reported a dance at Santa Clara Pueblo "in which the men and women exchange costumes." See Letters Received from Day School Teacher Clara D. True, 1902–7 (Entry 38), Box 1, Pueblo Records, NARA.

91. Dozier, *Pueblo Indians*, 157, 202–3. For the ways in which scholars have analyzed European carnivals as occasions for temporarily reversing hierarchies, see M. M. Bakhtin, *Dialogic Imagination: Four Essays by M. M. Bakhtin*, ed. Michael Holquist (Austin: University of Texas Press, 1981), and Terry Castle, *Masquerade and Civilization: The Carnivalesque in Eighteenth-Century English Culture and Fiction* (Stanford CA: Stanford University Press, 1986). For more on the function of "symbolic inversion," see Barbara A. Babcock, ed., *The Reversible World: Symbolic Inversion in Art and Society* (Ithaca NY: Cornell University Press, 1978). In this book, in "'A Tolerated Margin of Mess': The Trickster and His Tales Reconsidered," *Journal of Folklore Research* 11 (1975): 147–86, and in "Arrange Me into Disorder," Babcock argues that symbolic inversion such as that of Pueblo clowns cannot be understood simply as a "steam valve," that is, as an outlet for otherwise inappropriate behavior. She argues instead that the ambiguity and paradox inherent in symbolic inversion serves as a means of promoting creativity. In Babcock's view clowns do not just promote conformity to social norms but also "prompt speculation about, reflection on, and reconsideration of the order of things" ("Arrange Me into Disorder," 122).

92. Alfonso Ortiz, "Indian/White Relations: A View from the Other Side of the 'Frontier,'" in *Indians in American History*, ed. Frederick Hoxie (Arlington Heights IL: Harlan Davidson, 1988), 12. Alison Freese's "Send in the Clowns: An Ethnohistorical Analysis of the Sacred Clowns' Role in Cultural Boundary Maintenance among the Pueblo Indians" (Ph.D. diss., University of New Mexico, 1991) also looks at the role of clowns in dealing with Catholicism, the Spanish, and the first white anthropologists. See also Jill D. Sweet, "Burlesquing 'the Other' in Pueblo Performance," *Annals of Tourism Research* 16 (1989): 62–75, and J. Sweet, *Dances of the Tewa*, 33–34.

93. Fergusson, "Laughing Priests," 662.

94. Fergusson, *Dancing Gods*, 43, 51–52. Pueblo clowns have continued to ridicule whites, especially tourists, in their dances. See, for example, Deirdre Evans-Pritchard, "How 'They' See 'Us': Native American Images of Tourists," *Annals of Tourism Research* 16 (1989): 89–105.

95. Elizabeth DeHuff quoted in Coolidge, *Rain-Makers*, 167; Elizabeth DeHuff, "Dancing for Life," clipping from *Southwest Review*, n.d., 378, Box 9, DeHuff papers. Perhaps with unintended irony, only a few pages earlier, DeHuff described her own similar shopping spree at a pueblo.

96. Laski, *Seeking Life*, 80; Austin, *Land of Journey's Ending*, 258.

97. Elizabeth DeHuff, "The Pueblo Indian Corn Dance," in *St. Anthony Messenger* (December 1933): 347, Box 9, DeHuff papers; DeHuff, "Dancing for Life," 378; DeHuff quoted in Coolidge, *Rain-Makers*, 167.

98. Fergusson, "Laughing Priests," 658.

99. Quoted in Coolidge, *Rain-Makers*, 168.

100. L. R. McDonald to P. T. Lonergan, 11 May 1915, Exhibit D, Sweet collection. McDonald mistook men dressed as women for women.

101. Statement of Mrs. J—— B—— S—— of Bernalillo, New Mexico, made to Mrs. Adelina Otero-Warren, 4 May 1924, IRA papers, Reel 40. The woman Mrs. S—— describes in the scene was undoubtedly a male clown dressed as a woman.

102. Fass, *Damned and the Beautiful*, 302.

103. Statement of Evelyn Bentley, 30 September 1920, Exhibit C, Sweet collection.

104. Statement of Siventiwa, 10 December 1920, Exhibit B, Sweet collection.

105. E. M. Sweet to William Layne, 6 February 1921; and statement of Judge Hooker Hongeva, 9 December 1920, Exhibit B, both in Sweet collection.

106. Keith H. Basso, *Portraits of "the Whiteman": Linguistic Play and Cultural Symbols among the Western Apache* (New York: Cambridge University Press, 1979), 4, 5. Sam Gill has noted that one function of the clowns is to "act Kahopi, that is non-Hopi," thereby teaching the distinctions between Hopi and non-Hopi behavior. See Sam Gill, *Beyond "The Primitive": The Religions of Nonliterate Peoples* (Englewood Cliffs NJ: Prentice-Hall, 1982), 95. See also Hieb, "Meaning and Mismeaning"; and Ortiz, "Ritual Drama." Joann W. Kealiinohomoku argues that Hopi clowns actually administer a dose of Hopi-style "medicine" to cure inappropriate behavior. Thus *kahopi* clowning cures *kahopi* behavior among the Hopis. See her article "The Drama of the Hopi Ogres," in *Southwestern Indian Ritual Drama*, 58, 64.

107. The foremost theorist associated with the concept of ethnic-boundary maintenance is Fredrik Barth. See the introduction to his edited collection *Ethnic Groups and Boundaries: The Social Organization of Culture Difference* (Boston: Little, Brown, 1969), 9–38. As Sylvia Rodríguez has noted, "Boundary maintenance through time is the essential feature of ethnic persistence, whereas specific cultural content changes more or less continuously." See "Land, Water," 315. For other examples of ways in which Native Americans have used humor to mock whites, see Madronna Holden, "'Making All the Crooked Ways Straight': The Satirical Portrait of Whites in Coast Salish Folklore," *Journal of American Folklore* 89 (July–September 1976):

271–93; Thomas P. Lynch, "The Honkey Dance: White Dancers at Indian Pow-wows," presentation, California Folklore Society Conference, Santa Rosa, California, April 1990.

108. Otto Lomavitu to Editor, *Cococino Sun*, Flagstaff, Arizona, 29 August 1923, clipping in Carton 1, Folder: "Indian Religious Persecution Correspondence," CLAI papers.

109. Interview with Martin Vigil, 10 December 1970, Box 19, Folder 754, and 26 January 1971, Box 19, Folder 764, Duke collection; Pablo Abeita, "The Pueblo Indian Question," *The Franciscan Missions of the Southwest* (1916), 8. This publication seems to have had a more tolerant attitude toward the Indian dances.

110. Statement of Judge Hooker Hongeva, 9 December 1920, Exhibit B, Sweet Collection. H. Sekaquaptewa, *Me and Mine*, 106.

111. Sally Hyer, *One House, One Voice, One Heart: Native American Education at the Santa Fe Indian School* (Santa Fe: Museum of New Mexico Press, 1990), 20, 27. Indian boarding schools seemed to have encouraged the same trend that was evident in the rest of American society in the 1910s and 1920s—a shift from homosocial, intergenerational social relations to heterosocial peer relationships. On this point, see Smith-Rosenberg, "New Woman as Androgyne," and Fass, *Damned and the Beautiful*, 200–202, 260–90.

112. Grant, *Taos Indians*, 101. Elizabeth DeHuff, who was married to the Santa Fe Indian School superintendent, John DeHuff, commented that at the school, the Indian children were "encouraged in co-operative social life by their teachers and scout masters. In the pueblo, such familiarity is not tolerated." See DeHuff's "Pueblo Episodes," 29, unpublished manuscript, Box 6, Folder 48, DeHuff papers.

113. Leo Simmons, ed., *Sun Chief: The Autobiography of a Hopi Indian* (New Haven CT: Yale University Press, 1942), 76, 134. For more on Hopi sexual tales, see Malotki, *The Bedbugs' Night Dance*.

114. L. Simmons, *Sun Chief*, 78–79, 112–13.

115. Dockstader, *Kachina*, 135, 136.

116. Qoyawayma, *No Turning Back*; H. Sekaquaptewa, *Me and Mine*, 117–18; L. Simmons, *Sun Chief*; Schlegel, "Adolescent Socialization," 455–56.

117. See Sophie Aberle, manuscript, "Pueblo of San Juan," 33, 35, 46–47, Box 2, Folder 1, Aberle papers; Parsons, *Taos Pueblo*, 49–50; and Parsons, "Waiyautitsa," 96.

118. L. Simmons, *Sun Chief*, 103.

119. Proceedings of Council of Santa Clara Indians with Assistant Commissioner E. B. Merritt, 22 October 1927, Collier papers, Reel 29. In 1924 the Progressive Party at Santa Clara held its own election. The Conservative Party boycotted the election and chose their own governor, so that the pueblo then had two governors. See *Indian Truth* 2 (January 1925), 3. See also Dozier, "Factionalism," 172–85, which describes

the genesis and development of the conflict in this pueblo between 1894 and 1935; Clara True to Matthew Sniffen and Clara True to Edgar Merritt, both letters, 2 January 1928, IRA papers, Reel 44, and Clara True to Samuel Brosius, 5 May 1929 and 28 October 1929, IRA papers, Reel 45. Factionalism became even more complicated at Santa Clara in the 1930s when both the Progressive and Conservative Parties divided into two wings. See Dozier's "Factionalism" and Elizabeth Shepley Sergeant, "Memorandum on the Santa Clara Situation," summer 1935, Collier papers, Reel 29. For more on the sexual division of labor among the Tewa pueblos, see Marriott, *María*, 8, and S. E. Jacobs, "Continuity and Change."

120. Proceedings of Council of Santa Clara Indians with Assistant Commissioner E. B. Merritt, 22 October 1927, Collier papers, Reel 29.
121. Joseph Tafoya to Samuel Brosius, 24 September 1929, IRA papers, Reel 45.
122. Proceedings of Council of Santa Clara Indians with Assistant Commissioner E. B. Merritt, 22 October 1927, Collier papers, Reel 29.
123. Proceedings of Council of Santa Clara Indians with Assistant Commissioner E. B. Merritt, 22 October 1927, Collier papers, Reel 29.
124. Joseph Tafoya to Samuel Brosius, 24 September 1929, IRA papers, Reel 45.
125. Clara True to Samuel Brosius, 16 December 1926, and Clara True to Herbert Welsh, 17 December 1926, IRA papers, Reel 43; True to Matthew Sniffen, 2 January 1928; True to Edgar Merritt, assistant commissioner of Indian affairs, 2 January 1928; and True to Sniffen, 12 January 1928, IRA papers, Reel 44; and True to Brosius, 27 November 1929, IRA papers, Reel 45. For other examples, see Matthew Sniffen, IRA papers, letter to the editor, *New York Times*, written 1 November 1924, in Collier papers, Reel 9; and Kate Leah Cotharin, chair of the Indian Committee for the Women's Auxiliary to the National Council of the Protestant Episcopal Church, letter to the editor, *The Independent* 116 (1 May 1926): 531–32.
126. Antonio Abeita to Mary Austin, 1 September 1923, AU 806, Box 53, and Sotero Ortiz to Mary Austin, 29 December 1923, AU 4247, Austin papers–HUNT. For letters from Pueblos to the NMAIA, see folder 109, Indian correspondence, 1922–23, NMAIA papers. The minutes of the meetings of the NMAIA (Folder 37, NMAIA papers) also reveal the way in which Indians made use of the new activists for their own agendas.
127. Rodríguez, "Art, Tourism," 77–99; also Rodríguez, "Land, Water," 352. For another account of Taos Pueblo's attempt to recover Blue Lake, see R. C. Gordon-Mc-Cutchan, *The Taos Indians and the Battle for Blue Lake* (Santa Fe NM: Red Crane, 1991). In recent years, by arguing that the land is sacred to them, the Hopis have also tried to stop the expansion of the Snow Bowl ski area on the San Francisco Peaks near Flagstaff, Arizona. See Loftin, *Religion and Hopi Life*, 91.
128. Parsons, *Taos Pueblo*, 15; Zumwalt, *Wealth and Rebellion*, 236, 246–47. Anthropologists could be ruthless in their exploitation of impoverished Indians. As Rosemary

Zumwalt characterizes her, Elsie Clews Parsons "could be devious and secretive, meeting with informants far away from their pueblos and working with them for days at a time in order to extract as much information as possible" (241). To Parsons, obtaining this secret information for science took precedence over the desires of the pueblos that it remain secret. As she wrote to her husband, "This week I have cleaned out one woman and last night started with her as interpreter for her uncle" (244).

129. Dockstader, *Kachina*, 135.
130. Telegrams, True to Matthew Sniffen, 13 and 23 June 1924, IRA papers, Reel 41. For True's campaign against Atwood, see Grace Baer to officers of the GFWC, 30 August 1924, IRA papers, Reel 41. See also Ina Sizer Cassidy to Mrs. John D. Sherman, president, GFWC, 25 August 1924, Ina Sizer Cassidy papers; "The Big Biennial," *General Federation News* 5 (July–August 1924): 20–21; "Bureau Did Not Know Indians Were Going," *General Federation News* 5 (October 1924): 8; "What is the Truth?" *General Federation News* 5 (October 1924): 9; "New Mexico Dissents from Indian Program; Convention Unanimous," *General Federation News* 5 (November 1924): 3.
131. True to Matthew Sniffen, 1 July 1924, IRA papers, Reel 41.
132. Seymour, "The Delusion of the Sentimentalists"; Austin, "The Folly of the Officials"; Hertzberg, *Search for Identity*, 205.
133. See *Indian Truth* 2 (March 1925): 2, and Herbert Welsh to Clara True, 24 September 1924; Clara True to Herbert Welsh, 9 December 1924; a series of letters between Welsh, Sniffen, Brosius, and True; Welsh and Board of Directors; True and Board of Directors; and Minutes of Board of Directors, February to December 1925, IRA papers, Reels 41 and 42.
134. "Pueblos Have Right to Run Own Affairs, Court Decides," *Santa Fe New Mexican*, 15 August 1925, clipping from Cassidy papers; Matthew Sniffen to William Johnson, 20 August 1924, IRA papers, Reel 41.
135. Proceedings of Council of Santa Clara Indians with Assistant Commissioner E. B. Merritt, 22 October 1927, Collier papers, Reel 29.
136. See Reed-Crum, "Tolowa 'Hush.'"
137. See Box 2A, folders on EAIA, 1930–31 and 1932, White papers.
138. Vera Connolly, "End of the Road," *Good Housekeeping* 88 (May 1929): 170.
139. "Report of Division of Indian Welfare," Twelfth Biennial Council, [1927], 47, GFWC papers.

6. WOMEN AND THE INDIAN ARTS AND CRAFTS MOVEMENT

1. For more on the genesis and development of the arts and crafts movement in Britain and the United States, see Eileen Boris, *Art and Labor: Ruskin, Morris, and the Craftsman Ideal in America* (Philadelphia: Temple University Press, 1986); Lears, *No Place of Grace*, 60–96; and Orvell, *Real Thing*, 157–97. For the Indian arts and

crafts movement, see Brody, *Indian Painters*; Gibson, *Santa Fe and Taos Colonies*; and Kenneth Dauber, "Pueblo Pottery and the Politics of Regional Identity," *Journal of the Southwest* 32 (winter 1990): 576–96.

2. A notable and important exception to this is the work of Molly Mullin. Her dissertation, "Consuming the American Southwest: Culture, Art, and Difference" (Ph.D. diss., Duke University, 1993) deals extensively with gender.

3. Kenneth Chapman, "The von Blumenthal–Dougan Project, 1917–1919," unpublished memoirs—Santa Fe, Chapman papers–IARC. For an example of the large numbers of Pueblo women involved, see "Named Artists on IAF Collection Pottery," IAF Potters folder, IAF papers. The list contains few men. Most of the men included painted designs on their wives' pottery, as Julian Martinez did. See also Edwin L. Wade and Katherin L. Chase, "A Personal Passion and Profitable Pursuit: The Katharine Harvey Collection of Native American Fine Art," in *The Great Southwest*, which notes the increasing role of women in collecting Indian art (150–51).

4. Luhan, *Edge of Taos Desert*, 68; Henderson quoted in Erna Fergusson, "Crusade from Santa Fé," 386. One scholar has noted schisms in the promotion of arts and crafts between art patrons/collectors and traders/dealers that he illustrates in the battle between these two groups over the use of natural versus chemical dyes in Hopi and Navajo blankets and rugs. See Edwin L. Wade, "The Ethnic Art Market in the American Southwest," in *Objects and Others: Essays on Museum and Material Culture*, ed. George W. Stocking Jr., History of Anthropology, vol. 3 (Madison: University of Wisconsin Press, 1985), 167–91. This schism is somewhat related to the division I describe here between women who sought to preserve Pueblo culture versus women who hoped to "uplift" through promoting arts and crafts. Unlike traders and dealers, however, noneconomic motives also compelled female "uplifters."

5. The primary example of this approach is Brody, *Indian Painters*.

6. Brody, *Indian Painters*, 43–45. Parsons, "Zuñi La'mana," 42.

7. Brody, *Indian Painters*, 66–67, 76; Ruth L. Bunzel, *The Pueblo Potter: A Study of Creative Imagination in Primitive Art* (New York: Columbia University Press, 1929), 80–82; Lydia L. Wyckoff, "The Sikyatki Revival," in *Hopis, Tewas*, 68–69.

8. Brody, *Indian Painters*, 67–68, 85; Bunzel, *Pueblo Potter*, 82–83; Marriott, *María*, 152, 155–57. Patrons referred to the first group of Indian painters they encountered as "self-taught" artists, connoting that they had received no formal training.

9. On Chapman, see "Story of the Indian Arts Fund," ca. 1965, 1:92, IAF papers. On Collier, see Philp, *John Collier's Crusade*, 94, 101–2, 112, 185, 208, 225, 244; and Robert Fay Schrader, *The Indian Arts and Crafts Board: An Aspect of New Deal Indian Policy* (Albuquerque: University of New Mexico Press, 1983).

10. Brody, *Indian Painters*, 126; Gray, *Tonita Peña*, 12; Winona Garmhausen, *History of*

Indian Arts Education in Santa Fe: The Institute of American Indian Art with Historical Background, 1890–1962 (Santa Fe: Sunstone, 1988), 34.

11. E. DeHuff, "The Renaissance of Southwest Indian Art," unpublished manuscript, ca. 1926, Box 6, Folder 50; E. DeHuff, "American Primitives in Art," unpublished manuscript, ca. 1924, Box 6, Folder 3; Elizabeth DeHuff to Mrs. [Dorothy Dunn] Kramer, n.d., Box 10, Folder 31; Elizabeth DeHuff to Mother, 11 March 1919, Box 10, Folder 25; Fred Kabotie "to whom it may concern," May 1940, Box 7, Folder 24, all in the DeHuff papers. See also Kabotie, *Fred Kabotie*, 27–29; Coolidge, *Rain-Makers*, 103; Brody, *Indian Painters*, 101; Garmhausen, *History of Indian Arts Education*, 34.

12. Chapman, "The von Blumenthal–Dougan Project"; Bunzel, *Pueblo Potter*, 68.

13. "Story of the Indian Arts Fund." In 1925 the IAF stated as its goals: "[T]o encourage and promote Indian Art among the Indians of New Mexico and elsewhere; to preserve, improve and revive their ancient arts and crafts, to collect and preserve modern specimens of Indian arts of every character, and to perpetuate and disseminate Indian art in all its fazes [*sic*] and manifestations."

14. Ina Cassidy, "Mary Austin's Casa Querida," *Examiner* magazine section, 18 June 1939, clipping in Box 2, Folder 26, Pearce papers; Mary Austin to Mabel Dodge [Luhan], 25 May, ca. 1922 or 1923, Luhan papers. Austin frequently claimed credit for initiating almost every popular movement of the early twentieth century, a tendency her peers tolerated but also ridiculed.

15. "Story of the Indian Arts Fund"; Ann Nolan Clark, "From Basement to Basement, ca. 1965, 1:93, IAF papers. Also see IAF Report, ca. 1963 or 1964, Appendix: Board of Trustees, 1:88, IAF papers, and Margaret McKittrick to Kenneth Chapman, 22 November 1927, NMAIA correspondence, Chapman papers–IARC. For more on White's work, see Folder: "ISHAUU, Correspondence, 1923–29," Box 1D, and Folder: Exposition of Indian Tribal Arts, Inc., 1931, Box 3D, White papers.

16. Meriam, *Problem of Indian Administration*; Garmhausen, *History of Indian Arts Education*; Margaret Connell Szasz, *Education and the American Indian: The Road to Self-Determination since 1928*, 2d ed. (Albuquerque: University of New Mexico Press, 1977), 3, 19–24, 48–76; Hyer, *One House*, 31; Brody, *Indian Painters*, 126–28, 132; brief biography of Mabel Morrow, Morrow papers; Jeanne Shutes and Jill Mellick, *The Worlds of P'otsúnú: Geronima Cruz Montoya of San Juan Pueblo* (Albuquerque: University of New Mexico Press, 1996).

17. Bunzel, *Pueblo Potter*, 49, 53; Mary Austin, "Indian Arts and Crafts," unpublished article [1932], enclosed with letter to Paul Kellogg, *Survey Graphic*, 5 February 1932, Austin papers–UCLA; "She Learned from the Corn, the Rain and the Buffalo," *The Providence Sunday Journal*, 27 August 1933, clipping in Box 3D, Folder: Misc. Clippings, 1931–33, White papers. See also Dilworth, *Imagining Indians*, 154–56.

18. Austin, "Indian Arts and Crafts"; Dorothy Dunn, "Indian Children Carry Forward Old Traditions," *Indians at Work* 2 (1 May 1935): 25. Brody notes similarly that revivals of Pueblo ceramics involved an emphasis on antiquity (*Indian Painters*, 70). Collectors of other forms of so-called primitive art have also put a premium on "oldness." Historians assert that this value on antiquity derived from a reaction against modernization, primarily the rise of "the machine" in America and Europe. See Torgovnick, *Gone Primitive*, 137; Orvell, *Real Thing*; Lears, *No Place of Grace*.

19. E. DeHuff, "American Primitives in Art," unpublished manuscript, Box 6, Folder 3, DeHuff papers; "Story of the Indian Arts Fund," IAF papers; Dolly Sloan quoted in Helen Johnson Keyes, "Tribal Arts for American Homes," *Christian Science Monitor*, 16 January 1932, clipping in Box 3D, Folder: Misc. Clippings, 1931–33, White papers.

20. "Presentation of the Indian Achievement Medal to Marie [*sic*] Martinez," *Indians at Work* 2 (15 September 1934), 23; Catherine K. Bauer, "Indian Tribal Arts," *New Republic*, 30 December 1931, clipping in Box 3D, Folder: Misc. Clippings, 1931–33, White papers. Sally Price, in *Primitive Art in Civilized Places*, has also found this belief to be common among other white patrons of "primitive" art (56–67).

21. Austin, "Indian Arts and Crafts"; Edward Alden Jewell, "In the Realm of Art," *New York Times*, 6 December 1931, clipping in Box 3D, Folder: Misc. Clippings, 1931–33, White papers. According to Sally Price, many white patrons held a similar view of all "primitive" artists. Price, *Primitive Art*, 32.

22. "To the Aid of Indian Artists," *Indians at Work* 1 (1 January 1934): 32–33; Elizabeth DeHuff to Mrs. [Dorothy Dunn] Kramer, n.d., Box 10, Folder 31, DeHuff papers; E. DeHuff, "The Renaissance of Southwest Indian Art," manuscript, ca. 1926, Box 6, Folder 50, DeHuff papers; Brody, *Indian Painters*, 91, 134, 147–48.

23. Annual Announcement, Santa Fe Indian School, 1935–36, and "Earth Colors" handout, USIS #1, Dunn papers. For DeHuff's belief that only dances should be painted, see Brody, *Indian Painters*, 134.

24. Dean MacCannell, "Tradition's Next Step," in *Discovered Country: Tourism and Survival in the American West*, ed. Scott Norris (Albuquerque: Stone Ladder Press, 1994), 167; Brody, *Indian Painters*, 134; Garmhausen, *History of Indian Arts Education*, 41–51; Bruce Bernstein, "Art for the Sake of Life: Dorothy Dunn and a Story of American Indian Painting," in *Modern by Tradition: American Indian Painting in the Studio Style*, ed. Bruce Bernstein and W. Jackson Rushing (Santa Fe: Museum of New Mexico Press, 1995), 3–25. In the same volume, W. Jackson Rushing, in his article "Modern by Tradition: The 'Studio Style' of Native American Painting," contends that Dunn's approach was well intentioned but prescriptive (32).

25. Marriott, *María*, 157; Margaret McKittrick, NMAIA, to Mary Austin, 20 June 1930,

AU 4135, Austin papers–HUNT; IAF Bulletin #3, 1928, IAF papers; Bunzel, *Pueblo Potter*, 88.

26. IAF brochure, 1938, IAF papers. See also IAF Report, 20 June 1932, IAF papers.

27. IAF brochure, 1938, IAF Report, 20 June 1932, and "Story of the Indian Arts Fund," IAF papers. For a particularly disturbing "collection story," see Clark's "From Basement to Basement," IAF papers, on the acquisition of a Navajo blanket from Chief White Antelope, a victim of the Sand Creek Massacre in Colorado in 1864. A soldier removed the blanket from Chief White Antelope after the massacre, took it to Denver, and sold it for $375 to the mayor. The IAF obtained the blanket from a descendant of the mayor in 1929. As Clark recounts this episode, the method by which the blanket was attained does not concern her; her main concern and delight is with the authenticity and longevity of the blanket.

28. Austin, "Indian Arts and Crafts"; Box 1D, Folder: "ISHAUU, Correspondence, 1923–29," White papers.

29. Boris, *Art and Labor*, 28.

30. Letter to Friends of Indian Art from Dorothy Stewart, Gina Knee, and Margretta S. Dietrich, New Mexico Association on Indian Affairs (NMAIA), 5 July 1940, IAF papers.

31. Letter to Friends of Indian Art, 5 July 1940, IAF papers.

32. Arts and Crafts Committee, NMAIA, "Indian Fair Premium List," 1934, Indian Fairs—1934 folder, Chapman papers–IARC. See also "Premium List—Intertribal Indian Ceremonial," Gallup, New Mexico, 1933, Indian Fairs, 1933, Chapman papers–IARC; "Premium List—Eighth Annual Southwest Indian Fair," 1929, Indian Fairs, 1929, Chapman papers–IARC.

33. Margaret McKittrick (NMAIA) to "Governor" [of Pueblos], 6 June 1931, Southern Pueblos Agency, General Correspondence, 1911–35 (Entry 90), Box 5, Folder 047, Pueblo Records, NARA. Also see Ralph Ely, State Fair Commission, to Indian Agent, Santa Fe, 19 August 1913, Day School Correspondence, 1913–14 (Entry 42), Box 1, Folder N, Pueblo Records, NARA; Indian Fairs 1934 folder, Chapman papers–IARC; Molly Mullin, "The Patronage of Difference: Making Indian Art 'Art, Not Ethnology,'" *Cultural Anthropology* 7 (1992): 405–9. For more on the genesis of the Santa Fe Indian Fair and its development into Indian Market, see Bruce Bernstein, "From Indian Fair to Indian Market," *El Palacio* 98 (summer 1993): 14–18, 47–54.

34. Amelia White to Mike Kirk, 22 January 1924, Box 1D, folder: "ISHAUU, 1923–1929," White papers. Pablo Abeita was a prominent Isleta Pueblo Indian who was involved in the All-Pueblo Council. I have not found evidence of who "the Princess" was.

35. Lewis, *When Harlem Was in Vogue*, 98; MacCannell, "Tradition's Next Step," 162.

36. Address of Turin B. Boone, Entry 90, Box 5, Folder 047, Pueblo Records, NARA; Fynn, *American Indian*, 157. Interestingly, between 1896 and 1915, the clubwomen

who took part in the thousands of arts and crafts societies that sprang up across America also promoted art as a means of "uplift." However, to them, this meant that art as a source of home decoration served an uplifting function. They did not necessarily see it as uplifting for the laborers who produced it. See Boris, *Art and Labor*, 91–98.

37. Schrader, *Indian Arts*, 3–5; L. G. Moses, "Wild West Shows, Reformers, and the Image of the American Indian, 1887–1914" in *South Dakota History* 14 (fall 1984): 193–221.

38. Clara True to Superintendent Crandall, 28 September 1902, Letters Received from Day School Teacher Clara D. True, 1902–7 (Entry 38), Box 1, Folder: 29 August 1902–31 December 1902, Pueblo Records, NARA; Clara True to Mrs. Markoe, Board of Indian Rights Association, 22 April 1925, IRA papers, Reel 41.

39. "The Use of Indian Designs in the Government Schools," U.S. Office of Indian Affairs Report, [ca. 1930], Chapman papers–LAB.

40. T. F. McCormick to Cleto Tafoya, 3 April 1929, Northern Pueblos Agency, General Correspondence, 1911–35 (Entry 83), Box 80, Folder 904, Pueblo Records, NARA. The Maisel Company case in 1933 brought out the importance of this concern. The Federal Trade Commission accused the company of restraining trade by claiming to be "Indian-made" but using factory methods that took business away from small craftspeople. The FTC ruled against the Maisel Company, but the Maisel Company ignored the order and appealed the case, eventually overturning the ruling of the FTC. See Schrader, *Indian Arts*, 53–57. Also see "Maisel Jewelry Is Ruled Imitation," *Southwest Tourist News*, 7 September 1933, Box 1D, Folder, "United Indian Traders Assoc, 1931–33," White papers.

41. Stella Atwood, "Indian Welfare," excerpt of speech at the Sixteenth Biennial Convention, 1922, GFWC papers; Annual Announcement, Santa Fe Indian School, 1935–36, USIS #1, Dunn papers.

42. Elizabeth DeHuff, "Marie, the Indian Pottery Maker," *Everybody's Magazine* (April 1926), clipping in "Maria Martinez," Box 2, Item 37, Women of New Mexico collection.

43. Southwest Indian Fair Committee, Report on Shiprock Fair, 1933, Indian Fairs, 1933, Chapman papers–IARC; Kenneth Chapman to F. W. Hodge, 21 June 1933, Chapman papers–IARC.

44. Bunzel, *Pueblo Potter*, 5, 56, 58, 64.

45. "The Exhibit of Contemporary Indian Art at the Century of Progress," *Indians at Work* 1 (15 July 1934): 29; Luhan, *Edge of Taos Desert*, 68.

46. Henderson quoted in Fergusson, "Crusade from Santa Fé," 386; Parsons, *Taos Pueblo*, 120.

47. Bunzel, *Pueblo Potter*, 5.

48. Luhan, *Winter in Taos*, 94–95.

49. Mrs. Charles Collier, "The Success of the Macy Sale of Indian Arts and Crafts," *Indians at Work* 2 (1 February 1935): 31–32; "News from Indian Artists under the Public Works of Art Projects," *Indians at Work* 1 (1 April 1934): 38; and "A New Step in Merchandising Indian Arts and Crafts," *Indians at Work* 2 (15 December 1934): 19.

50. Austin, *Taos Pueblo*.

51. Boris notes that the same set of ideas regarding the "craftsman ideal" could be used to either challenge the alienation of labor or to bolster the dominant social order (*Art and Labor*, 193). For all their critique of modern society, antimodern feminists fell into the latter category.

52. Mary Austin to Ina Sizer Cassidy, ca. December 1923, Austin papers–BANC.

53. Leach, *Land of Desire*, 103, 105, 169–70, 324–26. Leach also points out that this cooperation between businesses and museums worked both ways. In his own exhibits for the Brooklyn Museum, Culin utilized the methods of modern merchandising he learned from his business associates.

54. Mary Austin to Mabel Dodge, 28 September [1920], Luhan papers.

55. Julia Blanshard, "If You'd Have Your Home 'Earliest American,'" NEA Service syndicated article, and Keyes, "Tribal Arts for American Homes," clippings in Box 3D, Folder: Misc. Clippings, 1931–33, White papers.

56. Trennert, "Fairs," 144–50. As if to signify the parallels between all nonwhite primitives, the exposition's most popular exhibit, the Philippines Reservation, complete with twelve hundred scantily clad Igorots, occupied the space adjacent to the American Indian exhibits. See Robert Rydell, *World of Fairs: The Century of Progress Expositions* (Chicago: University of Chicago Press, 1993), 19–22.

57. Clara D. True, "The Mantle of Black Mesa," *New Mexico Magazine* 16 (April 1938): 15–17, 38; Clara D. True, "Shrines of a Thousand Years," *New Mexico Magazine* 16 (July 1938): 12–13, 42; Clara D. True, "Cochiti Holiday," *New Mexico Magazine* 18 (October 1940): 10–11, 31–32; and Clara D. True, "Toast for New Mexico," *New Mexico Magazine* 17 (March 1939): 22. See also her articles "Forgotten Capital," *New Mexico Magazine* 16 (March 1938): 10–11, 41; "The Valley of Onate," *New Mexico Magazine* 16 (August 1938): 12–13, 54, 56. True mentions this planned book in a letter to Mrs. Markoe, a board member for the IRA, 22 April 1925, IRA papers, Reel 41. I have found no other references to this book.

58. See "Interesting Westerners," 38, and "Here Is Our Only Woman Dude Wrangler: She Guides Tourists to the Wild Spots to See Picturesque Indian Rites," *Philadelphia Record* (3 January 1926), both clippings available in Box 15, Scrapbook 1, Fergusson papers.

59. See "Interesting Westerners" and "Here Is Our Only Woman Dude Wrangler." See also Thomas, *Southwestern Indian Detours*, 75–77, 80–88; Weigle, "Selling the

Southwest," 214–16; and Marta Weigle, "Exposition and Mediation: Mary Colter, Erna Fergusson, and the Santa Fe/Harvey Popularization of the Native Southwest, 1902–1940," *Frontiers* 12 (1992): 117–50.

60. Amy Hurt, "The Koshare Tours: How Two Women Run a Sight-Seeing Business," *Woman's Home Companion* (May 1923), in Box 15, Scrapbook 1, Fergusson papers. Fergusson resigned in 1927.

61. Luhan, *Lorenzo in Taos*, 80. For more on the Lion's Clubs' exploitation of the San Geronimo feast day at Taos, see Luhan, *Winter in Taos*, 227. For more on Luhan's foray into dude ranching, see Box 15, Scrapbook 2, Fergusson papers; Rudnick, *Mabel Dodge Luhan*, 233.

62. Fergusson, *Dancing Gods*, 162–63; Coolidge, *Rain-Makers*, 117.

63. True to Board of Directors, IRA, 28 February 1925, IRA papers, Reel 41. See also "Museum Events—Entertainment by Santa Clara Pueblos," *El Palacio* 18 (1924): 241.

64. Fergusson, *Dancing Gods*, xxiii, xxv.

65. Margaret McKittrick to "Governor," 6 June 1931, Entry 90, Box 5, Folder 047, Pueblo Records, NARA; Pamphlet, "Southwest Indian Fair, Santa Fe, NM," n.d., [ca. 1929], Indian Fairs, 1929, Chapman papers–LAB.

66. Bunzel, *Pueblo Potter*, 64. Barbara A. Babcock has also noted that the arts and crafts movement glorified Indian women as both exotic and domestic. See "A New Mexican Rebecca," 429.

67. "New Mexico Indian Squaw Earns $5,000 a Year Making Pottery," syndicated article [ca. 1931], clipping in Box 3D, Folder: Misc. Clippings, 1931–33, White papers. See also Dilworth, *Imagining Indians*, regarding how the romanticization of Pueblo women artists in the Indian arts and crafts movement spoke to issues of women's labor in American society (125–26, 162–63), and Boris, who notes that the arts and crafts movement was often used to reproduce rather than to challenge the sexual division of labor (*Art and Labor*, 99–121).

68. Morrow, "Arts and Crafts," 18.

69. Bunzel, *Pueblo Potter*, 2, 62. Male art patrons also lamented that "the young generation of Pueblo women are growing up in comparative ignorance of the art of their mothers." See Saunders, *Indians of the Terraced Houses*, 231.

70. Clara True to Superintendent Crandall, 20 January 1904, 18 February 1904, 31 March 1904, 14 April 1904, 16 April 1904, and 19 April 1904, Entry 38, Box 1, Pueblo Records, NARA.

71. For examples of female moral reformers' resentment of their segregation from public life, see Mary Dissette to Herbert Welsh, 10 February 1906, IRA papers, Reel 18; Clara True to Herbert Welsh, 19 April 1922, IRA papers, Reel 38.

72. For a similar analysis, see Mullin, "Bryn Mawrter's," 31–98. Elsewhere Mullin contends that these women insisted on authenticity because they feared the disorder and chaos they believed attended the rise of mass-produced commodities. Mullin insightfully points out that while these art patrons championed cultural difference, they implicitly feared and crusaded against class differences. See Mullin's "Patronage of Difference."

73. Marriott, *María*, 54–55, 61, 152; Elizabeth DeHuff, "The Procession of the Pots," *New Mexico Morning Examiner*, 5 March 1939, Box 9, DeHuff papers. Rick Dillingham's *Fourteen Families in Pueblo Pottery* (Albuquerque: University of New Mexico Press, 1994) confirms the assertion of many Pueblo women that pottery making was passed down from generation to generation.

74. DeHuff, "Pueblo Episodes."

75. Letter from Sarah Smith to Henrietta Burton, included in Report on Navajo Women's Conference on Rugmaking, 1933, Chapman papers–LAB.

76. Seymour Anderson, Principal, Santa Fe Indian School, to Commissioner of Indian Affairs, 1 December 1930, and Statistical Report, Industries, Total for Arts and Crafts, n.d., [ca. 1930], Entry 83, Box 80, Folder 904, Pueblo Records, NARA.

77. Clark, "From Basement to Basement." For an example of hard bargaining between a white collector and an Acoma Indian, see the letter from "Reuter" to Kenneth Chapman, n.d. [ca. 1929], Correspondence, 1929, IAF papers.

78. Kenneth Chapman, "Maria Martinez and the 'Butterfly' Motif," in unpublished memoirs, Santa Fe, "Stories Leading to the Founding of the IAF, 1919–1920," Chapman papers–IARC.

79. Marriott, *María*, quotes, 167; story of black-on-black ware, 173, 201–2. For other ways in which Pueblo artists "respond to tourists' needs for cultural significance by telling them just what they want to hear," see Evans-Pritchard, "How 'They' See 'Us,'" 95.

80. Schlegel, "Adolescent Socialization," 452–67; Schlegel, "Male and Female," 246–50; Young, "Women," 440–42.

81. Marriott, *María*, 190, 198–99, 215.

82. Gray, *Tonita Peña*, 52.

83. Letter from Sarah Smith to Henrietta Burton, included in Report on Navajo Women's Conference on Rugmaking, 1933, Chapman papers–LAB.

84. Marriott, *María*, 119, 157.

85. Marriott, *María*, 19.

86. Biographical information from Gray, *Tonita Peña*, 7–20.

87. Gray, *Tonita Peña*, 45.

88. Gray, *Tonita Peña*, 20–21.

89. Gray, *Tonita Peña*, 51.

90. Sally Hyer, "Pablita Velarde: The Pueblo Artist as Cultural Broker," in *Between Indian and White Worlds: The Cultural Broker*, ed. Margaret Connell Szasz (Norman: University of Oklahoma Press, 1994), 276–77, 280. See also Gray, *Tonita Peña*, 52–54.

91. Hyer, "Pablita Velarde," 281, 289; Gray, *Tonita Peña*, 55. Velarde's daughter is Helen Hardin.

92. For the conflict engendered by Maria Martinez's success, see Wade, "Straddling the Cultural Fence," 243–54. For Peña's problems, see Gray, *Tonita Peña*, 18–19. For Velarde's difficulties, see Hyer, "Pablita Velarde," 284, 289, 293, quote, 287. For more on Santa Clara Pueblo's rule that excludes the children of Santa Clara mothers and the non–Santa Clara fathers from full participation and membership in the pueblo, see Anderson, *Changing Woman*, 83–85.

93. Elizabeth DeHuff, "Sketching Pueblo Friends," unpublished manuscript, n.d., Box 6, Folder 56, DeHuff papers; Susan Peterson, *The Living Tradition of Maria Martinez* (Tokyo and New York: Kodansha International, 1977), 85.

94. Gray, *Tonita Peña*, 24–25.

95. Klein and Ackerman, *Women and Power*; Ford, "Native American Women," 42–68; Shoemaker, *Negotiators of Change*.

96. For the effect of the wage economy on Pueblo women's roles, see S. E. Jacobs, "Continuity and Change," 204; Young, "Women," 443; Schlegel, "Male and Female," 265. For other interpretations of the effect of the arts and crafts movement on Pueblo women, see Wade, "Straddling the Cultural Fence," 252–53; Babcock, "Marketing Maria," 150; Naranjo, "Cultural Changes," 194; Reynolds, "Women, Pottery," 279–300.

CONCLUSION

1. Ortiz, "Dynamics," 301–2.

2. "Seeing the Southwest the Koshare Way," brochure for Koshare Tours, Box 15, Scrapbook 1, Fergusson papers.

3. Indian Detours Brochure, n.d., Box 15, Scrapbook 1, Fergusson papers. Santa Fe touted itself as "the ancient city," an attempt to reach the same tourists who were drawn by the "antiquity" of the Pueblos. See Weigle and Fiore, *Santa Fe and Taos*, 11.

4. Frederick Simpich, "New Mexico Melodrama," *National Geographic Magazine* 73 (May 1938): 529–69.

5. Hyer, *One House*, 37, 40, 54. See also Anderson, *Changing Woman*, 73.

6. Quoted in Gillette, "On Her Own Terms," 86.

7. Quoted in Peterson, *Living Tradition*, 187.

8. Rudnick, *Mabel Dodge Luhan*, 149.

9. Morrill, *Taos Mosaic*, 10.

10. For a critique of the New Age movement's appropriation of Native American culture, see Deloria, "Playing Indian," 403–6; Wendy Rose, "The Great Pretenders: Further Reflections on Whiteshamanism," in *The State of Native America: Genocide, Colonization, and Resistance*, ed. M. Annette Jaimes (Boston: South End, 1992), 403–21; Laurie Anne Whitt, "Cultural Imperialism and the Marketing of Native America," *American Indian Culture and Research Journal* 19 (1995): 1–31; and Green, "The Tribe Called Wannabee," 30–55.

11. Morrill, *Taos Mosaic*, 10.

12. Letter from the All-Pueblo Council to Superintendent Crandall, 18 August 1924, in "The Pueblo Indians and Constitutional Government," Carton 1, Indian Religious Persecution Correspondence, CLAI papers.

13. Tedlock, *Beautiful and the Dangerous*, 43–45; Freese, "Send in the Clowns," 1–2, 22–25.

14. Elizabeth Shepley Sergeant to Mabel Dodge Luhan, 14 January 1954, Luhan papers.

Bibliographic Essay

The endnotes contain detailed descriptions of every source used. The following essay is intended as a guide to the sources most frequently cited.

I. WHITE WOMEN, PUEBLO INDIANS, AND FEDERAL INDIAN POLICY

Though dated, the most comprehensive work on Maria Martinez is Alice Marriott, *María: The Potter of San Ildefonso* (Norman: University of Oklahoma Press, 1948). For background on Pueblo culture and history, see Joe S. Sando, *Pueblo Nations: Eight Centuries of Pueblo Indian History* (Santa Fe: Clear Light, 1992); Edward P. Dozier, *The Pueblo Indians of North America* (New York: Holt, Rinehart, and Winston, 1970); Edward H. Spicer, *Cycles of Conquest: The Impact of Spain, Mexico, and the United States on the Indians of the Southwest, 1533–1960* (Tucson: University of Arizona Press, 1962); *Southwest*, ed. Alfonso Ortiz, vol. 9 of *Handbook of North American Indians*, ed. William C. Sturtevant (Washington DC: Smithsonian Institution, 1979); Alfonso Ortiz, ed., *New Perspectives on the Pueblos* (Albuquerque: University of New Mexico Press, 1972); Alfonso Ortiz, *The Tewa World: Space, Time, Being, and Becoming in a Pueblo Society* (Chicago: University of Chicago Press, 1969); Frederick J. Dockstader, *The Kachina and the White Man: The Influences of White Culture on the Hopi Kachina Religion*, rev. ed. (Albuquerque: University of New Mexico Press, 1985); John D. Loftin, *Religion and Hopi Life in the Twentieth Century* (Bloomington: Indiana University Press, 1991); Harry C. James, *Pages from Hopi History* (Tucson: University of Arizona Press, 1974); Scott Rushforth and Steadman Upham, *A Hopi Social History: Anthropological Perspectives on Sociocultural Persistence and Change* (Austin: University of Texas Press, 1992). One of the most recent works that deals with interactions between the Spanish and the Pueblos is Ramón Gutiérrez's *When Jesus Came, the Corn Mothers Went Away: Marriage, Sexuality, and Power in New Mexico, 1500–1846* (Stanford CA: Stanford University Press, 1991). This work has elicited both praise and criticism from scholars and controversy among Pueblo peoples. See "Commentaries: *When Jesus Came, the Corn Mothers Went Away: Marriage, Sexuality, and Power in New Mexico, 1500–1846* by Ramón Gutiérrez," compiled by Native American Studies Center, *American Indian Culture and Research Journal* 17 (1993): 141–77.

Except for Gutiérrez's controversial work, there is very little work available on changing gender roles and relations among the Pueblos. A few anthropological works deal with these topics among the Western Pueblos (Zuni and Hopi). See M. Jane Young, "Women, Reproduction, and Religion in Western Puebloan Society," *Journal of American Folklore* 100 (October–December 1987): 436–45; Alice Schlegel, "Male and Female in Hopi Thought and Action," in *Sexual Stratification: A Cross-Cultural View*, ed. Alice Schlegel (New York: Columbia University Press, 1977), 245–69; and Alice Schlegel, "The Adolescent Socialization of the Hopi Girl," *Ethnology* 12 (1973): 451–53. One article that deals with Tewa gender roles and relations is Sue Ellen Jacobs, "Continuity and Change in Gender Roles at San Juan Pueblo," in *Women and Power in Native North America*, ed. Laura F. Klein and Lillian A. Ackerman (Norman: University of Oklahoma Press, 1995).

Recently, scholars have been very interested in examining how the status of women in Native American societies was affected by contact with Europeans. For general studies on this topic, see Nancy Shoemaker, ed., *Negotiators of Change: Historical Perspectives on Native American Women* (New York: Routledge, 1995), 1–25; Ramona Ford, "Native American Women: Changing Statuses, Changing Interpretations," in *Writing the Range: Race, Class, and Culture in the Women's West*, ed. Elizabeth Jameson and Susan Armitage (Norman: University of Oklahoma Press, 1997), 42–68; and Laura F. Klein and Lillian A. Ackerman, eds., *Women and Power in Native North America* (Norman: University of Oklahoma Press, 1995).

There are many studies of federal Indian policy from the era of assimilation to the Indian Reorganization Act. For more on assimilation policy, see Frederick Hoxie's *A Final Promise: The Campaign to Assimilate the Indians, 1880–1920* (New York: Cambridge University Press, 1984), and several books by Francis Paul Prucha, including *American Indian Policy in Crisis: Christian Reformers and the Indian, 1865–1900* (Norman: University of Oklahoma Press, 1976), *The Churches and the Indian Schools, 1888–1912* (Lincoln: University of Nebraska Press, 1979), and *The Great Father: The United States Government and the American Indians*, vol. 2 (Lincoln: University of Nebraska Press, 1984). To examine the origins and policy of the Indian New Deal, Lawrence C. Kelly's *The Assault on Assimilation: John Collier and the Origins of Indian Policy Reform* (Albuquerque: University of New Mexico Press, 1983) and Kenneth Philp's *John Collier's*

Crusade for Indian Reform (Tucson: University of Arizona Press, 1977) are particularly helpful. For firsthand perspectives of this era in Indian reform and policy, see Lewis Meriam and Associates, *The Problem of Indian Administration*, Institute for Government Research, Studies in Administration (Baltimore: Johns Hopkins Press, 1928), and John Collier's works, including "The Red Atlantis," *Survey Graphic* 2 (October 1922): 15–20, 63, 66, and *From Every Zenith: A Memoir* (Denver: Sage, 1963). For overviews of changing white attitudes and Indian policy, see Robert F. Berkhofer Jr., *The White Man's Indian: Images of the American Indian from Columbus to the Present* (New York: Knopf, 1978), and Brian Dippie, *The Vanishing American: White Attitudes and United States Indian Policy* (Middletown CT: Wesleyan University Press, 1982).

Scholars have also generated many studies regarding changes in anthropological theory and practice from the late nineteenth to the early twentieth century. To learn more about the first years of American ethnology, see Robert Bieder, *Science Encounters the Indian, 1820–1880: The Early Years of American Ethnology* (Norman: University of Oklahoma Press, 1986); George Stocking Jr., *Victorian Anthropology* (New York: Free Press, 1987); and two works by Curtis M. Hinsley Jr.: "Ethnographic Charisma and Scientific Routine: Cushing and Fewkes in the American Southwest, 1879–1893," in *Observers Observed: Essays on Ethnographic Fieldwork*, ed. George W. Stocking Jr., History of Anthropology, vol. 1 (Madison: University of Wisconsin Press, 1983), 53–69, and *Savages and Scientists: The Smithsonian Institution and the Development of American Anthropology, 1846–1910* (Washington DC: Smithsonian Institution Press, 1981). For a classic source on cultural evolution, see Lewis Henry Morgan, *Ancient Society: Researches in the Lines of Human Progress from Savagery through Barbarism to Civilization* (Chicago: Charles Kerr, 1877).

The work of George Stocking Jr. offers many insights for those interested in the development of cultural relativism. See in particular "The Ethnographic Sensibility of the 1920s and the Dualism of the Anthropological Tradition," in *Romantic Motives: Essays on Anthropological Sensibility*, ed. George Stocking, History of Anthropology, vol. 6 (Madison: University of Wisconsin Press, 1989), 208–76, and *Race, Culture, and Evolution: Essays in the History of Anthropology* (New York: The Free Press, 1968). Elazar Barkan's *The Retreat of Scientific Racism: Changing Concepts of Race in Britain and the United States between the World Wars* (New York: Cambridge University Press, 1992) also provides an analysis of the rise of cultural relativism. For one of the classic works of cultural relativism, see Ruth Benedict, *Patterns of Culture* (Boston: Houghton Mifflin, 1934).

For more on white women anthropologists in the Southwest during this era, see Nancy J. Parezo, ed., *Hidden Scholars: Women Anthropologists and the Native American Southwest* (Albuquerque: University of New Mexico Press, 1993), and Barbara Babcock and Nancy Parezo, eds., *Daughters of the Desert: Women Anthropologists and the Native American Southwest, 1880–1980*, an illustrated catalogue (Albuquerque: University of New Mexico Press, 1988).

Many scholars have studied the growing romanticization, beginning in the late nineteenth century, of the Pueblos. A particularly astute article is Richard Frost's "The Romantic Inflation of Pueblo Culture," *The American West* 17 (January/February 1980): 5–9, 56–60. The works of two male writers—Charles Lummis and Charles Saunders—provide evidence of an emerging sentiment among white Americans that favored the preservation rather than the assimilation of Pueblo cultures. See Charles Saunders, *The Indians of the Terraced Houses* (New York: G. P. Putnam's, 1912); Charles Lummis, *Bullying the Moqui*, ed. Robert Easton and Mackenzie Brown (Flagstaff AZ: Prescott College Press, 1968); and Lummis, *Mesa, Cañon, and Pueblo* (New York: Century, 1925).

For more on the artists' and writers' colonies in Santa Fe and Taos, see Van Deren Coke, *Taos and Santa Fe: The Artist's Environment, 1882–1942* (Albuquerque: University of New Mexico Press, 1963); Marta Weigle and Kyle Fiore, *Santa Fe and Taos: The Writer's Era, 1916–1941* (Santa Fe: Ancient City, 1982); Kay Aiken Reeve, "Santa Fe and Taos: An American Cultural Center." *Southwestern Studies*, monograph no. 67 (El Paso: Texas Western Press, 1982); and Arrell Morgan Gibson, *The Santa Fe and Taos Colonies: Age of the Muses, 1900–1942* (Norman: University of Oklahoma Press, 1983).

For more on the role of the Santa Fe Railway, the Fred Harvey Company, and other tourism promoters in enhancing the romantic image of the Pueblos, see T. C. McLuhan, *Dream Tracks: The Railroad and the American Indian, 1890–1930* (New York: Harry Abrams, 1985); D. H. Thomas, *The Southwestern Indian Detours: The Story of the Fred Harvey/Santa Fe Railway Experiment in "Detourism"* (Phoenix: Hunter, 1978); Marta Weigle and Barbara Babcock, eds., *The Great Southwest of the Fred Harvey Company and the Santa Fe Railway* (Phoenix: The Heard Museum, 1996); and Leah Dilworth, *Imagining Indians in the Southwest: Persistent Visions of a Primitive Past* (Washington DC: Smithsonian Institution Press, 1996).

A vast literature exists regarding changes in gender roles and sexual mores from the late nineteenth to the early twentieth centuries. For debates regarding sexual norms versus social practice in the nineteenth century, a good beginning place is Estelle Freedman's "Sexuality in Nineteenth-Century America: Behavior, Ideology, and Politics," *Reviews in American History* 10 (December 1982): 196–215. For opposing views on the topic, see Carl Degler's "What Ought to Be and What Was: Women's Sexuality in the Nineteenth Century," *American Historical Review* 79 (December 1974): 1467–90; and Carroll Smith-Rosenberg's "A Richer and a Gentler Sex," *Social Research* 53 (summer 1986): 283–309. Ronald G. Walters' *Primers for Prudery: Sexual Advice to Victorian America* (Englewood Cliffs NJ: Prentice-Hall, 1974) sheds further light on prescriptive literature. Two books deal in particular with social movements regarding notions of nineteenth-century sexuality: David Pivar, *Purity Crusade: Sexual Morality and Social Control, 1868–1900* (Westport CT: Greenwood, 1973); and, focusing on a very different movement, William Leach, *True Love and Perfect Union: The Feminist Reform of Sex and Society* (New York: Basic, 1980).

For studies that deal with the transformation of Victorian sexual norms in the early twentieth century, see John D'Emilio and Estelle Freedman, *Intimate Matters: A History of Sexuality in America* (New York: Harper & Row, 1988); Kathy Peiss and Christina Simmons, eds., *Passion and Power: Sexuality in History* (Philadelphia: Temple University Press, 1989); Paul Robinson, *The Modernization of Sex: Havelock Ellis, Alfred Kinsey, William Masters and Virginia Johnson* (New York: Harper and Row, 1976); Michael Gordon, "From an Unfortunate Necessity to a Cult of Mutual Orgasm: Sex in American Marital Education Literature, 1830–1940," in *The Sociology of Sex: An Introductory Reader*, ed. James M. Henslin and Edward Sagarin (New York: Schocken, 1978), 59–83; and Pamela S. Haag, "In Search of 'The Real Thing': Ideologies of Love, Modern Romance, and Women's Sexual Subjectivity in the United States, 1920–40," *Journal of the History of Sexuality* 2 (1992): 547–77.

Changing notions of female sexuality proved integral to transformations in how women perceived themselves and their options in the early twentieth century. For more on changing conceptions of womanhood in this period, see Kathy Peiss, *Cheap Amusements: Working Women and Leisure in Turn-of-the-Century New York* (Philadelphia: Temple University Press, 1986); Nancy Cott, *The Grounding of Modern Feminism* (New Haven CT: Yale University Press, 1987); Rosalind Rosenberg, *Beyond Separate Spheres: Intellectual Roots of Modern Feminism* (New Haven CT: Yale University Press, 1982); Carroll Smith-Rosenberg, "The New Woman as Social Androgyne: Social Disorder and Gender Crisis, 1870–1936," in *Disorderly Conduct: Visions of Gender in Victorian America* (New York: Alfred Knopf, 1985); Paula S. Fass, *The Damned and the Beautiful: American Youth in the 1920s* (New York: Oxford University Press, 1977); Elaine Tyler May, *Great Expectations: Marriage and Divorce in Post-Victorian America* (Chicago: University of Chicago Press, 1980); Joanne J. Meyerowitz, *Women Adrift: Independent Wage Earners in Chicago, 1880–1930* (Chicago: University of Chicago Press, 1988); William O'Neill, *Divorce in the Progressive Era* (New Haven

CT: Yale University Press, 1967); Ellen K. Rothman, *Hands and Hearts: A History of Courtship in America* (New York: Basic, 1984); Judith Schwarz, *Radical Feminists of Heterodoxy: Greenwich Village, 1912–1940*, rev. ed. (Norwich VT: New Victoria, 1986); Elaine Showalter, ed., *These Modern Women: Autobiographical Essays from the Twenties* (New York: Feminist Press, 1989); Ruth Rosen, *The Lost Sisterhood: Prostitution in America, 1900–1918* (Baltimore: Johns Hopkins University Press, 1982); and Peter Gabriel Filene, *Him/Her/Self: Sex Roles in Modern America* (New York: Harcourt Brace Jovanovich, 1975).

A small number of researchers have been interested in the question of how white women have used representations of Indian women as a means to define white womanhood and feminism. Two excellent articles on this topic are Deborah Gordon, "Among Women: Gender and Ethnographic Authority in the Southwest, 1930–1980," in *Hidden Scholars*, 129–45; and Gail Landsman, "'The Other' as Political Symbol: Images of Indians in the Woman Suffrage Movement," *Ethnohistory* 39 (summer 1992): 247–84.

2. UPLIFTING INDIAN WOMEN

On the subject of female moral reform, I rely primarily on Barbara Leslie Epstein, *The Politics of Domesticity: Women, Evangelism, and Temperance in Nineteenth-Century America* (Middletown CT: Wesleyan University Press, 1981), and Peggy Pascoe, *Relations of Rescue: The Search for Female Moral Authority in the American West, 1874–1939* (New York: Oxford University Press, 1990). Blanche Wiesen Cook's "Female Support Networks and Political Activism: Lillian Wald, Crystal Eastman, Emma Goldman," in *A Heritage of Her Own: Towards a New Social History of American Women*, ed. Nancy Cott and Elizabeth Pleck (New York: Simon and Schuster, 1979), 412–44, is also helpful. For the professionalization of women's moral reform work, see Regina Kunzel, *Fallen Women, Problem Girls: Unmarried Mothers and the Professionalization of Social Work, 1890–1945* (New Haven CT: Yale University Press, 1993).

Regarding women involved in Indian reform, there are several scholarly works on both the Women's National Indian Association (WNIA) and the field matrons and female schoolteachers who worked for the Bureau of Indian Affairs (BIA). On the WNIA, see Valerie Mathes, "Nineteenth-Century Women and Reform: The Women's National Indian Association," *American Indian Quarterly* 14 (1990): 1–18; and Helen M. Wanken, "'Woman's Sphere' and Indian Reform: The Women's National Indian Association, 1879–1901" (Ph.D. diss., Marquette University, 1981). As for white women field matrons, see Helen M. Bannan, *"True Womanhood" on the Reservation: Field Matrons in the U.S. Indian Service*, Southwest Institute for Research on Women, working paper no. 18

(Tucson: Women's Studies, 1984); Lisa Emmerich "'To respect and love and seek the ways of white women': Field Matrons, the Office of Indian Affairs, and Civilization Policy, 1890–1938" (Ph.D. diss., University of Maryland, 1987); and Susan Peterson, "'Holy Women' and Housekeepers: Women Teachers on South Dakota Reservations, 1885–1910," *South Dakota History* 13 (fall 1983): 245–60. For a unique case of an independent female reformer who worked with Native Americans, see Margaret D. Jacobs, "Resistance to Rescue: The Indians of Bahapki and Mrs. Annie E. K. Bidwell," in *Writing the Range*, 230–51. For images of native women that moral reformers promulgated, see David D. Smits, "The 'Squaw Drudge': A Prime Index of Savagism," *Ethnohistory* 29 (fall 1982): 281–306.

For white women BIA employees who seemed to resist the civilizing and uplifting mission, see Patricia A. Carter, "'Completely Discouraged': Women Teachers' Resistance in the Bureau of Indian Affairs Schools, 1900–1910," *Frontiers* 15 (1995): 53–86; and Mary Ellicott Arnold and Mabel Reed, *In the Land of the Grasshopper Song: Two Women in the Klamath River Indian Country in 1908–09* (New York: Vantage, 1957; reprint, Lincoln: University of Nebraska Press, 1980). In "'The Tales Those Nurses Told!': Public Health Nurses among the Pueblo and Navajo Indians," *New Mexico Historical Review* 65 (April 1990): 225–50, Sandra K. Schackel notes how professional public health nurses gradually replaced field matrons.

Paralleling female moral reformers' efforts in the United States to uplift Native American women, European and American women also sought to "uplift" non-Christian women in other parts of the world. See Barbara Welter, "She Hath Done What She Could: Protestant Women's Missionary Careers in the Nineteenth Century," *American Quarterly* 30 (winter 1978): 624–38; Joan Jacobs Brumberg, "Zenanas and Girlless Villages: The Ethnology of American Evangelical Women, 1870–1910," *Journal of American History* 69 (September 1982): 347–70; Leslie A. Flemming, ed., *Women's Work for Women: Missionaries and Social Change in Asia* (Boulder CO: Westview Press, 1989); Jane Hunter, *The Gospel of Gentility: American Women Missionaries in Turn-of-the-Century China* (New Haven CT: Yale University Press, 1984); and Antoinette Burton, *Burdens of History: British Feminists, Indian Women, and Imperial Culture, 1865–1915* (Chapel Hill: University of North Carolina Press, 1994).

Virtually the only published source that discusses Clara True is Harry Lawton, *Willie Boy: A Desert Manhunt* (Balboa Island CA: Paisano, 1960), which deals with her tenure as superintendent of the Morongo Reservation in southern California. The Pueblo records of the National Archives and Records Administration—Rocky Mountain Region in Denver, Colorado, however, are full of

True's letters, as are the Indian Rights Association papers, available at the Historical Society of Pennsylvania in Philadelphia or on microfilm (Glen Rock NJ: Microfilming Corporation of America, 1975). Plentiful sources written by and about True's friend Mary Dissette can also be found in these two archival collections. In addition, the *Home Mission Monthly*, published by the Woman's Executive Committee of Home Missions for the Presbyterian Church, contains some writings by Dissette.

On native women's experiences of the assimilation mission, two recent books on native women in boarding schools are prescient. See K. Tsianina Lomawaima, *They Called It Prairie Light: The Story of Chilocco Indian School* (Lincoln: University of Nebraska Press, 1994); and Devon A. Mihesuah, *Cultivating the Rosebuds: The Education of Women at the Cherokee Female Seminary, 1851–1909* (Urbana: University of Illinois Press, 1993). For firsthand accounts of assimilation policy from Pueblo women's points of view, see Helen Sekaquaptewa, *Me and Mine: The Life Story of Helen Sekaquaptewa*, as told to Louise Udall (Tucson: University of Arizona Press, 1969); and Polingaysi Qoyawayma (Elizabeth Q. White), *No Turning Back: A Hopi Indian Woman's Struggle to Live in Two Worlds*, as told to Vada Carlson (Albuquerque: University of New Mexico Press, 1964).

3. FEMINISTS AND CULTURAL RELATIVISM

There are many biographical works on Mary Austin, including Esther Lanigan Stineman, *Mary Austin: Song of a Maverick* (New Haven CT: Yale University Press, 1989); Peggy Pond Church, *Wind's Trail: The Early Life of Mary Austin*, ed. Shelley Armitage (Santa Fe: Museum of New Mexico Press, 1990); T. M. Pearce, *The Beloved House* (Caldwell ID: Caxton, 1940); T. M. Pearce, *Literary America, 1903–1934: The Mary Austin Letters* (Westport CT: Greenwood Press, 1979); Helen MacKnight Doyle, *Mary Austin: Woman of Genius* (New York: Gotham, 1939); Augusta Fink, *I-Mary: A Biography of Mary Austin* (Tucson: University of Arizona Press, 1983); Richard Drinnon, "The American Rhythm: Mary Austin," in *Facing West: The Metaphysics of Indian Hating and Empire Building* (New York: Schocken, 1980); and Willard Hougland, ed., *Mary Austin: A Memorial* (Santa Fe NM: Laboratory of Anthropology, 1944).

Mary Austin was a prolific writer of fiction, nonfiction, and essays. The books I found most useful to this study were her outstanding autobiography, *Earth Horizon* (Boston: Houghton Mifflin, 1932); her nonfictional study of the cultures and history of the Southwest, *Land of Journey's Ending* (New York: Century, 1924); her collection of short stories, *Stories from the Country of Lost Borders*, ed. Marjorie Pryse (New Brunswick NJ: Rutgers University Press, 1987); and her collaboration with Ansel Adams, *Taos Pueblo*, photographs by Ansel Easton Adams (San Francisco: Grabhorn, 1930). The papers of Mary Austin are housed at a number of archives. The largest collection is at the Huntington Library in San Marino, California. Smaller collections of Austin's papers also exist at the Bancroft Library, University of California, Berkeley; the Center for Southwest Research, General Library, University of New Mexico, Albuquerque; and Special Collections, University of California, Los Angeles.

Mabel Dodge Luhan's writings on her life in New York and the Southwest include *Movers and Shakers*, vol. 3 of *Intimate Memories* (New York: Harcourt, Brace, 1936; reprint, Albuquerque: University of New Mexico, 1985); *Edge of Taos Desert: An Escape to Reality*, vol. 4 of *Intimate Memories* (1937); *Lorenzo in Taos* (New York: Knopf, 1932); and *Winter in Taos* (New York: Harcourt, Brace, 1935). For a fine biography of Mabel Dodge Luhan, see Lois Palken Rudnick, *Mabel Dodge Luhan: New Woman, New Worlds* (Albuquerque: University of New Mexico Press, 1984). Luhan's personal papers are cataloged at the Beinecke Rare Book and Manuscript Library, Yale University, New Haven, Connecticut.

Elsie Clews Parsons was also an immensely prolific writer. For the purposes of this book, I found the following works by her to be most relevant: *Fear and Conventionality* (New York: G. P. Putnam's, 1914); *The Old-Fashioned Woman: Primitive Fancies About the Sex* (New York: G. P. Putnam's, 1913); *Taos Pueblo*, General Series in Anthropology no. 2 (Menasha WI: American Anthropological Association, 1936); and Barbara Babcock, ed., *Pueblo Mothers and Children: Essays by Elsie Clews Parsons, 1915–1924* (Santa Fe: Ancient City, 1991). The American Philosophical Society in Philadelphia owns Parsons's personal papers.

For biographical information on Parsons, see Rosemary Lévy Zumwalt, *Wealth and Rebellion: Elsie Clews Parsons, Anthropologist and Folklorist* (Urbana: University of Illinois Press, 1992); Desley Deacon, *Elsie Clews Parsons: Inventing Modern Life* (Chicago: University of Chicago Press, 1997); Peter H. Hare, *A Woman's Quest for Science: Portrait of Anthropologist Elsie Clews Parsons* (Buffalo NY: Prometheus, 1985); Rosalind Rosenberg, *Beyond Separate Spheres: Intellectual Roots of Modern Feminism* (New Haven CT: Yale University Press, 1982); entry for Elsie Clews Parsons, in Babcock and Parezo, *Daughters of the Desert*; and Louis A. Hieb, "Elsie Clews Parsons in the Southwest," in *Hidden Scholars*, 63–75.

For some of the other women who seem to have also held an antimodern feminist philosophy, see Mary Roberts Coolidge, *The Rain-Makers: Indians of Arizona and New Mexico* (Boston: Houghton Mifflin, 1929); and the writings of Erna Fergusson, including her "Crusade from Santa Fé," *The North American*

Review 242 (winter 1936–37): 376–87; *Dancing Gods: Indian Ceremonials of New Mexico and Arizona* (New York: Knopf, 1931); and "Laughing Priests," *Theatre Arts Monthly* 17 (August 1933): 657–62. Fergusson's personal papers, which particularly illuminate her role in New Mexico tourism, are housed at the Center for Southwest Research, General Library, University of New Mexico, Albuquerque. For more on Fergusson's literary works, see Robert Franklin Gish, *Beautiful Swift Fox: Erna Fergusson and the Modern Southwest* (College Station TX: Texas A & M University Press, 1996).

<h4>4. FEMINISTS' REDEFINITION OF GENDER AND RACE</h4>
Sources cited for chapter 3 serve as the primary sources for this chapter as well. Scholarship on the transition from Victorianism to modernism is vast. Some recent significant works include T. J. Jackson Lears, *No Place of Grace: Antimodernism and the Transformation of American Culture, 1880–1920* (New York: Pantheon, 1981); Miles Orvell, *The Real Thing: Imitation and Authenticity in American Culture, 1880–1940* (Chapel Hill: University of North Carolina Press, 1989); Daniel Joseph Singal, *The War Within: From Victorian to Modernist Thought in the South, 1919–1945* (Chapel Hill: University of North Carolina Press, 1982); Daniel Joseph Singal, ed., *Modernist Culture in America* (Belmont CA: Wadsworth, 1991); Ann Douglas, *Terrible Honesty: Mongrel Manhattan in the 1920s* (New York: Farrar, Straus, and Giroux, 1995); Adele Heller and Lois Rudnick, eds., *1915: The Cultural Moment: The New Politics, the New Woman, the New Psychology, the New Art and the New Theatre in America* (New Brunswick NJ: Rutgers University Press, 1991); George Cotkin, *Reluctant Modernism: American Thought and Culture, 1880–1900* (New York: Twayne, 1992); and Stanley Coben, *Rebellion against Victorianism: The Impetus for Cultural Change in 1920s America* (New York: Oxford University Press, 1991).

Many scholars have also devoted much thought to probing the connection between primitivism and modernism. See Marianna Torgovnick, *Gone Primitive: Savage Intellects, Modern Lives* (Chicago: University of Chicago Press, 1990); Elazar Barkan and Ronald Bush, eds., *Prehistories of the Future: The Primitivist Project and the Culture of Modernism* (Stanford: Stanford University Press, 1995); Deborah Root, *Cannibal Culture: Art, Appropriation, and the Commodification of Difference* (Boulder CO: Westview Press, 1996); Helen Carr, *Inventing the American Primitive: Politics, Gender and the Representation of Native American Literary Traditions, 1789–1936* (New York: New York University Press, 1996); and Leah Dilworth, *Imagining Indians.* Philip Joseph Deloria's "Playing Indian: Otherness and Authenticity in the Assumption of American Indian Identity" (Ph.D. diss., Yale University, 1994) is a provocative work that also, in part, probes the relation between primitivism and modernism.

5. THE 1920S CONTROVERSY OVER INDIAN DANCES

Primary sources regarding the 1920s dance controversy can be found in the Indian Rights Association papers, Historical Society of Pennsylvania, Philadelphia; the John Collier papers, Manuscripts and Archives, Yale University, New Haven, Connecticut; the California League of American Indians papers, Bancroft Library, University of California, Berkeley; the E. M. Sweet collection of the National Anthropological Archives, Smithsonian Institution, Washington DC; and the Pueblo Records, Record Group 75, National Archives and Records Administration—Rocky Mountain Branch, Denver, Colorado. Published primary sources regarding the alleged immorality of the Pueblos' dances include the 1924 issues of *Indian Truth*, a publication of the Indian Rights Association; Flora Warren Seymour, "Our Indian Problem—The Delusion of the Sentimentalists," *Forum* 71 (March 1924): 273–80; William E. Johnson, "Those Sacred Indian Ceremonials," *The Native American* 24 (20 September 1924): 173–77; and G.E.E. Lindquist, *The Red Man in the United States: An Intimate Study of the Social, Economic and Religious Life of the American Indians* (New York: Doran, 1923).

Very little has been written about the dance controversy. Lawrence C. Kelly's *The Assault on Assimilation: John Collier and the Origins of Indian Policy Reform* (Albuquerque: University of New Mexico Press, 1983) and Kenneth Philp's *John Collier's Crusade for Indian Reform* (Tucson: University of Arizona Press, 1977) each contain a section on it, and David M. Strausfeld treats the subject as well in "Reformers in Conflict: The Pueblo Dance Controversy," in *The Aggressions of Civilization: Federal Indian Policy Since the 1880s*, ed. Sandra Cadwalader and Vine Deloria Jr. (Philadelphia: Temple University Press, 1984), 1943. In "Documents in Hopi Indian Sexuality: Imperialism, Culture, and Resistance," *Radical History Review* 20 (spring/summer 1979): 99–130, Martin Bauml Duberman quotes from the Secret Dance File.

To learn more about the role of ritual clowns in Pueblo dances, see Louis Hieb, "Meaning and Mismeaning: Toward an Understanding of the Ritual Clown," in *New Perspectives on the Pueblo*, ed. Alfonso Ortiz (Albuquerque: University of New Mexico Press, 1972), 163–95; Alfonso Ortiz, "Ritual Drama and the Pueblo World View," in *New Perspectives on the Pueblos*, 135–61; Alfonso Ortiz, "The Dynamics of Pueblo Cultural Survival," in *North American Indian Anthropology: Essays on Society and Culture*, ed. Raymond DeMallie and Alfonso Ortiz (Norman: University of Oklahoma Press, 1994); Alfonso Ortiz, *The Tewa World: Space, Time, Being, and Becoming in a Pueblo Society* (Chicago: University of Chicago Press, 1969); Emory Sekaquaptewa, "One More Smile for a Hopi Clown," in *The South Corner of Time: Hopi, Navajo, Papago, Yaqui Tribal*

Literature, ed. Larry Evers (Tucson: Sun Tracks, 1980), 14–17; Barbara Babcock, "Arrange Me into Disorder: Fragments and Reflections on Ritual Clowning," in *Rite, Drama, Festival, Spectacle: Rehearsals Toward a Theory of Cultural Performance*, ed. John J. MacAloon (Philadelphia: Institute for the Study of Human Issues, 1984); Vera Laski, *Seeking Life*, Memoirs of the American Folklore Society, vol. 50 (Philadelphia: American Folklore Society, 1958); Jill D. Sweet, *Dances of the Tewa Indians: Expressions of New Life* (Santa Fe NM: School of American Research Press, 1985); and Charlotte Frisbie, *Southwestern Indian Ritual Drama* (Albuquerque: University of New Mexico Press, 1980). A Ph.D. dissertation by Alison Freese, "Send in the Clowns: An Ethnohistorical Analysis of the Sacred Clowns' Role in Cultural Boundary Maintenance among the Pueblo Indians," (University of New Mexico, 1991) provides insights regarding the historical role of ritual clowns in Pueblo cultures.

Several studies were helpful in theorizing about how the Pueblos sought to make sense of cultural contact with white women. Fredrik Barth's edited collection, *Ethnic Groups and Boundaries: The Social Organization of Culture Difference* (Boston: Little, Brown, 1969) provides a useful theory of cultural interaction. Keith Basso's *Portraits of "the Whiteman": Linguistic Play and Cultural Symbols among the Western Apache* (New York: Cambridge University Press, 1979) highlights how the Apaches use humor to define Apache identity. Basso's insights seem relevant to the Pueblos as well. Elizabeth Brandt's "On Secrecy and the Control of Knowledge: Taos Pueblo," in *Secrecy: A Cross-Cultural Perspective*, ed. Stanton K. Tefft (New York: Human Sciences, 1980), 123–46, contends that the main reason the Pueblos have been so secretive about their religious ways derives more from a desire to maintain secrecy among different groups within the pueblo than to prevent outsiders from learning of Pueblo religion.

6. WOMEN AND THE INDIAN ARTS AND CRAFTS MOVEMENT

For research on the American arts and crafts movement as a whole, see Eileen Boris, *Art and Labor: Ruskin, Morris, and the Craftsman Ideal in America* (Philadelphia: Temple University Press, 1986); Lears, *No Place of Grace*, 60–96; and Orvell, *The Real Thing*, 157–97.

For the Indian arts and crafts movement in New Mexico, see J. J. Brody, *Indian Painters and White Patrons* (Albuquerque: University of New Mexico Press, 1971); Kenneth Dauber, "Pueblo Pottery and the Politics of Regional Identity," *Journal of the Southwest* 32 (winter 1990), 576–96; and Edwin L. Wade, "The Ethnic Art Market in the American Southwest," in *Objects and Others: Essays on Museum and Material Culture*, ed. George Stocking Jr., History of Anthropology, vol. 3 (Madison: University of Wisconsin Press, 1985), 167–91. Molly Mullin's "Consuming the American Southwest: Culture, Art, and Difference" (Ph.D. diss., Duke University, 1993) is one of the few works thus far that has studied the marketing of Native American arts and crafts from a gender perspective. Her article "The Patronage of Difference: Making Indian Art 'Art, Not Ethnology,'" *Cultural Anthropology* 7 (1992): 395–424, also contains an insightful class analysis of the movement.

For the role of John Collier's Indian New Deal in promoting Indian arts and crafts, see Robert Fay Schrader, *The Indian Arts and Crafts Board: An Aspect of New Deal Indian Policy* (Albuquerque: University of New Mexico Press, 1983). For more on the Santa Fe Indian School's arts program, see Winona Garmhausen, *History of Indian Arts Education in Santa Fe: The Institute of American Indian Art with Historical Background, 1890–1962* (Santa Fe NM: Sunstone, 1988); Jeanne Shutes and Jill Mellick, *The Worlds of P'otsúnú: Geronima Cruz Montoya of San Juan Pueblo* (Albuquerque: University of New Mexico Press, 1996); and Bruce Bernstein and W. Jackson Rushing, eds., *Modern by Tradition: American Indian Painting in the Studio Style* (Santa Fe NM: Museum of New Mexico Press, 1995).

For primary sources on the Indian arts and crafts movement in New Mexico, see the Amelia Elizabeth White papers, Catherine McElvain Library, School of American Research, Santa Fe, New Mexico; the Indian Arts Fund papers and the Kenneth Chapman papers at the Indian Arts Research Center, Santa Fe; and the papers of Kenneth Chapman, Ina Sizer Cassidy, Dorothy Dunn Kramer, and Mabel Morrow at the Archives of the Laboratory of Anthropology/Museum of Indian Art and Culture, Santa Fe. The papers of the New Mexico Association on Indian Affairs (which later became the Southwest Association on Indian Affairs), New Mexico State Records and Archives Center, Santa Fe, also contain information related to the arts and crafts movement. See also the Erna Fergusson papers and the DeHuff Family papers at the Center for Southwest Research, General Library, University of New Mexico, Albuquerque, as well as Clara True's letters and other miscellaneous letters in the Pueblo records of the National Archives and Records Administration—Rocky Mountain Branch, Denver, Colorado. Ruth Bunzel's *The Pueblo Potter: A Study of Creative Imagination in Primitive Art* (New York: Columbia University Press, 1929) offers a glimpse into the perspectives of white women who sought to preserve Pueblo pottery skills.

There have been many recent articles and books that deal with tourism in the Southwest. In addition to the sources on this subject cited in chapter 1, the following articles were helpful: Marta Weigle, "Exposition and Mediation: Mary Colter, Erna Fergusson, and the Santa Fe/Harvey Popularization of the Native

Southwest, 1902–1940," *Frontiers* 12 (1992): 117–50; Marta Weigle, "From Desert to Disney World: The Santa Fe Railway and the Fred Harvey Company Display the Indian Southwest," *Journal of Anthropological Research* 45 (spring 1989): 115–37; Robert A. Trennert Jr., "Fairs, Expositions, and the Changing Image of Southwestern Indians, 1876–1904," *New Mexico Historical Review* 62 (April 1987): 127–50; Sylvia Rodríguez, "Art, Tourism, and Race Relations in Taos: Toward a Sociology of the Art Colony," *Journal of Anthropological Research* 45 (spring 1989): 77–99; Sylvia Rodríguez, "Ethnic Reconstruction in Contemporary Taos," *Journal of the Southwest* 32 (winter 1990): 541–55; and Sylvia Rodríguez, "Land, Water, and Ethnic Identity in Taos," in *Land, Water, and Culture: New Perspectives on Hispanic Land Grants*, ed. Charles L. Briggs and John R. Van Ness (Albuquerque: University of New Mexico Press, 1987), 313–403.

For more on Pueblo artists, see Edwin L. Wade, "Straddling the Cultural Fence: The Conflict for Ethnic Artists within Pueblo Societies," in *The Arts of the North American Indian: Native Traditions in Evolution*, ed. Edwin L. Wade (New York: Hudson Hills, 1986), 243–54; Fred Kabotie with Bill Belknap, *Fred Kabotie: Hopi Indian Artist* (Flagstaff: Museum of Arizona Press with Northland Press, 1977); and Rick Dillingham's *Fourteen Families in Pueblo Pottery* (Albuquerque: University of New Mexico Press, 1994). On Pueblo women artists, see Samuel L. Gray, *Tonita Peña: Quah-Ah, 1893–1949* (Albuquerque: Avanyu, 1990; Sally Hyer, "Pablita Velarde: The Pueblo Artist as Cultural Broker," in *Between Indian and White Worlds: The Cultural Broker*, ed. Margaret Connell Szasz (Norman: University of Oklahoma Press, 1994), 273–93; Alice Marriott, *María: The Potter of San Ildefonso* (Norman: University of Oklahoma Press, 1948); Susan Peterson, *The Living Tradition of María Martinez* (New York: Kodansha International, 1977); Barbara Babcock, "Marketing María: The Tribal Artist in the Age of Mechanical Reproduction," in *Looking High and Low: Art and Cultural Identity*, ed. Brenda Jo Bright and Liza Blakewell (Tucson: University of Arizona Press, 1995), 124–50; Tessie Naranjo, "Cultural Changes: The Effect of Foreign Systems at Santa Clara Pueblo," in *The Great Southwest of the Fred Harvey Company and the Santa Fe Railway*, ed. Marta Weigle and Barbara Babcock (Phoenix: Heard Museum, 1996); and Terry R. Reynolds, "Women, Pottery, and Economics at Acoma Pueblo," in *New Mexico Women: Intercultural Perspectives*, ed. Joan Jensen and Darlis Miller (Albuquerque: University of New Mexico Press, 1986), 279–300.

CONCLUSION

The legacy of antimodern feminists' representations of Pueblo women and Pueblo gender relations can be found today in the New Age movement and one wing of the feminist movement. For sources that critique this phenomenon, see Deloria, "Playing Indian," 403–6; Wendy Rose, "The Great Pretenders: Further Reflections on Whiteshamanism," in *The State of Native America: Genocide, Colonization, and Resistance*, ed. M. Annette Jaimes (Boston: South End Press, 1992), 403–21; Laurie Anne Whitt, "Cultural Imperialism and the Marketing of Native America," *American Indian Culture and Research Journal* 19 (1995): 1–31; and Rayna Green, "The Tribe Called Wannabee: Playing Indian in America and Europe," *Folklore* 99 (1988): 30–55.

Index

cult of true womanhood, 25–29, 38–39, 46, 198–99 n.1
cultural differences, views of, 83, 97–98, 98–99
cultural evolution, 11
cultural pluralism, 15, 71
cultural relativism, 14, 57, 69, 71, 82–83
Cushing, Frank Hamilton, 13–14

Dabb, Edith, 121
dances, Plains Indian, 108–9
dances, Pueblo Indian, 18–19, 109, 125, 135–39, 233–34 n.90; condemnation of, 30, 106–7, 109–10, 114–15; controversy over, 18–19, 107–8, 112–48; representation of women in, 119–20, 228 n.38
Dancing Gods (Fergusson), 82
Dawes Act, 11, 19, 180
Dawes, Senator Henry, 33
DeHuff, Elizabeth, 97, 100, 102, 104, 136–37, 152–53, 155, 156, 161, 172, 235 n.95, 236 n.112
Deloria, Philip Joseph, 220 n.51, 221–22 n.65, 222 n.74
department stores, and Indian wares, 163–64, 167
Dilworth, Leah, 20, 102, 245 n.67
Dissette, Mary, 1, 11, 12, 24, 53, 60, 62, 81, 94, 171, 200–201 n.14; and campaigns against the BIA, 42–44; and dance controversy, 109, 120, 121, 123; and feminism, 41–42; and interactions with Pueblos, 29–40, 46–47, 54–55, 202 n.20, 204 n.45, 205 n.62
divorce: in Pueblo cultures, 73–74, 115, 117, 214 n.68; in white society, 63, 122
Dixon, John, 88, 217 n.17
Dockstader, Frederick, 142, 146
Dodge, Edwin, 66, 67, 79
Dougan, Rose, 153

Dozier, Edward, 12, 17, 93, 116, 132, 134, 135, 218 n.31, 224 n.9
Dunn (Kramer), Dorothy, 154, 155, 156, 161, 177

Eastern Association on Indian Affairs (EAIA), 17, 19, 112, 154
Eastman, Crystal, 67
Eastman, Max, 71
Edge of Taos Desert (Luhan), 76
education, and Indians, 32–33, 35, 50–51. *See also* assimilation; boarding schools
Eggan, Dorothy, 88
Ellis, Havelock, 67, 99, 121, 217 n.12, 220 n.55
Emmerich, Lisa, 22, 201 n.18, 204 n.50, 206 n.75
The End of Desire (Herrick), 70
epidemics, 30–31
Epstein, Barbara, 21, 26, 40
eugenics, 99–100, 220 n.55, 221 n.56
Evans, Hiram, 99, 221 n.56
Evans, Karl, 66
Exposition of Tribal Arts, 154, 164

fairs, national and international, 3, 133, 165, 167, 170
Fall, Albert B., 18
The Family (Parsons), 70
Fass, Paula, 120, 212 n.45
Faurote, May, 54–55, 202 n.26
federal Indian policy, changes in, 1–4, 11–12, 19. *See also* assimilation; Bureau of Indian Affairs; Meriam Report
feminism: and antimodernism, 22, 58; connotations of, 67; among Indian reformers, 33–34, 41–42, 46; and moral reform, 1–2, 21, 25–26, 33–34, 41, 200 n.13; and primitivism, 16; and "sex expression," 57; and sexual difference, 85–86. *See also* an-